NEWS FROM THE BORDER

Jane Taylor McDonnell

NEWS FROM THE BORDER

A Mother's Memoir of Her Autistic Son

Afterword by Paul McDonnell

New York 1993   Ticknor & Fields

For information about permission to reproduce selections
from this book, write to Permissions, Ticknor & Fields,
215 Park Avenue South, New York, New York 10003.

Library of Congress Cataloging-in-Publication Data

McDonnell, Jane Taylor.
News from the border : a mother's memoir of her autistic son /
  Jane Taylor McDonnell ; afterword by Paul McDonnell.
p.   cm.
ISBN 0-395-60574-1
1. McDonnell, Paul — 1972–   2. Autistic children — United States —
  Biography.   3. Autistic youth — United States — Biography.
4. McDonnell, Jane Taylor — Family.   I. McDonnell, Paul, 1972–   .
II. Title.
RJ506.A9M43   1993
618.92′8982′0092 — dc20
[B]   93-15711
          CIP

All photographs are courtesy of Jane Taylor McDonnell
and Jim McDonnell, unless otherwise credited.

AUTHOR'S NOTE: All the names of medical professionals and educators have been
changed except for Sheila Merzer, Lyle Chastain, Jerry Gregorson, Barbara
Clark, Molly Moodley, Mrs. Gellie, and Jim Brothen. In addition, most of the
other names have been changed except for Jan Albers, Molly Woehrlin, Sandra
Bartels, Allen, Roxanne, Chrissy, Bill Steele, and Bill Frykman.

Printed in the United States of America

DOH 10 9 8 7 6 5 4 3 2 1

The author gratefully acknowledges permission to quote from the following
sources: *The Empty Fortress: Infantile Autism and the Birth of the Self* by Bruno
Bettelheim. Copyright © 1967 by Bruno Bettelheim. Reprinted by permission of
The Free Press, a Division of Macmillan, Inc.; *Seven Little Rabbits*. Text Copy-
right © 1973 by John Becker. Illustrations Copyright © 1973 by Barbara
Cooney. Used by permission of Walker and Company, 720 Fifth Avenue, New
York, New York 10019, 1-800-289-2553; *Indefensible Weapons* by Robert Jay
Lifton and Richard A. Falk. Copyright © 1983 by Basic Books, Inc., Harper-
Collins Publishers, reprinted by permission of Stoddart Publishing Co. Limited,
Don Mills, Ontario; "He Wishes for the Cloths of Heaven," *The Poems of W. B.
Yeats: A New Edition*, edited by Richard J. Finneran (New York: Macmillan,
1983).

CONTENTS

For Paul's grandparents
Mary Brennan McDonnell
and
Frank Eugene Taylor,
whose wise and steady love
saw us all through difficult times

ACKNOWLEDGMENTS

Many people have helped in the writing of this book, and many more have sustained us as we lived through these experiences. Among those who read earlier versions of the manuscript, I would like especially to thank the following: Sigrun Leonhard, Paulette Bates Alden, Julie Landsman, Jan Albers, and Clare Rossini. Valuable assistance was given by Christina Baldwin and the Split Rock workshop members, in particular Charlotte Smith, Ron Powers and the nonfiction workshop at the Bread Loaf Writers Conference, and especially Vivian Gornick and her Minneapolis Loft seminar. Nuala Ní Dhomhnaill provided information on changelings and other Irish "migratory legends," Sylvia Tomasch gave me material on mapmaking as metaphoric activity, and Michael Flynn supplied information on Broca's area.

I would like to thank my agent, Bonnie Blodgett, and the Lazear Agency in Minneapolis. Very special thanks goes to my editor, Jane von Mehren, who always believed in this project and who helped me through massive revisions of the book.

Among those who helped us understand and deal with autism, I would especially like to mention Sheila Merzer and Lyle Chastain, as well as Kathy Holahan and Deb and Bruce Lundgren and the other parents of autistic children, who became friends and with whom we have shared the absurdity of our lives. Very warm thanks go to Molly Woehrlin, whose expertise and fighting spirit helped me find the best educational resources for both my children, and to Barbara Clark, without whom neither Paul nor I would have survived his high school years. Also thanks to Marilyn Mason for helping me get past many obstacles. Paul wants to acknowledge his gratitude to Jim Brothen for believing in him and giving him hope for the future. We both want to express our thanks to Nancy Casper for helping in so many ways, including saving five month's worth of weather reports and Garfield cartoons. Of the many other sustaining friends, two in particular — Sandra Bartels and Linda Morral — have seen me through the writing of this book and the living of this life, and to them I owe a debt of gratitude I can never repay.

I want to thank all the members of Jim's family and my own, especially Frank and Ellen Taylor. My daughter, Kate, in particular I want to recognize for a wisdom far beyond her years. And to my husband, Jim — who always believed in my right to tell our common story in my own way, even at the risk of partiality and incompleteness — I am grateful beyond words.

CHAPTER I

Beginnings

I AM STANDING in front of the theater marquee in our small town. It is seven o'clock in the evening and the lights are flickering rapidly. I am holding the hand of a beautiful two-year-old boy, my son, who stands entranced by the lights, fixated, hardly moving. Each night at seven he insists on coming to watch them, and I bring him willingly, cheerfully explaining to our friends as they enter the theater why I am there, how much he loves these lights. At first I see nothing strange in this. Paul loves lights. He turns them off and on for hours each day. He knows where every light switch is in our house and the houses of our friends and in many of the stores downtown. His world is lights and light switches.

I remember another scene. Two years earlier. In the delivery room, we watch the first moments of this new baby. Taken up in a bundle of loose blankets, he is placed on the warming table. Crying, rolling vigorously from side to side, he kicks, breaks free of the folds of the fabric and opens his eyes. Most newborns that I have seen are curled in on themselves, as if they need to fold themselves away from the onslaught of the world for fear it be seen too soon, too suddenly. Not this one. This baby seems to open his eyes to the full sense of things all at once. Eyes opened wide, he stops crying and stares at the lights on the ceiling. "He's a keeper," exclaims the attending nurse, and in my new mother's egotism, this seems like a wonderful omen. I think I have never seen such sudden sense, such full, startled awareness, such awakening to the world.

A third scene. Paul, now two and a half, is sitting on the floor of the kitchen with his back to us as we work around the stove, roasting a chicken for dinner. Jim speaks to him by name. No response. Paul doesn't turn around or indicate in any way that he hears us. Jim calls him again by name. Again no response. And again and again, until in utter frustration, Jim shouts at him, "You dummy!" and drops the chicken. It falls out of the pan and slides in its grease all the way across the floor. We eat dinner in frightened silence, feeling as if we have broken through some membrane of consciousness and are face to face with something neither of us is ready to face — a child who unaccountably doesn't even know his own name at the age of two.

When did we begin to worry? Later, I often looked back over these early months, searching for signposts that may have been missed at the time. But even when we did start to worry, our reasons were vague. We took him to his pediatrician when he was nine months old. We had small complaints, hardly formulated. "He seemed slow to develop gross motor skills, but not very slow." "He was content to sit in one place." "He didn't explore the world the way another child did who was born on the same day." We worried but felt guilty about worrying, as if we shouldn't. The pediatrician sent us away with a reassurance that failed to reassure. "You aren't raising a racehorse," he pointed out — a comment that stung.

We spent Paul's first summer in France and England, and should have been very happy. I have a picture taken at this time: June 1973, our garden on the edge of the little village of Contignac in the south of France. Paul, at ten months and just learning to stand, is holding onto one side of a metal lawn chair. My seventy-three-year-old father, who has come with us to babysit while Jim and I write our dissertations, stands on the other side of the chair. He is looking at Paul. He has just taken a pebble from the corner of Paul's cheek. The sun comes through the green leaves of the lime trees; it shines through the wispy blond curls at the baby's neck. Both faces have a look of open innocence.

Every morning at that time, my father took the baby down the hill to greet an old man. This old man belonged to the farming family, and he was put out by his daughter to sit all day by the side of the road or, if it was raining, in the mouth of the mushroom cave. My father spoke no French; the old French man, who was deaf and senile, spoke no English. But with the baby, together they communicated. For them it was enough.

Looking at that picture now, I want to pick up the baby, to re-enter that time. I want to blow kisses through his silky hair, to plant them on his small, hard skull. I didn't know then the fragility of that moment, over which already the dark wing was passing. I didn't know, and wouldn't know for another fifteen years, that the brain cells had clumped differently at the base of that little skull, that the cerebellum was too small, the cisterna magna too large.

During that summer I repressed my worries, but I continued to notice things. In a restaurant in our little town, we put Paul on the floor to crawl at our feet. Another baby, there with its parents, was also placed on the floor. They were the same age, but the little French baby crawled around Paul, around and around, as he just sat there, in his little peaked sun cap with fish hanging from the crown. They babbled together, and the French couple pointed out that now their sounds were the same, but soon they would be differentiated, as they learned their respective languages.

Paul's babblings did not become differentiated, however. He did not start to imitate the sounds he heard around him; he did not begin to speak English. Later that summer, in Cambridge, where he had his first birthday, I showed him the lights in our rented house, switching on and off the light in the hallway, showing him how to make it work, and saying over and over: "Light, light." He appeared to comprehend, looking from the light to the switch to my mouth as I formed the word. He reached for the light, opened his mouth, made sounds, seemed to try to form the right sound. A friend commented that *light* has been the first word of so many babies, and it seemed so appropriate to us, so basic, so fundamental: "Let there be light." We remembered his wonder at the light on the delivery room ceiling and thought surely this would be his first word also.

It seemed that he was about to say "Ight, ight!" Later, I wondered if it was just my imagination that he seemed so very close to speaking, so comprehending and ready for communication. Language was there. And then it was just out of his reach.

In fact, language was to remain out of Paul's grasp for another eighteen months, until he was two and a half. During that time, he seemed not to know that he had a name or that we had names. There was no "Mama" or "Dada." He did not point for a long time; he never asked for what he needed by trying to make sounds. He did not understand that sounds had meaning or that they could be used deliberately and could help him gain some control over his world. He seemed not to communicate in other ways.

*

Looking back later, we realized that other things were different. In Cambridge, Paul began to explore his world, but with a difference. He learned to climb the stairs of our rented house, a very typical, normal activity for an eleven-month-old baby. At the top of the stairs, he patted the floor. Following him, I also patted the floor. He patted the floor more loudly and enthusiastically. I did the same. After that, every time he climbed the steps, he patted the floor on the same spot before he moved on. Then he took the same path each time past the toilet, where he looked in fearfully at this thing that made so much noise, then to the separate bathroom.

At the top of the steps, he never omitted the pats, nor did he ever turn right instead of left. He never climbed the steps to get to his room, which was just at the top of the stairs on the right and where there were toys, nor did he move on to explore our room farther down the hall. He was able to crawl outdoors to the garden in back, but he invariably went to the same spot — a small stake at the edge of the asparagus patch. There, he would haul himself up and hang on that stake, laughing and shouting, where he knew we could always count on finding him whenever he disappeared from the house.

Over the next year, between Paul's first and second birthday, we felt more and more anxious. His pediatrician suggested that I was "doing too much for him, not giving him a chance to ask for things for himself." So one day I withheld a banana from him as he sat in his high chair. I knew he was hungry. I held the banana just out of reach, saying clearly over and over, "Banana, banana," then adapting and playing with baby sounds, "Ba ba ba, ba ba ba."

I thought, If I get any kind of sound out of you, I'll give it to you. Just open your mouth. Say something. Anything! Paul became more and more agitated, squirming in his chair, bouncing up and down, reaching for the banana, watching my mouth, trying to say something, struggling to speak.

Finally he burst into tears. He fell back in the chair and sobbed. He sobbed in the most abandoned tones I had ever heard from him. Feeling guilty about my own behavior and angry at the doctor, I picked him up and held him close against my shoulder. I gave him the banana and swore I would never, ever try this particular experiment again. It seemed so clear to me at that moment that he was trying to speak, trying to give me what I wanted. It was also crystal clear that he couldn't.

CHAPTER 2

A Watched Child

SUNLIGHT is streaming across our bed. Slowly I wake up and from the room next door I hear Paul babbling in his crib. "A bah bah," he says, and I picture him holding up his panda bear. "A bah bah. Bear. Teddy *bear!*"

Now I am awake. I sit up in bed. "Teddy. *Up. Down.* Uuuuup. Doooown." He must be swinging his bear up and down. "*Down.* All gone!" Then the soft sound of Teddy hitting the floor. "Bye. Bye-bye."

Slowly I creep around the door of Paul's room, and there he is standing in his crib, surrounded by his toys and stuffed animals. He sees me standing there and starts to bounce up and down, his wet diapers making a squishy sound inside his rubber pants. "Fish," he says, pointing to the fish on his mobile. "Fish swim." He pushes the mobile and it swings around his head.

Dumbfounded, I approach his crib. "Paul! You fraud." I reach out to hug him. "How long have you been talking? Why didn't you tell me?"

I rolled over and looked at the illuminated dial of the clock. It was three in the morning and dark, deadly quiet. I was covered with a cold sweat. Slowly I started to cry, the hot tears running down my cheeks. Jim stirred and his hand brushed my cheek. In his sleep, he drew me to him. "I know, I know," he said. "It's all right. It will be all right. You'll see."

Over and over again I had this dream, or some other like it, wish-fulfillment dreams of Paul beginning to speak. Maybe words, long words, complicated sentences, would come pouring out of him. Maybe like Lord Macauley, a little after the maid had spilled scalding tea on him, he would suddenly say, "Madam, the agony is abated." I began to cherish such stories, part of the folklore of every generation: stories about Einstein not speaking till he was five, about the grown-up children of friends, now lawyers or college teachers, who were late to speak.

Language seemed to us so basic, so central to the human condition. For a long time Jim laughed with our friends who asked about Paul. "He's still just humanoid," he would say, and I knew he was referring to the fact that Paul wasn't speaking. Now, as Paul approached his second birthday, Jim didn't say that anymore. It wasn't a joke any longer. I wondered sometimes if we didn't overvalue language. After all, we were two English teachers. We lived in a world of words.

Jim and I met over a seminar table in graduate school in St. Louis. We met over books and words, over writing and teaching, a shared space for two very different people from two very different backgrounds. We truly believed we were remaking ourselves through literature and the intellectual life, which seemed at times to be our only common ground. Like many young adults, we felt that through deliberation and will and hard work we could have just the kind of life we both wanted. And by the time Paul was born, we did have much of what we both wanted out of life. Jim and I had new jobs at a prestigious liberal arts college in a little river town in Minnesota where we had many friends. We had bought a mid-nineteenth-century house, which we worked on in the summer — painting, papering, refinishing antique furniture. In a very real sense, the world was all before us. All we needed now was a child, the kind of child we both had been.

We were both very conscious of wanting children. On our first date, Jim had talked about "our kids." At first I had been puzzled, alarmed, then realized that he was talking about his five younger brothers and sisters, especially the last four who were much younger than he was. He spoke of them with such pride, showing me tattered black-and-white pictures he carried everywhere with him in his wallet. " 'When Mum tells me to go to bed, I know I don't have to,' " he quoted his youngest sister as saying. " 'When Dad tells me to go to bed, I know I don't have to. *But when Jimmy tells me . . .*' " And I could picture little Mary rolling her eyes and scuttling, running for cover to her bedroom. "Jimmy," I gathered, was the real father in this household, the one with authority, but also with warmth, kindness, generosity of spirit. He had come home from school when he was sixteen to care for everyone so his mother, in her last pregnancy, could stay in the hospital and recover from high blood pressure. I had been very attracted to this image of Jim, the older brother, the young "father," the responsible one who every day cooked four pounds of potatoes and saw that the children got off to school on time.

I had grown up as the daughter of an Associated Press reporter who worked on the Hill, in Washington, D.C., a much-loved father who was only just able to keep his family of four alive in suburban Virginia on his poorly paid ability to use words. My father sometimes joked that he had really wanted to be a latter-day gentleman farmer, the kind who sat on the porch drinking bourbon, watching the mountains, and reading Thoreau. My mother had grown up on a "real" farm, and for her the suburbs of Washington were a place of exile. She never wanted to leave the land in the Shenandoah Valley that her family had farmed for more than two hundred years.

Mother's family was Scotch-Irish, a modern-day clan that had stayed in the valley, dozens of them, since the eighteenth century. They were worldly, assertive, cheerful, hardworking, successful. Her father, a member of the Virginia state legislature, was a "good shot," but, blind in one eye, he never wanted to waste his vision on reading books.

My father's family also lived a Southern agrarian myth, but they were otherworldly, deeply religious, poetic, great readers. They no longer owned the land they once had had. Living in poverty in Macon, Georgia, my father grew up playing with his two sisters and his friends in Civil War trenches still visible in the fields behind the house. The children never had enough to eat, but what they did have was served on antique Meissen china. My father remembers once stealing a whole loaf of bread and climbing the chinaberry tree in the back garden to eat it secretly. He told me he dreamt of Hershey bars (someday he would have a whole one all to himself) and of Welch's grape juice (an unheard-of luxury).

They were never safe from the "wolf at the door," yet my father's family, I could see even as a child, was a family bound together by a warmly self-deprecating humor, a joy in life, a rare love that held steady against all assaults from outside. They were almost a whole culture, a country to themselves. Words were what they knew best, what made them their livings, what brought them their deepest satisfactions. As a child, I was thought to take after that side of my family.

In many ways I was a special child. Forbidden by my father to read Nancy Drew mysteries and given *Alice in Wonderland* instead, I longed to be "ordinary" like my friends. Sometimes I hid out in their houses all afternoon reading Nancy Drew, then walked home feeling both sated and unsatisfied, trudging through the gardens and climbing over the back fences of our modest postwar neighborhood, wanting to be special again.

My younger brother and I grew up reading and acting out our books on the back porch "stage," or in the woods at the bottom of the hill, or on the "pirate ship" in the compost heap with the telephone pole "mast" at the end of the garden. Frank eventually decided he was more interested in physics than in literature, and when we were teenagers, he set up a laboratory in the basement with oscilloscopes and enough electricity to "electrocute the whole county," in my mother's words of grumbling admiration. During those years, I climbed onto the roof to hide from Mother and to write poetry in the style of Shelley's "Ode to the West Wind."

I went to Bryn Mawr, then to Chapel Hill for an M.A. in American literature at the moment when the civil rights movement was just beginning and when the English department was still holding on to the Southern agrarian mythmaking that was so familiar to me from my own family. Afterward, I went to teach in a pretentious undergraduate college in California modeled (Disney-style) on Oxbridge. In 1965 I went to Washington University in St. Louis to work on a Ph.D. in English.

And there I met Jim, who had grown up in the west of Ireland in a poor Catholic family for whom Protestants — "your ilk," as he was fond of saying — were "dirty Prods." At the age of two Jim had been evacuated from London and the Blitz to live close to his mother's family in County Mayo. He lived there for eight years with his mother and his brother, while his father built runways for the RAF.

In the little two-room Irish cottage, there was no radio, no electricity, no books, no toys except the ones given on Christmas Day and which were broken the day after. Jim remembers his mother sitting by the turf fire long after the boys were in bed, knitting and talking aloud to herself in her loneliness. At three Jim learned to read from his mother's knitting magazines, and for the next few years, while his brother Tommy learned to dig in the garden or to explore the countryside, Jim preferred to play "offices" on the doorstep. The old people were alarmed at this precocious young intellectual. His grandmother, coming to visit one day, stopped to watch Jim arranging his papers and his pebble money on the front steps. Shaking her head sadly, she told her daughter, "You'd better keep that one in school because he will never amount to anything."

Moving back to postwar London, Jim and his family returned to a privation unknown even in dirt-poor, rocky Ireland. His father captured a slum house for his family only because he happened to be walking past just as the previous family was being thrown out on the sidewalk, furniture and all. They moved into this house with no electricity, no hot water, and with only gas light.

Within a year of moving to London, Jim had been discovered by the parish priest. He was sent to a private Catholic school in the healthy countryside of Hertfordshire. A scholarship boy, recognized and singled out by family and the church as brilliant and promising, he was of course intended for the priesthood. He became top scholar and head prefect, then was sent, again by the church, to Cambridge for a degree in English. There he entered the orbit of F. R. Leavis and read D. H. Lawrence. In their different ways, they spoke to him of his own condition, and, of course, the expected happened. The old faith broke apart; the old self broke apart. When I met Jim in St. Louis, there also to get his Ph.D. in English, he was reeling from an old life, from centuries-old beliefs, from a lost country, two lost countries, from a lost worldview.

I had never met anyone so richly and vividly alive, so different from myself. And yet, of course, here again was someone in exile, someone whose family had struggled with poverty, another special child bearing the not entirely welcome burden of family expectations. I didn't see any of this at the time, could never have connected Jim's family to my own, his life history to mine. All I thought was that Jim needed someone to stand beside him as he put himself together again, to make a new vision out of the literature we both loved.

Now, of course, I can see that Jim and I were two uneasy "special children." We both longed to be ordinary, but also exceptional, singular, set apart. Born in a far more privileged time than our parents, we wanted to be the intellectuals we both had become and which was expected of us, yet we also longed to be of the earth, earthly, rooted in the soil of the families we both loved so much yet had left so far behind. There was, however, nothing in Jim's life history and nothing in mine which prepared us for a child like Paul.

When Paul was twenty-two months old, we took him to his pediatrician in the Twin Cities. As always, the doctor seemed delighted with this beautiful, alert child. Paul — bright-eyed, active, energetic, obviously healthy — was put on the floor to walk around after he had his shots. He inspected the medicine cabinet but couldn't get the door to open. He moved over to the examining table and started to pull out the metal extension. Dr. Skye tried to show him what to do, but Paul brushed him aside and moved back to the cabinet drawers. The doctor intervened again with a toy doctor's bag that he kept in the room. "Look, Paul." He showed him the little rubber reflex hammer and tapped him gently on the knee. Paul looked briefly at the doctor and moved away again, this time to the wheels on the bottom of a stool. He bent down to examine them, then started to drive the stool across the floor.

Giving up with a sigh, the doctor turned to us. "Do you have any worries?" he asked. We told him that we were worried that Paul still wasn't speaking. Dr. Skye turned to watch Paul again as he bent to pick up, with precise finger-to-thumb movement, the tiniest bit of lint from the floor. The doctor listened thoughtfully as we told him about our concerns, then remarked that Paul was still young, that he was obviously bright and well developed. All children are different, and speech would come, he assured us.

Then the conversation turned to Dr. Skye's own son, a senior at the college where Jim and I taught. He was very worried about his son, who was not happy with his major and was at a loss about what to do with his life. Jim and I listened sympathetically. We liked this doctor a lot, partly because he treated us as equals, as professionals ourselves, but even more because he let us know that he too was a parent, that we were all in this thing together. There was something comforting in this thought, and we trusted Dr. Skye, valuing his judgment precisely because he was willing to be vulnerable with us.

When his letter arrived three days later, I was not prepared: "I have thought about Paul frequently since you were here last. I am concerned that Paul is having a 'block' in his speech development which is psychic in origin. I say so because of a 'feeling' I had about him when I was with him. I got poor eye contact from him and he seemed more interested in things than in me. He didn't seem to have any very strong feelings about me and this concerns me."

Dr. Skye went on to suggest that I read *Dibs: In Search of Self,* the story of a very bright child who had a block in speech but learned to talk under the care of a therapist. I was devastated. I had read this book. It was the story of a child rejected by his surgeon mother, who had had to give up her work when her child was born. This mother so deeply resented her child's existence that she succeeded in depriving him of his very "self." *Dibs* was the story of a child who was very bright, but because he was so deeply disturbed he retreated from reality until a caring doctor reclaimed him and helped him to develop the strong, healthy personality that his mother had taken from him.

Dr. Skye thought that I was, in some way, perhaps unconsciously, rejecting my child. Paul's seeming brightness, his normal looks and clear, fine features, made it appear that he *could* learn to speak if he just *would*. So why did he lack the motivation to learn? It must be because of an "emotional block," as the doctor's letter said.

Had I caused my child to withdraw from reality? All the ghosts that I had pushed aside since becoming a parent came crowding back. I remembered an aunt's surprise when I told her I would continue to teach after Paul was born. "But won't that cause asthma?" she wanted to know. No more was said, but the guilt was planted, from that and from a thousand other injunctions I had heard all my life. Asthma, hyperactivity, school problems, delayed development, allergies, psychological withdrawal, autism — all came from working mothers. The first two or three years are absolutely critical in the development of a child; the personality is set by the age of six. A mother can never be too careful. So much, so very much, is at stake.

I forgot that my own mother had worked full-time in an office for most of the first three years of my life and that I was cared for, during that time when we lived in Richmond, Virginia, by a loving black woman. If I had stopped to think, I might have remembered that Virgie was my other mother and that it was her presence that I would find at the very deepest layer of my consciousness. It was Virgie's ample lap that I sought when I ran too close to the edge of the dining room table and blacked my eye. It was Virgie who put butter on my eye to bring down the swelling, who put a tobacco poultice on my foot when later I ran across the lawn barefoot and stepped on a hornet.

I might have remembered this large woman standing for hours in the kitchen, ironing the ruffles on my dresses, her sore, swollen feet in soft, flattened-out, maroon carpet slippers. It was Virgie's broad shoulder that sheltered me when the grocery store owner tickled me under the chin and I didn't know how to answer "Cat got your tongue?" And it was this other mother who held me up to the mirror to chastise my tears when I didn't want to play with Stompy, my friend from down the block who bored me sometimes: "Ain't you shamed! Look at your face." I had looked at my face in the mirror by the front door, my small white face, reddened now with angry tears, next to her glistening black face. "Now you run along and play nice with your little friend what's come to play with you!"

It is these memories that run like a broad river of love in the rocks underground; they are there beneath the sharper, more focused memories of my mother and father, who, I knew, also cherished me and loved me but (it almost seems) came a little later. But when Paul was a baby, these memories were not present to me. I yearned to be with him, as I know my mother yearned to be with me, and out of that longing I made a moral imperative that simply did not exist. As he started to slow down in his development, I began to read back into the past a maternal neglect that had never been there.

At the same time, I seemed to forget my own emerging feminism, my conviction that motherhood need not be an exclusive full-time job, that mothers, like everyone else, need meaningful work or at least a social life outside the home. I had never intended to take time off from teaching and I had always planned on finishing my dissertation. But now it seemed that two absolute and incompatible ideals — love and work — were at war in my head. And it seemed that there would never be any way of bringing them together.

I remembered Paul's first year when I had rushed off to teach, then back home the four blocks from my office or classroom to nurse him. I remembered how Jim and I, with the aid of babysitters and household help, spelled each other at home, how we held conferences at the kitchen table, baby on lap. And now I searched my memory for all those times I had left Paul. Coming home once, I found Paul's babysitter working her calculus problems in our dining room and holding him in the crook of her arm as he sat on the edge of the table. Paul was waving around a sheet of paper and banging her on the shoulder with it. Just as I walked in, she paused to nuzzle his neck, to kiss his round cheek, and he was hunching his shoulders, laughing and hitting her head with the crumpled paper. Could Paul have been damaged by that? Surely not.

Or by leaving him with another babysitter — a young man from South Africa, whose missionary parents had worked with Zulus all his life, an anthropology major already deeply awakened to the injustices of the world? I remember coming home one day, after a rain, to find Steve holding Paul out by the clothesline. Steve was carefully gathering a raindrop, a little rainbow shining in the sun, onto his index finger. Paul was reaching for the drop, a look of wonder on his face.

Could Paul have been damaged by such times without me? It seemed impossible to believe, and yet, I still felt deeply threatened by Dr. Skye's letter. I had waited so long for this child. I had lost two other children before Paul, and the pregnancy with him had been unusually difficult. All of this I had pushed underground at the moment of his birth. I had told myself that none of this mattered anymore, but I was carrying an enormous burden of anxiety and unresolved guilt from this troubled pregnancy which I was only just holding at bay.

Reading the letter, I remembered only my own exhaustion, distraction, worry, during the months after Paul's birth. I thought of all those moments when I had had no time for him. I saw myself standing to grade papers at the mantelpiece as Paul crawled around me on the floor and pulled himself up by hanging onto my legs. I pictured him in the bathtub as I sat next to him on the floor, grading English comprehensive exams when this was the only way I could buy even one hour of work time on a babysitter-less weekend.

Dr. Skye's words — "I am concerned that Paul is having a 'block' in his speech development which is psychic in origin" — came to me now as blame, not as worry; as criticism, not as the honest expression of the doctor's own care for this child. None of our long talks about his own son, none of his appeal to us as parent professionals, stood me now in good stead. The Trojan horse had been let in, the gift taken through the gates to spill out the enemy within. I couldn't handle this letter. It had a thousand hooks that attached themselves to a thousand suppressed anxieties.

At the back of my mind was the word *autism*. Wasn't *autistic* the name for the withdrawn child who doesn't speak, the child abandoned by a rejecting mother? I remembered the first time I really thought about this condition. When I was in graduate school in St. Louis, a friend, another graduate student, told me about a child who she said was made autistic because she hadn't been touched enough as a baby. Laughing, she jumped up and ran across the room to her own sleeping baby, to stroke his cheek and to kiss him on the forehead. His eyelids fluttered and he woke to smile briefly into her eyes before falling asleep again.

"*This* one won't ever be autistic," my friend said, confident that she had surrounded her child with the protective care that wards off the evil of autism. Now I wondered if I had failed to do that. I must have failed my child in some nameless, unidentified way.

Reading the doctor's letter, Jim pulled back and said simply, "This isn't a diagnosis. We still don't know what the problem is. But if it is an emotional block, and not some neurological damage, the prognosis is very good. Don't all these children recover in the end?" But I couldn't hear this or any other comfort. I had damaged my child.

During this time, Jim was very steady, but I felt I was spinning out of orbit. Also, in ways we could hardly identify, the tension was building between us and the old spontaneous warmth Jim used to show Paul was beginning to be damped down. It was a long time before I even began to notice this. But by the time he was two, Paul had become the child of troubled, not proud, parenting: a watched child.

Jim was staying later and later at work, or returning to his office most evenings. Weekends were gone also. There were always papers to grade, class preparations, endless meetings, and in the summer, both of our dissertations to finish. We worked most of the time. But increasingly, Jim worked in his office; I carried work home in the afternoons to be with Paul as much as possible.

My life had become a series of interruptions. Child care interrupted academic work; academic work distracted me from taking care of my child. By Paul's second year, Jim had made a choice, the only one he could have made, given his personality and the demands made upon him: his work came first. I couldn't do that and so remained bound by ambivalence. And suddenly, it seemed, Jim was no longer there.

Sometimes I thought about the first year of Paul's life: our pride and pleasure, our wish to be with him most of the time, our sense that anything was possible with this marvelous, bright child. I remembered Jim coming home from work. "Where is the bob-a-somes?" He called his pet name for Paul from the kitchen as he dropped his briefcase down on the floor and threw off his coat. "*There* he is! De bob-a-somes, de bob-a-somes, de Daddy bob-a-somes," Jim chanted, as he swung Paul high above his head, as he brought him down and kissed his cheek. "De *Daddy* bob-a-somes."

Paul would squeal and wriggle and laugh that fat baby laugh we both loved so much. Jim would settle him into the crook of his arm and sit down on the sofa. "And how is my son today? Read any good books?"

Just after Paul was born, Jim read a book called *A Child's Mind*. He avidly studied the development of visual attentiveness, the onset of visually directed reaching and the social smile. He read about RNA and DNA and the intraneuronal theory of learning, the measurement of intelligence and the development of concepts and language. He was fascinated.

After the first year, Jim didn't read books about children anymore. I went on reading Dr. Spock and the Gissell Institute books and talking to friends, other mothers, about what to expect from a baby. And by now, when Paul was approaching his second birthday, Jim had grown to depend on me to interpret any sign of illness, to mark the milestones of growth and development, to decide whether something was "normal" or not. This was part of mother lore, I knew that. But we had started out so equitably, two equally engaged and responsible parents, just as we were two equal professionals. I began to feel a double loss — one of Paul, the child I thought we had had, the other of Jim, the father I thought Paul had had — a loss it would take me many more years to recognize and admit.

I was now the one who initiated consultations with doctors. I called and made appointments, sometimes took Paul there alone, and came back to discuss the results with Jim. And with this added responsibility came added power. I was now the one with definitional power, the one who had talked face to face with the doctors, who filtered what they had said, who interpreted the results to Jim. More and more he was left out, and I was leaving him out. But again, it was years before I began to see this.

All during this time, I was drinking too much. In the evenings after Paul was in bed, I drank sherry or beer as I folded the laundry or washed the dishes, as I picked up toys and vacuumed the living room floor. I wanted to shut down, to hang a sign across my face, CLOSED FOR THE DAY. I didn't want to feel any more anxiety, the constant jumping at my nerve endings, the too alert watchfulness as I studied Paul's every move. But even more than that, I didn't want to feel a new and terrible sense of deprivation, a suspicion that some profound loss, still unknown to me but looming larger than life itself, was gathering just ahead.

CHAPTER 3

Doctors and Diagnoses

T wo months after Dr. Skye's letter, Paul had his second birthday: a happy, cake-smeared occasion, which we celebrated with my father, who was visiting us for the month of August. Paul still wasn't talking. He remained a sweet little boy, mostly happy, very affectionate, curious about the world, but he was silent. He could point now, and he showed pleasure and distress with a high-pitched "eeee" for happiness and a low "ummm-mummm" for unhappiness, but he had no words, and he never made any attempt at all to imitate our speech. He sometimes turned away from us when we tried to talk to him or to get his attention by calling his name, but usually he wanted to share his interests with us, to include us in all his play. To communicate, he took us by the hand, led us at a gallop across the room, then threw the hand at whatever object he wanted — the box of cookies, the refrigerator door, the toy on a high shelf. He stood for hours, it seemed, on chairs by light switches, flicking them on and off, on and off again. This gave him the most intense pleasure he seemed to know.

I didn't want to return to Dr. Skye and decided instead to take Paul to our family doctor in town to see if we could get a referral to other pediatric experts. Dr. Thorsten gave him an examination — ears, throat, chest, eyes, reflexes — then lifted him to the floor. Paul ran for the stool and quickly pushed it up to the wall. Before I could get to him, he climbed up on the stool and flicked off the light switch just inside the door. The fluorescent light went off, and the examining room was plunged into darkness, then the light flickered slowly back on again. "Eeeee!" Paul turned to us to see if we appreciated what he was doing.

"No, Paul!" I grabbed him at the waist and swung him off the stool. I shoved the stool into the center of the room, then backed up against the wall to hide the light switch. Paul hesitated, and the sides of his mouth started to pull down. Then he turned to the stool as it came to rest by the examining table. He shouted *"Eeee"* again, and turned the stool upside down, spinning the little wheels on it around and around.

Dr. Thorsten watched him thoughtfully. Paul's back was to him, his curly head bent over the stool, the palm of his hand rapidly brushing the wheels, making them spin faster and faster. "Eeeee!" Paul, smiling broadly, glanced at both of us.

Finally, the doctor looked at me and chuckled. "Well, obviously the wheels are turning around inside his head!" He looked back at Paul to consider him again, adding slowly, "But maybe he has a hearing problem. That might explain why he is still not talking. Because otherwise, he seems to be a very bright little boy."

Dr. Thorsten gave us a referral for a full workup, including auditory, neurological, and psychological testing, at a clinic in the Twin Cities. That October, I went with Paul alone to see the first doctor, a neurologist. I felt numb by this time and was just going through the paces, hardly thinking we would learn anything new about Paul. So once again, I was unprepared, unguarded, not ready for the blow to come.

Dr. Tremain was a young man, with a pale, drawn face and an abrupt, almost dismissive manner. Instead of taking a history of Paul's development, something the other doctors had so carefully done, he gave Paul the briefest of examinations, ears, throat, reflexes. Then he carried him down the hall and set him on the floor. Paul ran back to me, in his sturdy little toed-in way. He covered the full length of the hallway, squealing with joy as he leapt into my arms. I buried my face in his curly hair, then turned back to the doctor, inquiringly. What was he after?

"They usually do that," Dr. Tremain remarked, and disappeared behind a door. The nurse smiled and said he would see me in a moment in his office. I stood there, puzzled. What was the doctor getting at? Was he trying to see if Paul missed me and recognized me, or was he checking his gait? Paul did run in that funny, rather awkward way, but on the other hand he did recognize me and clearly loved me with all his heart. Of course he did, but by then I was proud to note even this obvious small truth.

Dr. Tremain opened his office door and, staring at the floor, gestured with his hand for me to come in. Just inside the door, Paul pushed a chair against the wall, climbed onto it, and reached for the light switch. I took him down and tried to hold him in my lap.

"I believe your son is retarded" was what the doctor was saying.

I stared at him, but his face was blurred and seemed far away, even though I knew he was right there, just across his desk on the other side of this bright, expensively furnished room. Dimly, I became aware that Paul was struggling in my arms. I was holding him too tightly and I loosened my grip. Paul wiggled his shoulders and tried to slide out of my grasp and onto the floor, but I lifted him back onto my lap and stared at the doctor over his head.

The sound of the doctor's voice seemed to be coming to me in waves. I caught "probably only moderately retarded," then heard "need to run some tests."

Retarded. Suddenly, and intensely, I wanted Jim there beside me. But then I knew I didn't want him there. None of this could be true without Jim there to hear it. I stared at a heavy crystal ashtray on the table beside me. Paul picked up the ashtray and was about to drop it on the glass-topped table. I caught it just in time.

Retarded. The dread word for all parents. The word, of all words, I didn't want to hear. Deafness, learning disabilities, almost any other diagnosis would be easier. Retardation seemed so final and so hopeless.

"But Paul knows where all the light switches are," I began. Dr. Tremain stared at me. "He knows where the light switches are in our house, and even in some of the stores downtown . . ."

I trailed off. Clearly this had no meaning for the doctor. And then something flipped over in my mind, and I saw the other side. And that's when I thought — grimly, but with determination — Well, this is it. At last we have something definite, something to hang on to and get used to, something to deal with and get on with. Something to understand.

I know we talked for a while after this, but I don't remember anything of what we said. I was numb to the bone, hardly more than a robot. I would get through this somehow, but what it was exactly that I would get through, and how it was that I was going to get through it, I didn't know. I knew only that I was standing up, saying good-bye to the messenger that I now hated so much, and I was leaving his office.

Sometime later I read in the doctor's report: "The mother seemed to accept her child's handicap readily enough. In fact, she showed an unusual maturity and resourcefulness. She mentioned other retarded children in her community and commented that the family have a number of friends to turn to for advice and help in dealing with such a child."

Instead of being grateful, I read these words of praise with a sinking heart, with a sense that I had somehow betrayed my child. How could

I have thought, even for a moment (as if it were up to me), that Paul was retarded? And later also I realized that this initial dazed acceptance was typical of my way of handling bad news. I trusted authorities at first; then as I took time to reflect, I usually questioned them and felt in the process that I had given in too quickly, hadn't taken the time to consult my own feelings and intuitions. What I thought of as my independence of judgment and strength of will usually came later and sometimes meant I had to go back and retrace my steps.

But even as I drove home from the doctor's appointment, crying all the way, the diagnosis didn't make sense to me. I knew little about retardation, particularly about high-functioning Down's syndrome children. I was resistant to this diagnosis, as all parents are, but also Paul *looked* too bright. There was such a look of understanding in his eyes most of the time. He was too interested in the world, too curious, even though the objects of curiosity were themselves rather "curious." How could a retarded child have found all the light switches? Irrationally, I held on to this strange little detail.

Jim's reaction when I told him that evening was incredulity. Retardation didn't make any sense at all to him. After dinner and after Paul was tucked into bed, we built a fire in the fireplace and drank a bottle of wine together. We talked late into the night. At some point that evening, I remember we put on a record. I'm not sure now what it was, something by Bach I think, perhaps the B Minor Mass. Then as we listened together to the slow, early chords of the opening Introit, curled up together on the couch before the fire that had burned down now to embers, we both began to cry.

"What if it is true?" I could hardly bear now to look at the raw pain on Jim's face.

Jim considered, taking my question as a real question. "If it is true," he began slowly, smoothing the hair off my forehead, "if it *is* true, then Paul . . ." And he waved his arm, taking in the room, the fireplace, the music, the books of poetry. "Then all of this, everything that brings us comfort at a time like this" — and I knew he meant the intellectual and feeling life that we shared, the books we both loved, the music we were now listening to — "then none of this will help Paul. If he is retarded."

A month later we took Paul to the university hospital for the first test, a sedated electroencephalogram. We were shown into a small room, a cubicle with glass walls and a slippery plastic couch. I held Paul as he was given a shot of Seconal, then gently lowered him to the couch so the technician could begin to glue the electrodes to his scalp. Jim sat at the bottom of the couch, holding Paul's feet.

Sensing my feelings, the technician talked to me quietly as she worked. "The glue, the collodion, will come off easily later. It will dry and just peel off. You can easily wash it out of his hair with shampoo." She glanced at me and stopped, knowing I found it hard to hear her, hard to think. When one of my tears fell onto Paul's sleeping face, she gently brushed it away and went on with her gluing. Jim reached out to take my hand, but I knew he was as unhappy and confused as I was.

Finally, the electrodes were all in place. But I wanted to cry out: This is all wrong. He doesn't need this test. Look at him. Paul's cheeks were so pink, his head so beautifully formed, his legs so sturdy and well muscled now that he had begun to lengthen out of his baby roundness into a new little boyishness. This small form, in Osh-Kosh B'Gosh dungarees and high-topped leather shoes, was such an image of health and competence. Paul clutched his panda bear loosely in his arms, his bear that had gone all ragged and thready at the knees from so much love. Soon he would be up and running again. But the wires, those wires . . . I had to turn away from this small baby monster and leave the room.

I went into the main room where the technician was now fiddling with dials and watching the wavy lines tracked by the needles on a long strip of paper. She started to mark some places on the paper and to fold it as it spilled out of the machine. I knew she saw something. There were answers to our questions on that piece of paper, messages that I couldn't read.

"Why are you marking that part?" I asked.

"We have to wait for the doctor to interpret this," she reminded me, but her voice was kind and I knew she would have liked to give me some answers now.

What are they looking for, I wondered. A seizure disorder? Localized damage to one part of the brain? A brain tumor? And suddenly I saw Paul in a high-sided white metal hospital crib. I saw him lying there, his head shaved and bandaged, a tube down his throat, IV lines in his arms. I saw him lying there unconscious. Not responding to our touch, our voices. Maybe dying of an invasive tumor that had grown past surgery. Maybe facing radiation or chemotherapy.

Dr. Tremain, who had ordered this test, walked into the room and paused to watch the needles squiggling their little lines across the page.

"Doctor . . ." I started to say.

He turned to peer into my face. "Don't take it so hard. Most parents are very grateful."

"Grateful?" I didn't think I had heard right.

"Of course. Grateful. When we find a brain tumor."

I must have looked disbelieving, because he paused for a moment. "When we find a brain tumor we can treat." He turned and left the room.

"So I'm an ungrateful mother," I muttered, turning to Jim, who grimaced in sympathy, then put his arm around my shoulder, as together we watched the last of the lines traced across the paper and the machine was turned off.

"You can take him home now." But when I scooped Paul up in my arms, his head rolled suddenly to the side, then flopped to the back. Never, even when he was a tiny baby, had he flopped about like this. His arms and legs were rubbery, and it was hard to hold a child who couldn't mold his body to mine.

He woke up slightly and tried to hold his head up as we walked through the waiting room and out to the car. He was restless, trying to fight off the drug. He must look very odd, I realized, seeing faces turned toward us, then quickly away, as we walked to the exit. Through the haze of my tears, I could see that people were wondering what was the matter with this child. "Just a brain tumor," I wanted to hiss in their faces as we walked past. "Or maybe a seizure disorder. If we are lucky."

Another one of the tests Dr. Tremain ordered was a skull x-ray. We returned to the university hospital, expecting a routine x-ray, without sedation, without trauma. I brought Paul into the x-ray room and lifted him to the metal table. He reached up to touch the equipment hanging above his head. "Dah," he said, pointing with interest. "Dah!"

He was so relaxed and trusting. And why not? He couldn't turn anything on. Two minutes of exploring and he would have been satisfied. But no, the technician was in a hurry, they didn't have time for a child to explore.

"Lie down, Paul."

He didn't. Of course.

"Lie down," she repeated. Nothing. "Look, honey, you have to lie down so we can take a picture of your head."

Still nothing. The nurse pushed on his shoulders. When this didn't work, she knocked his feet out from under him, with one clean sweep of her arm against the back of his knees.

Paul sat down with a thunk, startled. With a sharp intake of breath, he started to cry and tried to rise again.

"No, I said *no*. Lie down."

I tried to help. "Lie down, Paul. It's all right. I'm right here." I tried to hold him down with my hands on his chest, my head down next to his head. But by now he was crying too hard to hear me.

The nurse turned to me. "You'll have to leave."

"But he'll do better if I stay."

"I'm sorry. We have another patient in ten minutes."

Held forcibly down on the table now, Paul was beginning to cry loudly in great rasping sobs and to throw his body from side to side.

"Down, I said *down*." The nurse called another attendant in and together they held Paul down.

"I can put a lead apron on," I said. "I'm not pregnant."

"No. You have to leave." They meant it. Reluctantly, I backed out the door and joined Jim outside, just arrived from parking the car.

"What's going on in there?"

"Paul wouldn't lie down and they are forcing him down. He's frightened. He doesn't understand. They wouldn't let me stay. The bitches. *The bitches*."

Together we stood outside the door to the x-ray room, listening to Paul's panicky screams. This was wrong, all wrong. All my suppressed anger at Dr. Tremain and at the whole abusive, heartless medical system came to the surface, and I was shaking.

"I'm going in." I started toward the door.

"No. You'll just interrupt the x-ray, and they'll have to do it over again."

We paced down the hall and back again, the sobs growing softer, then louder again.

This time it was Jim. "Let's go in there. This is terrible."

"No. They're almost finished now."

We stood there. I felt awful. I had betrayed my child by letting him be called retarded. Then I had willingly handed him over to these monsters in white coats. And for what? A skull x-ray that I didn't think would show anything at all.

At last the door opened. "You can come in now."

We rushed in and took Paul in our arms. "It's all right, lovey. You're all right." His hair was damp, his face mottled red and white and streaked with tears. But seeing us, he stopped crying instantly.

Compared with the skull x-ray, the audiologist's test and the speech pathologist's examination were a snap. Paul enjoyed the little soundproof room and the test for his hearing. And the interview with the speech pathologist was nothing less than a treat.

Sarah Bartlett came into the waiting room and stood close to Paul, who was putting together a puzzle. She watched him for a moment as he rapidly, expertly inserted each wooden piece. "Paul," she called softly just behind him. He didn't turn around but instead flipped the puzzle over to knock the pieces out, then started over again. "Paul." No response.

Gently, she put a hand on his shoulder, then stooped down beside him to pick up a piece of the puzzle, the smokestack of the train. She handed it to him with a smile. "Paul, when you are through with this I want you to come with me."

He turned to look her briefly in the eye, then finished the puzzle, and took her hand to be led into her office. Once he glanced back at us, then seeing the light switch just inside the door, he climbed up a chair and started to flick it off and on again. *"Eeeh."* He turned to her to share his pleasure in this discovery, and she closed the door behind him.

Half an hour later, Sarah returned holding Paul by the hand. He went back to the puzzles, and she sat down beside us. "You noticed," she began, "he didn't turn around when I said his name. All through the test, I felt he responded to noises by jerking suddenly. He showed that he heard them, but he didn't ever look around to search for the source of the sound."

We nodded. This was familiar to us.

"He doesn't seem to be attuned to language. In fact, he seemed not to respond even to the simplest of auditory commands. He had to guess what I wanted by my gestures or by looking at the materials. He watched what I was doing, in other words, to figure out what I wanted from him. Actually, he did extremely well, way above age level, with puzzles and the other materials he could manipulate. But have you noticed, does he ever try to imitate speech sounds? Because he didn't with me."

"No. He doesn't."

"Does he like music?"

"Yes, loves it." And we told her about the little windup record player he carried around with him everywhere, playing "Humpty Dumpty" and "London Bridge" and "Camptown Races" over and over and over again.

"That's a good sign. But have you noticed any unusual behaviors in him? For example, does he rock a lot in his crib?"

"Well, yes, now that you mention it. He's happy to rock maybe half an hour at a time. Longer, if we let him."

"Does he turn toy cars upside down and spin the wheels?"

A vivid memory of Paul playing recently with another little boy came back to me. Richard, who was also two, drove the cars down pretend roads, he crashed the cars into each other, he brought out ambulances and fire trucks, he made vroom-vroom noises. Paul turned cars upside down and spun their wheels. I felt a chill as I remembered this. "Yes, he does."

Sarah went on. "He seems to be very interested in lights, am I right?"

"As you can see." Jim chuckled. "But what do you think the problem is? It's not his hearing?"

"We need to wait for all the tests to come back, but I will tell you that it's a hopeful sign that he responded so well to me. His eye contact was good, he was very curious about the testing materials, he clearly trusted me. He showed a variety of appropriate responses, including frustration when he couldn't make something work or couldn't understand me. All that is good. He seems to be a happy child, am I right? And very affectionate?"

"Oh, yes." We looked over at Paul playing, and he glanced at us with a smile. "Eeeh, eeeh." He brought over a toy telephone and placed the receiver to Jim's ear as he dialed. "Eeeh, eeeh," Paul repeated. Jim smiled and spoke into the receiver, "Time to go home now, Paul."

Sarah sent her report to our house a few weeks later, before we had received the other test results. She noted in her letter many of the things she had shared with us. Paul responded to noises, but "did not sustain interest or retain the stimulus long enough to actively search for the source of the noise." And even though she felt that he used "adequate eye contact" with her, she did not feel that he was "responding even to simple auditory commands but rather was reading the intent of the situation" by watching her gestures and the materials she was using.

The report also described Paul's available speech: "His expressive language consisted of a high-pitched 'eeh' utterance, a happy sound ('eh he he'), and a whiny 'uh uh.' He watched the examiner's mouth, but no attempts to imitate sounds were noted."

She concluded, "Although the parents report a significant amount of rocking in the crib, attention to music, interest in lights and wheels on toy cars, I did not feel that this youngster was using autistic defenses in the evaluation session. He related easily to the examiner, asked for help appropriately, and showed a variety of appropriate affective responses (pleasure, surprise, frustration, pain, etc.). The parents also report that Paul is a happy child who adjusts to changes in routine and environment easily." She recommended further tests to rule out "hearing impaired, aphasic language syndrome, or delayed language associated with mental retardation."

Later we were to realize that Sarah Bartlett had narrowly missed an accurate diagnosis. She was about to name Paul "autistic," yet she rejected this diagnosis because Paul was too sociable, too friendly, too attuned to other people. No one in the early seventies believed an autistic child could be so friendly. And yet it was one of the lower-status professionals, a speech pathologist, not a neurologist, whose job and whose predilections led her to spend time with Paul and to watch him closely, who almost made the diagnosis. It would be many more years before Paul was named "autistic-like," and at that time it would also be a woman, again without a higher degree, who was willing to observe closely and to learn from Paul himself what he was and what he needed.

Two months after Paul's first battery of tests, we were called back to the neurologist's office. We returned with a mixture of hope and dread. At last we would know exactly what was the matter with Paul: the test results would tell us conclusively if he was retarded, or hearing impaired, or emotionally blocked. Some days we felt certain that Paul was perfectly normal and that the test results would show this fact. On other days, usually after we had seen him with other children his age, we were terrified, thinking of how he didn't speak and didn't really play, but instead stood for hours on a chair flicking a light switch on and off.

After we were seated in Dr. Tremain's office, he looked down at his desk. He began, not looking at us, but reading instead from the papers in front of him: "The testing so far has shown a normal skull x-ray series and normal sedated sleep electroencephalogram."

Jim and I both leaned forward. My chest felt tight, and I could feel my heart pounding in my throat. "Does that mean he isn't retarded?" we both started to speak at once.

Barely glancing at us, the doctor continued, almost as if we weren't in the same room with him and he was talking to himself, musing out loud. "The audiogram has also come back negative." He paused again, picked up a pencil, and tapped the eraser end against the papers, then glanced at us again. "Your child doesn't appear to have any hearing loss. But we also did a urine metabolic screen for inborn errors of metabolism."

"Yes?" Jim prompted. This was taking forever. Go ahead and get it over with! I wanted to shout at Dr. Tremain. But at the same time I wanted to hold off that evil moment of absolute knowledge, that moment that I knew would forever separate us, Jim and me, from our former selves. Any official knowledge might remove our ambivalence, but it would also remove our innocence, our hope, our trust in a dependable natural order. We would no longer have the child we thought we had when Paul was born.

Dr. Tremain went on, reading the paper before him. "The tests included sulfur-containing amino acids, the indican test, mucopolysaccharides, Dextrostix, reducing substances, ferric chloride, and 24-DNPH."

"Did you find anything the matter with him?" My voice sounded strange, choked, even to my own ears.

The doctor stared at me briefly. "There is no definite evidence to indicate global retardation syndrome at this time."

"You don't think he is retarded?"

"No."

We stared at Dr. Tremain. Looking uncomfortable, he went on, "We found no evidence of retardation or of hearing loss."

"You didn't find anything?" I wanted to hear this, and I didn't want to hear it.

"No, we didn't find anything." Dr. Tremain stood up abruptly and, stepping around the desk, started to move us toward the door. I knew there were many, many more questions to ask, but at that moment, I couldn't for the life of me think of what they might be.

So that was it. The case was closed. Not finding anything clinically the matter with Paul, Dr. Tremain was no longer interested. He had no suggestions, no predictions, and no advice. Jim and I left feeling greatly relieved but just as perplexed as before.

After this, I could almost, almost allow myself to hope again. But Paul's behavior still seemed to be a map of a foreign land, of a country so puzzling and strange and unknown that I could never find my way around it. I needed a legend, an explanatory caption down in the lower left-hand corner. I needed a translation into my own language of what light switching meant, of what Paul's silence meant. And I wasn't sure that I would ever get one.

*

One day shortly after our interview with the doctor, Jim and I were driving, with Paul in the back in his car seat. It was a cold, snowy day, the first of the season. I turned to Jim and said, "I miss the green." Suddenly, from the back of the car, came a clear, sweet tune: "Greensleeves." The music, but not the words. Paul sang through the first several measures.

I was so startled that I pulled the car over to the side of the road and turned around to stare at Paul. Jim also stared at him, then at me. Paul stopped singing and looked at us, then turning back to the snowy landscape outside the window he patted the window, leaving an impression of his handprint on the foggy surface. He started humming the "Greensleeves" melody to himself again.

Jim and I said nothing to each other. We almost held our breaths as I pulled back onto the road, and from the back seat of the car came the exquisite singing. Perfect pitch, a clear tone, accurate rhythm. No words, only music, but music that spoke, music that *was* speech. Paul had heard me say "green," and he had understood it and was singing "Greensleeves" in response.

Over the next several weeks, Paul began to sing "Hickory, Dickory Dock" when he heard the word *clock,* and "London Bridge Is Falling Down" when he heard us speak of London. Always the clear, sweet tune, the perfect pitch, but no words, never any words. Yet the songs were provoked by words. He sang them in response to words, so clearly he must be understanding some speech.

Years later I was to read about Broca's patients, who lose the ability to speak but retain the capacity to sing. These patients have damage to "Broca's area" in the left temporal lobe, an area of the cerebral cortex. They can sing a melody or enunciate words clearly when they are sung, but they have lost most of their capacity to speak. Like Paul, they haven't lost the urge to communicate, but must use other methods such as music. I didn't, however, know any of this when Paul was two. I knew only that this child had found a way to communicate, had found his own exquisite, clear speech.

When Paul was almost two and a half, I found that I was pregnant again and things were not going well. I had had an IUD removed eighteen months before and for the last year and a half had been treated with powerful antibiotics for a lingering infection that never seemed to go away. Now, three months pregnant, I was admitted to the hospital and the next day I miscarried. I didn't call the nurses immediately but sat there in my hospital bed for a while, holding this small human shape in my hands. This was Paul's little brother, tiny and perfect, but limp, lifeless, eyes sealed shut, never to open on the world. I held him in my hands, our fourth child, spilled, like two others before Paul, into the world too soon. I didn't want this to be a medical occasion; I wanted to be alone for a little while with this new loss.

What was wrong with me? I had had a series of intractable infections, and before that my incompetent cervix had almost caused the loss of Paul. But I began to wonder if there was some deeper incapacity in me, something more, something as yet undiagnosed. When my doctor came in, I was angry and close to despair. "One swallow does not a summer make," he remarked. But I wondered if there weren't many swallows by now, and if they weren't beginning to add up to something.

I was far sicker than I realized. With a falling blood pressure, I was going into shock and had to be quickly taken into surgery for a D and C, then placed on strong intravenous antibiotics to combat rapidly spreading strep and anaerobic and staph infections. I had puerperal fever, in fact, childbed fever, one of the few cases to appear in modern sanitary conditions, until they became more common with the advent of IUDs.

I recovered quickly, but when I got home a few days later, I was still in pain and shortly afterward the doctor diagnosed thrombophlebitis, a blood clot following the trauma of the miscarriage and repeated infections. I was in and out of the hospital three more times with complications following the miscarriage, once with a dangerous reaction to antibiotics.

Jim called his mother to come over from London to care for Paul, and I finally settled in at home to stay and to convalesce slowly over the next two months. I was told by my doctor that I absolutely must stay off my feet and that I could not teach for the rest of the term. Two colleagues took over my classes, the "Romantic Poets" and a literature course, "The Woman as Artist." I continued to grade papers and exams at home, but my kind friends did the hard work of meeting classes, giving lectures, or guiding discussions.

When I got home after the last hospital visit, I was so startled and then glad to find myself still alive that I spent weeks in utter stillness of spirit. I started lying awake at night, not reading, hardly even thinking. Something important had happened to me. I was a survivor. And I needed to dwell on all my experiences, to turn them over, sort them out, just live with them. I had not died. I would go on living.

One day shortly after I returned home from the hospital for the third time, I was lying on the couch in the living room when Paul walked into the room. He carried a small metal canister of Twinings English Breakfast tea.

"Tea," he said clearly, pointing to the canister. "Tea!" He smiled into my face and leaned up against me. "Tea. Tea."

We knew, of course we knew, that this was nothing more than what all children do. One fine day they recognize and reproduce a meaningful sound: "tea," "daddy," "ice," "mama." After all their babbling, the months of making human sounds, they begin to speak recognizable words, and to use them appropriately in a social context. Just about all children do this and then go on to try out many more new words.

But for Paul, the discovery of speech, the revelation that sounds had meaning and connected with objects in the world, was different, and not just because he was so slow to learn to speak. For him, the discovery was astounding. The look of wonder that came over his face, the reverence with which he said "tea" over and over, his utter, comprehending delight, was striking.

A few days later, he pointed to our red kettle on the stove. "Tea dah," teapot, he said. He started carrying the kettle around with him everywhere, whispering "tea" and "tea dah" over and over. He took it with him when he went to swing next door, he carried it with him to our offices, and the offices and homes of our friends and colleagues. I remember laughing about it and saying most children carry a teddy bear or some favorite toy or a blanket. Not Paul. A teapot was to him the most wonderful object in the world because it *signified*.

Later, as language appeared slowly but steadily, he still tended to repeat words over and over lovingly, caressingly. He walked around the house whispering to himself, "Bah wee wah wah, bah wee wah wah." We had no idea what he meant. Only much later did we realize that he was saying "bunny rabbit, bunny rabbit," one of our affectionate names for him. He repeated it endlessly, under his breath, chuckling with pleasure.

The *fact* of words was to him wonderful, even startling. One evening at dinner, he made a joke. "Bad mama," he said, then "banana," as he picked up the banana from the tray of his high chair. Then over and over, "Banana, bad mama, bad mama, banana!" Increasing excitement, wilder laughter, finally almost hysterical laughter. It was a joke, a wonderful joke because the sounds were so nearly alike, yet they meant very different things. Paul clearly loved the sense of sameness and difference, congruence and incongruity. And it was words that gave him this sense.

At that moment, we relaxed a little. Any child that could make a joke, then appreciate his own humor so vigorously, had possibilities, real possibilities. He was on his way.

CHAPTER 4

"Here Be Dragons"

D E, D E," said Paul, pointing to the street. *Dangerous*. He stood on the curb and pointed into the gutter, ignoring the cars as they sped down Hemingford Road, Islington, northwest London. "De, de," he said more emphatically, and looked up into my face. He was proud of himself for having learned my lesson so well, but he was puzzled. He couldn't figure out why the asphalt and gravel were so dangerous.

"Cars, Paul." I pointed to them as they zipped down the small hill past the late Victorian terrace houses, the newsagent on the corner, the Lamb and Flag pub just opposite our flat. "Cars. Trucks. Buses. *Lorries!*" I knelt down beside him on the curb and turned his face toward a large truck rumbling, bumping past us, its tailgate open, chains at the back clanking on the pavement. Paul glanced at it briefly, then stared again at the surface of the road. He drew his shoulders up, then let them down, sighing with satisfaction. He pointed again at the road and announced with more determination. *"De de."* I knew, although he had learned a different lesson from the one I had intended, that he would not be stepping into the street alone.

I was delighted to be in London. We were here for a whole year's sabbatical. Paul had had his third birthday in August, two weeks before we left for London. And because he now had a little more language, I felt somewhat hopeful about his development. I thought the move to London would be good for him, or at least not harmful, because he had always accepted change before this.

The day before, we had flown into Gatwick, then taken the train through Sussex and south London into Victoria Station. After Paul fell asleep on the seat beside us in the train, Jim and I had bought paper cups of strong, milky tea from a vendor who swayed through the cars with a cart full of cheese and tomato sandwiches, fish paste and cucumber sandwiches, crumpets, raisin scones. Dipping my scone in the steaming tea, I stared out the window at the rows of flats, the long lines of terraced houses just coming awake in the early morning light. I felt brimful of excitement, as if I were seeing the world for the first time.

Each house had its narrow garden backing up to the tracks, its little shed, the line of wash, the French doors opening onto cabbages and roses — all that riot of bloom which in England seems to grow every-where, even in soot and cinders. As the sun moved higher, here and there I could see an old man dig in his garden, a baby in its pram outside a kitchen door. Then a woman, holding a child by one hand and a string bag in the other, crossed the street by a Midlands Bank, headed perhaps for the greengrocer, or the postbox, or the shop on the corner for an ice lolly for the little boy. The child looked the same age as Paul, and I thought of the pleasure we too would have going to the bank, or the greengrocer, or the park. How much fun it was going to be just to walk through London, just to watch the street life, the Indians and Pakistanis in saris, the Greeks and Turks opening their shops in the morning, the Jamaicans playing steel drums on the corner.

Sussex and south London seemed to glow in the freshness of the early morning light. The sunlight, falling cleanly from the upper air, touched the pavement washed by a recent rain, the purple lobelias and the pink geraniums still wet in their hanging baskets on the front of the bank. A man in a white apron cranked down the green-and-white-striped awning above the tables of a Greek restaurant. Staring through the grimy window of the train at all that brightness, I wanted to hold onto that moment when I was shot into a new time, a new day, arriving just past exhaustion for a new beginning.

We had signed a lease on a small garden flat in a renovated early Victorian house. One floor of our flat was a combined living room, dining room, and kitchen, with a beautiful big window at either end, opening onto the garden in back and the street in front. Beneath the main floor, we had two bedrooms in the basement. Paul's room had a Dutch door opening onto a little sunken terrace in the back garden.

The first night we were in our flat, I helped Paul unpack all the toys we had mailed ahead. We laid them out in his room and the living room: his plastic clock with the removable numbers, the Etch-A-Sketch, the trays of colored numbers and letters, Mao Tse-tung, the little stuffed mouse whose tail had been almost chewed off. Then I spent a long time reading to Paul and tucking him up with Baba, his panda bear. I tried to explain about the "new house," telling him we would be going back to the "old house" later that year. Paul kept kicking his quilt off and hopping out of bed. He ran wildly around his room, flicking the light switch on, then off again. He seemed not to understand anything I was saying. I wanted to believe that, because his world was so small, all he needed was his two parents and a few favorite toys. I thought he would soon settle down.

The first week we were in Islington, we got in touch with London Babysitters Unlimited for a couple of regulars who could come several days a week for a few hours, and we took out a joint subscription at the London Library. Having finished my dissertation the year before, I was starting now on a new project on nineteenth-century women's fiction. Jim began to teach the twenty students he had brought over for a London English department program, and I started to write a review I had promised to do on a new book about Victorian women's literature.

Paul, however, seemed to become more and more disturbed. He started to travel with a screwdriver. "Oo ah ah," he called it, and the yellow screwdriver was "Eh oh oo ah ah." First his bed came apart, the guardrail on the top bunk swinging loose. Then chair railings and coat hooks came down in the kitchen. Then a bicycle left in the hall by our upstairs neighbor was found partly dismembered. I tried to answer the phone one day, but the receiver came apart in my hands. More alarmingly, Paul began to work on lights and electric wall sockets in his room before we came to get him in the morning. I found him once with most of the plaster removed from around the socket, as he struggled to get in to where the wires and screws were. Several times, he was probably in real danger, so we took the screwdriver away from him when he went to bed.

As soon as Paul understood that he was not to touch the electric wall sockets, he started to tackle the doorknobs. One evening, we entertained all twenty of Jim's London seminar students in our flat. After dinner, they found they were unable to leave by the front door, as the knob no longer worked. Finally, they used our basement bedroom door and climbed over a front wall and iron fence to get out to the street.

"Tay, tay par, hah down." Take, take apart, fall down, Paul often said at this time. Family and friends, including Jim's brother's wife's father, brought him old telephones, typewriters, various office machines that had been thrown out. They went to a lot of trouble searching in dumpsters and asking around businesses for used office machines that were scheduled to be replaced. Paul took them all apart, and this kept him happily occupied for hours.

Did we think of taking the screwdriver away from him? Oddly, we didn't. I think I sensed that it was too central to his very identity at that time. And we became used to things falling apart around us. Only once did Paul ever put anything back together again. Jim's family decided to remove the staircase carpeting when they redecorated their front hall. They saved the risers for Paul. Each step had its bronze border clamping the carpet in place, and each metal border was held in place with screws, many screws. They called us over with Paul and his screwdriver. He set to work, carefully removing all the screws. It took him all morning. We left him, happily occupied and safe. Checking on him later, we discovered that he had carefully replaced all the screws he had removed earlier.

Such fine dexterity, such total concentration and dedication to task, such narrowness of focus, I had never seen in another child. For months all during that fall in London, Paul seemed not to see most of the world except for all the screws within it. Like a hawk or eagle surveying the total landscape to find the one small detail — the mouse running under the leaves — he looked for the tiny screws that he needed so desperately to find.

Later I read of the remarkable capacity of the brain to keep out stimuli as well as to let it in. "Our brain is so constructed," Robert Jay Lifton writes, "as to limit what we can eventually feel, lest it be so overwhelmed as to lose its capacity to organize or to respond at all." We must "do considerable psychic work" to organize mentally and recreate everything we take in. And this work can be overwhelming at times. Perhaps for Paul at three, the work of organizing the stimuli of his world was too great. A narrow (even bizarrely narrow) focus was the only way he could avoid becoming totally inundated and overwhelmed. He had to work hard to screen out anything extraneous that would keep him from the all-important work of organizing stimuli into meaning. And for Paul in London, screws had become intensely meaningful.

Trying to find ways of amusing him and hoping to find other children, I took Paul to a nearby park almost every day. It was a beautiful place located in the center of an elegant but decaying crescent. Every third house was being renovated, but the ones in between were boarded up with corrugated sheet metal, the windows and floors knocked out to prevent squatters from living there. LEB, London Electricity Board, O F F signs were painted crudely across the fronts. The poor were slowly being squeezed out of their neighborhood, as professionals, theater people, doctors, American academics like us, moved in.

The park, however, was a green oasis, kept up at public expense in the midst of the urban decay. It had a formal rose garden, a little wooded area, and a garden house for the park keepers. Every day I saw two old men whose only function seemed to be to keep an eye on the park and drink tea in their tiny house. I watched them as they came out of the little house, knocked the leaves from their pot, and drew water for fresh tea. I waved to them. Eventually they became a kind of spirit of the place for me, woodland creatures who had their being only in the tiny cottage on the edge of a park, a comforting presence from a simpler, more secure world.

There was a large play area for children, with slides, swings, a sand pit. Paul loved going down the high slide. One day, however, he came down the slide too fast and fell onto the loose gravel. Picking him up, I could see that he was all right, but the old men came running, flapping their arms, exclaiming, "That was a nasty bump! The poor little lad." They circled him, and suddenly the back of my own eyes began to prick with the tears I had been denying for weeks.

I hurried home before I began to bawl. After weeks of holding together as the beds and doors and telephones fell apart, I was starting to cry because of the kindness of two old men in a park.

One day in mid-September, Paul and I set out with the grocery cart to stock up on supplies for a dinner we were giving for Jim's students. We stopped first at the greengrocer, where I bought watercress, avocado, Bibb lettuce, and some fine Cox's Orange Pippin apples, the slightly sour apples that were the only ones Paul would eat.

Just as the greengrocer handed me my bags, Paul pulled an apple from the bottom of the pyramid and suddenly there was a rumble of apples, a whole avalanche cascading to the floor. I ran to pick them up, as the greengrocer and his assistant shored up the remaining apples, but then Paul started to cry and ran out the door.

I went after him, pausing just long enough to stuff the bags into my cart. "Doan wan appulls. Doan wan appulls." He was sobbing and jumping up and down, flapping his arms.

"It's all right, Paul." I bent to comfort him. "It's all right." But I thought bitterly that now he probably wouldn't eat apples for a long, long time. Now he would be down to only three foods: milk, eggs, and raisins.

When Paul calmed down slightly, I led him sniveling down the street to Tescos. Inside the grocery store, I parked my canvas cart among all the others at the door and found a wire shopping cart, the only one left, and lifted Paul into the seat. Then we started down the crowded aisles. It was worse that day than ever before. I had never seen so many people, nor heard so many crying babies.

Immediately Paul started to cry again. "Doan wan appulls. Doan wan appulls." He started to stand in the cart, clutching my sleeve. I pushed him down again, rather harder than I should have, and he started to cry in earnest. Several people turned sharply to look at me with real disapproval on their faces. Paul was crying louder than any other child, and now he was kicking the cart and reaching for the food on the shelves, lashing out to try to throw things on the floor.

"Stop it, Paul." I bent low to hiss in his face, "Just stop it!" I pushed hard on his shoulders to keep him down in the cart.

Grimly whipping around the aisles (I *had* to finish this shopping), I stuffed food almost at random into the cart, running to find the few things Paul would eat and the supplies we needed for dinner that night. Mint sauce, raisins, milk, rice, Cheddar cheese.

By now it was hard to ignore the panic in Paul's voice. Several times other shoppers, staring at me with stony faces, seemed about to say something, then quickly glanced away. Other children had stopped their crying and were staring with fascination at Paul.

Coming up at last to the checkout lines, I saw they were all full. I would have to stand here and wait with this screaming child. I kept shoving Paul back down into his seat. Then feeling terribly guilty, I would try to comfort him. But he was beyond comfort, way beyond it.

Then I caught sight of a display of lollipops, the candy that Jim sometimes used for bribing Paul. I had been very determined to try to keep this candy away from Paul and was even rather censorious with Jim and his mother when they gave him sweets. But now I snatched a lollipop, the biggest one of all, off the rack. Tearing the wrapper loose, I stuffed it into Paul's mouth.

He gagged slightly, and started to take it out of his mouth, to howl again. But he stopped, midhowl, and started sucking on the lollipop, pausing just enough to catch his breath in hiccups. His face was streaked with tears and dirt. He looked a most forlorn, lost little boy, and I noticed other shoppers still watching us in a covert and deeply disapproving way.

Suddenly, I felt very sorry for Paul and very guilty about my own behavior. I also noticed for the first time that he had grown out of his trousers. They were too short and one knee was slightly torn. His hair was also too long, his beautiful curly light brown hair, and it looked chopped unevenly where I had tried to trim it because I knew he would never sit still in a barber's chair.

Biting back my own tears, I somehow managed to pay for my groceries and stuff everything into our canvas shopping cart. Then, taking Paul by one hand and pulling the cart behind me with the other, I started for the crosswalk, the zebra crossing. But he wasn't ready to be cooperative. He lagged behind me, so that I had to drag him into the street as soon as I saw the crossing light. And then the light changed just as we were halfway across. I looked up and saw a large lorry bearing down on us. I knew the driver had time to brake, but he probably expected us to cross and he slowed down only slightly.

I took all this in in a flash. Abruptly Paul broke free of my hand and lay down in the middle of the street. The truck stopped, but only just in time, and now cars were screeching to a stop and honking. I tried to pull Paul up and also hang on to my cart, which was starting to roll away from me. I couldn't do both. And then, there at my elbow was an old woman, so small that she hardly came up to my shoulder.

"Here, love, let me help you." She took the cart, and I bent to pick up Paul and carry him across the street.

At the other side, I put him down, and through my tears turned to thank her.

She smiled, the sweetest smile I had seen in weeks, and reached out to pat my arm. "That's all right, dear. I have a retarded son, too. I know what it's like. I remember."

And then she was gone and I stood staring. "Retarded?" But Paul's not retarded.

Or was he?

All the rest of the way home, the old woman's words rang in my ears. She had appeared at my shoulder like an angel of mercy, yet she had said those awful words, those words meant to comfort but which had hurt so terribly.

Maybe her words were true. How could I be so sure that Paul wasn't retarded when he was hardly speaking and seemed to understand so little of what went on around him? I walked home, stumbling through a haze of tears. Inside our flat, I shut the door and bent to unzip Paul's coat.

When he ran away to look for his yellow screwdriver, I slid down on the floor, my back to the door. I sat there for a long time in the darkening twilight and stared into the emptiness that lay all around me.

I began to realize how badly Paul needed a nursery school and time with other children. He was as isolated with me as I was with him. Even with two regular babysitters, I was feeling very confined; Jim was away teaching every day, and three evenings a week he went to the theater with his students. With the help of our landlady, we learned about a nursery school not far away. I made an appointment and set out the next Monday morning with Paul in his pushchair, hoping to persuade them to take this child who had little speech and who was not toilet-trained.

I had never felt so vulnerable, nor so desperate for others to help me. Jim and I had had a fight the night before about the nursery school, and the memory of this fight made me feel even more fragile.

"They're not obligated to take him, you know," Jim had reminded me as we were clearing up in the kitchen late at night. He put down the skillet he was drying and turned to face me. "They don't have to take him. We aren't residents, and it's a private nursery school."

"I know all that." I turned away from Jim and wiped the counter with a cloth. With the edge of my thumbnail I tried to scrape off some dried egg. "Don't think I don't know it. You don't have to lecture me. But he *needs* this school."

"I'm not lecturing you. Here you are, going off on one of your crusades again." Jim turned back to the sink and stared out the window at the pub across the street.

"So what if I am 'on one of my crusades,' as you put it? Here is a child who needs other children, and I'm going to march in there tomorrow morning and convince them of that fact."

"Oh, are you?" Jim turned from the window. "And how are you going to do that, if they don't intend to take him?"

"They *have* to, it's as simple as that." I shoved the milk into the refrigerator and slammed the door shut. I turned to face Jim and glared at him. "Why do you have to be my enemy too? Can't you be with me for once and help me with this?"

"I *am* with you. How can you possibly think that I'm not? I'm just reminding you that we are not residents and we have no rights in the matter."

"Rights! A child has needs, not rights. I don't care if he is a citizen or not. That's immaterial to me."

I had insisted on arguing from the standpoint of need, not obligation. Although I didn't know it at the time, this was to be the first of many battles in which Jim took the position of reason, of law or contractual agreement, and I argued from emotional or even socialist standards: "From each according to ability, to each according to need." I so firmly believed this — where there was need it must be met — that I refused to accept defeat, at this time or any other in the future when Paul's welfare was at stake.

I also knew, and here I felt great sympathy for Jim, that behind his argument lay the experience of being the poor Irish boy in postwar London. He had been dependent on the goodness of others, the priests who "saved" him by sending him to a school where he could have a good education. But they had done this, Jim had always insisted and I knew he was right in this, not out of simple charity but because he was very bright and very "good." Good priest material, in other words. Jim had *deserved* his good fortune, and he had to work hard to deserve it. And now, when he repeated that the nursery school was not obligated to take Paul, I knew he was right.

The Beatrix Potter Nursery School was within walking distance, set in a little square behind some high-rise cement-block flats. I found it easily enough that Monday morning, as I walked past the cement building, where each flat had its tiny balcony piled with washing and broken toys and bicycles. I thought this was a dismal place, most unpromising. But rounding the corner, I came upon the school. It was a beautiful brick building. Tall trees grew near the front, and a late-blooming clematis climbed a trellis near the entrance.

Inside the school, the headmistress greeted me warmly and invited me into her office with Paul. Miss Gray was a very tall woman who spoke with a rattling quickness in a bright, chipper upper-middle-class accent. She had a long, plain, rather horsey face, and she wore a simple, no-nonsense smock.

We sat down in her office, and I looked around with pleasure at the blooming plants on the windowsill, the children's bright artwork pinned to the walls, the clutter on her desk. This seemed to be such a relaxed, happy atmosphere.

Drawing a deep breath, I started to explain what Paul was like, that he was not toilet-trained, but that he had enjoyed a small nursery school the year before. But then I noticed that Miss Gray's attention seemed to be wandering. Or rather, she seemed fixed on Paul. I turned, and there was Paul behind the desk, taking apart her phone. He had climbed up on her chair, and stood there, one knee braced precariously against the side of the desk. The receiver was partly dismantled, and he was working to unscrew the other part.

"No, Paul!" I jumped up and rushed behind the desk. "No, you can't take that apart."

I lifted Paul from the desk and turned anxiously to face Miss Gray.

"Tay, tay par. Tay, tay par!" Paul wailed. I put him down and tried to screw the receiver back together again.

Miss Gray intervened. "That's all right," she said. "We can put it together again. Here, let me take Paul out to the other children, and then we can talk in peace."

Paul let her lead him out, and Miss Gray and I talked a little longer. She was very uneasy about taking him on because he wasn't toilet-trained, and the school had a requirement that children be trained before they could enter the program. To this I argued that the staff didn't have to change him during the three hours he would be there. I also talked a lot about his loneliness, the fact that we didn't know any other children and couldn't find them easily because we were just here on a sabbatical. This argument had some weight with Miss Gray, and rather reluctantly she agreed to take him.

I was terrified that Paul would be afraid of this new school; throughout our interview, I had listened for sounds from the classroom outside the office. But all seemed quiet and we stood up at last to go and find him.

The large classroom was beautiful. One whole wall was glass and looked out onto a well-equipped playground. Colorful artwork hung on the other walls, and children occupied different little play areas: a sand table, a water table with toys for pouring, a playhouse area, and a wooden climbing gym in one corner. There were easels for painting, a piano, puzzles and books, and tables for eating. It was all one large, bright area, abuzz with activity.

I noticed all this as I walked into the classroom, and then I noticed Paul standing by himself in one corner, looking bewildered. A teacher was showing him a little toy construction set composed of different colored balls with sticks for attaching them. Suddenly Paul shouted with delight, "Boo bah, bee bah" (blue ball, green ball). His delight seemed out of all bounds, and Miss Gray stared at him, then at me. I started to explain that he had had something just like this at home in America. I didn't tell her, however, that for six weeks he had carried around "boo bah" and "bee bah," until finally he had lost them and had then cried for days. Clearly Miss Gray and the other teachers at the nursery school had never seen a child like this. But she had accepted Paul and we filled out all the forms. There was no turning back now.

When I returned to our flat with Paul at lunchtime, I was surprised to find Jim there waiting for us.

"Why are you here? Don't you have a class?"

"I canceled it." Jim looked both sheepish and anxious.

"Why?"

"I just had to find out what happened at the school. Did they take Paul?" Jim reached down to unbuckle Paul from his pushchair.

"Yes, they took him." I grinned at Jim and couldn't resist adding, "I knew I could make them take him."

Jim's face relaxed into a broad smile. "Good for you! I know how persuasive you can be. Don't think I don't know that or appreciate how hard you work for him."

"I know that." I smiled back at Jim. I realized acutely at that moment that Jim wanted Paul to have the right school as much as I did. The evening before, he was just defending himself against the possibility of disappointment. He often tried to set his expectations low so he wouldn't have to suffer the terrible swings of hope and despair I seemed to be laying myself open to.

To help the teachers cope with Paul, I wrote out a "glossary" of his vocabulary. He had about forty-five words at the time, mostly only vowel sounds, "eh oh oo ah ah" (yellow screwdriver), and *b* sounds. Along with "boo bah" and "bee bah," "Baba" might mean variously his panda bear, which went everywhere with him, but also might mean "sugar" or "mama." "Baba boo" was chocolate milk, with an egg beaten up in it, which was almost his only food at the time.

I thought that because he had so few sounds and many of his words sounded alike, this glossary of Paulspeak might help his teachers in the difficult task of interpretation. I wanted them to get to know him quickly, so he might begin to feel secure there without me. But even with the glossary, Miss Gray felt that I should also stay with Paul at school for two or three months, if necessary, until he "settled down." I resisted, but not openly. I learned to watch for the moment when the teachers' backs were turned, then to say good-bye to Paul, who didn't seem very unhappy to see me go. Then I would flee before Miss Gray could see me.

But I still felt guilty. I didn't know anymore if I was doing the right thing. Our neighbor from the upstairs flat, the father of a retarded son, was delighted with this story, however. He told me I was doing the right thing, reminding me that Paul would never develop relationships with the teachers and children at the school as long as I was there. I chose to believe him, but my belief rode uneasily over a deep uncertainty.

One day as I arrived to pick up Paul at school, Miss Gray asked to talk to me. I went into her office and sat down on a hard plastic chair, feeling a little frightened of what I might hear. She shuffled some papers for a few moments, avoiding my eyes.

"Lately I've been noticing something very interesting about Paul," she began. "He runs to the toilets every day as soon as his coat is off. He puts his head down close to the toilet bowl, and he flushes it over and over and over again. He would do this for hours if we let him."

I started to say something, but she waved me aside. "I think I know what this means," she continued. "And it's not as strange as you might believe. Once we had another child who behaved like this, and it turned out she was deaf. This child was also fascinated by the toilets flushing."

"But Paul was tested last year by an audiologist, and the test turned out negative," I began, and then stopped. Suddenly I liked this idea: Paul was deaf. That would explain everything — his difficulties speaking, his difficulties understanding. Slowly I began to muse out loud. "If this is true, it might mean that he has normal intelligence? And there would be a way of reaching him and helping him learn?" I realized I very much liked this idea.

Seeing the relief and pleasure on my face, Miss Gray went on eagerly. "I have observed deaf children a lot. In fact we have one little boy here at the moment. Paul's behavior seems at times to be strikingly like his. I suspect he is deaf only to certain pitches and frequencies. He responds to certain musical instruments and not to others. I noticed the other day that he likes some of our drums but not others. And he turned sharply toward the tambourine with his face all lit up."

I went home that day halfway hopeful. I trusted Miss Gray's judgment. After all, she said she had observed other hearing-impaired children and Paul behaved like them. They had gotten help and had done well later in school. Miss Gray had promised to tell the school pediatrician about Paul when she came for her biannual visit in November.

For days after this, I allowed myself a flicker of hope. "All shall be well, and all manner of things shall be well" ran as a refrain through my head. Jim had often quoted these words of Julian of Norwich to me at some of my lowest moments. Even though I had never read this fourteenth-century Englishwoman whose mystical revelations showed her God as a mother, her words appeared now to run through my head like a shibboleth, a password leading to courage and hope.

I was determined that deafness or retardation, or whatever it was that was holding Paul back, would not prevent him from learning, or me from teaching. As we walked to school and back again, I often stopped to point things out to him. I paused sometimes to rub his hand across different textures. "Rough," I would say, as together we touched a stucco wall, and "smooth," I repeated over and over as I trailed his fingers across brick or wood. He listened attentively. It seemed that he heard me.

One day, soon after the conversation with Miss Gray, I stopped to talk to another mother. As it happened, this was the mother of the deaf boy now enrolled in the school. I was delighted to have a chance to meet her and to talk to her, and even more delighted with the way Paul and her son were playing at the letter slot in the door. One went outside and peeked in as the other laughed and jumped up and down; then they switched places. Watching them, I laughed with pleasure. At last, here was some real interaction with another child.

But then Miss Gray appeared and told the children they were not to walk out the front door unless they had permission. "Now, you know that, don't you?" She wagged her finger at the two boys. "Remember what we told you?" Paul stared at her. He clearly didn't understand. The other child was led away by his mother.

Miss Gray turned to me. "Now *there* is a sensible mum," she said. "Her little boy is deaf and *look* at him. He is doing just fine. His mother is very sensible," she repeated with more emphasis, and I began to understand that she was drawing a contrast between me and this more capable mother.

"Paul is getting more and more frustrated and difficult in school." Miss Gray's voice was thin with suppressed anger as she asked me once again to come into her office to talk for a moment. When she had closed the door, she turned to explain more fully. "Today Paul couldn't make a toy work, a little fire engine that makes a siren noise, and he threw it across the room. Just threw it! Slung it to the other end of the room. It might have hit another child. This could have been quite serious, you know. You know that, don't you?"

I was flabbergasted. Yes, I knew a child might have been hurt, but what could I say?

Then Miss Gray started to quiz me on how many hours I spent in the library every day. "How many hours do you leave him?" she asked pointedly.

"Only for three or four hours a day," I began, but by then I felt very defensive and angry. And yet I felt I couldn't defend myself because I was also deeply uncertain. Maybe I wasn't doing enough for Paul. Maybe we shouldn't have come to London at this time.

Then Miss Gray began to tell a story of Paul on the playground one day the previous week. From the way she told it, she seemed to think this story had great significance, that it proved something about Paul which I failed to grasp, that it demonstrated that something was deeply wrong with this child — and maybe also with me.

"Last week, Mrs. Peters dropped something heavy on her foot. She broke her toe. She was in the playground at the time, and of course, all the children were very interested and curious about what had happened. But Paul . . ." Miss Gray paused to fix my eye. "Paul . . . well, you would hardly believe. . . . He just kept coming back to Mrs. Peters every day after that, every morning, first thing when he got to school. Every time he pointed to her toe and winced and he made the same sounds. He did this over and over again. I mean, it was last week, and he just won't let it go. He goes on and on worrying about that toe. It's long after the pain has gone away."

"Well," I began, "Paul has always been a very sensitive child —"

Miss Gray cut me off. "Sensitive? Well, maybe, but this has been exaggerated out of all proportion. He seems pretty . . ."

She stopped and stared at me, considering if she should go on. "Also, his eye contact is poor, very poor. I'm sure you've noticed that. We just can't get his attention half the time."

I left soon after this, without ever defending myself, or Paul. I felt overwhelmed by a confusion of emotions: I was defensive and hurt because Miss Gray seemed to doubt me as a mother so completely, but I also felt a scalding anger at her because of her own callousness and lack of understanding. Swamping all these other feelings, however, was the even greater worry and anguish about my child. Perhaps there *was* something deeply, immovably wrong with him, something worse than deafness, something I had done to him. And yet I thought his concern over the broken toe just showed his great empathy, his fine sensitivity, and his dearness, his utter sweet dearness as a human being.

Several times after this, I stayed to watch the children sing and recite nursery rhymes, dance, act out stories, and follow complicated directions with comprehending looks on their faces. One day I sat cross-legged on the floor, with Paul on my lap, and together we watched ring-around-the-rosy and London Bridge. Paul twisted around and stared limply off in space. When the children started a clapping game with Mrs. Peters, I held his hands in my own and tried to clap them together.

"See, Paul." I held on to him tightly, bringing my cheek close to his. "Let's clap together."

But Paul wailed, "No cap!" He jerked his head back against my jaw and, wrenching free from my arms, ran off into the bathroom. In a moment, I heard the toilets flushing.

I never tried again to force Paul to participate. Eventually he refused even to watch the other children. He knew, he must have known by that time, his difference.

As I walked home with Paul in his pushchair through smoky Islington, I looked into the steamy windows of the tiny flats we passed. I watched the little boys kicking their footballs in the gutter and suddenly it was they, not Paul, who were the odd ones. It was the other children who began to look like geniuses to me. Every little boy in the street, arguing with his friends, seemed to have a surprising, almost preternatural gift for speech.

For years I had read about the remarkable capacity for language and social learning in the human infant, a gift for "humanness" which seems to come out of nowhere and to blossom under any conditions. For years, teaching literature, I had taken this capacity for granted and thought no more of it than of my heart beating, my lungs inflating and deflating as I breathed.

Now I began to look at class in another way. It was these other children, not Paul, whom I saw as having class privilege. Because these children were neurologically intact, they seemed to me to have everything — all possibility, the most basic grounds for a fulfilled life. I began to see mental capacity as the most fundamental of all privileges. Nothing we could give Paul would ever make up for this loss or restore what was gone.

Feeling blamed by his teachers and responsible for his disability, confined in my unique relationship with him as his mother, isolated from other mothers who had gone through similar experiences — indeed believing that no one ever *had* gone through such an experience — I became more and more depressed and frightened. What was the problem with my child? No one seemed to know; many people in fact said there was nothing to worry about, which was even more confusing.

I was afraid. Afraid of something as yet unknown, unidentified. It is said that when medieval mapmakers did not know an area, they wrote in that spot, "Here be dragons." They did not leave that part of the map blank. They did not fill it in with mountains or marshes or dark forests or a city on a hill, or any feature of the known world; the empty spots, the unknown landscapes, contain fearful creatures of our imagination, not more of the same, humdrum world.

And so I felt about the unknown that I was encountering daily in my child. In the absence of an explanation, I began to furnish one, veering from one diagnosis to another. I visited a specialized bookstore near the University of London Medical School. I found a newly published textbook which seemed to be a standard for medical students on disorders of speech in children. In my desperate quest for some answers, some guidance, and some sense of what to expect in the future, I read it from cover to cover, carefully marking passages that seemed to have most relevance for Paul. Was he suffering from hysterical aphonia? Receptive aphasia? Articulatory apraxia? Ataxia or auditory agnosia? Dyslalia? Or a psychosis?

In spite of the earlier tests, which had turned up nothing, I settled on hearing loss or developmental aphasia. But no single diagnosis made much sense. Every one of them contained some traits that Paul simply did not have.

Under the heading "Autism and Speech," the book explained that autistic children can speak but will not. They are unaware of the need to communicate with others. The child with developmental aphasia, on the other hand, feels a strong need to communicate, yet is often frustrated. This child, the book pointed out, then exhibits temper tantrums, withdrawal, or other signs of frustration at the inability to communicate with others or to express ideas or needs.

Sitting in our little flat in London, trying to read about aphasia and autism, I was pulled by Paul, who had me by the arm. "Eh oh oo aah aah," he said. Then more insistently, "Eh oh oo aah aah."

"Just a minute, Paul. I'll help you in a minute."

Increasing frustration, increasing anxiety.

"In a minute, Paul." But by then he was flat on the floor kicking his heels and screaming. "Eh oh oo ah ah."

Was this the child who refused to talk, who *could* speak and make himself understood but felt "no need to communicate" with other people? "As the desire to communicate with others is lacking, it is not surprising that these children have little use for speech," said the book. I read over these passages describing the autistic child or "schizophrenic syndrome in childhood," with interest, but dismissed them as ultimately not relevant to Paul.

I would not have survived that year if it were not for Jim's mother. She came to Islington to stay with Paul for a few hours every Thursday, and on Sundays we went to her house for dinner.

Taking a train through north London on a Sunday, we arrived in Acton and walked down her street, past the bombed-out house still not rebuilt after thirty-five years, the car repair shed, the other abandoned houses, the Indian grocery store on the corner, the Pakistani newsagent. At her house, we picked up Prudence, the cat who stood at the doorway flipping the letterbox flap in a vain attempt to be let in. We knocked, and Mum answered the door. "*There* you are," she exclaimed, and bent down to cup Paul's cheeks in her hands. "There you are. Oh, you *lovey.*" She kissed him, and he jumped up and down, flapping his sleeves.

"Come with me, Paul. I have something for you." He followed her into the front room, where she kept his favorite toys, a salt shaker and pepper grinder.

Jim's father sat close to the fireplace and the TV, smoking his pipe and knocking his ashes into the grate. "*Hello.*" He grinned as Paul settled down on the hearth rug to take the pepper grinder apart. "Tay, tay par." Paul looked up to smile at us, pointing to the little wheels inside. "Wow ah wow," he said, as he moved them round and round.

Jim settled on the couch with the Sunday papers to read his way steadily through the afternoon. I moved to the kitchen to help Mum make tea, then to take the roast lamb from the oven, to help her serve the roasted potatoes, the mashed potatoes, the cauliflower with cheese sauce. A delicious feast, which we ate from trays on our laps in the front room. One of Jim's brothers came in, then his two sisters, then a married brother and his wife, who lived upstairs on the top floor.

The front room was crowded now, full of talk and laughter. The TV was on, as well as a radio in the kitchen and another radio in an upstairs bedroom. Paul played quietly in the midst of it. He had stopped banging doors, running from one room to another, whining, clinging to me. His usual weekday self had gone and another self had appeared — calmer, more focused, happier. We all drew closer to the fire and to the TV and to each other.

The warmth and acceptance of this household, the simple, straight affection they all showed Paul, gave me something I desperately needed. When they asked questions about him, they were loving questions, not critical ones. Never did they suggest that I was to blame for Paul's differences. To them he was special, a sweet little boy who could take almost anything apart, who had a vivid personality, who was affectionate and curious and very clever. And even though I knew they were sometimes worried, they seemed not to expect Paul to be different from what he was. Jim's brother Tony had even started to use Paul-speak. "Mama, *hah* (help)!" he would complain when he couldn't make something work. Or, "Uh, uh high. *Hah* down (fall down)," Tony would laugh when he put his coat on top of a stack of coats and they all fell down.

"Don't worry," Jim's mother would tell me over and over again. "Don't worry. He'll be just fine in the end. *You'll* see." And she kissed the top of Paul's head as he came to lean against his Hahi, as he called her.

More tea and talk. On these Sundays, I never wanted to go back to Islington. I wanted to stay here forever and be one of Mum's daughters, looked after and loved, years after my own mother had died. Often Mum told me stories about her time as an Irish servant girl on Philadelphia's Main Line so many years ago, about the long gray crossing across the North Atlantic and the great divide from home with only occasional letters to bind the hurts. Seven years away from her family. She told me about how she cried herself to sleep every night dreaming of her father's hand-cut stone house, the gorse turning yellow in the spring, the sheep on the hill. About her mother and how they loved to tease her until she flashed with anger: "Get on wid ye! I wasn't born yesterday. I wasn't hatched under a hen, you know."

How separated she was from her mother's life; how separated I also was from my own mother's life. I talked to Mum about my time at an expensive women's college a little farther out on the Main Line from where she had once lived as a servant girl. We talked about my family, who were too poor (although we didn't call it that) to visit me even though I was less than two hundred miles away. My mother and father worked a twelve-hour day commuting from Virginia to Washington. It was a comfort to me to share all this, and the terrible history of my mother's high blood pressure, her nephritis, her bursitis, her allergies, her exhaustion, her early death.

One night after we had returned to Islington, I dreamt of those times: young Mary, the Irish serving girl on Philadelphia's Main Line. In the dream, I see her getting up, eyes still stinging, in the half dark to set the house going again, to start the kettles boiling, to spread the table, to soothe the baby. But when I try to speak to her, to tell her about Paul and the terrible, urgent need to find out what is the matter with him, she has turned away from me. I watch helplessly as she turns toward the window, her beautiful auburn hair gleaming, catching fire from the sun as it rises.

But, strangely, in the dream, this is the same dawn I am watching from the smoker where I have typed, all night, a paper about Cordelia and her immovable heart. A paper about obedience and love and their terrible toll. And now the dawn breaks in blank light on the hard stone of Rockefeller Hall. Somehow Paul is there playing in the crumpled papers at my feet. But he is crying. He is exhausted and I can't help him.

And I know my mother is there if I can just reach her. But she is not there. She is two hundred miles away, which is also three thousand miles across the Atlantic. She is rising in utter weariness to work another day at the office of Health, Education and Welfare. And in the dream I know I will never see her again.

CHAPTER 5

The Changeling

EARLY IN NOVEMBER, our landlady offered us the use of a cottage in a small town in south Devon. The house would be empty for a week around Christmas and she would let us have it for the cost of the utilities. I thought it was just what we needed to pull ourselves, body and soul, back together again. Suzanne let us see the description of the cottage that she had used in an earlier advertisement. "For rent: two-hundred-year-old stone cottage, set in orchard of mature apple and pear trees. Fireplace, beamed ceilings in lounge/dining area, deep windows set in two-foot-thick walls, modern, fully equipped kitchen, bath, all the amenities. Cottage is on edge of beautiful fishing village, $\frac{1}{4}$ mile from harbor. Near Dartmoor, prehistoric sites, pony trekking, footpaths."

All through November and the early part of December, I held onto this image of the cottage set in an orchard. It was my dream material, my one spot of hope to get me through the dreariness, the sinus infections, the frequent bouts of hopelessness. Islington seemed more stark and bleak now that the leaves were falling. Fogs had moved in, and many days it rained too much to go to the park. A damp wind blew grit in our faces every day as Paul and I walked to school.

I hoped that by getting away from London and from Paul's school I could also get away from the constant, unremitting anxiety I had felt for the last three months. I was looking for a quiet place where I could gather my thoughts, get some perspective, think through what we might do next. But really I didn't want just clarity; it was hope I was after, even unreasoning hope. I wanted to find something, some energy, some conviction, that would carry me forward through the next months.

Even though I would hardly admit this to myself, I still hoped that Paul might yet be perfectly normal. Deep down, at the bottom of my heart, I knew there would be no sudden breakthrough, no miraculous recovery, but I still sometimes hoped for one. I scorned what I called drugstore miracle-cure books, the accounts of children suddenly talking because of crawl therapy, "patterning," or changes in their diet. And yet, and yet, I always bought such books and read them avidly. I grabbed onto every bit of information about deafness, autism, food sensitivities, emotionally lost children who were found again.

The cottage in Devon may have seemed like my salvation, but I knew it would probably be far different for Paul. Any change was now very stressful for him, and we would have to prepare carefully before we left London. Paul had recently discovered flashlights and preferred them to any toy we could give him. So the weekend before we were to leave for Devon, I went to a local hardware store and bought five flashlights, beginning with the tiniest penlight size, on up to one that was about ten inches long. On the trip to Devon, sitting in his car seat in the back, Paul could take the flashlights apart. I knew this would keep him happy for hours as he unscrewed the bottom, took out the batteries, and removed the light bulb and the spring behind the batteries. Then he could put them back together again.

The sun was setting as we drove into the lovely little town of Dittisham-on-the-Dart set on a steep hill near the sea. But even with the map given us by Suzanne, we had trouble finding our way, until finally, we located the narrow lane that was supposed to lead to the cottage. We started down, driving between the high hedgerows. The car's headlights picked out the deep color of a few late blackberries, sloe, and elder. But the lane was very narrow, and the thorns closed in, scratching the car and finally choking our way so we could move no farther.

Jim backed up the rocky lane between the steep hedges and out onto the bigger road. There we found an old man with a lantern and a dog, walking down the steep hill toward the harbor. The man wore a large overcoat that hung below his knees. We stopped him to ask if he knew the cottage we were looking for.

"Arrgh, Tracer!" He slapped his thigh to call his dog back to his side. Tracer returned and sat obediently by his feet. "Sure I do. It's not far down this lane, but you can't get a car down there."

We told him we had already discovered that, and he paused to consider for a moment. "Do you have a torch?"

We laughed and showed him Paul's flashlight collection, but the old man said he would lead us down the lane with his lantern. We picked our way slowly over the rough stones and finally, at the end of the lane, we saw the dim outlines of the cottage.

Paul and I stopped outside, while Jim and our guide went in to find a light. I sat on a low stone wall and took Paul on my lap as we waited in the deepening night, far from any lighted house or streetlamp. All around us was a smell of woodsmoke, and a lovely, damp, earth-and-mushroom scent, so different from the exhaust fumes on Hemingford Road in Islington.

Suddenly Paul started to cry. "New new how," he sobbed. "Doan wan new new how."

I tried to explain that we would not stay here long, that we would return to London and to "new house." This "new, new house" was a temporary change, things would soon be back to normal, at least to our "new normal" life. But how could I explain? "New new how," he continued to cry. "Doan wan new new how."

But once the lights were on, Paul's bedroom settled on, and he was tucked in with Baba, all was well. In our week at Dittisham, he grew to love "new new how." With its two-foot-thick stone walls, the cottage was impossible to heat with electricity or with the unseasoned wood we tried to burn in the fireplace. We didn't care. We wore our coats indoors or warmed up by going outdoors and taking long walks through the town, down to the harbor, and over the moors on the hills. We drove through Dartmoor, stopping at the little villages where wild ponies came to topple garbage cans and eat the grass on the green. We stopped at the barrows and prehistoric portal tombs on windswept hilltops. My sinus infection went away after a couple of days in the clear cold air, away from traffic fumes, and we all started to feel healthier, more hopeful.

One evening as we were walking back to the cottage, we saw a light inside the village church and went in to find the organist and another man working on the organ. The workman was on a stepladder, making some adjustments to one of the pipes, and the organist sat pulling out stops, pressing keys, and testing the sound. Tall vases of holly stood just in front of the dark rood screen, the red berries, dark green leaves, and thorny stems making a dim tracery in front of the delicately carved screen. Other Christmas greens gave off a spicy scent that mingled with the smell of the cold dusty stone. The nave of the church was in darkness, and only one low electric light illuminated the choir.

The organist had a candelabra with three candles that swayed and flickered in the movement of air in the cold church. Seeing us come in, he turned to smile at us and invited us to stay for a while. Then he swung back to the organ and started playing a Bach prelude and fugue. The other man carried the ladder away, and Jim and Paul and I sat down on one of the pews near the front. Paul was very quiet and seemed content just to sit and listen.

At the end of the Bach fugue, the organist started a passage from "Ode to St. Lucy's Day." We sat there listening to Purcell's beautiful music written for the winter solstice, for that darkest, shortest day of the year, that day which had just come and passed. I thought of how the Northern Hemisphere had already started its slow tilt back toward the sun, turning toward the light again and a new spring to come. We huddled together in the dimly lit church, and the clear, rich tones of the organ seemed to draw us all into a charmed circle, a circle of light and hope and peace.

We sat there for a long time, listening to the music. Finally, the organist turned back to us. "That's all, friends. My fingers are getting stiff with the cold." We knew he had been playing for us. We thanked him warmly and got up to leave.

Near the door, we stopped to leave a donation. On a table next to some pamphlets and postcards was a model of the church, with a sign announcing that it was a collection box for building restoration. Somehow we had failed to notice it as we came in, but now we stopped and stared with fascination. Even in the low light, we could see that the model was a perfect little replica, exact and precise and accurate down to the last detail. Small stones had been stuck to the outside of the walls and stained glass windows had been carefully painted with vivid, true colors, deep cobalt blue, turquoise, and crimson. A few leaning gravestones, spotted with pieces of sponge that looked surprisingly like gray-green moss or lichen, stood in the cemetery outside.

Jim lifted Paul up to drop a coin into the slot on the tower. As he did so, tiny, flickering lights went on inside the church and a little bell rang faintly in the bell tower. Paul drew his breath in sharply, transfixed by the little fairy church. He leaned his head down closer to the bell tower and dropped another coin in the slot. The bell rang again, a faraway, tinkling sound. The lights flickered again.

This was better even than light switches. "Eh oh oo ah ah," Paul demanded, wanting a screwdriver very much so that he could take apart this wonder and see what made it work.

"No, you mustn't touch it. Just put the money in the slot."

"Iigh oon."

"The light goes on, doesn't it?"

"Bow eeeh."

"And the bell rings."

"Dee don bow. Dee don bow."

"Ding dong bell."

"Oh eeh. Bao oo oh eeh ii."

"That's right! Paul puts the money in."

"Dee don bow. Dee don bow."

"Ding dong bell. You want more money to ring the bell?"

"Mow moh-eeh. Iigh oon!"

Jim laughed and, putting Paul down, he reached into his pocket and pulled out all his coins. I opened my purse to look for more money.

Jim lifted Paul again, and slowly, one by one by one, he dropped all our coins into the church tower. Each time he put his eye to the rose window at the east end to watch the flickering lights inside or twisted around to put his ear to the west tower. We probably spent five pounds on that little church, but it was just too beautiful to resist.

We walked home that evening through the frosty silence, taking the little path single file across the meadow to our cottage in the orchard. After we put Paul to bed, Jim and I tried to make a green stick fire and this time succeeded in getting a flickering flame, which we fed with newspapers and cardboard. Pulling a quilt off our bed, we wrapped ourselves together into a single cocoon and sat up late before the fire, marveling over how much Paul had talked in the church.

A stranger, dropping in on us at that moment, might have thought we were crazy, exclaiming over six or seven new words in a three-year-old, in a child who should have had hundreds of words by then. But to us, it was a marvel. A child who could learn six new words could learn. Period.

For months, taking Paul to school or to the park or to his grandparents, I had talked and talked and talked to him, explaining the world to him, as if he could understand. As if. During those months, I never knew if I could reach into a core self that might later thrive and flourish. I simply acted on the faith that he could understand because that was all I could do. But I never knew if I could believe in my own act of faith. That evening in Devon, I almost did believe.

Jim began to muse out loud, to say that Paul reminded him of the old Irish legend of the changeling, the fairy child left behind in the cradle when the real child is stolen away. "Paul looks like an other-worldly child, a child strayed into our world from a different order of being. The changeling was always a very beautiful child, perfect in every way, but somehow disconnected. Paul is so beautiful, so perfect, yet he doesn't seem to be with us, of us."

"Maybe tonight, the real child came back across some boundary," I began, slowly. "Maybe tonight Paul joined us in our world. That little church gave him so much speech, it was almost as if he was joining us for the first time."

"Ummm. Maay-be." Jim stared into the fire, then went on. "You know there are many stories in Ireland about crossover people, threshold people, people who could move back and forth across the border of reality, who were at home in both worlds. I remember hearing them when I was a child."

"Maybe Paul is one of them."

"Maybe."

The next day, we drove into Dartmouth and spent the day there shopping and visiting the castle guarding the mouth of the river. At the end of the day we felt too hungry and tired to drive back to Dittisham, so we set out down the high street to look for a restaurant or a pub that offered an evening meal.

At first, Jim wanted to stop at a fish and chip shop. I told him I didn't like the idea of greasy cod and vinegary chips in newspaper. Jim pointed out that Paul might act up in a restaurant. I pointed out that it was too cold to eat take-away food outdoors. Jim said we could easily go back to the car and eat. I said the car was too cold. Jim said we could turn on the heater. I said Paul wouldn't eat fish and chips anyway. Jim pointed out that we had muesli in the car. I pointed out that we had no bowl, or milk, or spoon for eating it.

We had been marching up and down the high street. Paul, who was very cold and hungry by this time, was whimpering against Jim's shoulder. Suddenly, Jim stopped in exasperation, swung around, and faced me squarely. We were just outside a lovely pub-restaurant.

"All right. You want a good meal in a beautiful place. Here is a beautiful place, and I'm sure they have good food."

We looked in the big bow window. Oak-beamed and brick-walled, the pub had an open fireplace, so large that you could sit inside it on a bench. Its walls were hung with gleaming copper and brass pots and kettles. Dried flower arrangements stood in the deep embrasures of the windows. A few people sat by the fire and near the front windows, but it was early still, before the crowd, a good time to eat.

"Okay." I looked defiantly back at Jim. "Let's eat here."

We went in, stooping under the low lintel, pausing just long enough to read a brass plate that said The George and Dragon was built in the sixteenth century. We found a small table near the fireplace.

"Iiii," Paul said, walked over to the hearth, and held Baba out at arm's length, too close to the fire.

"No, Paul! De de. Dangerous!"

"De de." Paul accepted that and came back to his chair.

"Now, you sit here, Paul, and be a good boy, and we'll get you some food." Jim, I could see, was nervous and uncomfortable.

We waited, and waited some more, but even though the place wasn't crowded, no one came to take our order.

Paul picked up his knife and fork and marched them across the table. Then he swept them off the table. They clattered onto the brick hearth.

"No, Paul! Now, you stop that, there's a good boy." Jim brought his face close to Paul's and hissed, "Stop! There's a good boy."

I tried to intervene. "Paul, come here. I'll tell you a story. Once upon a time, there was a little boy, and his name was Paul."

Paul swung his shoulders back and forth and slid onto the floor, lying stomach down on the hearth. He kicked his heels against a copper washtub full of dried flowers, making more noise.

Still no waiter. Jim reached down and dragged Paul up by one arm, sitting him down in his chair. "Now, you sit down here," Jim said between clenched teeth, adding almost automatically, "there's a good boy."

"Let's give him something to eat." I began to search my pockets for raisins, crackers, anything that would hold him for a few minutes until food arrived.

"His food is in the car," Jim reminded me, an edge to his voice. This had been my idea, not his, and he didn't want me to forget it. But then Jim added: "Maybe we can get him some crackers."

"Crackers will take his appetite. Maybe they will bring us some milk."

"Hah iigh. Hah iigh!"

"You want your flashlight?" I started searching my pockets for one of the small flashlights, then turned to Jim. "Have you got his flashlight?"

"No, I thought you had his flashlight."

"HAH IIGH. HAH IIGH!"

"But you're the one that's supposed . . ."

"Sir. Madame." A waiter at last materialized out of the ether and stood before us. He wore a white jacket over black pants. His dark hair was slicked back so close to his head, it looked as if it were painted on. Holding his upper body stiff, he bent forward slightly at the waist. He looked like a puppet carved out of wood.

"Madame. Sir."

"Yes?"

He bent closer to us, and in a very low voice said, "I'm afraid I must ask you to leave."

Jim was already standing and dragging Paul up.

"You are disturbing our other guests. I must ask you to leave."

Jim and Paul were out the door. I mumbled something as I bent to pick up Baba and Paul's coat and mittens, then I hurried after them.

Jim turned to wait for me at the corner. "I've never been so humiliated in my life."

"Well . . . so what? They could have served us sooner."

"I told you we should never have gone in there."

"No you didn't."

"Well, you should have known."

"Known what? We were hungry and went in to buy dinner. Like everyone else. We had a perfect right . . ."

"No we didn't. Not with Paul."

"But what are you supposed to do if you've got kids? Starve? Eat nothing but fish and chips?"

But Jim was already marching off to the car. "Yes, eat fish and chips," he flung back over his shoulder. "I told you!"

When we got back to Dittisham, we made a meal of sausages and beans. I pulled out the sherry bottle and poured a big glass for myself. Jim watched but didn't say anything about the sherry. Instead he muttered, "I've never been so embarrassed in my life. How can you think of taking a child into a fancy restaurant? That's your stupid American obtuseness again. You always think you are right about everything."

"Well, why do you get so embarrassed at other people's opinions?" I glared at Jim, then turned back to the stove to flip the sausages.

Choking down my meal, I remembered a story Jim had once told me. When he was eleven and new to St. Edmunds, the other first form bóys would meet secretly after dinner. Then they would come to Jim and, on some pretext or another, they would entice him to the boot blacking room, a little room behind the refectory, out of hearing from the rest of the school. Once in that small room, away from the teachers, the headmaster, the prefects, they set to. Goading Jim with the skillful cruelty of schoolboys, with the comments about being Irish, about being a poor scholarship student, about being always very "good," they buzzed and buzzed around him, stinging again and again just where it hurt the most until, maddened by their stupidity and their skill, Jim would explode.

And that, of course, was just what they wanted. As soon as Jim was out of control with rage, they would dance around him gleefully, having made of him just what they wanted to see in him — a poor boy with an Irish temper, a poor boy with intelligence and strength of character who could still be cut down to size. To them, Jim was an Irish boy perversely endowed with all the gifts of nature that had been denied those more deserving in their wealth and English respectability. Anger, Jim told me, became from that time on, very, very dangerous.

Anger was dangerous, and so was being Irish (or American) among the snobbish middle-class English. Jim was always most nervous, most ill-at-ease, when he couldn't easily fit into an upper-middle-class setting. Being shamed in front of English respectability was the hardest, the very hardest thing for him to handle.

I had never been able just to walk away from his anger and embarrassment. I became defiant, superior, almost censorious when Jim was embarrassed and angry. At these times I always knew best, knew what Jim should have done, should have felt — which made me insufferable.

But my own anger was also confused and impure, mingled with feelings of shame and humiliation and hurt and a sense of abandonment. I was afraid that from now on Paul would keep me from eating where I wanted to eat, from going where I wanted to go. I was afraid that now, with Paul, I would forever be separated from the life I wanted to go on living. But I couldn't really identify these feelings, let alone talk about them. Instead I poured sherry on them. Then I left Jim to put Paul to bed and slammed out of the cottage to go for a walk by myself.

It was a chill, damp December evening, but being the south coast of Devon, a few late roses still bloomed over hedges, and the winter flowers, narcissus and crocus, were just coming up, showing here and there through the grass. Wandering down the lanes at random, I paused to look into the garden of one of the cottages. Large cabbages grew there, winter vegetables, and I could just make out their deep, purply green showing in the warm light from the kitchen window. The grass on the path beside them gleamed with the cold dew.

On the outskirts of the little village, I came to the church that we had visited the evening before. It was dark and utterly quiet, and the gravestones were barely visible in the cold light of the moon. I paused under the roof of the lych-gate, the roof they had used in the past for sheltering coffins on their way to the churchyard. I leaned against the old wood of the gate, swinging it slightly in and out and feeling the grain where it had risen up from the damp.

This is where I want to be, I thought suddenly, remembering our happiness here just the night before when we had sat and listened to Bach and Purcell and had poured all our change into the little church. I wanted to recapture some of that earlier feeling of hope, when we had all come together and it had seemed that Paul would talk like any other child, that he would grow and learn like any other child. Even as I thought this, I knew, with one part of my mind, that I was drunk, must be drunk to go trailing around churchyards in the middle of a damp December night. Nevertheless, I swung the gate in and started up the path.

The graves were nothing but dim humps in the moonlight, and I stumbled as I walked over the hummocky grass, feeling for the leaning, lichen-covered stones to guide me. Finally I came to one gravestone under a large yew tree, a very dark, spreading tree by the wall of the churchyard. This one was just right. I slid down, the damp, mossy headstone to my back, and drew up my knees to try to get warm. Resting my chin on one knee, I looked around the churchyard, as gradually my eyes grew more and more used to the dim light under the tree. All around me I could smell the dank earth.

I sat there for a long, long time, waiting for the tears to come. I settled in for a good, long cry, a proper cry in a proper setting. But somehow the tears seemed wrong, illegitimate, worked-up, dishonest. At last, I got up and started back to our cottage. I was very ashamed of this drunken evening and still confused and angry about our day in Dartmouth. I couldn't sort through my feelings, didn't know why I was still so angry at Jim. Above all, I was afraid my hopefulness the evening before had been a sham.

Jim's image of the changeling, the beautiful silent boy left behind when the fairies stole the real child away, kept coming back to me, only now I saw it as an image of despair, not of hope. Maybe Paul was such a child, a crossover child, a threshold child who had strayed into our world across some border. Maybe he didn't belong here, and maybe he never would learn to speak.

Trailing back through town, as the church clock struck eleven, I thought, I too am just a traveler, just a tourist passing through my own life.

Before we returned to London, we visited a monastery in Hereford-shire, on the edge of Wales. David, Jim's best friend from the years they had both been students at St. Edmund's, was a monk who taught in the boy's school attached to the monastery. He had arranged for us to sleep in a dormitory and to eat in the refectory.

Over big bowls of sweet, milky tea at breakfast the morning after our arrival, Jim and I talked with the monks about all those modern conveniences Americans don't have. "No, we don't have towel warmers," I answered their questions. "Well, a few rich people do. But most people don't." They asked about electric tea kettles. "No, we don't have those either. Except maybe some rich people."

I looked around the big refectory. Even with an electric heater blazing away not far from us, the big stone room was cold. Moisture fogged up the tall windows and was beginning to run down the glass in tiny rivulets. Paul wore his snowsuit coat over a sweater and corduroy pants. He had finished eating his cereal and was standing beside Jim on the bench, dropping packets of sugar into an empty bowl on the table.

"Airing cupboards?" David was asking. "Surely you must have airing cupboards?"

I laughed. "No, we don't have those. And we don't have Bovril, Marmite, or McVities Digestive Biscuits."

They were amazed. "But I thought Americans had everything!" one young monk sitting across the table from us exclaimed. His hair was tonsured, and a few pimples peppered his forehead. He looked about seventeen years old. I could picture him on a motorcycle or lounging against the wall of a pub with his friends.

"We do have warm rooms." I laughed as I drew my sweater around my shoulders and cupped my hands around the warm bowl of tea, blowing steam from the top.

The monks turned their attention to Paul. He had brought his little plastic Fisher-Price record player with him, and all through breakfast, he slapped on one record after another: "Camptown Races," "London Bridge Is Falling Down," "Greensleeves." He also had his Scratch-and-Sniff book with him. David and the others were fascinated by both the record player and the book. They scratched each page of the book, marveling at all the different smells: banana, strawberry, apple, pine.

David, sitting next to Paul, tickled him under his arm. "You're a scratch-and-sniff boy," he said. Paul giggled and, pulling his arms close to his sides, swung his shoulders back and forth, brushing him off. "A scratch-and-sniff baby, and I'm going to *scratch* you!" Paul laughed and ducked out from under his arm, sliding off the bench.

"Hah iigh. *Hah iigh.*" Paul suddenly remembered that he didn't have his flashlights with him.

David stared at him.

"*Hah iigh!*" Paul started to scream.

"Here, Paul," Jim reached into the pocket, looking embarrassed. "Here. Here's your flashlight." Jim's voice was low, urgent. "Come here. Here's your flashlight."

"Hah iigh," Paul said more quietly, sitting down on the stone floor to take the spring and light bulb and batteries out of the flashlight. Jim turned back to David and relaxed slightly.

The monks began to discuss what treats a three-year-old might like and decided finally to take Paul to the top of the church's bell tower. Right after breakfast we set off, Jim, Paul, and I, with the monks in their black robes. Up the spiral stone steps just off the nave we went, then out onto the platform in the square tower itself and onto the wooden steps and scaffolding built around the clockworks. We could hear whirring and clicking sounds as we passed the cog wheels of the clock mechanism and the bells of graduated sizes that hung in the tower. We were afraid that the bells would ring when we were too close to them. I imagined Paul, carried by Jim over the high, open-backed wooden stairs, suddenly terrified by the bells all ringing at eleven, and twisting out of Jim's arms to fall down the entire flight. Then of the sound beating in our heads until blood spurted from our noses and ears. Silly fears, but we had watched *The Nine Tailors* on Masterpiece Theatre and knew that someone had died in just this grisly fashion.

David led us up and several monks followed. Finally we reached the top of the tower. We could see the soft Welsh hills purpling the distance, the green Valley of the Wye at our feet: a magical place. The monks swooped down on Paul, swinging him high in their bat-wing arms and setting him down again as they reached into their sleeves for candy bars. And Paul ate Milky Ways and Smarties, candy we usually never allowed him, up there under the open Welsh sky, on the tower that Pugin had built.

We stayed at the top of the tower for a long time, well past the hour of eleven, waiting for the bells to ring. Finally we gave up. Later we learned that the bell mechanism (but not the clockworks) had been turned off, perhaps because of our climb.

Many years later, visiting David again, we talked about that earlier time. We questioned him about Paul, asking for his impressions of this child at three. David thought for a moment, then said simply, "I thought he was retarded, and I thought the two of you were making heavy weather of it."

Thinking of this comment, I wondered at the absolute distance between being the parent of a child and observing the child of another, even of a dear friend. Making heavy weather of it, Jim and I were? How could we not be? Paul was the axis of our lives. Our lives — full in other ways with teaching, friends, family, manifold interests — still turned on him, rotating slowly on this mysterious, troubling center. I have rarely seen young parents do otherwise, although I have seen them far less burdened than we were. I wondered later, Should we have been less concerned? Should we have cared less? Gone our own way more? Been less preoccupied with him? Would that have been healthier? Therapists were to tell us so in no uncertain terms much later, but at this moment we were deeply, deeply invested in our child. For us the planets swung slowly around his little head.

On our way back to London, we also stopped by Stratford for two days of sightseeing. We took Paul with us when we visited New Place, Shakespeare's daughter's house, and Trinity Church. On a cold day with few tourists, we walked slowly through Shakespeare's birthplace, admiring the worn oak floors, the timber-framed walls and raftered ceilings, the samplers and tapestries, the dressers and joint stools, the spit and drip pan in the massive kitchen fireplace, the funny little babyminder set up to keep toddlers out of the open fire.

In the birth room upstairs, Jim and I paused to examine the wattle and daub, which had been exposed in one place in the wall to show us how buildings were constructed in the sixteenth century. We stopped to read the signatures etched in the window glass — Sir Walter Scott, Ellen Terry, Thomas Carlyle, Washington Irving. Turning around, we saw that Paul had slipped under the rope to walk over to the cradle. He was standing there, slowly rocking Baba. We froze. Then looked around quickly, but we were the only visitors and there were no guides nearby. Quietly, we watched Paul rock Baba back and forth, back and forth. His hand rested lightly on the carved hood of the cradle. The worn oak rockers made a slight thump, thump on the raffia rug.

I turned to Jim and knew he had the same thoughts I did. Maybe some magic from the cradle of one of the best users of the language would rub off on our almost wordless child. Maybe some blessing, some aura not quite used up in four hundred years of secular pilgrimage to this spot, would settle on this little boy, and he would yet have the gift of understanding.

CHAPTER 6

"A Cup Is Not a Hat"

W E RETURNED to a foggy London. Islington, with its sulfur yellow brick houses, seemed even more bleak than when we left. The overflowing garbage cans, the broken paving stones, the traffic fumes, all seemed to have grown in our absence. Back in London I missed the dark green of the Devon cabbages and the misty green of new growth on the hedges, all those greens in that pocket of southwest England warmed by the Gulf Stream.

There was one good thing about our return, however. The first week back we learned that Paul had been accepted into a small, experimental language-learning program at the Wolfson Centre. I had written the Wolfson Centre the year before, having heard of its remarkable success with the child of a friend of ours, but no one had answered my letter. When we had first arrived in London, I called and was told that the speech therapy classes had been canceled due to lack of funds. I thought then that the Wolfson Centre would be another dead end and never expected to hear from the school again.

But now, the school was offering us a very special placement in a highly expensive program that had accepted just six little boys. And it was all because of the pediatrician who had visited the Islington nursery school in November. Dr. Headly had been intrigued by Paul. She had not thought the broken toe episode so peculiar but had told me very pointedly that she thought it was a very good sign indeed. She had listened carefully to Miss Gray and to me, as we both explained Paul to her. Evidently, she had then recommended him to the Wolfson Centre for this new program beginning in January.

So now Paul was to be one of only six children, aged three and four, in all of London, to go to this language learning program. He was to have the concentrated attention of his teacher and the help of a pediatrician, a speech consultant, and other early childhood specialists from the Great Ormond Street Hospital, which ran the program. Because it was an experimental program, it was there not just to teach the children, but to teach the teachers and all the consultants about how these most exceptional and different little boys learned speech.

When we first heard of our good fortune, we felt the need to tell the people at the Wolfson Centre that we were Americans, or that at least Paul and I were. And Jim, although still a British subject, had lived in the United States for many years as a "resident alien," so he did not pay British taxes. We felt we had to tell them all this because strictly speaking we weren't entitled to this specialized program, which was funded through the National Health Service. But something else was at work here. They *wanted* Paul, they wanted him not just for his sake, but for theirs. They felt they could learn from him.

Jim and I went to the Wolfson Centre together on the day Paul was to take some tests. I had dressed Paul in some new blue overalls with a little red anchor appliquéd to the front and had carefully brushed his curly brown hair. For once in his life, he had eaten a good lunch, and he seemed cheerful and relaxed as we drove to Mecklenburgh Square.

We arrived early, anxious to make a good impression on these marvelous people, whose help we so desperately needed. After finding a parking place in the quiet cul-de-sac off the square, with its beautiful Georgian houses, we looked for the school and finally found it behind a tall wire fence. The low cement slab building was a most unprepossessing place. But appearances didn't matter. They could teach Paul in an empty warehouse as far as I was concerned.

After introducing ourselves at the front desk, we were told to have a seat in the waiting area, a little space in a corner of the front hallway, where there were a few broken toys scattered on the linoleum floor. Paul immediately started looking for one he could take apart and found a piece of airplane wing with different colored bolts and screws, red and green and yellow and blue. "Eeee!" He was delighted with his find.

A beautiful young Indian woman came up to us and introduced herself as Molly Moodley. I was startled, so different did she seem from the tall, precise, pursed-mouth English schoolmarm type I had come to expect. Molly's skin was a deep terra cotta, and her short black hair seemed to glint with blue-black highlights. Thin and quick and agile, she was dressed simply in nondescript Western clothes, slacks and a sweater. Around her neck, however, was an Indian silk scarf of purple and red crinkly cloth, shot through with threads of gold and silver. I stared at her with admiration: she had a sheen of health and youth and energy, a glow from within that I felt I had lost. Molly put out her hand and smiled. She had an open, direct look. I liked her immediately.

"I'll be Paul's teacher," she told us. "And now would you introduce him to me?" This was so different from our first interview at the Islington nursery school, and seemed so "adult" to me, that I was at first taken aback. Then I thought, of course, Paul trusts us, and our introduction of a new teacher to him is just what he needs to learn to trust her.

We crouched down by Paul on the floor, and I spoke to him. "Paul, this is Molly" (she had told us she preferred Molly to Mrs. Moodley) "and she will be your new teacher." Paul looked up into her smiling, dark face, then he looked down at her brown hands, then back up to her face again. "Nanny doity hands," he exclaimed loudly.

Molly laughed with delight. "Yes, it *does* look like the lady has dirty hands." She seemed to understand his speech immediately and not to be offended.

Molly left Paul playing on the floor and took us over to some chairs in the corner to talk for a moment. "We need to assess his level of development before classes begin," she began. "As you know, this is an intervention program for preschool children with delayed language development. And we think of language not as a separate form of learning but as integral to all forms of intellectual development."

Jim and I nodded. This was nothing new to us.

"Specifically," Molly went on, "language is important in concept formation and as a directive function."

"Directive?"

"Yes, we'll explain more of this later, after Paul is tested. But for now, I'll just say that children go through stages, not just of language learning but also of attention control. We want to assess Paul's level of attention and then help him move on to use language as a directive-integrative function."

Molly stood up and took Paul by the hand to lead him down the hall to the room where he would be tested. She told us to follow and showed us a little glass cubicle where we could watch through a one-way glass. Jim and I perched on the high stools in the stuffy room. I reached across the space for his hand, and he gave mine a squeeze. We leaned closer to the glass, as Molly dragged two chairs up to a small table. Paul sat in one, but Molly's chair tipped and she got up to exchange it for another.

"It's broken, Paul. I need another chair." She put the broken chair in the corner.

Paul hopped up to follow her. "Eee bowooh air!"

"You want to see the broken chair? Here, look at it. The leg is loose."

Paul crouched down to study the leg and, finding a loose screw, he demanded, "Ooo aah aah."

Molly was puzzled.

"Ooo aah aah." Then more insistently, *"Eeh ooo ooo aah aah!"*

"Uh oh." Jim and I squirmed behind the glass. We looked at each other. "Should we go in and tell her what that means?"

"No, better not. Let her figure it out for herself."

We looked back at Paul, who was wailing loudly now. His voice sounded tinny and metallic in the microphone amplifying the sound from the testing room.

"Eeh ooo ooo aah aah," Paul repeated. Then, noticing Molly's hand, he took it and examined her thumbnail. Then carefully he fitted her nail into the top of the loose screw and started to rotate her hand.

Molly laughed. "You want a screwdriver to fix the chair, don't you!"

"Ooo aah aah," Paul repeated, more relaxed now.

"Oh, you clever child!" Molly laughed again and gave Paul a quick, little hug. "We don't have a screwdriver, but I want to show you something else that's interesting."

She tried to lead Paul back to the table, and very reluctantly he went with her. "Eee bowooh air. Eee bowooh air," he kept repeating, but he did sit down on his chair at the table.

Molly brought out a pegboard and put it on the table. "Here, Paul, would you make a fence around the edge?"

Paul stared at her.

"I'll show you." Molly started to put the pegs around the outer edge of the board.

Quickly, Paul seized the board from her and started placing pegs around the edges. He worked carefully, with a precise pincer grip, shifting from his right to his left hand, then back to the right again. Finishing, he looked up at Molly and clapped his hands together. "OOO OYE!"

"Yes, good boy! That was very good, Paul. Now find the red pegs."

"Eeh." Paul went unerringly to the red pegs.

"Now find the blue ones." Paul found the "boo" pegs, and the "bee" (green) ones, the "eeh ooh" (yellow), and the "iigh" (white) ones. He was good at this, and he knew he was good.

Next, Molly asked Paul to build a bridge with blocks, and he did so quickly and confidently. He started to build a tower. "Uh uh eye-eeh."

"Up, up high! That's right, Paul."

Jim and I watched with amazement. We had never seen anyone catch on to Paul's language so quickly. We understood most of what he said because we spent so much time with him. But it had taken the teachers at the other nursery school a long, long time to begin to understand Paul, even with the help of my glossary.

"Hah dow-oo!" With a sweep of his arm, Paul wiped the blocks off the table.

"Fall down. That's right, Paul. Now it's time for something else." Molly held Paul's hands down on the table with both of her hands and restrained him for a moment, speaking slowly and quietly. He was getting a little excitable.

"I want you to do one more thing for me, Paul." Molly spoke slowly and distinctly. Gently, she placed her hand under his chin and tipped his face so that he was facing her. She held his chin until he was making eye contact, and slowly she reached under her chair for a small doll and some dollhouse furniture.

"Put the dolly in the chair."

Paul slapped the doll into the chair and giggled.

"Now give the dolly a cup of tea. She wants a cup of tea."

Paul looked around for the cup and, finding it, brought it up to the doll's lips.

"Now put the doll in the bathtub."

Paul found the bathtub and put the doll in it. Then he braced his arms against the table and suddenly shoved his chair back.

"You've had enough, haven't you, Paul? You've been very good. We'll go now and find your mum and dad."

Molly brought Paul out of the testing room. Catching sight of me, he ran into my arms, and I scooped him up and hugged him. "Eee bowooh air." Paul took me by the hand and dragged me back into the room to see the broken chair.

Jim laughed, and turned to Molly: "If he could have all this, and his mama too he would be quite happy." He paused, and then he added with a grin, "And also a screwdriver, if you just happen to have one lying around somewhere."

Molly snorted, then put her hand over her mouth, turning to see if

Paul had heard. "You saw that! Paul is something else again. An original! I've never seen one like him."

Molly explained that because Paul was getting tired, they would schedule the pediatrician's examination and the speech therapist's for another day. We stood in the hall with her for another few minutes, just enjoying the warmth of her company. I felt an enormous relief seep into me. Here I was a good mother once again, and here Paul was an "original," not a freak. Best of all, here there was hope and understanding and warmth and respect for this different little boy.

We left, Paul walking between us, hanging onto our hands. "Uh uh eye-eeh!" he demanded, and we swung him up high, jumping him over the cracks in the linoleum floor. Molly saw us to the front door and stood there waving as we got into the car and drove away.

After Paul had had the other examinations with the pediatrician and the speech therapist, they called us back for a conference to tell us what they had found. They were all there, Molly, Dr. Reston, the pediatrician in charge of the program, and Heather O'Neal, the speech therapist.

Dr. Reston began by explaining their theory of language learning. "It's connected with attention control. We have found that immature attention control is a very common difficulty for children who have a language delay. If a child cannot attend to one thing for long enough to learn, then all intellectual development will be slowed down. Also if a child's attention is inflexible, if he or she is rigid or intolerant of interference," Dr. Reston paused to see if Jim and I were with her, "then the range of learning opportunities is severely limited."

"Screwdrivers," I said.

Dr. Reston looked puzzled, and Molly leaned toward her. "I think I told you about Paul and the screwdriver."

"Oh, yes." Dr. Reston laughed. "Yes, Paul and the screwdriver. Exactly! That's exactly the kind of thing I'm talking about. Anyway, we believe the first stage of attention control is typical of babies in the first year of life. Babies are entirely at the mercy of environmental stimulation. Their attention is focused on whatever is the dominant stimulus at the moment. And they are distracted by any new stimulus, the phone ringing, the dog barking, the light turned on.

"Now, at the second stage of attention control, occurring usually at the second year of life," she went on, "the child's attention is held rigidly by his own choice of concrete task, and he won't be shifted by someone's voice or effort to redirect him, unless you remove the material holding his attention." Dr. Reston stopped to grin at us. "That's the stage of Paul and the screwdriver."

"That makes a lot of sense to me," Jim said, "but what can you do to move him on?"

"There's a lot we can do. We want to move him along to the next stage where he will be able, voluntarily and deliberately, to transfer the focus of his attention. With the help of adult control, he will learn to switch his attention from a concrete task onto a demonstration or a verbal direction, and then back again to the concrete task. That's where Molly comes in, and there is a lot she can do.

"At that stage, stage three, the child's attention is single-channeled so there must be a complete transfer, not a division of attention. The child's whole attention, visual and auditory, must be focused on the adult, and then back on the task. At this point, the child can't yet integrate two channels of attention at once.

"Later, in stage four, the child learns to control his own attention. He can stop what he is doing, focus completely on the intervention, and then transfer his attention back to the task. Stage five is typical of the immature-to-average school-age child. This child can carry on a task and assimilate directions at the same time — at least for short periods of time and with simple materials. We prefer that they be at stage six, where they can fully integrate two channels of attention at the same time. This is the level expected of children in a large classroom."

Dr. Reston paused and asked us if we had any questions. Then Molly gave us the results of Paul's testing.

"We found, as you heard, that he is at about level two in attention control. He is easily distractible, but he will accept adult control. We also found that he can manage perceptual tasks quite a bit above age level, but his visual-motor abilities are lower, closer to his age level. He was, however, quite good in symbolic understanding."

"How did you test that?" I wanted to know.

"Do you remember the doll-play material? Yes? And matching pictures and toys. He was fine there, showing that he has symbolic understanding and an understanding of representational objects. He was also quite good with concept formation, which is very encouraging intellectually. But as you know all too well, his verbal comprehension shows a serious delay. Maybe I should let Heather tell you about the results of her speech evaluation."

Heather leaned forward. "Paul's speech is very deliberate, and he has a lot of trouble finding words. In our time together, mostly he took me by the hand and pointed toward objects. He could use some single words and two-word combinations, but he failed to do some of the object-by-name tasks in the test I gave him, and he also had a lot of trouble identifying objects by use."

"How do you mean?" Jim asked.

"Well, he couldn't show me what you use when you wash your face, or when you dry the dishes, or when you mow the lawn. That kind of thing."

They finished explaining the results of the testing, and stood to shake our hands. We left, feeling very impressed by their knowledge and feeling that we had learned a lot. We liked the way they shared everything with us and included us in their plans. Molly had told us a little bit about the teaching methods she would use. She said she would be doing some auditory training but would work mostly on attention control. She repeated the invitation to come and watch Paul at any time.

When Paul started classes, I took Molly up on her offer and watched the classroom from the observation booth. Unlike Miss Gray, she told me I could not stay with Paul in the classroom because he would remain dependent on me if I did. So, perched on a stool inside the little cubicle behind the one-way glass, I watched Molly and another teacher work with the children. Here the richness of the teaching belied the seeming poverty of the physical setting. Used to the large, well-equipped nursery school in Islington, I had been afraid at first that here they had no physical, material resources for the children. But they did: hidden away in closets were puzzles, paints, books, construction toys, playhouse toys, puppet theaters, all the apparatus thought necessary for a three-year-old's learning.

The teachers would take objects off the shelf one by one and use them as an integral part of their teaching. I began to see why. These were very distractible, learning-disabled children, and it helped them to focus if they had just one or two objects available to them at any one time.

The teachers gave time for free play, they read them books, and they had circle games and songs for the whole group at the end of the day, but in the middle they worked with each child individually. In these sessions, actions always accompanied language. They never used language to direct the child's attention to something that was not present. And all learning was involved with play.

I watched Molly teach "same" and "not the same," that most fundamental principle of language learning. She held pictures and toy objects up near her lips as she spoke slowly and clearly. I watched her laugh gently as one child took a toy cup from a little plastic tea set and placed it on his head. "A cup is not a hat. *Not* the same." She took the cup from the little boy's head and pointed again to the picture of a child drinking from a cup. She set the cup right side up on its little saucer, then picked it up and drank pretend tea from it.

One day I observed as Molly worked with Paul. The other children had been taken off to another room, and Molly was alone with him. She had some noisemakers: wooden spoons, keys, a bell, a comb, and a paper fan that made a small clapping sound when you folded it together and a whistling, sibilant sound when you unfolded it. She also had some party favors. There was one you blew through, which made a bleating sound as a long insect tongue unraveled. Another made a very rude sound, blowing raspberries.

Molly and Paul tried out each of these noises, and Paul squealed with delight, trying to vocalize each of the sounds. "Eeeeeh." He made a high-pitched sound after blowing the insect tongue. And then he blew through the little rubber tube that made the raspberry sound, and giggling, lowered his voice to try to vocalize that sound.

"Oowe noy-eeh," he repeated after each of the loud noises.

"Hah noy-eeh." He picked up the fan, folding it with a soft, clapping noise, then unfolding it with a soft, whishing sound. "Hah noy-eeh," Paul said in a soft voice.

"That's right, Paul, that's a soft noise."

Molly took some paper and rubbed two pieces together.

"Hah noy-eeh," Paul repeated. "Hay noy-eeh. Hay noy-eeh."

Then Paul took the wooden spoons and banged them loudly on the table. Putting one of the party favors in his mouth, he blew a bleating sound, banging the table at the same time. Spitting the favor out, he shouted, "Lou noy-ee. Lou noy-ee."

"Pau mai lou lou noy-ee." He collapsed in giggles and rolled on the floor, kicking the chair with his feet.

Molly slid down on the floor beside him. "Loud, loud noise. Paul makes a loud, loud noise." She reached over to tickle him. Paul giggled and rolled away from her.

"Time to go home now, Paul." Molly stood and pulled him up by the hands. "Time to put away the toys."

"Doan wan go ome. No go ome."

Watching from the little booth, I thought, is this the same child that turned his back on other people in the first nursery school? Is this the child that ran away into the bathroom and hid, flushing the toilets over and over and over again? For after the first few weeks at the Wolfson Centre, Paul seemed transformed. He was another child, a child who wanted to learn, who enjoyed learning, who didn't simply avoid new situations with all the old passive-resistant behaviors. Now Paul made active verbal demands; he did more than simply point or whine for what he wanted. He had even led the way in making up new noise games with Molly.

I started to climb down from the stool to go to meet Paul and take him home, but suddenly I felt a dull ache in my lower abdomen. The day before, I had visited a doctor who had confirmed that I was one month pregnant. Now as I eased myself off the high stool and hesitated by the door of the little booth, I paused for a moment to consider. The ache was becoming more insistent, and I knew quite well what it meant. I might miscarry, or I might continue with a troubled and unstable pregnancy. I realized at that moment that our lives would be very complicated for the next few months. This new pregnancy, if it was anything like the earlier ones, would claim most of my energy; it might even put me in bed and take me away from Paul. And it would certainly make Jim's life very, very difficult for the next few months.

When I said good-bye to Molly that day, I knew I probably wouldn't visit her or the Wolfson Centre for quite a while. But I said nothing to her, and even I didn't guess how many long weeks it would actually be before I was able to return to watch Paul again through the one-way glass.

CHAPTER 7

The Royal Free Hospital

T HE DOCTOR I had consulted the day before had been furious. "How can you dare to think of becoming pregnant again?" he had almost shouted at me when I told him about my suspicions. He started to stand up from his desk chair, then sank back and glared at me. "You just finished treatment for the thrombophlebitis a couple of months ago. You just finished taking anticoagulants!"

Sitting on the other side of his desk, I looked Dr. Culler in the eye. "Well I am. And I have been off the anticoagulants for two months. You said at the end of November that you thought I was completely cured."

Dr. Culler sighed and looked down at my folder. He scanned the top page, then looked back at me. "This is too complicated for me," he began. "I'll give you a letter to a specialist on Harley Street, an obstetrician who has a lot of experience with cases like yours." He closed the folder and stood up, extending his hand. "Congratulations, anyway." He gave me a wry smile. "And good luck." He hesitated, then added more seriously, "You'll probably need it."

The new doctor gave me a reservation at University College, London, for the birth of a baby in eight months, even though I said I would be back in America by that time. Then she forbade me all activity at least for the next couple of months until the cervix could be stitched up. "Complete bed rest. And don't even come out in the car, except to see me," Dr. Benstock added, noting my startled look. "No walking around. No car rides. Unless," she turned to the medical students smirking at her elbow, "unless you have a Rolls-Royce."

"But can't you do anything?" I pled with her, remembering an earlier diagnosis of luteal insufficiency and the progesterone I had been given to stop the bleeding in the pregnancy with Paul. But Dr. Benstock didn't believe in progesterone; in fact, she was well aware that the hormone in its synthetic form, although not in the form I had been given, had recently been found to cause birth defects in rats and was now contraindicated in human pregnancies. She didn't tell me any of this, however, and I went home in despair and terror, remembering how I had lost other children when I had not received the hormone, knowing that it was one of the things that had helped to sustain the fragile pregnancy with Paul.

I went back to Islington and to bed. And then the flu hit London — Victoria type A, then Hong Kong type A, then Victoria B. It lasted for weeks, and I had one ache after another. I stayed in our basement bedroom, the fumes from the busy street seeping in around the loosely fitting window frame and through the vent put in by Victorian legislation for proper air circulation in times of smallpox epidemic. I lay there staring at the deal dresser, the shoes of passersby on the street, the edge of the garbage cans by the sidewalk. Sometimes I sat in the bathtub and stared at the toadstools, the strange extrusions, fungal or plastic, that grew from the damp cracks between the tiles.

I sat there and thought, sat there and remembered. Once, more than three years before, when I was greatly pregnant with Paul, I was half lying, half sitting in the bathtub just like this. Beached, like some great blowfish on the shore, I was idly washing my stomach, when Jim walked in the door. There was a strange look on his face, something between joy and shock, something I couldn't interpret. "I just got a phone call," he told me.

"Yes." I sat straight up to prepare for whatever it was he had to tell me.

"It was the adoption agency. They have a baby for us."

This was the news we had waited two years for. We had kept our names on the list "just in case." But by then, of course, I was within three weeks of giving birth myself. "What did you tell them?" I asked.

"Of course I told them we are about to have our own baby."

And then, to Jim's amazement and even to mine, I burst into tears. "Why did you do that? Who is this baby? Is it a boy or a girl?"

But Jim had not learned any of this, so fixed was he on the healthy, active baby inside me. We never found out anything more about this other child of ours, the baby that got away. This son or daughter went of course to another family. But sitting in our Islington bathtub, pregnant with our second child, I thought again of that other child who was still joined with us, not in the here and now among the living members of our family, but rather among the ghosts of our own might-have-been babies.

I desperately wanted this new baby growing inside me, surprising myself with the sheer raw force of my feelings. I wanted another child, partly to help to redeem the earlier losses, partly because I wanted a sister or brother for Paul, but mostly of course because I just wanted another baby. And, confined to bed, I had plenty of time to think about it all.

Paul played around my bed, in my bed. He took out all the little plastic pegs from a pegboard puzzle and swirled them around and around. "Awe the peepo," he said. "All the people." This was a phrase he had recently learned, but he was repeating it as more than just a stock expression, a piece of rote learning. I thought I knew what he meant, and this was the beginning of representational play. He was referring to all the people in the street outside, in the park where he was taken every day to swing, in the underground, in the local Co-op and W. H. Smith's, at the greengrocer and the newsagents — all those places Jim and his babysitters continued to take him. All the people. Noisy, dirty London was beginning to get on his nerves. But out of his distress was emerging more and more representational or referential play.

One day Jim brought me some flowers, bright daffodils that were just beginning to open, a gift from the world of sunshine and fresh air. Slowly the buds opened, bright yellow fringes against the dull oatmeal walls. Seeing them when he came into my room, Paul was fascinated. As he approached the buds, I said to him playfully, "Shhhh, the flowers are asleep. Quiet, you might wake them up." Paul looked at me, startled. He approached the flowers fearfully, slowly, on tiptoe. He peered closely at them, hands held well away, then quickly moved back and away, a look of uncertainty on his face.

I remembered my father showing me snapdragons when I was about Paul's age. I had had a series of sore throats, tonsillitis, and was about to have a tonsillectomy. My father, in order to reassure me and perhaps to prepare me for the surgery, took me out to the back garden. There he opened the throat of a snapdragon, pulled down the tiny yellow jaw, and let me look inside at the little tongue-stamen, the little throat with its dusting of pollen. "You see," he said, "the snapdragon has a sore throat, too." And I was delighted. The whole world, it seemed, was full of sore throats.

But now in London, I realized I had done something wrong with

Paul. I had said something I shouldn't to this child who was having so much trouble telling people from objects, living things that moved from living things that did not move, sentient beings from nonsentient beings. Years later Paul told me he had been afraid of flowers when he was little. He didn't know why and thought that he must have been very "stupid." But I remembered the daffodils in London, and I felt I understood his fears. How is it that any of us make these distinctions so easily and so securely? How is it that I knew, and my father knew I knew, that the throats of snapdragons are really not the same as the throats of little girls, but are just another metaphor from this rich and various world of ours?

At the end of February I went for a routine checkup at the Royal Free Hospital on the edge of Hampstead Heath. By this time I had changed doctors. I had found a Harley Street doctor who practiced at the Royal Free and who was willing to prescribe progesterone, the hormone that had sustained my earlier pregnancy with Paul. We had discussed the drug fully, including my chances of losing this baby if I didn't take it versus my chances of having a handicapped child if I did take the hormone. I had also called my old obstetrician in Minnesota, a doctor well known for his treatment of infertility. He had told me, point-blank, that given my reproductive history, this might well be my last chance to have another baby. He also said that I had had a hormonal imbalance earlier and that progesterone, in its natural form versus its synthetic form, was *not* associated with birth defects. He felt so strongly that I needed the hormone that he was even willing to send me the medication in the mail.

At the Royal Free Maternity Clinic, I was seen by an assistant to my doctor. The young Indian doctor came in for a routine consultation, clearly expecting this to be a quick checkup — blood pressure, weight, urine check — before he moved on to the rest of a full waiting room. But, unknown to him, I had a lot to say.

I started with the cramping, the strong contractions I continued to feel. Then I went on to my medical history (it was clear this doctor didn't have it in his file), beginning with the recent bout of thrombo-phlebitis. The doctor's eyes widened. He listened closely, as I went on to tell him about my history of miscarriages.

"Goodness!" he said. "Just a minute." He put up a hand to stop me. "I'll be right back."

I waited, shivering slightly in the cotton hospital gown. Then the doctor bustled back into the room.

"I think," he said, "we should admit you to the hospital at once."

"But I'm not a National Health patient," I began, "and my American health insurance won't cover this kind of hospital cost."

"No matter. No matter. We'll see to all that." His warm brown eyes showed such genuine concern that I knew I could trust him.

Later that day I was admitted to the Royal Free Maternity Ward, only two months pregnant. Jim's mother went with me and sat beside me as forms were filled out for me to become a National Health patient, even though I wasn't a British subject. I felt a mixture of fear and relief. I was grateful that now I would receive the care I needed. I was relieved that other people would look after me, bringing my meals, making it possible for me to rest, watching for early signs of miscarriage. But I was very worried about Paul. How would he be with me gone all the time now? He had just started to settle down at the Wolfson Centre.

The first night I was in the hospital, my anxiety seemed to lie like an incubus huddled on my bed, crouched on my chest, drawing the air from the room, sucking the very breath out of my lungs. The room was hot and dry. I later learned that they kept this whole wing of the hospital at ninety degrees to provide enough warmth for the newborn babies. But for the rest of us, it was intensely uncomfortable.

I felt lonely and frightened and supersensitive to all the hospital noises: the telephone at the nurses' station, the ping of the elevator bell, the soft, padding sounds of nurses checking on us during the night, the rattle of metal rings as curtains were pulled back.

I was grateful when morning finally came and I could sit up, look around, and get to know my roommates. I learned that Jewel had high blood pressure. She was a big-boned, redheaded woman, very jolly and overactive. I quickly found out that she enjoyed looking after all the rest of us. Always hopping up to tell the nurses we needed something, or to fetch magazines for us out of the lounge, or to bring us news of what was happening down the hall in other wards, she clearly found it impossible to relax.

Penelope was a petite, dark-haired woman, very quiet and upper-middle-class, rather disapproving of Jewel, whose bed was next to hers. She was a devout Anglican, I later discovered very early in the morning on Ash Wednesday when I awoke to the wavering light of candles behind her drawn curtains, and her priest anointing her forehead with ash. She had had a stillborn baby two years before and preferred not to talk about it.

Toni was in the bed next to me, in the ward because of bleeding at seven months. Of all my roommates who were there when I came in, I liked her the best. We discovered we read the same books and had made similar marriages to bright sons from Irish families living in London. Toni had a strong suspicion of authority. She was convinced that the doctors knew very little and that my medical problems would disappear if I took the right minerals, magnesium or potassium or calcium, and I half believed her. She also, I discovered to my surprise during one of our late-night whispered confidences, believed in witchcraft and said she could sense immediately when she walked into an old church whether unquiet spirits still lingered there.

Because this was a room with four beds, the traffic was constant. Each of us had a separate doctor, and of course each of us had family members who visited once or twice a day. In addition, the Royal Free was a teaching hospital, so we were each assigned a young medical student who took our histories and explained our case before the whole class and the supervising teacher at least once a week during rounds.

I tried to read, but I had chosen the wrong books to bring. All fall and winter, I had been reading little-known books by nineteenth-century women writers — Geraldine Jewsbury, Harriet Martineau, Margaret Oliphant, Beatrice Webb, Lady Blessington. But now Harriet Martineau's novel *Deerbrook,* in a musty decayed leather binding, seemed incomprehensible to me. I couldn't read anymore. I couldn't eat. The food wasn't right, no vitamin C or calcium in it, I told Jim, who brought me milk and orange juice every day. I couldn't sleep. During the night I was suspended somewhere between dozing and stark, staring wakefulness; during the day I was suspended somewhere between wakefulness and dopey sleepiness. Every morning at six-fifteen, the tea cart banged against the corner of the door, and it was easier to give in and have a cup of strong tea, then another, than to lie there and try to force sleep.

I began to accept the "Valium-type" sleeping pills they handed out at night. "As far as we know they are safe," the nurses said. But still I never slept well, not a true, deep-down sleep. My contractions continued. "An irritable uterus," my Harley Street doctor told his students gathered around my bed. "An incompetent cervix and luteal insufficiency." These were his vague terms for conditions I knew neither he, nor anyone else, truly understood. And then he prescribed Scotch, which I kept by my bedside and drank with the orange juice "as needed" for the contractions.

Jim's mother came to see me every Thursday. She brought me flowers and magazines, and she sat with me for an hour or more, listening to my stories about the hospital and soon getting to know each of my roommates. Jim came to see me every evening after dinner. He brought Paul with him and told me that he had to drag him over the cracks in the sidewalk, as well as the "dog pooh pooh," which now terrified him. The teachers at the Wolfson Centre also reported that Paul was regressing in his behavior and in his ability to concentrate. This new change was affecting him badly and at times Jim seemed to be at his wit's end. Some evenings when he came to see me, he almost fell asleep in the plastic chair by my bed, as Paul ran around wildly.

"Wow up, wow down," he would say as he rolled my bed up, then down, up, then down. Then he would run into the bathroom and flush the toilet over and over. Then back he would careen around the bed to the lamp on the bedside table, flicking the light switch off and on. His behavior was more hectic, disordered, and it was harder to control him through language. Finally, Paul would settle down, and by the end of every visit, he was ready to snuggle against me in the bed as I read him a book. "Seven little rabbits walkin' down the road, walkin' down the road. One little rabbit said he was tired, walkin' down the road, walkin' down the road. One little rabbit said he was so tired . . ." And Paul would fall asleep against my shoulder.

One evening, as I read to him, he stopped me and remained fixated on one picture, refusing to let me turn the page. The picture showed one little rabbit holding up her sore foot that had been hurt by all that walking down the road. "Blister," I said, "that's a blister on her foot." Paul stared. "Plister," he said, then got up and moved to the lamp, pointing to the bulb. "Plister," he said, pointing to the light bulb. "Plister," he said, pointing again to the little rabbit's foot. I was confused, and then I saw how the hairs on the end of her foot were twisted and looked very much like the filaments in the light bulb. This was a different kind of "sameness" from the kind Molly was trying to teach him, but at least he was making connections.

The head nurse, Sister Murphy, popped in three or four times a day to check on us. "Let's listen to the bambino," she would say, and then she placed the primitive listening device, a metal rod with a cup, to each of our stomachs. Sister Murphy was small, determined, and Irish. She had gray hair, which she tucked up under her cap with the help of bobby pins, but it was always escaping, giving her a harried look as she rushed from one room to another, trying to keep us all in order.

Forced to lie in bed most of the day, allowed only to walk up and down the hall or to go to the TV room, my roommates and I felt very confined, and we reacted in childish ways. We were all hungry for news, for events, for anything at all to happen. A journalist from the BBC had a steady stream of visitors who came to drink brandy in her private room farther down the hall. We all got out of bed and stood around our door watching the hallway for celebrities. We hung inside the door frame, cackling together, until Sister Murphy marched in to shut us up.

"Back in bed, all of ye! Back, back." And she flapped her arms at us, as if we were hens, or geese, escaped from our pens. "I never!" And Sister Murphy would turn on her heels to flounce back out of our room.

Every day we became more and more hysterical. We worked hard at turning all these lives into soap operas, something we could walk away from and laugh about. The enforced passivity of our lives, as well as the enormous emotional pressure we each felt, had in a sense infantilized us, sent us back to immature versions of our present selves. So here we were, schoolgirls again, separating ourselves from the tragedies enacted daily around us. Any real feeling — anxiety, hope, memory — was too dangerous to us now. I for one thought I might be plunged into despair, if once, just once I opened the door to genuine emotion.

The hospital radio crew came to our floor one Sunday afternoon, trailing heavy cords and carrying sound equipment with them. They hoped to get a good story or two for the Royal Free radio station. I was confined to my bed and couldn't get up and run with my room-mates into the bathroom, where they had hidden behind the shower curtain, collapsed in helpless laughter. Two young men trailed in, looking thoroughly miserable. One stood at the foot of my bed, as the other tried to twitch the lines around the door. "Please help us out," the first one begged. "We have to put something on the air, and so far we only have one old woman up in the surgical ward. She wants to show everybody her gall bladder scar."

His coworker pulled the heavy cords up to the edge of my bed and held out the microphone. "Yeah, you've got to help us. Last time this old bird was on the air, she invited everybody up to the fifth floor to play strip poker with her."

I could hear my roommates giggling behind the door of the bath-room. Then Toni poked her head around the door, and I could see that Jewel was leaning over her shoulder, "Go on, Jane," Jewel sputtered. "Go on, you can't get out of this one!" She clutched herself and started to laugh so hard I thought she would fall on the floor. "Let's see her try to get out of this one!" Penelope was nowhere to be seen. I knew this was too undignified for her.

I looked back at the radio crew. "I'm Nigel," one of them said, leaning across the bed, his hand extended to shake mine, a broad smile on his face. He knew he had me trapped. He gestured to his blond coworker. "And this is Ian." They both looked so handsome, so young. And also so desperate.

"Okay." I gave up, feeling exposed. I pulled my robe over my shoulders, wishing I could get up and get dressed. "What do you want to know?"

"Where are you from? The United States?" Nigel began, and held the mike out to me. I told him that I was from a little town in Minnesota. Nigel didn't know where that was, so I started to explain: west of Chicago, near the Great Lakes, not too terribly far from the Canadian border, at least not far by American standards. Then he asked me about the weather there.

"Below zero this time of year. Sometimes it's below zero for several weeks at a time, that's zero Fahrenheit, not centigrade, that's — how do you explain it? — thirty, forty, fifty degrees of frost?"

"Noooo, that can't be!"

Nigel was having the right reaction, so I went on. "It gets so cold there that you can't touch metal doorknobs. You don't dare put a key between your lips."

"What would happen?"

"It would freeze, of course. When you pull the key away, it takes off the top layer of your lip!" I heard a loud snort from Jewel just on the other side of the bathroom door. Beginning to enjoy this more and more, I started to tell Nigel and Ian about the game Minnesota children play as they wait for the school bus on cold winter mornings. "They dare each other to lick the stop signs."

"They never!"

"They do! And then the mothers have to run out with pans of warm water and slosh the water on the tongues." I paused for effect, then went on in a lower voice. "Sometimes they have to call the police, the rescue squad. The tongues are still stuck even after the warm water treatment. Of course, the water can just freeze as it's falling to the ground."

"But that's bloody awful!" Nigel spoke into the mike, then held it back to me. He was enjoying this.

"We survive. Of course, we don't usually walk for more than a few streets. And when we go to the grocery store, we have to leave the key in the car and the car running. You wouldn't dare to turn a car engine off when it is thirty below."

"Don't your cars get nicked?"

"Stolen? Never. Anybody outdoors in that kind of weather has brought his or her own car anyway." I paused again, feeling more and more nostalgic for our little midwestern town locked in cold at this time of the year. "Anyway," I went on, rather wistfully, "we have no crime there."

"Really?" Nigel winked, then held the mike back to me.

"Nope. The weekly paper publishes the crime report, called the 'Police Log.' That's a record of all the calls the police department receives in one week."

"How many do they get?" Nigel genuinely wanted to know.

"They get about two calls a day." I paused for effect again. This time, Nigel just raised an eyebrow, and kept the mike close to me. "The calls are mostly about raccoons, sometimes deer, sometimes livestock."

"Raccoons!"

"Yes. They get in the garbage cans, into the rubbish bins." Behind me, Jewel snorted again. Nigel was also struggling. He took a deep breath, then dropped his voice a notch and spoke calmly into the mike.

"You say they get into the rubbish bins?"

"Yup. They can be quite vicious. Of course, people call the police to help them get bats out of their houses also. And many calls are about keys locked in cars."

Ian tapped his watch, and Nigel took the mike from me, even though I had much more to say. I wanted to tell them about our mid-nine-teenth-century house, one of the earliest to be built in the town, and about its owner who had fled the South during the Civil War with Confederate gold, which he stored in a bank just one block away. I wanted to talk about how the bank had been almost robbed in the last century by one of the most notorious outlaw gangs in the country.

"Thank you very much! That was Jane McDonnell speaking to us from the maternity floor of the Royal Free. We hope you have a super week, and we'll be back next Sunday afternoon for another glimpse into the private lives of the patients at the Royal Free Hospital. Cheerio, that's all for now."

My roommates spilled out of the bathroom, and I turned around to grin at them. "You never told us about the winters in America before," Jewel exclaimed.

Ian started to loop the wires around his hand and elbow, and Nigel reached over to shake my hand again. "You saved my life." He grinned. "We got something we could run this time."

"Better than strip poker?" I grinned back.

"You bloody well better believe it!"

A few days later a tall, lanky medical student came into our room and leaned back against the heat register under the window. His clothes were rumpled, and there were dark circles under his eyes. He took his stethoscope from around his neck and put it on the windowsill. Then he lifted himself up with his two arms and sat on the sill, swinging his legs. He looked exhausted, almost ill.

"One of you ladies has got to give birth soon." He looked around at each of us to make sure we heard him. "I mean," he said, brushing his hand through his hair in embarrassment, "what I mean is: one of you has to have a normal birth soon. Otherwise, I won't pass this year."

We all sat up in bed. This was interesting. This cast a whole new light on things. "You won't pass?" Jewel asked. "What do you mean you won't pass?"

"I won't pass the course. I haven't yet delivered a normal baby in a normal birth to a normal woman. If I don't, I won't pass OB. All of you ladies are so damn complicated."

"Well, you've come to the wrong place." Toni laughed.

But Colin came back every day to lean against the heat register and joke with us. He told Jewel to quit smoking. He also told us where the delivery rooms were, and when Penelope went into labor and was suddenly carted off down the hall, he arranged a signal for the rest of us, lights blinked on and off, twice for "She's all right." Three times for "She's not all right. Complications."

After Penelope left us with a healthy baby girl, a beautiful young Turkish woman was brought in one evening to give birth to her stillborn baby. The doctors had not been able to find a heartbeat, and they were scheduling the birth for the next day. Soon after she arrived, Gulchin called excitedly from her bed. "I've found it. I found the heartbeat," she said, pressing her hand to her side. We all looked up and smiled at her, but Toni said quietly to me, "It isn't her baby's heartbeat she's found. It's her own. She's pressing on her own artery."

After dinner, Gulchin's relatives began to arrive. They gathered around her bed, mother, father, husband, brother, aunt, grandmother. Suddenly the room was crowded. They were all talking excitedly. "If this baby is dead, why can't she give birth now? Why does she have to wait till tomorrow?"

When Jim came to visit, I got up and walked slowly around the hall with him. Sister Murphy caught up with us. "I hope she isn't bothering you," she said. "We can't schedule an induced birth when we are so short-staffed. It's too risky." She seemed to feel that she must explain to someone who would listen and understand. "No," I said, "she isn't bothering me at all. I think I understand what she's going through." But I felt her sadness so strongly that I needed to get up and walk away from it for a while. I was intensely grateful for Jim's presence, as together we walked down the hall to find a quiet place in a lounge for visitors. We just sat there, holding hands, not talking, but glad to be together.

Later, after Jim had left, I went back to bed. I wanted to go over to Gulchin and talk to her for a few moments, but I saw that the curtains were drawn around her bed. I felt a terrible, overwhelming sadness. I also felt the beginnings of real cramping, not just a slight tightening across my lower abdomen, but real pain.

I pulled the curtains around my bed. The contractions were getting worse, and they reminded me of that other time, that terrible time, when I was confined to bed for five weeks with ruptured membranes, yet still gave birth to the baby three months early. I had been so careful then, so conscientious about staying in bed. I had worked so hard to stay sane, hopeful, occupied, unself-pitying. Lying on my left side, I had written two chapters of my dissertation.

I had talked to friends who came almost every day with food, and books, and sometimes a cocktail shaker for a happy hour around my bed. Somehow I had held on, but it was all for nothing in the end. I wondered if I would lose this other baby now in the same way.

Lying in my London hospital bed that evening, I tried to relax, to breathe deeply, to send messages to my "irritable uterus" to be quiet. But I found I couldn't relax. The past kept rising up before my eyes: the sudden rush to the hospital years ago when the contractions had suddenly started for real; the alcohol drip I was hooked up with in the hospital; Jim's pale face as he tried to comfort me and keep his own anxiety in check, so as not to doubly burden me.

For five weeks, Jim had cooked, and mopped the kitchen floor, and brought me books from the library, and told visitors when they could come and when they couldn't, and sat beside me, and read to me every night to distract us both from sex, so that I wouldn't crawl into his arms and assuage my body's hurt in a way that would kill the baby. And yet all of this incredible effort was, in the end, lost.

And then the moment of the baby's birth: his first breath strangled in his throat. His dark, dark eyes stared into mine as I struggled to sit up on the delivery table and tried to reach for him with my arms under the sterile covers. I was told to lie down again and I heard then the awful sound of the suctioning down his throat, and that even more awful mewling, choked sound, that sound of a breath stifled at its very beginnings.

"Can't you put him on a respirator?" I had wanted to know.

And the doctor's impatient voice. "It would blow out his lungs."

The nurse quickly wrapped him, this tiny, tiny red boy, this boy we had already named Paul Thomas, in a blanket and ran out the door.

And that was the last I ever saw of him.

Later the nurse came to tell me that, for two hours as they waited for the ambulance to arrive from the university hospital, she had stood at the foot of his isolette. She had flicked the soles of his feet to keep him awake and breathing. She told me about how he had fixed his dark eyes on her, how he had struggled to breathe with lungs that collapsed after every breath. "I was sure he would live," she told me, the tears slipping down her cheeks. "Sure he would live. He was trying so hard." And she had turned aside, almost ashamed of her own grief in the face of mine.

Now that untimely birth rose before my eyes, as I lay on my side in the hospital bed in London and drew up my knees to try to ease the hurt in my lower abdomen. But the contractions had become much stronger, and the Scotch I had been sipping was simply not working. I reached for the nurse's bell, and in a moment Sister Murphy was beside my bed.

"What is it, love?" Her face held real concern.

"The cramping . . ." I started to cry. "It's so bad, and I'm so afraid."

"Be right back," and she was gone quickly down the hall.

Toni quietly got out of bed, and without saying a word, pulled up a chair. She reached out for my hand, and I clung on to it, tears streaming down my face. She reached over to wipe my cheeks, then she wiped her own.

We both laughed, a little hysterically. "We're a right pair, aren't we?" She sat there, holding my hand, until Sister Murphy came back with a hypodermic needle.

"Here," she said, "roll over. Your doctor wants you to have this. It's morphine. He says it's perfectly safe for the baby, and it will stop the contractions."

I felt so desperate that I accepted the drug. I felt that, without it, I would certainly miscarry. Half an hour later the hard contractions had stopped, and gratefully, easefully, I fell asleep.

At the end of March, when I was a full three months pregnant, surgery was scheduled to stitch up the incompetent cervix. The doctors hoped that after this my pregnancy would be more secure and that I could look forward to a full-term baby. Before the surgery, however, they wanted an ultrasound scan to see how the baby was doing. The doctors were, as always, very anxious not to interfere in a defective pregnancy, or one that would produce a child with major deformities. Primarily, they wanted to know that they were stitching in a real baby, not an empty egg sac, a fetus that had failed to develop.

I was taken by wheelchair down to the radiology department and asked to put on a cotton hospital gown. Ultrasound scans were new at the time, and I was anxious that my baby would not be hurt. I was also concerned about what the scans might show. I felt that a lot was at stake as I walked over to the high table and climbed onto it.

The technician poured the cool oil onto my stomach, then ran the flat edge of the scanner slowly back and forth across it.

"Watch the screen," she said. I turned to look at the television monitor set up next to the table.

There on the screen were fuzzy, cloudy forms, always moving, always shifting. The picture looked a little like the clouds on a satellite photo of the earth: the same swirling atmosphere so hard to read, yet so active. I watched, thinking about how satellite photos have shown us, for the first time, the living air above the earth. And I thought of how this scan was showing me for the first time another image of life, just as wonderful, just as marvelous.

"Look!" the technician pointed suddenly to the monitor. "There it is."

I watched closely. I could just make out a faint pulsing, and the outlines of a small cloud.

"That's the fetal sac, and there is the fetal heartbeat. How far along did you say you were?"

"Three months, almost exactly."

"It looks a little earlier than that. But not to worry, everything looks fine." She switched off the monitor and turned back to smile at me. "Everything looks just fine. Congratulations." And with a smile, she held out her hand to help me off the table.

CHAPTER 8

Anthem for the Foundling Hospital

T HE SURGERY, which I had shortly after the ultrasound scan, went well, but I was getting more and more tired of the Royal Free. Later, as spring progressed, I was able to talk my way out of the hospital, just as earlier I had been able to talk my way into it. I packed to leave and said good-bye to Jewel and to Toni. By this time, they were both very close to delivering full-term babies. We exchanged our London phone numbers and addresses, and I told them that I would write later when I had returned to America and again when my baby was born.

Somehow, in leaving the hospital, I misplaced Toni's phone number and address. I felt a lot of regret that I had lost touch with her, but Jim's mother told me later that she thought she saw someone who looked just like Toni wheeling a pram through the open-air market on Acton High Street. So her baby had survived. I knew that much at least.

Jewel and I exchanged Christmas letters for several years. She told me that she had had a baby girl, then a year or two later I learned that the child was slow to develop, especially slow to learn to speak. When the little girl was three or four, my Christmas letter was returned unopened. Jewel had moved, and I never was able to learn if her daughter was all right or not.

Gulchin I saw once in the outpatient clinic of the Royal Free when I returned for a checkup in the fifth or sixth month of my pregnancy. By this time I was large, obviously pregnant. As soon as I walked into the waiting room, I saw Gulchin sitting in a corner, flat-stomached and miserable. I started to go over to speak to her, but she looked away from me, averting her eyes from my big belly. She picked up a magazine and hid behind it. I hesitated for a moment, and then I sat down on the other side of the room. I remembered, oh how keenly I remembered, how terrible it was to lose a baby and then to meet a pregnant friend.

It was a glorious spring that year. After my months of confinement, I couldn't get enough of the sun, of the grass, of the flowers that popped out all over our little back garden. I walked around the streets a bit, but mostly I stayed in bed or sat under our flowering pear tree. Gradually I got stronger, my appetite improved, I slept better, and the contractions lessened, although they never went away completely.

Paul began to get better. He calmed down, adjusted to all these new changes, and acquired more and more language. Some months before, I had given up counting, after his vocabulary had reached seventy-eight words, all of which I could write in tiny script on one five-by-eight card. Now several new words were appearing every day.

Paul played beside me outdoors under the pear tree. One day he took his shoes off and, before I could stop him, he slung them over the high brick wall into our neighbor's patch of garden. "He-ooos!" he shouted. "Shoes!" He giggled as I lectured him on the disappearance of his new leather shoes and Jim ran next door to ring the front bell. Soon our neighbors appeared in the back to sling the shoes back over the wall. But every day after that, in spite of all my lecturing, Paul gleefully hurled his shoes over the wall, and our neighbors happily pitched them back. As always with Paul, a lesson once learned, a habit once acquired, would be forever repeated. To him, it was very funny to hurl his shoes over the wall, and he didn't stop for the rest of our time in Islington.

For the last year Paul had known the alphabet, and now he recognized letters in many different contexts. We tried to use letters as a way of reaching him. One day I wrote to my father: "Daddy: Paul is very eager to get a letter from you. If you do write, could you mention the moon, a train, a windmill, bells, a teapot, or one of his favorite letters — *i* for icecream or *w* for water. He can't pass a postbox without mentioning you or your letters."

A few weeks later, there came not just a letter, but a whole little book, bound, typed, and illustrated. "Dear Paul: This is my first letter to you for your very own," and there followed a story about an old man with a broken windmill, and a little boy who took a train to town to get a teapot for his mother and screwdriver to fix the windmill. In town the bells rang, and back at home the moon rose.

"When the little boy returned home, he saw the moon climbing higher and higher, and getting bigger and bigger." And there was a picture of the moon, with an explanation underneath: "Actually, this is a series of timed exposures of the moon, not taken all in one night but during the space of about two weeks." At the bottom of every page was this other story, the one for me and Jim.

The story concluded: "His mother thanked him for the teapot and gave him some ice cream. And his daddy fixed the windmill. And then they all had water to drink from the well." The picture showed a *w* and a glass of water, an *i* and an ice cream cone. Then under the picture: "The old man got a welder after all to fix the windmill. Screws do not hold in a wind. This view of the windmill was taken from a neighboring farm to obtain the proper perspective of windmill against moon. Fortunately, the disagreeable owner of the neighboring farm was asleep at the time."

Paul became a great favorite of Molly's, and the Wolfson Centre became a magical, healing place for him. Just before our scheduled return to America, we were called in for a final conference with the school staff. They would tell us the results of some final tests and give advice about next year.

We all sat down in a conference room — Molly, Dr. Reston, Heather O'Neal, and Jim and me. Molly gave me an extra chair to prop up my feet, and I leaned back comfortably. By this time, I felt much better, but I was also sad to have missed the whole late winter and spring at the Wolfson Centre, and now I would have to be content with just this final report.

Molly went first. "In some ways, Paul has made quite startling progress in his time here. In learning visual concepts, he made fifteen months progress in just six months. It's clear he has high perceptual abilities."

Molly grinned and paused to let this sink in, then she went on. "Paul's language, however, is still very slow and deliberate, without much variety in tone. It still requires a very conscious effort for him to translate his thoughts into words, but in spite of this, he has made quite good progress in language acquisition also. In attention control he is now at level three.

"At this level, Paul is only slightly immature for his age. In other words, he can now accept adult control, and he can assimilate verbal directions and relate them to a task. This is still hard for him to do, and he needs a lot of guidance, but he is now able to shift his attention back and forth between the adult and the task at hand."

Dr. Reston added: "Paul hasn't yet learned to use language as a directive-integrative function, but with more help, we think he should be able to attend a regular school at the usual time."

Heather told us that, although she worked with Paul on varying intonation, his speech was still singsong in quality. "We worked a lot on this," she said. "He loved to copy different intonation patterns, but for him this was just a game. He's not ready yet to incorporate the subtle differences of intonation into his regular speech.

"He enjoyed his individual sessions with me," Heather added, "but it was good for him to be in a group also, where a certain amount of conformity was demanded of him. Nevertheless, he did have trouble working with the group."

We weren't surprised at any of this. The picture they painted of Paul's high abilities and remaining deficits was just what we would have expected. We left the interview that day feeling much more hopeful than when we first went to the Wolfson Centre.

Years later I read that the Wolfson Centre on Mecklenburgh Square was on the site of a famous hospital for orphan children founded in the eighteenth century, and that Handel had written an "Anthem for the Foundling Hospital" to raise money for the children who lived there. Later Handel also gave them an organ, and he dedicated the proceeds of several performances of the *Messiah* for the benefit of the orphans.

This hospital, founded by Thomas Coram for the "maintenance and education of exposed and deserted young children" and built in 1742 on Lamb's Conduit Fields, had, however, been a place of appalling suffering. The children of desperately poor unwed mothers were taken there and abandoned. Beggars with donkeys were often paid by the destitute mothers to carry their babies in panniers, woven baskets slung on the sides of the donkeys, into London. The babies were deposited on the threshold between double doors so arranged that the giver need not be seen by the receiver. The hospital became famous and was quickly overcrowded. Most children died of smallpox or typhus, tuberculosis or cholera. Those who survived grew up to a life which doesn't bear thinking on.

At the end of the eighteenth century, the "city fathers" decided to close down the hospital. They did this not because of the overcrowding and the illnesses of the children, but because they felt in their "great wisdom" that the sinful ways of the mothers could no longer be rewarded. They wanted to discourage immoral women from having children out of wedlock, and they thought closing the hospital was the only effective way of doing that. A public outcry, however, soon restored the foundling hospital.

I often thought of the suffering experienced there, of the baby ghosts wandering among the flower beds and trees of present-day Mecklenburgh Square, now a calm center in noisy, distracted London, and of our own child born to a happier, more privileged time. For there Paul flourished. There was no "breakthrough," in the sense of a drugstore paperback miracle story, only quiet, steady progress, the slight beginnings of real, usable speech. We felt then, and always afterward, that without the intervention of those wonderful teachers at the Wolfson Centre, Paul would not have done so well. They gave him a precious gift: by helping him gain some control over his attention, to focus his attention at will and to shift focus, they helped him to learn to learn.

CHAPTER 9

The Clarity of Simple Babyhood

H ERE I WAS, staring into the lights of the delivery room, the same room, I suddenly realized, where Paul had been born four years before. Clamped into a pain that astounded me after three hours of the easiest labor imaginable, I thought I would break apart. And then I thought it was my mind, my spirit, my consciousness, that would break apart, would shatter into a thousand fragments. There was no way I could sustain this, no way I could survive what was happening to me. So shocked was I by this knowledge, that I almost missed the voice that was saying, "What an awful lot of black, curly hair!" and the other voice that said, "It's a girl's hair."

But then I could hear the suctioning, and that sharp cry, that wail of protest, that grabbing onto life, that sound so different from the stifled, snuffling cry of the six-months baby.

"It *is* a girl." I heard this, and at the same time I felt the most astonishing *absence* of pain. And then I saw the doctor wrap a slippery, squirming thing in a sheet and hand it to Jim. "Here. Take her."

Jim took her, this round girl baby, whose lungs, like a little tree of empty air sacs, had filled full of air, inflated all the way and were turning her now a bright pink. She was breathing! She was also angry, shocked right down to her toes, her face puckered up in protest against this strange thing that had happened to her.

"Would you like to cut the cord?"

"Oh, no." Jim looked startled. "I couldn't."

"Yes, you can. Here are the scissors. She can't feel a thing."

They had the clamp on the umbilical cord. And Jim took the scissors and cut.

I was afraid he might drop her in his excitement. But no, he moved over to my head. He held her down for me to see and a nurse supported my shoulders so I could peer into her face. A perfectly round, red face, and thick, long black hair, curly and matted against her head. Puffy eyelids. I wondered how she would ever open them. And then she did. She stared right into Jim's face. Our Kate. Our black-haired Irish Kate.

On that September morning, Kate seemed to be perfect. The doctors gave her a nine out of a possible ten on the Apgar score, the index of a newborn's general health and well-being. When Jim and I both exclaimed that Paul — who was just as healthy at birth, who had taken his first breath even sooner than she had — had received only an eight, the doctors said, "Oh, well, let's knock hers down to an eight also." Jim and I looked at each other, a little stunned at this way of keeping medical records.

But later I thought of that moment as symbolic. Not only was Kate born into a family where there was already an older child establishing the framework for her life and claiming most of the energies of her mother, but also she was asked in her first ten minutes to stop competing with her older brother, to scale back in her own expectations. I vowed then that she wouldn't be asked to do this again.

But there was another way in which Kate's birth got very special recognition, as I learned later that day. My physicist brother, who was working at Fermi Lab, heard the news from my sister-in-law Ellen some time after lunch. And before he went home that day, Frank logged Kate's birth into the official list of events recorded at the lab that day. I've often thought of Kate's appearance on earth recorded among the day's yield of bosons and positrons at Fermi Lab.

The day after she was born, I sat alone with Kate in my hospital room. She was completely relaxed, completely content, lying swaddled in a yellow baby blanket, arms and legs folded again into a tight little space. I thought I might allow myself to hope for this child because she seemed so perfect curled up against me, a satisfying, heavy warmth in my arms. I bent to kiss the top of Kate's head, to take in her clean, new-baby scent, and I tried to bask in the simple hopefulness that a new baby can bring. I wanted to think only good thoughts, to bring her only blessings, to keep from her unformed newness the dark shadows that had already gathered in her troubled family.

When you have one handicapped child and a history of troubled pregnancies such as mine, friends and family often wonder why you choose to have another child. I know many of our friends were very puzzled that I had been willing to put my own health and well-being at risk once again, or to risk having another handicapped child. Few dared to speak openly to me about their worries, but I always sensed it on their faces, in their voices, in what was *not* said.

Looking back now on that period of our common life, I often wonder myself why Jim and I chose to go ahead and have another baby. I think we acted out of a complex mixture of naive optimism, blindness, denial, and sheer unthinking courage. Maybe this blindness and this courage are necessary for the next generation to be born at all. I often wonder if I could act this way again, and I look with amazement at people who go on getting pregnant, who go on having children. But Jim and I also were once young and willing to embrace the special kind of vulnerability that comes only from having a child.

Holding Kate in that hospital room, I thought suddenly of a time when Paul was young, just ten months old, before we knew that he had a disability. I was afraid at that time, and watchful, but I didn't really know very much and I could still sometimes allow myself to feel a pure pleasure untainted with worry.

We were in the south of France and had gone with friends to a ruined Cistercian monastery. We went inside the fourteenth-century oratory and stood there for a long time in silence. The monastery was made of some local cream-colored stone, and the oratory was large and empty and very dusty. Suddenly a single shaft of light entered the small rose window high up in the western wall, and the whole vast, empty room seemed to fill with a smoky, golden pink light.

I put Paul down on the floor, and he started crawling toward the light. Then he stopped, a look of rapt attention on his face. Sitting back on his heels, he lifted his hand toward the light. "Bah," he said, that all-purpose baby sound, but this time it seemed to have a special resonance. Paul sat back and solemnly saluted the light. And we had laughed with pleasure at his happiness.

Holding this new young baby curled against me, I thought of that moment in the monastery as a time before, a time that was irrevocably lost to me now. I wondered if I would ever again be able to enjoy the clarity of simple babyhood, to appreciate the directness of a baby greeting the light. Would there always be an edge of worry, an edge of watchfulness to any pleasure I would take in this new child?

I knew too much now. And I was the one who had lost my innocence.

Because of her beautiful head of hair, Kate was chosen as the "bath demonstration model," and she gave the first performance of her life to a group of seven or eight new mothers. I went with them down the hall and took my seat in the little room to watch Kate being bathed.

I watched as this unknown little baby was unwrapped from her pink blanket, as she was gently lowered into the pan of tepid water, as her black hair was washed and brushed into a topknot. The nurse tied a little pink grosgrain ribbon around Kate's hair. Then, placing her on her stomach on the table, the nurse turned around to find the powder. In a moment, Kate was up on her elbows and had brought her knees almost under her stomach and was pushing off, shoving herself close to the edge of the table. Quickly, the nurse caught her. "Lesson number one, the most important lesson of all," she said, laughing, "is never, never leave a baby alone on the table even for a second."

It was so good to see the health and strength of this baby, but somewhere in the back of my mind was tucked away the knowledge of the "old brain" in a newborn baby, the brain which allows them to walk if supported, to hold themselves up with the grip of their tiny fists, to almost crawl off a table. I remembered, as I sat there watching the nurse bathe Kate, that this brain gets broken down, the cells reabsorbed into a new and more complex brain. And it's the new brain that must relearn the same skills and behaviors that were instinctual before. We would have to wait to see if Kate's new brain would re-learn the old skills.

Immediately, I censored this knowledge. Kate was new. Kate was not Paul. I need not worry about her just because I was worried about Paul. Any forebodings I felt at this time, I told myself, came from my experience with Paul, and I fought hard just to be happy with a new, healthy baby. It was good to nurse a baby again. It was good, during the days when I was in the hospital, to sit and stare at this beautiful, black-haired girl child, asleep in my arms.

The day we came home from the hospital, Paul, to my surprise, didn't run out to the car to meet us. Walking in the back door, through the kitchen and into the living room, I searched for him. Ellen, who had come with her own two children to stay with Paul and help me after I got home from the hospital, rushed to meet us and to take Kate from Jim's arms. At the playroom door, she knelt on the floor and called to Paul to come and see his little sister. There he was, behind the door, fitting together lengths of plastic pipe.

"Come see your little sister."

Paul dropped the pipes and sidled around the door. He looked so big. His high-top boots with the laces coming untied suddenly looked enormous to me, ten times the size of Kate's white knit booties. I didn't realize until now how big Paul had grown, and I wanted to wrap my arms around him, to hold him again and feel his taut boy muscles, his sharp little elbows. He stood next to Ellen and stared for a moment at the bundle in her arms. Ellen moved the blanket away from Kate's face and her eyelids briefly fluttered open.

"Would you like to hold her, Paul?" I asked him, and he nodded slowly. "Come sit with me. I want to see you." I patted the sofa, then gave him a quick hug as he sat down next to me, working his back up close to the cushions, his legs sticking straight out in front of him. Slowly, I lowered Kate into his arms, but he held them limply by his sides and wouldn't raise them to hold on to her. For a moment, Kate lay in Paul's lap as I supported her, and a little flicker of something like interest passed across Paul's face. But then he wriggled around and slid off the sofa.

Ellen laughed and sat down next to me, taking Kate again from my arms. In a few moments, Graham, her nine-month-old son, tried to climb into her arms, and she put Kate down to sleep in the baby carriage that was made up for her in the playroom next door. We sat on the couch for a while and talked, catching up on all our news, on what Paul and his cousins Charlie and Graham had been up to while I was in the hospital.

A few minutes later, we looked up and there was Paul pushing the carriage into the living room. In a flash, I took in the scene: covering the carriage, hanging over the side and off the hood, were Paul's plastic pipes, and he was bumping the carriage over the threshold of the playroom door. "Poipes!" he exclaimed, a broad grin on his face. "Baby see poipes." He came to a halt in front of us.

Ellen and I both jumped up to peer into the carriage. But Kate was sleeping peacefully, wrapped in her blanket, surrounded by Paul's collection of plastic pipes from the hardware store. Junction pipes, T junctions, pipes of many different lengths, together with the circular joining pieces — all of these were carefully tucked in around her, but none had been placed very close to her face or head.

"Poipes." Paul showed us again proudly, and he began to gather up the pipes to take them back to the playroom. At that moment, I knew that he had given Kate his most precious possession. And by showing his pipes to Kate, by draping them over her sleeping form, Paul had shown us, momentarily at least, that he accepted and welcomed her into the family. But more than that: Paul had now passed on to Kate whatever special luck or charm rested in the pipes. And having done this, he could safely take the pipes back and go off and play with them.

I was hoping that this new baby would redeem all the losses and all the anxiety that had gone before. But I was too exhausted to enjoy Kate or even to register this experience the way I wanted to. I wanted to sit under a tree, my back to the solid trunk, and nurse a baby in the dappled sunlight. Then I wanted to bounce up and care energetically for two children, and have time left over to read and write and prepare for the new women's literature class I wanted to teach later that year. But is it ever like that? And with me, not only was I exhausted by the usual demands of pregnancy and child care, but I found as soon as I came home that I had another infection. This one was very resistant to treatment, maybe because I had had so many infections before and was so debilitated. In the end I had to be treated with twice the usual dose of antibiotics.

Ellen worked hard, caring for Paul and her own two sons, cooking and looking after the housework. But even with all this help, I was too tired even to come downstairs on most days. The effort of getting dressed, the effort of simply sitting in the same room with three young children, was too much, so I stayed in bed for almost two weeks, until Ellen had to return home. I felt very guilty at not even being able to talk to her, to offer a little adult companionship, as she struggled with the task of caring for two four-year-olds, as well as a baby of nine months.

As soon as Ellen left, and I began to regain a little of my strength, we found that Kate was colicky. She nursed well, she grew well, she flourished in all other ways, but she cried and cried and cried. Four years before, when Paul was a new baby, we had been given a book by some very up-to-date, no-nonsense, childless friends of ours: *How to Raise a Baby at Home in Your Spare Time.* One chapter, called "For Crying Out Loud, What *Is* Colic?" explained that it was simply crying out loud, and crying out loud was of course colic. Nobody knew why some young babies, otherwise healthy, cried so much. The book advised us simply to put up with the crying, and it would go away in three months.

Now, with two-week-old Kate slung across my shoulder crying bitterly, I searched my study for this book. Paul had been such a contented baby that I had barely skimmed the chapter about colic. Now, in the clutter that was my abandoned study, I couldn't find it, and I thought, with some bitterness myself, that the book had been seriously misnamed anyway. Who ever dreamed of raising children at home in your spare time, like tomatoes or onions?

But at least I knew Kate was healthy, and I also had far more confidence in my own knowledge and skills now with the second child. Friends came forward with their own remedies for colic. "There's always brandy," one offered slyly, quoting the oldest doctor in town, the one who had cared for half the population when they were babies. Another said simply, "She's a walker." She's a walker and you'll have to walk her, and that's that.

So with Kate across my shoulder, I walked and walked and walked. I patted her back and pressed her gently into the warmth of my own body, and I walked some more. When Jim came home, he did the same. And then we started singing a little song to her, "Colicky, Colicky Baby," to the tune of the Irish children's song about the snail in its shell, "Shellicky, Shellicky Bukey."

I pulled a spare mattress into her room and put it on the floor. I made up my bed there to sleep beside her, so I could reach her while Jim still slept. He was teaching that term and I wasn't, so I thought this only fair. But because he was now closer to Paul's room, Jim always heard Paul first if he happened to cry in the night. Soon I began to hear only Kate's cries and Jim heard only Paul's, so we learned to help each other through those difficult nights.

One night we both woke from a deep sleep. Somewhere, far away, someone was crying. Finally I realized it was Paul, and he was sobbing uncontrollably. A train roared through town, sounding unbelievably loud through the open windows. Jim and I both stumbled into Paul's room. I scooped him into my arms: "It's just a train, Paul. It's all right." But his crying continued. He pointed to the plaid cover on his bed.

"Train. Train," he sobbed.

We were puzzled. "The train is far away, Paul." We listened as it moved farther and farther away, until we could barely hear it.

But Paul was still crying. "Train tracks," he said. He pointed again to the lines running parallel across his cover.

"Train tracks? Oh no, Paul." Light dawned on us suddenly. "Those aren't train tracks on your bed, just stripes." But Paul continued to cry quietly for a while. "Paul don't like stripes. Don't like stripes."

After that episode, we kept the windows closed on one side of the house to reduce the sound of the trains in the night. Paul never again woke crying about the trains, but he refused for years to wear striped clothes. All he would ever say was "Paul don't like stripes." But we knew trains, loud shrieking trains, were the origin of that fear of stripes. Other parents of children like Paul are not so lucky. Many never find out the origin of their children's strange fears — of dogs, shower curtains, flowers.

After this we became very aware that Paul was acutely sensitive to sound, or to certain sounds. A neighbor's lawn mower, the buzz saw at the lumberyard, trains, sirens — all of these sent him into a frenzy. "Loud noises," in fact, became his name for all forms of pain: "Paul have loud noises in his stomach," he would say when he had a stomachache. Sometimes I suspected he heard sounds at frequencies we couldn't hear. My sister-in-law Ellen reported the same thing of her son Charlie. "He cries whenever we go to the bank," she told me one day. "I think he hears their alarm system." Then later, she told me that he would go to certain stores only if she called ahead and asked them to turn off their security system.

The train track episode was the first instance I remember of Paul's sound sensitivity; it was also one of the first examples of his unusual and even rigid way of learning after he began to acquire language. He put together the sound of the train with the image of parallel lines going across his bed and that suggested to him train tracks. This seemed to be very creative to me, but the important thing here was that our reassurances that stripes were not the same as train tracks didn't work. Back in Minnesota, I wished we had Molly to explain to Paul that train tracks and lines on a plaid blanket were "not the same," just as a cup is "not a hat." But for Paul, the first context for learning a new concept remained the only context. If something was learned in a moment of fear, he would forever afterward remain fearful of it.

Gravity was the same. One evening I went with Paul to the day care center next to our house. It was after dinner, and the children had gone home for the day. We often came over here at this time. There was a swing on a huge old elm tree, a large sand pit nearby, and some other playground equipment, a jungle gym and a merry-go-round. It was a lovely evening and the sun was setting, sending long golden beams across the grass and slanting through the leaves of the trees. Paul played in the sandbox and I sat on the swing, reading a book.

"Want to swing." Paul left the sand pit and came over to me. "Swing. Now!"

"All right, Paul." I put my book down and pulled the swing way back, giving it a big push to start it forward. As usual when he was on the swing, Paul started talking. I had noticed this many times before. When he was swinging, he became calmer, more focused, more verbal.

"What pull Paul back?" he asked.

"Gravity. Gravity pulls you back."

"What gravity?"

"Gravity is a force that pulls you toward the earth. It holds you on the earth."

Paul was quiet, considering this. I pushed him back and forth, back and forth.

"What happen gravity go 'way?"

"Then you would fly off into space."

"But Paul fwye now. Swing."

"No, you won't fly off. Gravity is still holding you."

Paul was quiet again. Then, in a high-pitched, anxious voice: "But gravity go 'way? Gravity go 'way!"

I thought no more of this little conversation, except to be impressed at Paul's ability to learn an abstract concept. But later that night, after Paul had been in bed for a couple of hours, we heard him crying and went into his room.

"Gravity go 'way." He was sobbing and rocking back and forth on his hands and knees under the blanket. He looked up at us when we came into his room. "Gravity go 'way!"

"No, Paul." Jim and I both sat down on the edge of his bed. "Gravity won't ever, ever go away. Not ever!"

But Paul was still rocking and crying. "But . . . but gravity go 'way when Paul sleep."

"Oh, no." Jim and I almost laughed at this. "Gravity won't go away when you go to sleep."

We stayed with Paul and rubbed his back, and slowly he relaxed and went back to sleep. But after this he was still afraid gravity would go away and that he would fall up into the air and away forever. We were bewildered by these fears. Verbal reassurances helped a little bit because Paul was now talking and understanding more and more. But I had never met anyone so rigid in his habits, so fearful of new experiences, so traumatized by the small upsets that every child encounters in learning the world. Nor, I thought in my better moments, had I ever met a child so interesting, so fascinating because of the way he learned.

Even though he was now preoccupied with pipes and numbers, Paul had not forgotten about screwdrivers. As soon as we returned home from England, he got to work on the door handles. Jim and I, occupied for the last several months with my troubled pregnancy and then with a newborn, were always at least three steps behind him. He outwitted us every time we tried to hide the screwdrivers or to replace the screws in the doorknobs. Now almost every doorknob we tried to turn fell off in our hands. Jim, who has never been good with his hands, tried over and over to put them back again, or to buy new doorknobs, which usually meant he had to drill new holes for the hardware, which in turn meant endless hours of frustrated, fruitless work. Eventually, that winter, when the northwest wind blew the front door open for the thousandth time, Jim grabbed a hammer and nails.

"I'm going to nail that bloody thing shut," he muttered through clenched teeth. He pounded a row of large ugly nails into the door-jamb, then stepped back to admire his handiwork. "That bugger won't ever come open again!"

But even with that door nailed shut, Paul remained obsessional about screwdrivers — and then one day he discovered Jim's study light. A red draftsman's light screwed to the edge of the desk, this contraption clearly had removable parts and Paul was going to go after them. But this time, we decided to draw the line: Paul could not have Jim's study light to take apart. We were not going to sacrifice that light, and Jim and I made a solemn pact that whatever it took to save the light, we had it in us. We were going to hold firm. For months, if need be.

The siege began. "Want-a Dadd-ee stud-ee light-a!" The wail went up every day. We called this Paul's Italian phase because he was adding "a" to the end of most words. "Want-a Dadd-ee stud-ee light-a!" He marched every day into Jim's study and every day we removed him from the light.

"No, Paul, you can't have that light," I would say as I led him out of the room. "And that, my little skunk, is that!"

"Want-a Dadd-ee stud-ee light-a!"

We tried distracting him with toys that had removable parts, with his plastic numbers, with his set of plastic pipes which he could screw together and take apart. Nothing worked.

"Want-a Dadd-ee stud-ee LIGHT-A."

The siege did indeed last for months. Only the parent of a child like Paul would ever really understand what this meant — how little effect "no" had, how distractions and punishments, persuasions and re-wards, had no effect whatsoever. But this time, Jim and I had the willpower and determination to keep at it. Paul never did take that red study light apart. But he also never gave up trying, for weeks and weeks, and then for months.

*

For weeks after her birth, people came to the house to see Kate and to bring gifts. Those with some insight into children always brought Paul a little present also — a Matchbox car or a stuffed animal to go with the stuffed animal for Kate. One kind neighbor brought two koala bears with Velcro fasteners on their arms so they could hug each other.

Paul wasn't interested in any of this. He was interested, of course, in screwdrivers, but also in plumbing and toilets, his pipes and the mechanism in the tank of the toilet. "Oh, what a lovely baby," Paul would say, bending over Kate and showing her off to our friends. Then Paul would take them by the hand to the bathroom to examine the back of the toilet. "Oh, what a lovely potty," he would say to bewildered guests, as he stood on tiptoe to peer into the open tank. Some of our guests, longtime friends and babysitters of Paul's, weren't bewildered at all. They had since grown used to Paul and would peer with amusement into the toilet as the two of them flushed and watched the tank fill up again.

One day when Kate was about four months old, I sat nursing her in the rocking chair in the living room. We sat in a pool of sunlight, which shone through the stained glass at the top of the west windows and the leaves of the plants clustered below. At my feet Paul played with his plastic numbers, lining them up on the side of the carpet. He kept glancing up at us, then quickly away again, watching us but not wanting to be seen watching us, as he tried to place his numbers exactly at the edge of the carpet. He was having some trouble because one side of the carpet was smooth, but the other was fringed. I could feel the frustration building in him, but I didn't want to stop and help him. I was enjoying this peaceful moment with Kate and didn't want it to end.

I finished nursing Kate, then bent to kiss the top of her head and to curl her hair around my finger. She was wearing a little red suit, which made her dark hair seem even darker. The sunlight just touched her round cheek, and her skin seemed to glow with a delicate sheen. She leaned forward in my lap, craning to see what Paul was doing. She adored him, and showed it in a dozen ways every day. Paul, on the other hand, mostly ignored her.

"Do you want me to read you a story, Paul?" I knew he was feeling jealous and hoped I could defuse the tension in him.

He dropped his numbers and came close to me, pushing Kate out of the way to the other side of my lap.

"Little, tiny fingers," he said, taking one of her hands in his hand and bending her fingers back slightly, one by one, counting them.

"Little, tiny, *tiny* fingers," he said again. Kate smiled at him, utterly relaxed and trusting. Then suddenly Paul jerked her fingers back sharply.

"Paul!" Kate had started to cry, and I stood to hold her against my shoulder and away from him. "You mustn't do that. It hurts Kate when you do that."

He glared at me. "When Kate go 'way?"

"She isn't going away."

"But when Kate go *away?*"

I stared at him for a moment. "She isn't ever going away, Paul."

"But . . . *when Kate going away?*"

"She isn't going away. She's your little sister, and she's here to stay."

With that, Paul threw himself backward onto the sofa and sobbed.

CHAPTER 10

Another Diagnosis

O NE DAY when Kate was about six months old, I was out walking
with her in the stroller when I met an acquaintance, someone
who taught child psychology classes at our college. We stopped to talk,
and Melissa bent to look at Kate. She took her little mittened hand to
shake it playfully, then lifted her out of the stroller. She explained that
she liked to bring babies into class who were at various stages of
development. She had found a three-month baby, and a year-old baby,
but hadn't found a six-month-old yet.

Kate swung around sharply on Melissa's shoulder to keep me in
sight, then she reached out her arms to me, making a slightly pouting
face. Melissa laughed and handed her back to me. Then she asked me
what Kate was doing these days.

"Well, she isn't sitting up yet, and she isn't —" I started, then
stopped. Kate was batting at my cheek and putting her fingers in my
mouth, giggling at me as I pulled her fingers out.

I started again, "She likes to sit in her little sling chair and bounce in
it. She doesn't like to be on her stomach on the floor."

I stopped again. There was something here I didn't want to say, or
to look at. Brushing it aside, I laughed and said, "She's a quiet baby.
She loves to watch us and be a part of everything, but she doesn't really
want to move around much."

Melissa put out a hand and touched my arm, then touched a curl on
Kate's cheek. "They're all different," she said, but I could see her
studying Kate again, her eyes lingering for a moment, as she stood
there considering. She seemed about to say something else, then she
said she must be off, would talk to me later.

I started slowly walking home. Melissa was worried about something. I knew it. She had been about to tell me that Kate was behind.

She should be sitting up now and rolling over, maybe even beginning to creep. I thought of Paul at this age, how he loved to lie on his stomach and practice push-ups, how he propelled himself backward for a while, then forward, how he could roll over and push off and hitch himself around on his bottom.

I worried all the way home. Why wouldn't Kate lie on her stomach? She had always absolutely refused to sleep on her stomach, almost from birth. She cried, almost screamed, if I put her facedown in her crib. I had learned quickly to come back and turn her over.

Only that morning a friend had asked me why I never put Kate on the floor with some toys. I said I tried to, but she always fussed till I put her in her canvas sling chair. "Maybe she just likes to see what's going on. She doesn't want to miss anything that's going on around her." I had laughed and tried to make light of my own worries about all this.

Walking home with Kate in the stroller, I thought about how I often came into Kate's room in the morning to find her in her crib on her back, head lifted way off the mattress, feet and hands waving in the air, smiling at me. It seemed as if Kate could bend in one direction but not the other. She could lift her head forward and even hold it there for long periods, but she couldn't seem to lift it backward.

I talked to Jim that evening. "She's just fine," he said. He seemed so sure, but later that same night, he took Kate out of her sling chair and put her on her stomach on the floor with some toys. Paul brought her his numbers. "Look, Kate, three thousand, four hundred, and sixty-seven," he said, holding the numbers up one by one for her to see.

I listened from the kitchen where I was washing the dishes. Kate was fussing, working herself up to a full cry. "Look, Kate." I could hear Jim try to get her attention. I walked to the door to watch. Jim was squeaking a little yellow rubber porcupine near her face, but then she fell forward on her nose and started to cry steadily.

Jim picked her up and danced her around the room. "It's all right, lovey. It's all right, twiddlywinks." He held her against his shoulder, and slowly she stopped crying and popped her thumb into her mouth, still sniffling a little. Jim sat down with Kate on his lap. He handed her the porcupine, and she tried to reach for it. But her hands failed to come together around the porcupine, and she started to whimper again.

Jim looked up and his eyes locked with mine for one moment, then he bent to Kate once again. "It's all right, lovey. You're just fine, lovey-ducky. You'll be just fine." And he danced her around the room again.

I turned sharply and walked back into the kitchen. Plunging my hands into the hot, soapy water, I stood there and stared at my reflection in the dark window above the sink. Kate was giggling loudly now, trilling a beautiful, high laugh, as Jim galloped with her across the living room floor. She sounded so happy, but I wasn't so sure that Kate was just fine, not so sure at all.

I repressed my worries, for a while at least. That spring, shortly after the episode with Melissa, I went back to teaching. I was very involved with a new course and with starting a program in women's studies. But I still spent a lot of time playing with Kate, hanging interesting mobiles above her in her crib, playing music for her, and clapping her little hands together in rhythm. I went on reading to her and playing hide-and-seek with her under a blanket — "Where is Kate? *There* she is!" — all those things you do with a normal baby. All those things that Kate enjoyed, and that I expected her to enjoy.

By this time, Kate had started to stay up at night after Paul went to bed. I thought it was because she knew she could get my undivided attention that way, and I was delighted to have this time alone with her. Every evening, we folded laundry together, we watched television together. Sometimes I did my exercises with her, and she squealed with delight as I twirled her around. She was such a happy baby after her colic went away.

Another child who might have a handicap was more than I could consciously take in. Finally, however, when Kate was ten months old, and she had just learned to sit up, but still couldn't crawl or roll over from back to stomach, I could no longer ignore the signs that something was wrong. I got a referral to a pediatric neurologist at the University of Minnesota, one of several who had seen Paul briefly and one we liked and trusted.

This time, however, we were here with Kate, our beautiful, healthy baby girl who had been pronounced perfect at birth, whose pediatrician had reassured us at each of her well-baby checkups that she was just fine. Kate was our supposed-to-be-perfect daughter, but now once again we were sitting in the crowded waiting room, and once again we were being called down the same narrow hallway to the little examining room. I felt suffocated as we walked into the familiar room with the red-brown linoleum floor, the small black plastic couch, the dirty window that looked out on a parking lot.

Dr. Preston recognized us and asked first about Paul. We told him about the Wolfson Centre and about how Paul had started to speak. He was doing much better, we said. We didn't really want to get into our continuing worries about him.

Dr. Preston looked relieved, then he turned to Kate. "And how is the little lady today?" He picked her up and sat her on the examining table. Then, with his hands on her hands, he tried to lift her slowly to a standing position. Kate stood for a moment, then her legs buckled under her, and she sat down.

"How old did you say she was? Ten months?"

We nodded.

He turned back to Kate. "Let's just see what your reflexes are like." And he tapped her knees and various places on her legs with the little rubber hammer. "Hmmmm. Some briskness there."

Laying her flat on the table, he tried to rotate her legs at the hips. "Some stiffness here. Have you noticed that it's hard to change her diapers?" He turned to me, and I stepped up to Kate at the table.

I put a hand on her. "No, I haven't noticed that." I almost felt as if I should defend her. "I thought she was just fat. Her legs are so chubby . . ." I trailed off, noticing the worry on the doctor's face. He didn't seem to think she was just chubby.

Next he stroked the bottom of her right foot with his thumbnail. Kate's big toe curled out and her little toes curled in. He did it to the other foot. The same thing happened, but not in so pronounced a way.

Dr. Preston picked Kate up and then dropped her toward the edge of the table.

"What are you testing?" Jim asked. He seemed to have suddenly come to.

"This is called the parachute reflex. I'm trying to see if she will throw her arms out to catch herself."

"She didn't, did she?"

"No." The doctor's voice was subdued. "No, she didn't."

"You can get her dressed now." Dr. Preston's voice was kind as he turned back to Jim and me.

"But what . . . ?"

"I think there is some neurological involvement," Dr. Preston was starting to explain, but just then there was a knock on the door, and a nurse put her head around the corner. "Dr. Preston, could I see you for just a moment?"

"Be right there." The doctor turned to us and laid a hand briefly on my arm. "I'll be right back. Then I'll explain everything to you as fully as I can."

As soon as he was out of the door, I turned to look at Jim, and he took a step toward me. But I didn't want to see the raw pain in his eyes. I wanted to be strong, to be able to handle any problem that came my way, and I felt that if I shared my feelings with Jim at that moment I would collapse. I also thought that I couldn't take on Jim's pain as well as my own. But without really knowing what I was doing, I was shutting him out.

I turned from him, and just then I noticed, out in the hallway, a small wooden rack hanging on the wall. Inside was a set of leaflets: "Your Child and Cerebral Palsy." The moment I saw these, I knew this was what was the matter with Kate. I carried the brochure back into the examining room. "Cerebral palsy," I read out loud, "is a disability caused by brain damage before or during birth. The most common cause is oxygen deprivation during the birth process itself."

"But that can't be the cause." I looked up at Jim. "Her birth was perfectly normal." But I was shaking so hard, I could barely stand.

I sat down quickly on the chair. Jim took Kate from my arms and held her as I continued to read.

"There are different types of cerebral palsy — the spastic type, athetosis, and ataxia." I paused, then went on more slowly. "It also says that twenty-five percent of those affected suffer some degree of mental retardation."

I handed the pamphlet to Jim, but he looked so stunned, he couldn't take it from me.

When the doctor returned, we were simply staring at Kate, who was sitting on Jim's lap and who had snatched the pamphlet out of my hand and was chewing on the edge of it. I wheeled around to speak to Dr. Preston. "Is this the problem?" I held the brochure out to him. I felt numb, my hands and feet were beginning to tingle. A roaring had started up in my head.

"Well, yes," he replied.

I sat down again. Whatever were we going to do now? What hope was there now? Then I heard my own voice, which seemed faint and far away: "What should we do now?"

"Take her home and love her. Do whatever you are doing now."

Jim hadn't said a word. He was holding Kate too tightly, and she began to whimper in his arms.

I took another deep breath, but it was hard to speak through the roaring in my head, which was now almost more like paper crackling very close up to a microphone. "But isn't there something we can do to help her?"

"No, I don't advise one of those infant stimulation programs. I don't think she needs one." Dr. Preston pulled up a chair to sit close to Jim and me. His face, I could see, was lined with pain. He didn't want to give us this news any more than we wanted to receive it.

"But isn't there any way we can help?" I persisted.

"Not really. Her right side seems to be more affected than her left side. She will probably take the course of least resistance and become left-handed. We'll just have to wait and see about the rest. Probably the best prognosis you can hope for is that she will walk, but will have a shuffle all her life. She will drag her right foot."

I tried to take this in. Kate having trouble walking and running? Kate crippled?

Jim still hadn't said anything. He was stroking Kate's back now, running the edge of his thumbnail gently across her shoulders. He tucked his chin over the top of her head and stared out the window. There was a look of such pain, such bewilderment, on his face that I needed to look away from him and back to Dr. Preston, who I noticed had an ink stain on his breast pocket, just over his heart, just where many of Jim's shirts had similar stains.

"Her hearing and eyesight seem fine," Dr. Preston continued. "That's a good sign. But we will just have to wait and see what her mental development will be."

When we got home, Jim went back to his office to work. I got through the rest of the day somehow. The roaring in my head had stopped, but now there were bees buzzing and knocking inside the shell of my head. "Twenty-five percent of those affected . . . some degree of mental retardation . . ." The words ran like a chant through my head, but I didn't know what they meant, couldn't focus, couldn't think clearly.

Later that evening, as I was bathing Kate, getting her ready for bed, I collapsed. Leaning against the edge of the cold porcelain tub, I held her in my arms in the towel and started to sob. Kate too. My second child. My hope. My second chance. My last chance. Kate now, as well as Paul. Puzzled, she twisted in my arms and reached up to pat me on the cheek, a baby pat with the flat of the palm. I kissed her hand and dried my own cheeks. Then I put her to bed.

I remember nothing more of that day. But years later, I mentioned to Jim that Kate's diagnosis of cerebral palsy might have meant that she would be retarded. He stared at me. "Cerebral palsy? Retarded? What are you talking about? I don't remember that at all." I was so stunned by that admission that I began to wonder if, during those years, we had even inhabited the same universe. And indeed we did seem to live in different worlds, each locked in our separate sorrow.

"The Icicle Broke Off and That Was Paul's Head"

I WAS NOW THE MOTHER of two damaged children, and I began to think of myself as different, set apart. For the first time, I began to hesitate before I went out to the park. It hurt too much to meet other mothers, to talk over the heads of our littlest ones as we pushed them in the swings or exchanged stories at the sand pit. Earaches and tonsillitis and refusals to go to bed didn't interest me because we didn't have those problems in our family. But everything else had become a minefield. The simplest things, the most commonplace observations, became the opportunity, in my own mind, for invidious comparisons. Little Thomas had helped to sort the laundry and knew what clothes belonged to each member of his family; even smaller Chris had climbed out of her crib. I didn't want to hear about any of these mundane achievements because my own children were doing none of them.

Dimly, I sensed that I wanted to withdraw from the company of mothers for their sake, as well as for my own. Full of a smoldering envy, I felt I might pollute the very atmosphere if people only knew, only guessed what I was really feeling. I did not wish their children well, I did not take joy in their good fortune.

I remembered how I had felt when I lost the premature baby, when I had the two miscarriages. I would cross the street to avoid passing a mother with a baby in a stroller, I would duck into a longer checkout line to escape the toddler in the cart ahead of me. Now once again, I felt full of jealousy, and I thought this jealousy could easily turn into spite. I felt contagious, as if the corrosive resentment I was really feeling might some day spill out and hurt everybody around me.

At times only the beauty of my two children kept me going. I would sit and watch them: the light brown head bent next to the dark one, as they examined some toy together, their beautiful large brown eyes, their fine, delicate fingers. Kate had long, dark lashes and clearly defined eyebrows, giving her a wise look, much older than her ten months. With a small, precise mouth, and wide-open round eyes, she had a way of studying everything quietly, as if she were considering and taking it all in.

It surprised me a little that this physical beauty should mean so much to me. At the same time, I felt it was my one small compensation for the damage done to their minds. I took a fierce pleasure in these two small bodies, as if the sheer perfection of their physical selves was all I could ever hope for.

The beauty of these children confused other people who tended to think that such good looks had to mean complete normalcy. Hearing that we were worried about them, that we had taken them to neurologists and other specialists, they would express disapproval. "How can you think there is anything the matter with this one!" Our neighbor from down the street stopped me one day, as I was walking with Kate in her stroller.

Anne tickled Kate's tummy, and Kate squirmed and giggled. Anne wiggled her own shoulders back and forth. Then Kate wiggled *her* shoulders back and forth. Anne stuck out her tongue, Kate stuck out *her* tongue. Kate said, "Ga ga." Anne said, "Ga ga." Kate giggled, and repeated, "Ga ga."

"You see," Anne turned to me as if to prove me wrong, "she's imitating me. She's communicating."

"I know, but . . ." I started to point out that Kate's social development and her cognitive development seemed, as far as we knew, to be fine. It was her motor development we were worried about. But I stopped. I knew Anne wouldn't hear me, and anyway I felt torn. I wanted to believe that Kate was just fine, that there was really nothing seriously the matter with her. At the same time, I wanted other people to believe me, to listen to me when I told them about my worries.

Around this time, I hosted a women's experimental theater group who came to give a performance at the college, and I told them I would take them out to breakfast the next morning. Taking Kate with me, I picked them up early and we went to a restaurant downtown. The night before, one of the women had played the part of a baby, a huge baby sitting in an enormous high chair in the center of the stage. Now Delia wanted to study Kate in her little high chair in the restaurant. Kate obliged by banging the tray with a spoon, by chewing through a packet of sugar, paper and all, by swirling oatmeal and eggs together across her tray, by dropping the spoon on the floor and leaning way over to see where it had gone.

Delia laughed at Kate and stuck her own legs straight out in front of her chair, trying to make them look like Kate's fat little legs. Then she leaned forward, trying to balance and still keep her feet off the floor. Delia held her arms out stiffly and, without bending them much at the elbow, banged them on the table with a spoon in each fist.

"See, that's how it's supposed to be done." Delia laughed as the others watched. "Here's the expert." She jumped up from her chair and, sweeping a deep bow toward Kate, she said, "Thank you very much, Kate. My next performance will be much more convincing."

I laughed with the others and kept silent. Delia didn't see anything the matter with Kate, and none of the other women, some of whom were mothers themselves, saw anything wrong with her. Or if they did notice that she was a little slow, they didn't say so. I relaxed and just enjoyed Kate and the attention paid her. It was nice not to have to worry at every moment.

Kate's disability, unlike Paul's at this time, had a name, and therefore a clear course of treatment. I had not listened to the doctor when he said she didn't need an infant stimulation program. In fact, the day after our appointment with Dr. Preston, I had called our good friend Molly Woehrlin, the mother of a handicapped child. She had immediately called the Portage Project, an early intervention program for babies and young children with developmental delays, and they had sent someone to the house to assess Kate and to recommend some exercises I could do with her.

Now every day I put Kate stomach down on a large rubber ball, a brick red ball that was much bigger than she was. Holding her there with my hands on either side of her back, I rolled her and tipped her, head down, feet down, to the right, to the left. The occupational therapist had explained to me that this would help her develop the muscles needed for balance. On this ball, she would learn how to make all those minute adjustments of muscles in the trunk and arms and legs, she would learn how to move her body in space. She would also learn the parachute reflex, which she had failed to demonstrate to the neurologist. In fact, very soon Kate began to throw her arms out in front to catch herself as I tipped her head down toward the floor.

Kate loved this exercise. She didn't enjoy some others I did with her, however. I had been told to rotate her legs at the hip, turning them out, then in again, out, then in again. Her legs were stiff, and this seemed to hurt her a little. But even though she sometimes whimpered, I did these exercises every day with her. I also pushed on her legs, bending them at the knee, then extending them again.

Sometimes, Paul watched. "What Kate doing?" he wanted to know. I explained as best I could that her legs were stiff, and I was trying to make them more flexible, more bendable. Satisfied, Paul would drift away to his numbers.

Kate and I also listened to a record of clapping songs and animal cries. The rooster crowed (and I would shout "cock-a-doodle-doo!"), the cat meowed (and Kate would try "meooow"), the cow would moo (and this time Kate could really join in — "mooooo").

I remembered that Paul learned animal sounds as early as any child. Before he was a year old, I would tell him to roar like a lion, and he would roar into the phone to his grandfather in South Carolina, or his uncle and aunt in Illinois. Why, then, was he so late to talk? Would Kate be the same, fine now in her cognitive and social development at ten months, but after that slower and slower? I remembered how Paul's development was normal as long as I was nursing him. Later, when he started to eat solid food, he began to slow down.

Although Jim and I worried about Kate, we never worried about her as much as about Paul. And in fact, not long after I started the exercises, Kate did start to lie on her stomach and do push-ups. Then she started to creep, and then to crawl. She was reaching for objects and grasping them.

Years later a psychotherapist told me she had always been puzzled by my attitude toward Kate. I always seemed to minimize her handicap. Whenever it came up in our sessions, I always skipped over it quickly and went back to my obsessive worries about Paul. I thought, when she said this, she was criticizing me, telling me I was neglecting my daughter, not taking her as seriously as I took Paul. But then one day she said to me: "You were overloaded during those years. You were carrying too much pain, too much grief already. You couldn't afford to take in any more."

Even so, I disagreed with her, thought differently, and still do. Jim and I learned to trust our instincts, and we knew we were right about Kate. Her learning was different from Paul's, delayed yes, but deep down, we knew, somehow, that she would be all right. Some parent's instinct, some second sight, gave us both the unshakable conviction that Kate would begin to develop normally. Maybe it's true that we simply couldn't afford to think otherwise about a second child's handicap, but the deeper fear was still about Paul. Whatever it was that held him back was also making him very unusual and very fearful of the world. He was not like Kate, who always, even when she was slow to develop, seemed to be at home in the world. Kate was comfortable, exquisitely adapted in advance to what she was likely to find. She seemed to learn the way the world taught.

This was not true of Paul. At times, he seemed ravaged by fear of things we could hardly understand or credit. And when he did learn, he put things together in odd ways, he made a new and highly unusual sense of things, as in the train track episode. He resisted all new foods. He was upset by all changes. All his pajamas had to have spark plugs on them, just like his first pair of pajamas after he was out of baby clothes. The rest of his clothes had to have long sleeves and long pants, even in the summer. In the house, he followed me from room to room and would not let me out of his sight.

Our friend Jan, who often babysat for us during this time, made sweaters for the children the Christmas they were four and three months old. Paul's had little bears across the front, in an intricate pattern that must have taken Jan weeks to complete. When Paul was given the sweater, he started to wail, "Don't want bears. Don't like bears." He never would wear that sweater because none of his other sweaters had ever had bears on them. They didn't belong, the way spark plugs necessarily belonged on pajamas.

One day I was reading in my study upstairs. Paul was downstairs in the playroom watching "Sesame Street." The hour between four and five had become sacred to us both. It was a time when Paul was utterly absorbed in something that was "educational" but that didn't require me or his school. And for me it was a whole, precious hour to myself — to read, to try and take a nap, to just sit and think.

On this particular day I could hear, faintly, the sounds of the signature tune of the show. "Happy days. Sweeping the clouds away." But this time there was a subtle difference to the music, a difference in the rhythm, a slight syncopation. I listened: I could hear ukuleles in the background. "On my way to where the air is sweet. Won't you tell me how to get, how to get to Sesame Street?" But now there was a sudden wailing sound. And Paul was pounding up the stairs, sobbing.

I met him on the staircase and gave him a hug. Then I sat down beside him to try to find out what was the matter. But all Paul could say was, "No. Not right. Big Bird. Airplane." He took me by the hand and almost ran with me back to the playroom. But then he stopped and hung just outside the door, watching anxiously as I walked in to look at the television screen.

There on the TV screen, I saw Mr. Hooper and Big Bird finding seats on a 747. Big Bird was too big and they were having trouble fastening the seat belt around him. Eventually they got it on, and others came on board: Maria, Ernie, Bert, Cookie Monster. They were all very excited. They were on their way to Hawaii.

So that explained the changes in the signature tune. I went back to Paul, who now was hiding in the dining room. "It's all right, Paul. They're just going to Hawaii." But Paul was still crying. "Don't want Hawaii," he said. "Tell them to come back. Not right."

Paul wouldn't watch "Sesame Street" for more than a week after this event. Coaxing, careful explanations, sitting down in the playroom to watch it myself — nothing worked. So I left it alone, and eventually Paul drifted back. But any changes in the routine of "Sesame Street" continued to be disturbing. He would sometimes try to tell me that something wasn't quite right: Ernie and Bert had switched roles in some way, Oscar wasn't in his garbage can, the "Counter," as he called the Count who counted numbers, didn't appear.

But mostly, for several years "Sesame Street" was an utterly dependable institution in our household — reliable, predictable, and orderly in the midst of a confusing world. The same cast of characters appeared over and over, many even had the same silly and utterly predictable routines, which they did day after day, week after week. Oscar the Grouch was always grouchy, Ernie and Bert always misunderstood each other and fought, Mr. Snuffleupagus was always invisible to grown-ups. "The Man Who Easily Paints," as Paul called the workman who painted lines and numbers on the street, always "easily" painted. Variations were variations on themes, the themes remained the same. Newness was introduced gradually and always through repetition, endless repetition.

"Sesame Street," with its short, highly structured, and dependable learning routines, was ideal for Paul, who learned in patterns and through repetition. And for me it was a lifeline, a support system during the two or three years when we had so little to keep us going. One time, a year or so after the Hawaii incident, when "Sesame Street" was taken off the air for a whole week of fundraising, I called the station to complain. "You can't do this to me," I almost shouted into the phone. "We can't live without "Sesame Street" for a whole week!

You don't know what you're doing!" I know they thought I was crazy, but at that moment I was beyond caring.

Paul loved a "Sesame Street" book, one of many books he was very attached to when he was four. This book contained a story that Paul asked for over and over: "Princess Ruby," who so liked red that she asked that everything — flowers, furniture, food, clothes — be painted that color. Only when her face was painted red did she grow discontented and ask that everything be changed back to its rightful color.

"And so, Paul," I said one day, finishing the story, "in the end, Princess Ruby decided she didn't want everything to be her color, the color of her name. She must have called in the gardeners to hose off the plants, the furniture strippers to strip the red paint from the furniture. And she must have washed her face over and over again. What do you think of that?"

But Paul would flip the pages back to the beginning and point a peremptory finger to the first line. "Read. Read it again," and I would start all over again, although I was thoroughly sick by now of Princess Ruby and her brattiness.

Another favorite story from this time was Thumbelina, who also changed in the end, not back to her rightful color, but into a full-size little girl named Maia. He also loved the story of the Gingerbread Man, who popped out of the oven after he was baked and ran away from the old woman and the old man who had baked him: "Run, run, as fast as you can. You can't catch me, I'm the Gingerbread Man."

Unknowingly, I was reading Paul three stories about radical changes to the human body. Princess Ruby changed color, Thumbelina grew larger, and the Gingerbread Man changed from dough to human flesh. Many children's books show such metamorphoses, and children some- how accept them without becoming disturbed. Perhaps they don't really believe such stories, or maybe they are able to play with reality as a pleasurable activity. But Paul could not, as I was soon to discover.

At first I took Paul's fascination with these stories for a normal four- year-old's curiosity. Since he was two, Paul had been especially fond of books, and this to me was one of the most hopeful signs in his devel- opment. He loved the stories, he was showing signs of wanting to read, and even more importantly, books expanded his world. Sometimes I thought he learned more through books than through direct experi- ence. He certainly acquired more language that way than through listening to the spoken word.

But at times I did wonder what Paul was learning from his books. One day I invited a little girl from his nursery school and her mother to tea. The little girl was named Maia, just like Thumbelina after she became a little girl, but at the time I thought nothing of it. I served milk and gingerbread men to the children, but Paul, the confirmed sweets lover, wouldn't touch the gingerbread, not even to nibble at it.

A week or so later, his nursery school teacher, Rachel Loftis, called in some distress. She asked if I could come and visit the school one day soon and mentioned that Paul was getting to be more and more agitated and difficult to control. She didn't know what to do or how to handle him. Maybe I would have some suggestions.

I knew Paul missed the small protected environment of "new, new school" in London where he had made so much progress. I knew also that all the changes in his life recently — a new sister, a different school, a different house, even a different country — would set him back temporarily. But I didn't expect what I saw the next day when I visited his school.

I arrived at snack time. The school was in a church, in a pleasant and well-equipped large room. But this was the year the church was building an extension, adding rooms at the other end of the Sunday school building. As I climbed the steps, I heard a deafening roar just behind a thin partition: a power jackhammer breaking up cement. I walked down the hall and into Paul's classroom, but even behind the door, I could hear the high-pitched maddening whine of a power drill.

The children were getting ready for snacks, washing their hands at a little sink in the corner of the room. The two teachers laid the tables with crackers and Dixie cups of apple juice, then called the children to sit down. Everyone came promptly, except Paul, who was working on puzzles at the farthest end of the room.

"Paul, time for snack." He didn't move, but went on fitting pieces of a farm puzzle together.

"Paul!" Rachel went over to him and led him back to the table, but clearly he didn't want to sit down.

I joined the teachers and the children at the table. "Paul, come with me. Show me what you have to eat today."

But Paul twisted away from us. Rachel brought him back and pulled out his chair, then gently pressed on his shoulders until he was sitting sideways, but still sitting. Rachel went back to her place, and I pulled up a chair to be close to Paul, just behind him. "Mmmmm, this looks good. Can I have some too?"

Obediently, Paul started to drink from his paper cup, but a little drop of juice splashed out onto his chin, and he cried out, "Paul don't want to be Maia. Take the red off!" A rising wail of panic: "Don't want to be Maia!"

I was as startled as the teachers. Paul got up from his chair and ran across the room to the playhouse area, where he found a little hand mirror. He held the mirror up and scrubbed at his face with the other hand and with his sleeve. "Take the red off. Don't like red!"

"It's all right, Paul." I went to him and held him on my lap for a few minutes until he calmed down. By now snack time was over and the children, after watching Paul briefly, were gathering around the piano for music time. Paul sat on my lap and watched them, but neither the teachers nor I made a move to get him involved. At the moment, it seemed enough just for him to watch and to stop crying and rubbing at his face.

When the children went home at noon, I stayed behind to have a talk with Rachel. Paul returned to the puzzle corner to work on an alphabet form board, and Rachel and I went to the opposite corner of the room to talk away from his hearing.

"How long has he been doing this?" I asked.

"Just for the last week. Is he like this at home?"

"No, although he does have a hard time sitting down with us at mealtimes and eating."

"What do you think is going on?"

Suddenly I had an idea. "His books," I said.

"His books?"

So I told Rachel about Princess Ruby and the red on her face, about Thumbelina turning into Maia, about the Gingerbread Man that changed from dough into flesh and blood and ran away in the end, and finally about Paul's panic when I served gingerbread men to him and Maia.

"What do you mean?" Rachel leaned forward.

"I think he's putting all this together. Thumbelina changed into Maia, Maia came to our house to eat a gingerbread man, the gingerbread man became human, jumped out of the oven, and ran away."

Rachel nodded, and I continued. "Also remember Princess Ruby got very upset when her face was painted red. The paint had to be scrubbed off and she needed to look into a mirror to be sure it was all gone."

Rachel nodded. "But what about eating?"

"Remember Maia's visit and Thumbelina changing into Maia in the story? Then you add eating the human form, the gingerbread man.

Maybe he's afraid he'll change into another person if he eats in front of other people."

I was proud of my sleuthing, but none of this solved the problem of how to help Paul overcome his fears. In fact some of his fears seemed so profound, so metaphysical, so central to the human condition, that I was amazed at the complexity of thought required to put all the pieces together. Perhaps Paul truly did not know who he was, where he stopped and where other people began. Perhaps he did not understand that objects in the world remain where you leave them, that they are consistently themselves or that they change according to certain predictable and (to us) easily understood rules. A face turns red only when you paint it with red paint. No one can ever change into another person, except in fairy tales. But to this child, such things, apparently, were not so obvious.

Jim often remarked at this time that we didn't need to travel halfway around the world to study interesting customs or other ways of thinking. We could be anthropologists in our own living room. The strangest and most interesting human differences were enacted daily in our own household: all we had to do was stop and think about it.

But we didn't have that luxury. Jim was in his office or classroom a lot of the time, or if he was at home, I was in my office or classroom. At home we rushed from one crisis to another. I remember one day being *grateful* to the sink for clogging up and spilling water all over the kitchen floor. This crisis took precedence over others. I knew what to do about a clogged drain, where the persistence of personal identity and the reliability of gravity and other forces in the universe were beyond me. "It's a great life if you don't weaken," Jim's mother always said, and we started quoting her more and more. Stamina is all; sheer grit-your-teeth-and-get-through-it endurance.

Mealtimes, in particular, were becoming more and more stressful. Jim, especially, was frustrated at Paul's eating oddities. He began to stand over Paul, clutching the back of his chair and saying through clenched teeth, "You *will* eat your dinner!" Paul always ended up sobbing and running away from the table, having eaten little, and Jim and I always ended up locked in angry recrimination. I felt Jim was trying to force Paul; Jim felt I was giving in to Paul's eating oddities.

Paul's suspicions of food, which had been there since he was three, were becoming even more pronounced. Now, at the age of four, he wanted mostly "cheese numbers," Cheddar cheese cut up into numbers. I became very adept at cutting the cheese, particularly into ones, sevens, fives, and fours. Sometimes I would throw in a cheese sailboat for interest, or a broccoli tree, or a carrot log, or raisin pebbles.

My willingness to cut up cheese numbers for Paul, however, just drove Jim even more crazy. We held endless discussions over Paul's head, in his presence, as he played repetitively at something or as he flew out of control. "I think he's getting worse," Jim would say, "he's regressing." "No he's not," I would say. "Why do you say that? Maybe he's hungry; he hasn't had lunch yet." Or Jim would say, "I think he's really schizophrenic." And I would shout back at him: "How can you say that! He's not schizophrenic. How can you even think of saying that!" And Jim would shout back at me: "There you go again. You aren't listening to me. You're denying my feelings once again."

Our fears were terrible, but Paul's were even worse. On Christmas Eve, shortly after the Princess Ruby episode, Paul told me a bedtime story, a strange little fantasy. I was so impressed with this story that I went immediately to my journal and wrote it down. I rarely wrote anything other than letters during this time, but for once I was determined to capture and remember a remarkable incident. I was glad I did because years later my memory would not have credited it. My memory would have told me that Paul was too handicapped in his understanding and in his use of language to have been able to tell this story.

It took me a long time to put Paul to bed that night. He was excited about Christmas, of course, but something else seemed to be bothering him. Eventually, after I read him a bedtime story, sang him a lullaby, and rubbed his back, he began to tell me his story. And this is the way I wrote it down:

"Paul all alone on desert island. Cactus won't answer back. Sand never turn into snow, but sand burn and burn," he began.

Then: "Paul in a cave for twenty years, for forever. There's no key for the door, no key in *all* the universe."

I asked, "Are there any windows?" Answer, "No, no windows."

I said, "But Mama and Daddy are in a boat carrying a big golden key to unlock Paul's door."

Resistance: "No. No key IN THE WHOLE UNIVERSE to get Paul out."

I went on, saying Mama and Daddy had come in a boat with the key to unlock the door of Paul's cave on the desert island.

He said, "Yes. Now Paul climbing a mountain. Mama and Daddy pulling him over with a rope, but the rope broke and Paul fell down three hundred sixty-two miles."

Then a rather long dialogue with me saying, "Mama and Daddy

got Paul over the mountain," and Paul saying, "No! Paul fell down. Down into a hole. Underground."

Then, "Paul at the North Pole. Turned into an icicle. But the top of the icicle broke off and that was Paul's head. It broke off. Now, Paul has no head."

If he had tried, he could not have found better metaphors for his condition: All alone on a desert island, where the sands burn and burn and will never turn to snow; in a cave with no windows and no doors; falling off a mountain. Lost, alone, incapable of being rescued, maybe even resistant to being rescued. No key IN THE WHOLE UNIVERSE could get Paul out.

He feared this. And so did I.

CHAPTER 12

An Empty Spot in the Universe

I T WAS THE FALL OF 1977. We were having a reception at our house for a famous writer. She was a working-class woman who raised four children in conditions of poverty and who wrote standing up on the bus on her way to work. Not surprisingly she had written eloquently of the silences in women's writing careers — the silencing of women through lack of recognition, money, leisure, undistracted time. She had been holding a seminar at the college and was due at our house, along with twenty or thirty other guests, to have dinner before she gave a reading later that same evening.

Paul, who was now five, stood at the door with the bathroom scale. For months he had been weighing everything in our house: books, furniture, the cat, himself with clothes on, himself with clothes off, himself with cat in arms. He had found a way of placing one heavy chair leg on the scale as he piled the seat of the chair with dictionaries, encyclopedias, luggage, andirons from the fireplace, frying pans, lamps, anything he could get his hands on. The summer before, he had weighed everything at his grandfather's house. We narrowly saved other houses from their weigh-ins by rushing to hide the bathroom scale before he entered the door.

He wanted to know the exact weight of everything: *The Shorter Oxford English Dictionary* weighed more than *Webster's Dictionary,* which weighed just slightly more than the *Norton Anthology of English Literature, Major Author's Edition,* which in turn weighed a little less than the two-volume Norton.

Like many of Paul's behaviors, this one embarrassed us. And like most of his behaviors, it also controlled us. The last six months had been given over to scales, and we saw little relief in sight. Besides this obsession seemed relatively harmless. Over time we had grown used to finding the *Norton Anthology of English Literature,* volume I, the one we would be teaching from the next day, under the trash basket, beside the radio, in the chair on the scale in the living room. We had forgotten what it was like to live in a house where the bathroom scale was in the bathroom and the books were on the shelves.

Tillie Olsen walked in the door. Our guest of honor had finally arrived, and Paul was ready for her. Approaching her, he took her by the hand and led her to the scale. Without blinking, she stepped on the scale and waited quietly while he studied the wobbly hand. The wobbling stopped, he dropped her hand, and she stepped off and into the party.

Because he could not understand the world, Paul set out to weigh and measure it. The spring before, the district school psychologist, visiting Paul's nursery school to observe the children at the same time that they were weighed and measured, had noticed one little boy who was unusually interested in the scale and the measuring rod. This four-year-old without much usable speech was nevertheless fascinated by these instruments. The psychologist made a point of observing him in kindergarten the next year.

One day, Paul's kindergarten teacher called to say the school psychologist wanted to test Paul and asked if we would give our permission. We agreed readily enough. It never bothered us to have Paul tested. After the Wolfson Centre in London, we had been struggling to find help for him, but no one in our little town had ever seen a child anything like him. Later, after the testing, Paul's teacher called back to say that Mr. Anderson wanted to talk with us. We made an appointment and went to his office.

Mr. Anderson's office was a little room off to the side of some administrative offices in one of the older schools in town. I noticed, as we walked into the building, that familiar smell of grade schools, a mixture of library paste and dry radiators, of dust and wax and cleaning fluid. I had no idea what to expect of the interview, but I felt as we entered the room the return of an old feeling long buried, a tightening of the throat, a child's sense of helplessness, of being unprepared.

As we walked through the door, Mr. Anderson rose to greet us. A thin man with light hair and a receding hairline, he seemed very nervous. He had a book open on his desk, and it was turned to face us.

As we sat down I glanced at the page: "Checklist of Autistic Symptoms." Mr. Anderson pushed the book toward us. "I'd like you to read this," he said, "before we begin our discussion."

Jim and I bent forward. The checklist read: "(1) need for sameness in the environment; (2) withdrawal from people; (3) history of delayed speech; (4) normal or above-average intelligence; (5) ritualistic behavior; (6) problems with motor planning or integration with visual or other systems." I sat back and rubbed my eyes. The room seemed too bright. The glare from the large, unshaded windows seemed suddenly overpowering, a great, blank, bright sheet of white which made it hard for me to see anything at all.

I realized that Mr. Anderson was trying to get my attention. With difficulty I looked at him, but the windows behind him seemed to fog my eyes, making them smart. I had trouble focusing on this man who seemed almost to dance about in the dust motes.

". . . a number of similarities between Paul and children who are . . ."

What children was he talking about, I wondered. What does this have to do with us?

"For some time now . . ." he went on. "Unusual fears . . . mixed modalities."

What in the world was this man going on about? I made a greater effort to listen carefully, and this time I caught what he was saying.

"Paul has unusual fears. He has trouble interacting with the other children at school. He tends to be rigid, and he gets upset with changes in his environment."

He stopped and watched us for a moment. Dust motes floated all around his head, and I noticed that his hair stood up slightly on the top. Must be from static electricity, I thought to myself, because it's so damned hot and dry in here.

He went on. "Paul also has some unusual talents. For example, he is far ahead of other children his age in assembling puzzles." I nodded. "And math. He seems to have an unusual aptitude for math. Also he has a remarkable memory for some things."

Jim and I came to. "Yes." I leaned forward. "But what does all of this mean?"

Mr. Anderson paused, then went on. "All of this makes me suspect that Paul is autistic."

"Autistic?" I could hardly focus. "But will he be all right?"

"Will he be all right?" the words hung in the air between us.

"No." Mr. Anderson's voice seemed to catch on the word, and he swiveled in his chair slightly to face the window. "No." He cleared his throat and repeated more slowly. "No, they don't get better."

Mr. Anderson leaned forward and forced himself to look at us. "It's a lifetime condition. I did once know an autistic computer programmer. A very odd man. Never did learn to get on with people. But he was the highest-functioning autistic person I ever dealt with. Most have been institutionalized. They simply can't cope with the world. Fifteen, twenty years ago, the school system wouldn't even have tried to deal with Paul. He could not have gone to school, at least to a public, nonresidential school."

Mr. Anderson explained that he would make an appointment for us to see someone in the Twin Cities who dealt with autistic children. Dazed, unable to talk anymore, Jim and I left his office. We had long been exhausted by the effort of seeking a diagnosis for Paul. But this diagnosis, which seemed to carry with it such a bleak prognosis, was too much to absorb. A lifetime condition? An odd computer programmer who lived an isolated, lonely life: That was the best we could hope for? If we were lucky?

An enormous resistance started up in me. It was as if the white cells circulating in my bloodstream had found an enemy inside me and were suddenly swarming to destroy it. I felt as if I were fighting for my life, and for Paul's. I wanted more for my son. Something hard and rigid set in me that moment. This will not happen, I thought. I will not give up on my child.

But we kept our appointment, and a few weeks later we went, along with Paul's kindergarten teacher, to a special program in the Twin Cities for "Autistic and Other Exceptional Children" at the university. In the waiting room, Paul found a blackboard: 268,954,873,692 he wrote. "Two hundred sixty-eight billion, nine hundred fifty-four million," he began, pointing to each number. Sheila Merzer, codirector of the program, walked in the door. She stopped, watching quietly so as not to distract Paul. "Eight hundred seventy-three thousand, six hundred and *ninety-two!*" Paul finished triumphantly and turned around to see if we had noticed.

Sheila swung on her heel to face us. "I can tell you one thing right now." She smiled broadly. "He isn't retarded."

We relaxed a little. Maybe it was our egotism that was gratified, but we trusted Sheila immediately. She led Paul into the special classroom and gave us a place to watch the children behind a one-way glass. We were to observe the school for an hour while Paul joined the other children. After lunch Paul would be tested.

In the classroom we saw six children and four teachers. The children ranged from Paul's age, five or so, to ten or eleven, or even older. One ran wildly around the room on his toes, flapping his hands rapidly in front of his eyes. He shrilled a high-pitched "eee eeee." A teacher in jeans and sneakers sprinted after him and folded him in her arms. Gently she led him back to the small slide that the children were going down. One little girl, who must have been at least ten years old, was stuck in one spot. One foot slightly in front of the other, she rocked back and forth. She couldn't seem to move forward, much less up the steps of the slide. She stared straight ahead with a fixed, glazed look.

The others managed the slide, but not one of them "looked" like Paul. I was shocked but afraid to show it. Fascinated and horrified, I watched the little girl who was stuck. Back and forth, back and forth, she rocked. It was as if she were caught in some moment of time, some empty spot in the universe, some black hole she couldn't escape.

I wanted to cry. Jim was silent beside me, but Paul's kindergarten teacher, Mrs. Moore, said tensely. "It's a *shame* to label children too soon." I glanced at her. The line of her mouth was set. I knew what she meant; she was telling us that Paul was not like "them," wouldn't become like "them," didn't belong here with "them." I was grateful to her, absurdly grateful.

Suddenly I realized these children were a threat to me, a threat far beyond that of children with polio, or blindness, or heart defects. And they were a threat precisely because, in spite of myself, I sensed they were on a continuum somewhere with our own child. Desperately, I tried to distance myself from this particular human suffering, this particular human difference, because they were of a kind too close to our own.

A few years earlier, we had taken Paul for a speech evaluation at the university hospital. Paul, a rosy-cheeked two-year-old, had bounced down the wrong corridor and we had found ourselves on the outskirts of the children's unit. Grabbing Paul, Jim and I had paused for a moment outside of one of the doors. Inside there lay a child of about his size, immobile and bandaged, with tubes and IV lines running from various parts of his body. This, I thought, is a child in real pain and fear, who may grow up incapacitated by some terrible physical ailment, who might not even survive this injury.

Tears had filled my eyes. Tears both of gratitude and of compassion. This was an easy and ready compassion, and I knew I could afford the feeling. Because, I thought, here beside me is my own child, my boy who can't speak, who may never speak, but is just now running back down the hall. His golden hair is gleaming, his creamy skin is shining with a beauty that every day simply takes my breath away.

Now three years later, sitting in this stuffy little booth, back at the university, this time for an autism appraisal, I struggled to think of the little girl rocking back and forth as someone who, like the injured child, had nothing whatsover to do with my son. But now I could not.

When the children left, we had lunch. Then returned to the dark little booth behind the one-way glass and watched as a teacher led Paul back into the classroom for testing. She waited quietly for a few minutes while Paul played with a toy clock. He put the large hand on the twelve and moved the little hand to various numbers as he read the time out loud. He was accurate. We knew he knew how to tell time to the half hour.

The teacher took out a wand and a bottle of soap bubbles. She started blowing bubbles and Paul popped them. Then she gave the wand to Paul and told him to blow some bubbles. When she reached out to pop his bubble, he said quickly. "No. Don't do it. I *need* this bubble."

Behind the one-way glass, we relaxed a little. We began to enjoy the testing session and to hope Paul would show off all his skills. Forgetting that we were there for a diagnosis and for help, I began to want Paul to prove himself. I simply wanted him to excel, to show them that he was not autistic. Above all, I wanted to defy the prognosis of a lifetime disabling condition.

The tester took out a series of pictures showing a story about feelings. One picture showed a little girl crying and holding a broken vase. Another picture showed the same child smiling, holding an unbroken vase. Paul was asked what the little girl in the first picture was doing. He got agitated and started to fidget in his chair. The teacher asked again, "What is the little girl doing?"

"Crying," Paul answered, and got up to run across the room. He saw a set of large number cards on the floor, then ran to one of the work cubicles. He ran back with the "2" card and put it in the right place in the set of cards.

Gently, the young woman brought him back to the table and took out a puzzle with animal pieces. "Find the hippopotamus, Paul." He pointed to the hippo. "Find the pelican." He pointed to the pelican. Next she led Paul through a few activities that involved the sequencing of body movements, drawing circles, and building bridges. Finally, the tester led Paul back to us, and he ran over to me to climb in my lap. He was tired but happy. We turned to Sheila, who explained that the purpose of the evaluation was not to assess Paul's skills so much as to observe his functioning and "the dynamics of the learning situation" for him. She told us she would observe him in his classroom at home and then would submit a written report with suggestions for his educational program.

We went home somewhat relieved. Sheila had told us she wouldn't use the term *autism* with Paul. Later I learned that the term was narrowly defined at this point in time; Paul was said then to have "autistic-like tendencies." Later he was said to have pervasive developmental disorder, or high-functioning autism, or Asperger's syndrome. Only with the *Diagnostic and Statistical Manual, III, Revised* was *autism* as a term expanded to include children like Paul.

But at this point, when Paul was five, I was thoroughly confused. A diagnosis was to me, as it is to most parents, a prognosis, an indicator of what we might expect from Paul in the future. At least it was a rough indicator of the possibilities of his development. And these possibilities didn't look good. On the other hand, a label might bring with it a relatively clear course of treatment, an indication of what we might do with Paul. I didn't know if I wanted a label and a clear course of intervention — or hope, with no label. Autism still sounded hopeless to me.

CHAPTER 13

"*What Is Infinity Minus One?*"

W E W E N T H O M E to wait, and watch. I was always on the prowl for good signs. One day, Paul came home from kindergarten and complained of being bored with math in school. "Other children can't count," he said to me one day. "Only count to one hundred. Don't know negative numbers, don't know fractions or percentages. Can't multiply," he said.

Paul started going to bed every night with our calculator, and he worked with it before he fell asleep. During the day he often came to me to ask me to "count by sevens" or "count by fours." I could tell that he had worked out several multiplication tables.

He lined up his plastic numbers around the carpet in the living room, counting by hundreds, thousands, millions, billions, trillions, quadrillions, quintillions, sextillions, heptatrillions ... names we made up and gave to him all the way to "duodecatrillion."

One day Paul asked me, "What the highest number?"

"We don't have a number for it, Paul. We just have a word, and it's called *infinity.*"

"Infinity?"

"Yes, infinity is the name for everything that is."

"Infinity just everything that is," he repeated slowly after me, but he was clearly dissatisfied. He looked down at the numbers lining the carpet, then back up to my face.

"But . . . but want the *number*. Want the very, very, most highest number in the *whole* universe." Paul spread his arms wide and ran across the living room. He turned back to me to see if I had gotten the point. "The highest *number*. Not a word."

"I'm sorry, lovey." I knelt down beside him. I drew him to me and gave him a hug. "I'm afraid nobody knows the highest number in the universe. So they made up this name. Infinity. That's the best I can give you."

"Oh." Paul looked crestfallen as he returned to his numbers. He picked up a four and flipped it once between his thumb and fingers, then he laid it precisely on the edge of the carpet. "Quadrillion, quintillion . . ." I heard him muttering to himself. "Duodecatrillion. Infinity."

A few days later, he came to me as I was standing at the stove. "But —" He pulled on my sleeve. I could tell he was very excited about something. "But what is *infinity minus one?*"

Jim tried to help Paul out by leaving the calculator on all one night to see how far it would count, beginning at one. When they came downstairs the next morning, the calculator had reached only a few hundred thousand, even though it had been counting rapidly all night. After this, Jim estimated how long it would take for the calculator, counting by single digits, to reach a million, or a hundred million. And it was a very long time, many years in fact. Paul was very impressed by this.

Paul became very interested in maps. We gave him a globe for Christmas, and we bought him several sets of map puzzles, including one of the United States and one of the world. He loved these puzzles and put them together rapidly. Very quickly he learned all the states and all the countries of the world, the major oceans, mountains, lakes, rivers, cities. His memory for geographical detail was startling. For years after this when we made summer trips in the car, he always carried his map puzzles with him, holding the state we were driving through in his hand, flipping it, until the edges were worn away and the paper came off the backing.

At first the globe and the maps were tools for learning. Later they became almost sacred objects, totems with mystical properties. The globe became "Baby Earth," an object to be revered, almost to be feared. I didn't realize at the time that there are really magic moments when an autistic child can learn. With the first appearance of a new interest, there is a time when the child easily learns. Later the interest solidifies, becomes ritualized, patterns are set, and they become very difficult to disrupt.

Sheila visited Paul's school and made a number of recommendations. One was that Paul be taught to read. He was ready, she argued, and reading might give him a source of pride, something he could excel in.

She recommended that the school hire an aide and put Paul together with another little boy who was also starting to learn to read. Sheila felt that a good aide could build social interaction into the reading lessons. It might help Paul feel more comfortable with at least one other child. And he might then start to talk to the other children, to play in some of their games.

An aide was hired, and Paul started to read. He went to the back of the little stage in the kindergarten room for thirty minutes each day, and together with Matthew Olsen he learned to read. He clearly enjoyed these sessions and he began sounding out words at home when I read to him.

One morning a few weeks later, I visited the kindergarten class. It was in a large room in the basement. The morning was dark, rainy, the trees standing stark and bare now against low clouds. But inside it was warm, well lit, spicy with the smell of fresh-baked bread from the kitchen across the hall. This place seemed so safe and secure, but I wasn't sure it would seem so to Paul. Starting school had been difficult and stressful for him, especially because he was now taking the school bus and he was terrified of ending up on the wrong one. I hoped, as I walked into the classroom, to find Paul playing beside the other children, or at least watching contentedly. I desperately wanted to see him happy.

Mrs. Moore greeted me as she always did, warmly, generously, taking me in with the children. This was her last year of teaching, and Paul, she had told me, was her last great challenge. She was determined to make a difference in his life, and her face glowed with love whenever she spoke of him. She was proud of the progress Paul was making but a little worried that he still wasn't joining the other children in any of their games.

As the children found places in a big circle on the floor, I walked slowly around the large, bright room, examining the displays on the walls. There were stars by the names of all the children who had learned their phone numbers, their addresses, to spell their names, to tie their shoes. Paul, I noticed, had a complete set of stars, except for shoe tying.

Then I moved on to the artwork: bright pictures of suns and rainbows and children reaching into the sky, of wobbly bicycles as large as crooked houses, of cats and pumpkins and a witch on a broom. Then in the corner of the bulletin board, one picture caught my attention. It was a crude crayon drawing of stick children standing in a row, legs straight down, arms straight out, ending in huge round hands sprouting enormous fingers. But the truly arresting features were the faces. Each one had been blacked out with broad crayon marks, marks that dug so deep they had torn the paper. I peered into the lower right-hand corner of the picture. There, in faint printing, was written "Paul."

Paul was desperate for a friend. When the children of our friends visited, he shadowed them, never leaving their sides for a moment until they left. Then he ran after them and wept bitter tears as they climbed into their parents' cars. These children didn't care about Paul nearly as much as he cared about them, and mostly, they were too old for him, and far too advanced. Or they didn't share his interests, couldn't be bothered to line up numbers around the carpet in an endless quest for infinity. So I decided to invite the little boy who was learning to read with Paul, and his mother, over to our house one afternoon.

I was excited and hopeful the day Matthew and his mother were to come. I had prepared a little treat for the children, raisins and unsalted peanuts and sunflower seeds mixed together. I had read somewhere that sunflower seeds were especially good for autistic children. They contained some trace mineral that these children lacked. Also I wanted to impress Mary Olsen, whose child might be Paul's best hope for a friend.

The snack was laid out on the kitchen table. In the playroom, I had taken out all Paul's favorite toys, the ones he was so skillful with, the puzzles with dozens of parts, the plastic letters, the plastic numbers, the clock with removable numbers. The maps he already understood so well.

Mary Olsen came on schedule, looking much as I imagined she would. She was blond and tall, with sculpted features. Yet she seemed not to care at all about how she looked, wearing a plain red plaid skirt with a slightly mismatched pinkish blouse. She was clearly tense. Sitting on the edge of the couch in the living room, she was more preoccupied with watching Matthew and Paul next door in the playroom than she was interested in talking to me.

I watched too as Paul began to line up his numbers, flipping each one once in his fingers before placing it on the exact edge of the carpet. His back was turned to Matthew, and he wasn't saying anything. Listlessly, Matthew picked up a puzzle and began to put it together. Then he came into the living room and leaned against his mother. "When are we going home?" he asked.

"In a few minutes, Matthew." Mary looked nervously at me. "You see, he has his Suzuki violin lesson this afternoon. His teacher comes down from the Twin Cities on Thursdays. We really need to go in a few minutes." She looked away from me.

Suddenly, Paul got up and ran into the living room. "Outdoors," he said, grabbing Matthew's arm. "Swing!"

"It's fine," I said, "if they go next door to the day care center. It's safe, and the little children have left by now. Paul goes over there every day at this time."

Paul was jumping up and down. Then he turned and ran out the back door, with Matthew following. A few minutes later Matthew ran back in, with Paul following him. Then both of them ran out again. I heard Paul's laughter outdoors, high-pitched, excited, overexcited. He hadn't been so happy in months.

Bang. The back door slammed shut again. Paul and Matthew skidded around the corner of the kitchen door, knocking a chair over. More laughter. More jumping up and down. Then back outside again. I was so happy myself, I wanted to cry.

But Mary was standing up now and reaching for her coat. "We really have to go," she said, grabbing Matthew's arm as he swung by again. And they left. Just like that. And Paul stood at the door and cried. He cried for a long time, as I held him in my arms.

But I wasn't going to give up so easily, and next week I called Mary Olsen again. This time I had another treat planned, a far better one. I offered to take the boys to the circus. But Matthew had plans for that day, his swimming lesson, then a birthday party.

I called again the next week. "Would Matthew like to take a walk in the woods with us? And then go out for ice cream?" But no, Matthew was on a trip with his church group.

And then the frustration and anger of weeks boiled over. Gripping the phone so tightly that my wrist ached, I started in on her. "Why won't you let Matthew come over? Why do you keep making up excuses? Don't you know that Paul desperately needs friends? Haven't they told you at school? Why do you think Matthew is having those reading lessons anyway?"

I paused. My throat was so tight I could hardly breathe. My voice sounded thin, almost strangled. I didn't expect an answer, and I didn't get one. Mary mumbled some excuses, then quickly got off the phone.

Hanging up, I just stood there in shock. This was one of my lowest moments. I felt I could take rejection myself, but my child could not. He needed friends, and he needed them now. My deepest fear was that he would close down, that he would stop trying to make friends and retreat into his own little world. I was terrified that he was already beginning to do this on the days when he lined up his numbers around the carpet. But when Matthew had come over, Paul had reached out to this other child. He had done all the things I had so hoped he would do with another child.

But evidently Paul wasn't good enough for Matthew. This high-achieving child was being saved for other, more purposeful activities than playing with a lonely little boy, a little boy behind in his development who just wanted to laugh and run and chase.

I stood there, my hand resting on the phone. And then the hot tears started spilling down my cheeks. Quickly, before the children could see how upset I was, I ran up to our bedroom and shut the door. I couldn't talk to Jim, who had been standing there in the kitchen, overhearing this conversation. I couldn't talk to anyone at that moment. I just lay across the bed, sobbing, and stuffing my bathrobe in my mouth so the children wouldn't hear me.

Jim cooked dinner that night. I came down much later, after he had fed the children and they had gone off to the playroom. When I walked into the kitchen, Jim stood up from the table. I walked across the room and just leaned into him, resting my forehead against his chest. We were both exhausted, and by this time we were beyond words. But just standing there and holding each other was, at that moment, enough.

CHAPTER 14

Mothers and SS Guards

I WAS VERY PUZZLED about autism, this frightening condition that Paul might have, and I was worried about the pictures Paul had drawn in his kindergarten class. One day I went to the library to look for books that might enlighten me. Among a number of studies of communication disorders and childhood psychoses, I found one book that looked as if it had been checked out a lot. It contained long passages about autism. Three copies were on the shelf. And the title was catchy: *The Empty Fortress,* by Bruno Bettelheim. This all looked promising, so I checked the book out and took it home to settle in for a long read.

Opening the book at random, I found: "Turning to the origins of extreme situations in early childhood, it can be said that the mother's pathology is often severe, and in many cases her behavior toward her child offers a fascinating example of abnormal relations."

I read on. In this passage, the mother was described in more detail than the child. And Bettelheim evidently thought the mothers of autistic children caused their children's disability by not loving them enough. Sometimes the mothers didn't even realize they were rejecting their children (so deep was their own state of denial), but the children (who were far more perceptive than the mothers) could always sense the rejection.

I flipped back to an earlier page and learned that Bettelheim thought these mothers were similar to the SS guards in concentration camps. The "essential difference" between the autistic child and the prisoner of the death camps was that the autistic child "never had a chance to develop much of a personality."

By now I was shaking. Was I worse than an SS guard? Had I destroyed my child in the most callous and brutal way imaginable? Of course not, but the horrible thing was that this book, three copies of it, was in the library. Lots of people had checked it out. It was probably taught in developmental psychology or abnormal psychology courses in our college. That meant there were people who believed it. I closed the book and returned it the next day. And for a long time I didn't check out any more books from the library about autism.

No one ever suggested to me that I had caused Kate's developmental delay by not loving her enough, by rejecting her, then denying my rejection. They described her problems as physical in origin, as neurological, not as psychological and caused by bad mothering. This was one reason why I always found it easier to deal with her disability than with Paul's. I never felt conflicted, I never felt I had to prove to the world that I was a good mother.

Kate was now a year and a half, and I wanted to visit the early childhood intervention program where she would be going the following year when she turned two. It was also time to get a new assessment from the occupational therapist and the speech therapist. Kate looked especially beautiful the day I took her for the new evaluation. I had carefully dressed her in white tights and a little blue dress with bears on it. I braided her hair in two little pigtails and tied white ribbons on them. As it grew out longer and longer, her hair was becoming a dark auburn, or perhaps a deep chestnut. Her eyes, with their thick, heavy lashes, looked almost gray next to her blue dress.

Sarah, the occupational therapist, was delighted with Kate's progress. I told Sarah proudly that she was not only crawling, but that she had also begun to stand. She could pull herself up on furniture and could stand there for a few moments. Sarah lifted Kate gently by her two hands until Kate was standing. She stood there unsteadily with her feet several inches apart from each other. The bears marched in a row across the bodice of her dress. Sarah and I both laughed because Kate looked just like those fat little bears as she stood there on her stubby legs.

Sarah gently disengaged her hands from Kate's. Then she stopped supporting her and just touched the palms of her two little hands lightly so that Kate felt she had some support, even though she did not. Kate wobbled there for a moment, swaying slightly, then sat down suddenly and scooted away on all fours.

"Her gait is still too wide for walking," Sarah commented. "She seems to need a pretty broad base to stand at all, but it won't be long now before she walks." She smiled at me and continued. "You've done a wonderful job with her. I can't find any of the briskness she used to have on her right side. The exercises have done wonders." Then Sarah told me to get Kate a Jumping Jack chair, a little swinging chair I could hang from the lintel of a door. If Kate spent some time in the chair every day, just bouncing and jumping on her feet, she would strengthen the muscles she needed for walking.

I felt so happy at that moment, so welcomed, and so respected. Everyone was pleased with all the progress Kate had made, and they attributed much of this progress to my hard work. But visiting Kate's future classroom was unsettling. When I walked in the classroom door that day, I was not prepared for what I saw. One rather large child was packed in a big leather beanbag seat, propped up with pillows tucked in all around her. Her head lolled on her neck, but it was her hands and arms that I didn't want to see. Her arms were contracted, the muscles tightly drawn back so that her hands looked like claws. Another child lay on a mat as a teacher gently bent and stretched out his legs, one, then the other. This exercise I recognized because it was one I had been doing with Kate, but this child was bigger than Kate, and older.

Finding an empty mat in a corner, I sat down with Kate on my lap, to watch the classroom. Kate slid off my lap to crawl over to a little plastic dog. She sat back on her bottom and lifted the toy to her mouth. I watched the other children. One child, who must have been about three years old, seemed very competent. She sat on a rocking horse in front of a mirror and rocked back and forth, enjoying her reflection getting closer, then farther away, closer, then farther away. Maybe Kate would be like that in another year or so. Maybe she would be walking and climbing up on rocking horses, and sliding off again, and running across the room.

I concentrated on the child on the rocking horse and tried not to watch the child stuffed in among the pillows. These two children were at opposite ends of the spectrum. I guessed they both had cerebral palsy, but one looked like she would never walk, or even sit or stand. The other looked like she might be perfectly normal in the end. When I left that day, I felt very grateful that we had gotten help for Kate so early. And I was determined to be hopeful about her progress.

Around this time, I learned about a resource center on autism called the Institute for Child Behavior Research. It was run by Dr. Bernard Rimland, who himself had an autistic son. I wrote to the institute and received a questionnaire, a diagnostic checklist. The accompanying letter said that the researchers at the center wanted to develop improved methods of diagnosing children with severe behavior disorders and that they were developing a data bank based on thousands of responses from parents and teachers in several languages: English, French, Spanish, German, Hebrew, Italian, and Japanese.

I settled down to fill out the form. It began with a history of the pregnancy (troubled or not?) and the early medical condition of the child. Then it went on to ask questions about the usual developmental milestones. When did the child crawl, walk, talk? But then it asked some unusual questions: "During the child's first year, did he/she seem to be unusually intelligent?" (No one had ever asked me that.) "Before the age of three, did the child have an unusually good memory? For example, a remarkable memory for songs, music (humming only)?" On the other hand it also asked, "Did you ever suspect the child was very nearly deaf?" and "Is the child 'deaf' to some sounds but hears others?" This was spooky: it seemed that the questionnaire was designed with Paul specifically in mind.

I went on. There were many questions about the child's behavior, and once again, it seemed that whoever was posing them already knew Paul: Does he deliberately hit his own head? Does he rock? At three or four, did he seem to be distant, in a shell? Does he have eating oddities? Did the child take an adult by the hand to open the door, get cookies, turn on the TV?

Does he have unusual fears? I remembered the Princess Ruby episode, the fear of eating in front of other people, the train track episode, the changes in the "Sesame Street" tune, the fear of gravity going away when he went to sleep at night. Does he insist on taking exactly the same route, for example, to school? Does he insist that only certain words be used in a given situation? The answer was yes for all of these questions.

Then there were questions about unusual abilities exhibited between the ages of three and five: in assembling puzzles, in arithmetic computation, in perfect musical pitch. Again, it was yes to each of these. The questionnaire also asked if he could tell the day of a week a certain date would fall on. Once again it was yes. Just recently Paul had told me when we would have another Friday the thirteenth.

Did he line up things in precise, even rows and insist that they not be disturbed? (Had Rimland been watching Paul with his numbers around the living room carpet?) Is he fascinated by mechanical things? "Yes," I wrote beside that question, adding a comment about lights, humidifiers, telephones, anything he could take apart. Does he get upset at being interrupted, resist new clothes, get upset at things not being "right," adopt certain rituals? It was yes to every one of these questions.

Is he very good looking? Yes, very! After a delay, does he repeat words or whole sentences to himself? Yes, he often whispers them to himself. Does he refer to himself only in the third person or the second person, and have trouble learning the I/you distinction? I paused. Then I had a sudden, sharp image of Paul recently. I had long noticed that he called himself Paul or even you. Then one day a friend of mine, a mother herself, told me to try throwing a ball at him and saying, "I throw the ball to you." After that I was to ask him to say, when he threw the ball back to me: "*I* throw the ball to *you*." Paul did this a few times, obediently, by rote, just because I told him to. Then suddenly, he caught on. His face lit up and he clearly knew then that he was an "I" and I was a "you" to him. I had become a self, he had become a self. We were now equivalent centers of being, at least in terms of this verbal distinction.

I went on filling out the form. "Did he use one word or idea as a substitute for another for a long period of time?" Yes, I remembered the blister/plister used to mean the twisted filaments of a light bulb. And how about "loud noises" for pain? "Does he have unusual relationships to objects?" Again, yes, lights, maps, clocks, numbers, pipes, scales, thermometers.

"Does he look at objects from the corner of his eyes?" I didn't know it at the time, but shortly afterward he would begin to do this. "Does he spend hours at pointless tasks?" Yes, he hooks up his pipes together in the back yard and runs water through them. But maybe this isn't so pointless as some other things he has spent time on, for example, flicking light switches. "Is he intensely aware of odors?" Yes, he complains all the time that food smells bad.

This was uncanny. The people at the Institute for Child Behavior Research clearly knew about children like Paul. It seemed now that maybe he wasn't an "original," as Molly Moodley in London had called him. Maybe his very oddities, his differences from "normal" children, connected him with another group of children.

But some other parts of the questionnaire didn't fit Paul. He was "pliable," easy to hold as a baby, and he didn't have spells of inconsolable crying. He didn't chew or swallow nonfood objects. He didn't stop talking after once starting to talk. He didn't hold bizarre poses or postures. He *did* feel pain.

I finished the questionnaire, sent it off, and waited eagerly for Paul's scores for both speech and behavior. I knew a plus point would be given for each question (sign or symptom) characteristic of autism. In a few weeks Paul's score came back: plus-eight for behavior, plus-one for speech, a total score of plus-nine. I looked at the checklist score sheet. It explained that a score of minus-forty to plus-twenty indicated "autistic-type" children. A score of plus-twenty to plus-forty would indicate that the child was very probably a case of classic Early Infantile Autism. So, according to this questionnaire Paul was "autistic-like," which is exactly what Sheila Merzer had called him. But his score was definitely in the positive range, a very long way from minus-forty and normalcy, and uncomfortably close to Infantile Autism (just eleven points beneath it).

After receiving this test score, I felt oddly relieved. I didn't want to see how "autistic-like" Paul really was, yet now I knew that there were some other people in the world like him. This was a very far cry indeed from Bettelheim and the simplistic notion of mothers as SS guards. There was some hard truth to this diagnosis, and it made sense, it confirmed my own intuition about my child.

Nevertheless, I wasn't coping very well at this point in my life. All during this time I was drinking too much, still trying to blot out the consciousness of pain at the end of every day. And now I was beginning to worry not only about the children, but also about myself. I was so competent, so capable, as a mother: I knew that, in spite of Bettelheim and other writers. But underneath all my competence, I felt ravaged. I hardly knew who I was anymore.

I began to talk to Jim about going into therapy, family therapy, or at least some help for the two of us. Jim argued that we couldn't afford it and also visit his family in England the next summer. I knew he was right, and we began to plan our summer in Cambridge. We booked our flight, started the search for a house to rent, and agreed that we would look for a good babysitter the moment we got to Cambridge so that the two of us could go off to the library every morning. Then we would spend the afternoons exploring the countryside with the children. We would have a wonderful summer. But then a song started up in the back of my head: "Pack up your troubles in your old kit-bag, and smile, smile, smile." Obsessively, hypnotically, this song played and played, and it was many months before I could get rid of it.

The only person who answered the ad for babysitters in Cambridge looked exhausted, as if the blood had been drained from every cell of her face. But on the phone she had sounded mature and kind. She explained that she had just finished caring for an old woman and had been up every night with her. She didn't usually accept "childminding" jobs, but she needed something to tide her over this summer until she found another nursing job.

"We'll give it a try for a few days," I had told her on the phone. And now here she was on Monday morning at nine o'clock, looking exhausted, drained, every muscle of her body slumped. I hope this works, I thought, as Jim and I headed for the university library. Miss Prentice held Kate in her arms as she waved from the door. Paul stood on the sidewalk and was still watching us, I noticed, as the car turned the corner.

When we came back at lunchtime, Paul was sitting by himself halfway up the steps. He didn't run to greet us.

"How did it go?" I asked Miss Prentice.

"Not well," she answered. "Paul wanted to go to the park, and he wouldn't take no for an answer. He's a difficult child."

Paul started to kick the back of the stairs. He stared at Miss Prentice, but I noticed he held his hand out at arm's length to block out her face. I felt caught. I wanted to defend him against Miss Prentice, but we needed this babysitter so badly. We had come to Cambridge to get some writing done, and buying half a day of free time was important to us both. I wanted to make this work.

I took Miss Prentice into the living room and tried to explain to her what worked with Paul and what didn't work. We had been used to such excellent babysitters at home, college students with energy and dedication: understanding, accepting, loving people. I had almost forgotten that I needed to explain Paul to new people. Miss Prentice agreed to come again tomorrow and to try a different approach.

The next day, when Jim and I got in the car to drive to the library, Paul ran after us, down the sidewalk, crying all the way.

"Stop the car, Jim. We can't do this."

"He'll be all right. Give him a chance to get used to Miss Prentice. We've only left him for one day so far."

Reluctantly, I agreed to give it another try, but the image of Paul running after the car was burned on my retina. All morning I thought of him, and I simply pushed around papers, unable to concentrate at all.

At lunchtime, Miss Prentice met us at the door. She had obviously been watching for the car. "This isn't working," she said. Nothing else, just "This isn't working." We agreed, paid her, and breathed a sigh of relief as she walked out the door.

"Have we written you since Framlingham Castle?" I began a letter to my father. "Have we written you of Norwich, of the Norfolk coast and of Castle Rising, of Sawston Hall, of Hedingham Castle, of Saffron Waldon and the museum and castle, of Audley End House, of lunch in Puckeridge at an inn Pepys stayed in, of Colchester Castle and Dedham Vale and the the Valley of the Stour? I believe we have seen every Norman keep in East Anglia."

How jolly I made it sound. And what a liar I was. I sat down to write letters in the evening after the children were in bed and after I had had a good deal to drink. And at those times I almost, almost believed my own lies. I never wrote about Paul running after the car, tears streaming down his cheeks, or of my anguish at leaving him with a woman he had now started calling a wicked stepmother. I didn't write about how we never did find a satisfactory babysitter, about how we tried to take turns at the library, but never got any work done and just gave up finally, deciding to tour the countryside around Cambridge. I never wrote about how Jim and I fought all over East Anglia. Fought about where we would stay, what restaurant we would eat in, whose fault it was when we got lost, who was to blame when Paul misbehaved.

The only good thing about that summer was that Kate, at twenty-two months, started to walk and talk. After lunch every day, she picked up her Teddy and her blanket and headed for the front door. "Bye, bye, bruum, bruum." She would turn to see if we were ready for our daily excursion into the countryside of East Anglia.

At Colchester Castle, she held Teddy up to see everything: " 'ook, Teddy, 'ook." And at the end of the summer when we went to the Lake District, she and Paul and I climbed a low mountain, as Jim sat in a car repair shop waiting for the car to be fixed. I pushed her in her pushchair as far as the path permitted. After that it was up to her. Grasping a toothbrush in her hand, her inseparable companion that day, she tackled the last several hundred feet of the mountain. An old couple, striding down in their mountain boots, paused to consider her. "A young contender," they said admiringly. I smiled proudly at Kate, knowing the old couple spoke more truly than they imagined. She had conquered more than a mountain.

I wrote to my father about climbing the mountain, but I never wrote about how hard it was to amuse the children, to keep them safe and occupied. Nor did I mention the rusty tin cans in the tall grass in the back yard. Instead I said: "This house is very comfortable, especially if you go in for worn Persian carpets, hookah smoking, cooking with garam masala, eating tahini." I never wrote about how Paul wouldn't look anyone in the eye anymore, about how he held his hand out at arm's length to blank out the eyes of people looking at him. And I never described how he started to run rapidly down the sidewalk, head turned at an odd angle, eyes swiveled in his head the other way, watching the hedge go by, as he starting trying to see only with peripheral vision.

I sent a picture of Paul and me taken on his sixth birthday, August 12, 1978. I am sitting on the ground, smiling. Paul is sitting on my lap, head turned sideways, eyes rotated at an odd angle toward the camera. I never said that three nights before this I drank too much wine and swallowed a whole handful of aspirin, then quietly got into bed next to Jim, hoping he would hear the silence if my breathing stopped. I never wrote about the torn newspaper article I found in the trash basket that week, concealed by Jim who didn't want me to read about the death of a well-known activist mother of a handicapped child, who finally gave up and took all the pills she could find in the house.

At the beginning of September, we headed for home. I had a dream that I was wrapped in bandages, mummy wraps. Someone came and slowly started unwinding the sheets that held me. First my head, then my shoulders, appeared, then my arms and chest. Finally, my whole body lay exposed to the air. For a moment, I felt my body tingle all over in the too bright air. And then I dreamt that slowly I started to crumble, to collapse, to fall inward.

Until at last I was nothing but powder.

CHAPTER 15

Following Power Lines

T HE DAY AFTER WE ARRIVED HOME from England, I went with Paul to his new school, where he was to be in a special first grade class for developmentally delayed children called the Transition Room. This was the most modern school in town, built at a time when architects seemed to feel nostalgic for the old one-room schoolhouse. But instead of building a cozy little room for ten or twenty children, they had designed a one-room factory school for hundreds and hundreds of young children. The library and most of the classrooms were separated by a series of flimsy partitions that didn't reach the ceiling. Many of the windows had been blocked off, and the children sat under fluorescent lights.

The school year had already begun, and as we walked down the corridor, the noise got louder and louder. Fifty, sixty, seventy children were within hearing distance of each other. Some were working quietly at desks, but many others were leaning out of their chairs, punching each other or scribbing on each other's papers. We could hear three teachers in three different enclosures trying simultaneously to bring their students to order.

Paul suddenly dropped my hand and started running down the corridor, holding his head at an odd angle so he could watch the wall with his peripheral vision. I called to him, but he didn't stop. Just then a child carrying some construction paper rounded a corner between two partitions. She ducked out of the way just in time and stopped to stare at Paul as he ran by.

"Weird," I heard her say, as I ran past her in pursuit of Paul. "*Really* weird." She turned to grin at another child and make a circular motion with her index finger by her ear. At that moment, I wanted to kick her, or to stop and shake her until her teeth rattled in her head. I hoped Paul hadn't heard her.

I caught up with Paul and bent down to try to talk to him, but he looked away from me and squealed and hit the side of his head with his hand. I led him to the Transition Room, but there we were told that he would be taught separately from the other children in the room. For most of the day at least, he would be with two other little boys and a special education teacher in a little area off to the side of the larger classroom.

I was appalled at what I saw. This classroom was really just a closet big enough to hold a table, four chairs, and a blackboard. The teacher had made an effort to make the room livable. There were bright pictures and the usual letters and numbers above the blackboard. A very small bookcase held a few books. But there were no windows, and the room seemed almost claustrophobic.

Mrs. Carlson greeted us. She was big-boned, blond, Scandinavian, with a broad face and an open smile. Dressed for action in blue jeans and a red jersey, she seemed to be a warm, energetic person who enjoyed children and understood them, but I didn't see how anyone could teach in this little room.

We were introduced to the two boys. "This is Allen, and this is Ray." Allen was thin and blond, small for his age, a sweet-looking child, all elbows and knees. Ray was bigger and heavier. He burped suddenly, loudly, then grinned and ducked as Mrs. Carlson wheeled around to glare at him. She stood with her hands on her hips and made a face at him, half serious, half amused. He burped again, deliberately, more loudly, then clapped a hand over his mouth. "Oops," he said, and bent his head over the table. "*Excuse* me!" Allen giggled. Paul relaxed slightly, but his face still looked drawn and masklike.

Mrs. Carlson wagged her finger at Ray and said she would deal with him later, then paused at the door to talk with me for a moment. She promised that we would have a conference in the next few days. I knelt down to talk to Paul before I left, but he looked away, his face blank, his eyes flat. He moved his face from side to side, staring at the numbers above the blackboard through the corners of his eyes. He never even glanced at me as I left.

We had our conference, and I learned that Paul and Ray had begun to make animal sounds at each other. I was pleased, and started to say so. To me, this braying, barking, mooing, and meowing was progress, the first hopeful sign of social interaction, but Mrs. Carlson, not surprisingly, saw it as disruption. She told me she could get nothing taught to these children and that she had begun to carry a wooden paddle in her back pocket. She said she wouldn't hit them, would just use it as a threat. I didn't like the idea of the wooden paddle, but decided not to say so.

One day Mrs. Carlson called me to say Paul had started to use bad language. She said he had learned it from the other children, but they stopped when she told them to, or even when they saw her enter the room. Paul didn't; he just kept right on. She wanted to know if she should wash his mouth out with soap.

"Absolutely not!" I spluttered on the phone. "No. Please. Don't!"

"Just checking," she said. "I wouldn't have done it without your permission."

We had another conference. Paul's behavior was getting worse. He still ran with his head swiveled in the opposite direction so he could watch the wall out of the corner of his eye. I learned that he couldn't wait patiently in line at the cafeteria but made noises or hit his head with the flat of his palm. We decided that he should take a lunch box from then on. That way, he could go directly into the cafeteria and sit down and eat.

But Paul had started to attract the attention of the other children, and they had begun to sneer and laugh at him openly. When they did, Paul held out his hand rigidly to try to block the sight of their faces. The other children had started to say, "Here comes the weirdo" and to hold out their hands in front of their faces when they saw him. Or they hit their heads with the side of their hands, then collapsed in giggles.

At home, Paul was miserable. And more and more obsessive. He began to study temperatures with a vengeance. He learned the difference between the temperature of the sun at its core and on the corona, the temperature of a candle flame, and the differences among yellow hot, red hot and white hot. "What would happen to me at absolute zero?" he would ask, or "What would happen to me at the core of the earth?"

He began to call Time and Temperature on the phone dozens of times a day. Each time he called, he would step outside the back door to feel the temperature on his skin, then go back into the kitchen to phone again.

One day in November, it was seventy-three degrees. Instead of being pleased by the warm weather, Paul was outraged by this aberration.

"Is it summer or winter?" he screamed. "Tell me, is it seventy-three degrees, or not?" He walked outdoors, then slammed in again, redialed, slapped the phone back onto the receiver, and marched out. "Is it summer or winter? I ask you, which is it, summer or winter?" Watching him, Jim and I didn't know whether to laugh or cry. I think we did a little bit of both.

It was time to intervene. With the help of Molly Woehrlin, who had been active in the schools for many years, I at last convinced the administration to move Paul and the other two boys into the main Transition Room. These were three children with developmental delays who needed much more time to accomplish the simple exploratory tasks of early childhood. They needed to run, and climb, and play hide-and-seek, and make animal noises at each other. Primarily they needed to be out of that monk's cell.

Slowly, Paul began to get better in the Transition Room. He became totally absorbed in reading and begged his teacher for extra copies of work sheets, so he could take them home and do them all over again. His teacher gave him a big sheaf of papers, and he kept them all in order in his room, where he would fill them out ad infinitum. They were orderly, predictable, and he loved their patterns and slight variations. He became so attached to his first reader that I went out and photocopied the whole book for him. And he kept a running record in his head of each book in the series all the way through school. "After *Tigers*, I'll read *Lions*, then *Dinosaurs, Rainbows, Signposts, Secrets, Rewards, Panorama, Fiesta, Kaleidoscope, Images, Galaxies, Serendipity*," he would rattle the names off rapidly. It seemed to give him great pleasure to think of what he would be reading in second grade, or third, or fifth. I supposed at the time that it was very reassuring to him to know that there was something predictable about his future when so much of his world seemed chaotic and uncontrollable.

Paul's loneliness continued, however. He knew children at school and he was occasionally invited to someone's house, but he needed a close, best friend. Without someone reliable to play with, he was more dependent on me, and I spent more time on his obsessions than I wished. But I was always hoping I could use them to expand his world in some way. That particular winter of first grade we spent driving through the countryside looking for power lines and grain elevators for Paul to "collect," new towns and antique stores for me. Often in the afternoons after school, I would bundle Kate into her snowsuit and strap her into her seat in the back of the car. As we drove out of town, she often dozed off as Paul leaned toward the window, his eyes locked on the lines as they zipped past.

I could only guess at what the power lines meant to Paul. To me, this was the bleakest of his many obsessions, and it came just at the time when farmers were organizing in rural Minnesota to resist the seemingly inevitable march of the lines across their fields and meadows. No one in the whole state, it appeared, really liked power lines except for Paul, and for him, I supposed, they just formed yet another predictable pattern. They were evenly spaced, and one looked very much like another, yet Paul noticed and remembered each slight difference. Once again, repetition and variation, a predictable pattern that included the most infinitesimal deviance, seemed to soothe him, reassure him somehow. Perhaps he thought that if he could find and follow and map out the power lines, he might know and understand and possess some part of the physical world around him. Or so I thought at the time.

Now I wonder if there was more to it than this. I think that some visual disturbance, which had affected Paul earlier when he watched the flickering lights at the theater at age two, had become even more pronounced when he was six or so. He never flicked straws or his fingers before his eyes when he was young, as many autistic children do. Nor did he snake strings across the surfaces of objects he was trying to see, or sit for hours watching fans or spinning tops. But later when I saw *Rain Man*, I remembered that lonely winter when Paul and I chased power lines across the countryside. At the very beginning of the film, we see a Raymond's-eye view of the world which shows the spans of a bridge flitting by rapidly. That repetition of struts and telephone poles and signposts seen at an odd angle as Raymond rides by in a car made me remember Paul's early obsession. Maybe he was doing the same thing, seeing the world Raymond's way, when he was young.

One day I was driving alone with Paul to see power lines. His eyes were fixed on the lines, and he wasn't talking very much. A fine, powdery snow blew over the road as I drove from town to town: Little Chicago, Lonsdale, New Prague. A prairie wind blew steadily from the northwest, and the trees on the tops of hills were bent and stunted, deformed from years of prevailing winds. Following a truck down a rutted dirt and gravel road, I was trying to keep up a conversation with Paul to make this more than just a blind following of his obsession.

Suddenly the truck stopped and I stopped only just in time.

Just as suddenly I remembered another truck on another dirt road when I hadn't stopped in time. I was driving to a Bryn Mawr party for returning sophomore and new freshmen students. It was to be held in northwest Washington at the home of an alumna whose husband worked at the State Department. I recalled my reluctance that day. I did not want to go to the party. Never had I wanted to do anything less. I was a sophomore, and I was remembering the last year's party, which had been, for me, excruciating.

The year before I had worn a dotted swiss dress that I had worked on all summer, a navy blue straw hat, and the white gloves my mother thought were essential. I had turned up late, late and miserable. No one else had a hat. No one else wore gloves. But having shown up in them, I was even more afraid of taking them off than of leaving them on. If I took them off everyone would see that I thought them wrong, that I knew I had made a mistake, and then I would have betrayed my mother. I might have worn them bravely, but how do you do that in a room full of hatless, long-haired, laughing girls — the daughters of diplomats and senators?

You don't. I couldn't. So I sat there silently as everyone talked about Greek 101 with Lattimore, of Haverford boyfriends, of Lantern Night and the songs they planned for Step Sing. They were at home with Greek hymns, with Plato's dialogues and Bach cantatas and European summers. I had spent July and August working in a drugstore, where I sold cigarettes and talcum powder and laxatives, where I kept poems in the cash register to read secretly and to memorize as I rang up each purchase, and where I was almost fired for keeping the drawer open too much.

For a second time I was on my way to this back-to-school tea. Slowly I drove our old blue Plymouth down the dirt road, past the farmer whose guinea hens ran continually back and forth. The Plymouth, already ten years old, would have to last us through at least three more winters, my father had said the night before. Even with Mother's HEW salary, there was no way they could buy a new car and also send me and then my brother to college.

A truck rattled ahead of me. And then I noticed a bumblebee batting against the inside of the windshield. Better get it out before I have an accident, I thought. In the sudden stillness that followed, I noticed only smoke and dust. Then I saw that the rigid, heavy rear bumper of the truck was too high up. It was exactly the height of the car's radiator, not its bumper, and the Plymouth's whole front end had crumpled after I plowed into the truck. Neither of my front doors would open, so I climbed out over the back seat and out a back door onto the dusty road, just as the driver of the truck climbed out of his cab.

I leaned against the crumpled car door to catch my breath. I was shaking so much, I could hardly stand. I looked up, and there was the hen that had caused all the trouble. She was scuttling across the road again. She stopped once to tip her head and her beady eye toward us, then hunched her shoulders, fluffed and resettled her wing feathers, before she marched off, indignant, toward the barn. The truck had missed the hen, but I had not missed the truck.

Now, on that other rutted, snowy Minnesota road, I remembered the guilt I had felt at nineteen. The Plymouth was destroyed; my parents were forced to buy another car. The financial burden of that new car, added to the already heavy load of my tuition, was enough, I knew, to cripple my mother. Already ill and overworked, she now had to work even harder. Coming home from her long day at Health, Education and Welfare, Mother picked up her old insurance work and called clients at night. Often after my father called in his story to the AP office, she got on the phone to call old clients to try to talk them into a new household policy, a theft, fire, flood damage policy or an antique floater.

They both worked so hard: up early for the long commute into Washington, where my mother had to be at work one hour before my father. His job, on the other hand, ended one hour after hers did, so each had the extra time to wait. Then they had the long commute home, often stopping to pick up the cleaning, the groceries, the latest prescription, on the way. Then it was cooking, washing dishes, washing and ironing clothes for the next day.

Brought up short behind that truck in Minnesota, then picking up again the cold march of power lines across a bleak winter landscape, I thought, Is this what that expensive Bryn Mawr education has brought me to? Is this what my mother worked so hard for? To bump over frozen ruts, following a lonely child's obsession?

I couldn't shake the image of my mother, huddled on the bottom step of the staircase next to the phone, trying to read in the dim light the fine print of the Mariner's Insurance Schedule of Household Rates. Trying to talk someone into a new household policy, and wanting more than anything just to go to sleep.

CHAPTER 16

Three Hundred Seventy-Two
Light Bulbs

ONE AFTERNOON when I was sick with flu, I fell asleep on the playroom bed as the children watched "Sesame Street." I woke up to find Kate sitting on my head and Paul gone. Disappeared.

Stumbling around the house and then outdoors, I finally found him covering the side of the house with mud. It was November and mud was everywhere, especially on the path we had beaten from the garage to the house.

"Look. I'm painting the house burnt umber," said Paul excitedly. "And this part is raw sienna . . ." Seeing my face, he trailed off.

"Get in that house! This minute." I grabbed the hose and began to try to wash off the side of the house. But Paul started to cry, then to scream and dance up and down in the mud. I dropped the hose, which fell on the ground and made more mud. My socks, which I had run outdoors in, were now filthy. Paul was filthy, his jeans and shoes and shirt covered with mud.

My mood was now dangerous. "In the house," I shouted, pointing. But Paul just danced up and down in the same spot, screaming louder. I heard the panic in his voice and knew my anger was accomplishing nothing. But I couldn't help myself. I grabbed him by the arm and pulled him into the house. I pulled off my socks and left them in a puddle just inside the kitchen door. Then I stripped Paul and pulled him into the bathroom. I ran a warm bath and put him in.

By now my anger at Paul had gone and I was crying. I had shifted my anger to Jim, and I was feeling very sorry for myself. It was Jim's fault for leaving me alone with the kids all day. It was his fault for refusing to do his fair share of housework and child care, for working till midnight in his office every night. And above all, it was his fault for saying he couldn't be trusted around Paul, for saying that I, his mother, was more "suited" to take care of children. Why should I be left with all the responsibility? I bent over the tub to wash Paul, then leaned back on my knees, staring at the washcloth, which had shells around its border. Suddenly I was back in Richmond, Virginia, and I was five years old, staring at a washcloth similar to this one. My father was away, working in Washington, D.C.; my mother was ill, had recently had surgery, a hysterectomy. My brother, just turned two, was also recovering from an operation. It was wartime, and my mother had taken in boarders to make ends meet. One boarder had come down with diphtheria.

I knew all this, the way a five-year-old does, by realizing, without fully knowing. I sensed it the way you sense a change in the temperature, the way you sense a sudden drop in barometric pressure. I realized it on my skin, in my lungs, in the pressure behind my eyes. My mother was exhausted and overwhelmed. She needed help, and I was the only one there to help her.

Standing outside the door of the sickroom, waiting for my mother to come out, I knew something terrible was happening in there and that I wasn't ever supposed to go inside. I stood there waiting. My brother had just unlatched one side of his wooden playpen, folded it back, and crawled out. He toddled down the hall from his room, trailing his wooden train engine on its cord. The engine tipped over and the engineer fell out just beside the wastepaper basket Mother had taken from the sickroom.

Frank picked up the basket of used tissue and dumped it all out on the floor: dirty, balled-up tissue everywhere. He started to drive the train through the tissues. Maybe he thought they looked like snow. I had just bent down to help him when Mother came crashing out of the room.

Whapp! She slapped Frank away from the tissues and pulled him up sharply by the arm. He was shrieking now, dangling from her hand, his feet off the ground. She turned to me: "Out of that! Out, out!" Her face had gone patchy, mottled red and white. I didn't know this mother-become-monster.

She hauled us both off to the bathroom and started to scrub our hands under the running tap water. Using a fingernail brush, she scrubbed and scrubbed until our hands were raw, and still she scrubbed. Then taking a rough cloth, she set to on our faces.

Frank and I stood there, the tears rolling down our cheeks, quietly submitting, as Mother scrubbed, then patted our faces dry with the towel. Suddenly, she sat down hard on the edge of the tub, and buried her face in her hands. She pulled Frank to her and smoothed his hair over his forehead. "I'm sorry, I'm sorry," she kept repeating. "I didn't mean to hurt you. But why am I left with all this? Why? Why?"

Frank hiccupped back his tears, then crept off in search of his train. I stood there watching Mother. Her hair had come loose from the bun at the nape of her neck. Her full-length apron, with the lace-bordered ruffles over the shoulders that had been so fresh and crisp that morning, looked wilted and stained now. Her big blue eyes were puffy and red as she looked up at me, and asked again, "Why am I left with all this? It's so unfair!"

There was something I was supposed to do. I needed desperately to remember what it was. Mother needed me to help her, but I didn't know what it was I was supposed to do. I stood there for a moment, then I picked the washrag up off the floor. Carefully, carefully, I hung it on the towel rack. I arranged it so the sides were even, and the shells on the border were all in a row. Then I followed my brother down the hall.

I dried off Paul and helped him get dressed. As he settled down on the floor to play with his numbers, I went to the kitchen. Grimly I started to cook dinner. I sautéed the mushrooms, then deglazed the pan with sherry, sipping the sweet wine as I worked. And this was how Jim found me as he came in. I could see the uncertainty on his face as he came in the door, then the quick cover of anger as he saw the tears on my face, the sherry bottle beside me. These days my tears always made him angry. My drinking made him even angrier.

"What happened out here?" Jim said. "Did Paul do this? I told him not to play with the hose. He's obsessing again. He'll never change."

"Yes he will. Give him a chance." By this time I had completely forgotten my anger at Paul. I just wanted to defend him. Jim headed for the playroom, and I grabbed his arm.

"No. Wait. I've dealt with it. It's over with now."

With a sigh, Jim sat down and started to read the paper. I turned back to the stove. The moment had passed and I was relieved, but it was clear to me that we weren't talking anymore. This made me sad, but it also seemed too risky to try to talk. We always ended up blaming each other. By now I had noticed that when it came to Paul, we always had different reactions, different responses to what was going on around us. Usually I was more *optimistic* (my word) about Paul; Jim was more *realistic* (his word).

But now Jim and I had missed sharing a funny moment, or a moment

that might have been funny. I knew that Paul was "painting" the house
burnt umber because he was collecting every different color. He had a
box of sixty-four Crayola crayons and was memorizing each distinct
shade or tone. It was very important to Paul to discriminate each shade
from every other. He would often test the sky against his crayons,
holding turquoise and robin's-egg blue up against the horizon, with
powder blue a little higher up.

If I had not been so tired and stressed, I would have been amused
and impressed at his painting the house burnt umber, and maybe then
Jim and I would have laughed proudly together. But Paul had become
a pawn between us, and our anger at each other was too valuable a
weapon for either of us to consider giving it up.

Paul had been collecting, not just different shades of colors and pipes,
but also humidifiers and light bulbs. His light bulb collection had
grown to include not only incandescent household light bulbs, but also
fluorescent bulbs, black lights, infrared and ultraviolet bulbs, a car
headlight, Christmas tree light bulbs, and flashcubes: three hundred
seventy-two in all. He kept many of his light bulbs in a basket by his
bed, and every night he tried out different bulbs. He wanted to know
how many watts each had and how bright each one was, and of course
the relationship of wattage to brightness wasn't exact enough for him.

The Christmas tree lights, which came in so many different colors,
were especially precious. The collecting had started at Christmas, when
we visited my father and Paul had admired his tree lights. Admiration
and desire were enough to gain him the bulbs; my father gladly gave
them to him. No one questioned this at the time.

One evening around New Year's, Paul came running in our back
door, big moon boots clumping, skidding in the wetness on the kitchen
floor. He tried to slam shut the door as he ran through it, but a tall
man ran into the kitchen after him. Jim and I stood there staring. This
man was huge; he seemed seven feet tall at least. And heavy. And
angry: very, very angry.

He started shouting at Paul, "You stole my light bulbs. I know you
did. I saw you." He reached into the pockets of Paul's snowsuit —
three, four, ten, Christmas tree light bulbs fell out onto the kitchen
table. The man snatched them up, putting them in his pockets, a look
of satisfaction on his face.

I stared at this man, frozen and temporarily speechless before this
giant who had invaded our house, who was even now standing over
Paul. His mere presence was itself an intimidation, almost an assault.

Recovering my voice at last, I somehow got rid of him, assured him that we would have a serious talk with Paul, that Paul would not be on his lawn again near his outdoor Christmas tree.

But there was to be no discussion that day, no calm talk with Paul about the wrongs of taking someone else's property, no "reasonable" punishment. Jim, who had been standing still all this time, suddenly seemed to come to. "You stole those light bulbs, Paul." He leaned over him, fists clenched. "You stole them. And you are no son of mine."

Paul backed up until he was standing in a corner of the kitchen near the trash can. I saw his lower lip draw down and begin to quiver. He didn't take his eyes off Jim, who continued to advance on him.

"You hear that? You are no son of mine. If you ever, ever do that again, I will disown you. You understand?"

I tried to pull Jim away, but he brushed me aside angrily. "Stop interfering," he shouted at me.

Paul was beginning to sob, great rasping sobs as if he could hardly catch his breath. His face was pale and streaked with tears. He looked very small next to the tall trash can, next to Jim, who seemed now almost as tall as the giant who ran in our back door. I pulled at Jim again, and Paul ducked out from beneath Jim's arm. He ran into the dining room and stood there on the other side of the table.

"Can't you see he's terrified of you?" I shouted at Jim.

"He should be terrified of me! How is he going to learn otherwise?"

"That's not how children learn! That's not how my father treated us." As soon as I said this, I realized that it was the worst possible thing I could have said. I knew that making comparisons, holding up the example of my father, was not only grossly unfair but was also guaranteed to infuriate Jim, whose own father had been either absent or ineffectual throughout his childhood. This was an issue that had come up often between us, and it was a very touchy one for Jim.

I should have had the good sense to stay off the subject of fathers, but by this time, I too was past reasoned argument. Instead, I was remembering vividly a time in my own childhood when I felt this same sense of invasion that I thought Paul was feeling right now, and my father, unlike Jim, had defended me against a hostile world.

I was three or four, and we had rented a room to a mother and her daughter, Gloria, who was my age and who bit me. I suppose Gloria and her mother lived there before the diphtheria case. It was during the war, and Gloria's father was probably a soldier. I don't know if her mother was suffering the finality of her husband's death or anxiously waiting for his return from the horrors of war. In any case, hers must have been a miserable existence — poor, dependent, living resentfully in the midst of a family she hardly knew. I remember only my own feelings of invasion. And the sensation of Gloria's teeth sinking into my arm.

One day my father saw Gloria attack. He looked around for her mother and, not seeing her anywhere close by, hissed at me, "Bite her back. *Now!*" I bit her: quickly, before he could change his mind, because this command was so completely uncharacteristic of my gentle father, I chomped down on Gloria's arm. I still remember the satisfaction, the sense of vindication and adult protection for such a disreputable act. At that moment I lived simply in my own nerve endings, not in any thoughtfulness for another person's condition, not in any consciousness of right or wrong. I had broken one of my parents' most cherished rules — never bite anyone — and was still safe, protected from punishment. And, as a bonus, Gloria never bit me again.

Now, thinking of my father, who told me, "You come first — no matter what you do, I will still love you," I wanted the same for Paul. I wanted Jim to draw that same line and say to Paul that no matter what he did he was still loved. I wanted him to say, as I was trying to do, that Paul's behavior was wrong, that he needed to learn not to steal someone else's light bulbs, but that we would defend him against tall strangers who ran into our kitchen.

"Don't tell me how children learn," Jim was shouting at me. "He'll learn all right. I'll shame him into learning. He'll be so ashamed, he will never forget this as long as he lives."

Jim's face was purple with rage. And I felt I could explode with my anger, explode and splatter all over the kitchen. The blood pounded in my temples. My voice was hoarse and choked.

"Right!" I shouted back. "He'll never forget this as long as he lives. But I'm not so sure he's learned to stop stealing."

"He'll be so ashamed, he will never, never try this again."

"And how can you be so sure of that?"

"If he does, if he does steal again, it'll be your fault. You coddle him and make excuses for him, and now you're trying to undermine my authority."

"You're damned right I'm trying to undermine your authority." I glared at Jim.

Paul moved closer to the kitchen door. "You're fighting about me. I don't like it when you fight about me."

"See what you are doing to him?" Jim said to me.

"See what *you're* doing to him!" I glared back.

Finally, we were all so exhausted, we drifted away from battle, Paul up to his room, Jim out to do the shopping for dinner. I went upstairs to talk to Paul, to try to undo some of the damage, and there at the top of the steps I found Kate. She was sitting huddled against the wall, her thumb in her mouth. The hair ribbon had come out on one side, and her dark auburn hair spilled over her face. She had marked up her dress and her arms and legs with a blue Magic Marker, which she was still holding in one hand. Across her face and her chest and her white tights there were blue lines. She looked as if she were tangled up in blue yarn.

I sat down next to her. Suddenly I felt exhausted beyond exhaustion, sad beyond all possible sadness. I put my arm around Kate, and she leaned into me. Then she sat up straight again and took her thumb out of her mouth. "Kate is very good," she said. This was the longest sentence she had ever said.

"Yes. Yes, you are very good." I hugged her, then turned to stare at her for a moment. "Maybe you are too good."

Kate nodded, tears slipping down her cheeks. "Too good!" she repeated and butted her head against my shoulder.

"Are you sad about Paul?"

She nodded.

"Would you like to come with me and talk to him?" She nodded again and we went together into Paul's room.

Two days later I received a phone call I had been half expecting. It was from a hardware store two blocks away. "We have your son, Paul. We caught him stealing a Christmas tree light bulb. We're keeping him in the manager's office. Because he's so young, we decided not to call the police. Please come down and get him."

Jim was not at home. I rushed down to the hardware store. "Don't tell my dad," Paul was pleading with the manager as I walked into the office. Paul's face was pale and streaked with tears. "Please don't tell my dad." Seeing me come in, he repeated, "Don't tell Daddy."

I stood there, staring at him. Paul was backed up against some packing cases, twisting his hands together. What should I do? If I told Jim, he would be angry out of all proportion, especially now that Paul had been caught stealing in public. Jim would be ashamed and embarrassed and infuriated. Yet Paul had to learn not to steal light bulbs.

"I'll have to tell him, Paul," I said slowly. "But not now. Later." I thought I would have to tell him eventually, but how and when and with what consequences, I didn't know. I was ashamed to admit, even to myself, that I too was deeply relieved that Jim had missed this call. From now on maybe I had better deal with these crises by myself, I thought, as I led Paul out of the store. I felt caught in a double bind, torn by ambivalence, but I was beginning to think that I must sacrifice our relationship, Jim's and mine. Whatever the cost, I must put Paul first.

CHAPTER 17

Falling

THERE WERE FEW PLACES I could visit with Paul. Most of my friends didn't have children his age, and I was worried about taking him to other people's houses. I even began to avoid inviting people to our house. We had a number of dedicated student babysitters who loved and accepted Paul and who had become friends of the family, but now it seemed we rarely saw our older friends. During the lonely days, when I hurried home from work to look after the children, I missed adult company. I especially longed for other mothers of children who were the ages of mine, and for another little boy like Paul. And then I met another mother at a school open house. Jesse was a poor farmwoman, with a special needs child a little older than Paul who was in the elementary school Resource Room.

I called Jesse one cold, dark day when the sky looked bruised and I couldn't face the effort of a walk to the park. "Come over," she said. "Please, please come over. I'm putting on the pot for tea this very minute."

Jesse greeted me at the door. She was pregnant but also very skinny, as if the pith had been sucked out of her to go into the making of this baby. Her two boys, Mike and Harry, were rough-and-tumble farmboys: blond, freckled, obviously coordinated. "Can we take Paul on our three-wheeler?" they wanted to know.

"Three-wheeler?" I looked at Jesse for guidance.

"It's an all-terrain vehicle. Mike and Harry ride it over the hills. It's pretty safe."

I looked at Paul, considering. He seemed awfully small compared to these two strapping boys, both of whom were bigger and older than he was. Seeing us watch him, Paul suddenly held out his hand to block Mike's eyes, then Harry's.

"No, I don't think so," I said slowly. "It would be better if you stayed close to the house."

"Can we show him the barn?"

"Sure."

The boys went outside, and Jesse poured tea into two chipped mugs. Then we sat down at the scrubbed oak table by the window next to the smoky stove. We drank tea and talked and looked out over the flat fields stubbled with brown, at the clouds hanging low with unspent snow. Kate played contentedly at our feet, turning sticks of kindling into a house, clothespins and spoons into a family to live there.

After a while we heard the boys just outside the door. I got up to check on them. Paul was jumping in the mud and Harry and Mike were sliding down the slanted cellar door into the snow and mud. All three were filthy.

"Look at this, Jesse. Only you won't want to see it!"

Jesse walked over to the window to look out also. "Holy moley!" She grimaced. "We might as well let them. They can't get any dirtier."

"True." I was so glad to see Paul standing and watching the boys sliding down the cellar door that the mud didn't bother me. "As far as I'm concerned, any play is better than no play," I told Jesse. "What's a little mud, compared to loneliness?"

I watched for a few moments longer. Paul wouldn't talk to the two boys, but at least he stayed outside with them.

Jesse's dreams, I was to learn that day, had dried up even more thoroughly than mine. And sitting there in her kitchen, drinking tea out of the cracked mug, I began to recognize my own feelings of frustration, which I had refused to look at for so long. The book about nineteenth-century women's fiction, which I had been writing for the last three years, was going nowhere. I still worked on it in the summers, but rarely accomplished very much. Every summer Jim and I thought we would have lots of time for writing, for reading, for reworking our courses, and every summer we hired a college student for three or four hours a day to watch the children and take them to the park. But then Jim and I spent weeks scraping and painting the outside of the house, putting up a fence, papering the bedrooms, sweeping the sand out of the kitchen, folding laundry, clipping the hedge, and cleaning out the garage. I wondered how other people seemed to manage so well when my life was always verging on chaos. Everything of mine — house, children, back yard, our cat — was labor-intensive. And this didn't seem to be the case with anyone else at all, only with us.

Once a student asked to interview me on the college radio station. She wanted me and another woman faculty member to comment on how we combined work and family. I agreed readily enough, without ever thinking through my own ambivalence, my tangled, confused, distorted, agonized feelings. When I appeared at the station, the other faculty member, a young woman who taught religion and who had *three* children, began telling the radio audience about how easy and wonderful it was to be a mother and a full-time teacher.

Lilly announced that she kept the crib in her office, that the baby slept there peacefully some days when she had conferences. Her two older children went to an after-school program where they painted the most marvelous pictures, or made potholders and paperweights as little gifts to present to her later. They were doing very well in school. Lilly told us that she had given three papers at conferences that year, and everyone had managed very well at home in her absence. Then she mentioned, in passing, that, yes, she had always had a housecleaner and someone to take care of the lawn and garden.

Lilly brushed her short black hair back from her cheek and tucked it behind her ear. She sat up straighter as she finished her statement. "When I come home from my office at about five or so, the children have finished their homework. They look after the baby while John, my husband, cooks dinner. That's when I get to take a long, long soak in the tub. That's *my* time." She sat back and smiled sweetly in my direction as she slid the microphone toward me.

I sat there, in the QWIRK radio station, my hands sweating against the microphone. What could I say now that it was my turn to answer the questions? How could I say that Paul would never be happy in a regular after-school program, nor would they be happy with him. And the school district had never funded an afternoon program especially for learning-disabled or behavior-problem children? How could I tell the listeners that Kate had been expelled from her first regular nursery school because she wasn't potty-trained, yet it was her cerebral palsy that had caused her delay. The world wasn't set up for children like Paul or Kate, but sitting there in the radio station I could only think that it was my fault for not training them better, for not keeping more control over my children.

The student who had set up the radio program sat across the table smiling encouragingly at me, waiting for my story. Sarah was one of my most enthusiastic students: she had taken every course I had ever taught, and she had written an article about me and the women's studies program for the student newspaper. She stopped by my office regularly to tell me about her problems at home, her troubles with her boyfriend, her roommate. Her face as she leaned toward me was so open and trusting. How could I disappoint her?

How could I tell Sarah and Lilly, and the whole radio audience, that for recreation, Paul and I drove around the countryside looking for power lines? That every day when I came home from my office exhausted and with piles of papers still left to grade, I tripped over Paul's pipes? That our back yard was always littered with piles of sand and rocks? How could I tell them that once city hall told us that our neighbors had complained about the condition of our lawn and that I hadn't felt any better at all when a Jewish friend of mine tried to reassure me: "It's just that you don't have a good Christian lawn, Jane. Not to worry, my friend."

I had to say something. I bent toward the microphone and muttered something about home and work, about the joys of children and the pleasures of teaching, about the wonder of watching children grow and young minds unfold. "Liar," I whispered to myself, under my breath. "You fraud. You craven coward."

I had tried to forget the whole radio show incident, but now, sitting at Jesse's table, I remembered it. Maybe it was because Jesse was so straightforward and accepting. Maybe it was because her yard and her house were in far worse condition than mine, and this didn't seem to bother her at all. After we finished our tea, she took me to a cold, unheated room at the back of the house. There I saw dozens of canvases stacked against the wall. Hardened paints in half-empty tubes lay on the windowsill and on a small table in the middle of the room. An easel was set up, but the canvas was turned back side out.

"Can I see some of them?" I asked.

"No, no." Jesse waved her hand dismissively. "You don't want to see them." She took me by the elbow and led me to another room.

"Ta dah." She swept the door open with a flourish. Inside I could see an improvised darkroom set up in an old bathroom. Jesse showed me the rows of chemicals that had evaporated, the torn black curtain across the window.

"You're a photographer too?" I asked incredulously.

"Was. And was very good. At one time. Doing very well freelancing. That was B.C." She grimaced and patted her belly, "You know. Before children."

One day in March, we were taking a walk on campus, Jesse, with her two boys and the baby in a stroller, and I, with Paul and Kate. All afternoon Mike and Harry had been goading Paul, running too close to him, zooming in with arms spread out like airplane wings, then sideswiping him at the last minute so that he would lose his balance, trip, and fall. Then Paul would scream and hit the side of his head with the palm of his hand and run after the two boys with a rock. Over and over again, Jesse and I tried to control the boys but nothing seemed to work, and reluctantly we had decided to give up and go home. I was strapping Kate back into her stroller by the side of the lake when I heard the splash.

Jesse was in the water before me. And Paul's head was going under. Then I was in the lake and I realized that my heavy, Irish fisherman's knit sweater was drinking up the water, absorbing it so fast that it was weighing me down, but I had to get to Paul. His head bobbed under again. Then he came up with a weed streaking across his cheek, then he went under again.

Jesse reached him first. But I saw that Paul himself was paddling for the shore ahead of her. I reached Paul just after Jesse did, but he had managed to move by himself to the rocks at the edge of the lake. Jesse started to push him ahead of her, one hand on his back, but I could see, we both could see, that Paul had made it all by himself to the shore.

We pulled ourselves up onto the rocks, shivering, beginning to shake all over in the Minnesota cold. We were too shocked to say anything, then Jesse and I collapsed into each other's arms and around Paul. He stood there dripping between us, weeds and bits of grass draped across his head and shoulders.

"The car! Let's get to the car and turn the heater on."

We all ran for the car, a very subdued Mike and Harry pushing the baby in her stroller. In the car, Jesse turned around to confront Harry. "I saw you do that! Don't think I didn't see you push Paul in the water."

Harry slid down in the back seat, scrunching way back in the corner.

"You're going to have to do something special for him after this. You're going to have to give him something favorite of yours! Something favorite like your Godzilla!"

Harry didn't say a word, just scrunched down lower in the seat. But later that week, Jesse appeared at my back door, Harry beside her. And in Harry's hand was Godzilla. "Here," he said, thrusting Godzilla into Paul's hands.

"And what else?" Jesse prompted.

"And I'm sorry," said Harry, not looking particularly sorry.

Paul took Godzilla. We could hardly have refused a gift of that symbolic importance, although Godzilla meant little to him. But after this, it seemed more and more clear that Paul and Mike and Harry did not get on well together. Jesse and I got together after school less often than we used to do. It was just too difficult keeping control over the boys, and gradually we began to drift apart. And after that, it seemed that Paul was even more dependent on me, that I could rarely get away from him.

One Sunday morning I was sitting in the Congregational church next door to our house. It was a beautiful sunny day. This hour during the service was almost the only hour I could count on all week when I could be alone with my thoughts. Jim was at home with the children. I sat there enjoying the motes in the stained-glass sunbeams, enjoying also the waxy smell of the pews, enjoying above all the notes of a Bach partita. The church was full that day, quiet, everyone focused on the beauty of the music.

The heavy door to the side of the sanctuary opened very slowly, then slammed shut. A toddler walked in. She was in a dirty tee shirt that should have been washed days ago. She was barefooted and had a tear-stained face.

Kate. It was Kate. I rushed up to her before everyone's head turned in that direction and I bent down to talk to her.

"Mama, Paul is bobbering me," she said, then took me by the hand to lead me back home to resolve the latest crisis.

CHAPTER 18

The Gods of Destruction

I T W A S twenty-five aspirin tablets, maybe thirty or thirty-five. Anyway, I knew I had taken a whole fistful. I leaned my head against the bathroom mirror, trying to swallow my sobs. And Jim was outside the locked door, begging me to tell him what I was doing, to stop whatever it was I was doing, to come out and call a doctor, to talk to Malcolm, our new therapist. "Come out. I don't know what is happening to you in there," I could hear him pleading.

And then Jim left to call the doctor himself. He came back to tell me the doctor thought I was being manipulative. Just plain manipulative. Satisfaction began to edge out panic in Jim's voice. Or so I thought. I could hear in his voice just a little bit of pleasure taken in my sheer stupidity. He wasn't the only crazy one. I was probably crazier than he was and the doctor knew it and sympathized with him.

Jim left again to talk on the phone, and I sat down on the toilet seat to think. The week before, after a terrible fight when Jim said Paul was a liar and no son of his, when he said he would leave him if he ever lied again, when he slapped him across the face, and I slapped away Jim's hand and screamed at him to stop, when Jim turned on me and said I was always interfering, that I was the reason Paul couldn't learn right from wrong, on that day I had thrown my rings down this same toilet. Stripping off my wedding ring and my engagement ring, I had hurled them into the bowl. Then I flushed and flushed, gloating as the engagement ring, heavy with its tiny diamond weight, its weight of promises lost, was caught easily in the whirlpool and snatched away into the pipes, into the sewers, gone. Miraculously, the wedding ring, a simple gold band with no diamond, floated to the bottom of the toilet bowl and obstinately remained there until the water turned still again. I had reached in to retrieve it. At the time I had taken this for a sign.

Now, sitting on the closed toilet seat, I picked up the Greenpeace newsletter, which was lying on the edge of the tub. That's what I want, I thought: "to annihilate all to a green thought in a green shade," a lovely, cool, spreading, green shade. And suddenly, I felt very sorry for myself. Maybe I can get just one day to myself, I thought, just one day in the hospital, in a soft, clean bed in sheets that someone else has washed. One day in a lovely bare room that someone else has cleaned. Three meals that I haven't cooked, brought to me by kind nurses. Someone else to answer the phone. No tantrums to calm, no terrified child to comfort, no disapproving neighbors to ignore. Green peace.

I opened the door and walked out. Jim, with both tears and anger on his face, handed me the phone. "It's Malcolm. Will you talk to him?"

At that moment I couldn't afford to look at the pain on Jim's face, the anger, the bewilderment. As I handed the phone back to Jim, I told him I would meet Malcolm in his office in ten minutes. "Can you stay here in case the kids wake up?" I asked. I didn't want to say more to Jim. I felt unreal. My hands were beginning to come loose, to separate from my body. I was starting to tingle all over, as if sand were running through me.

I put on a dress, the nearest at hand. It was an old maternity dress that I hadn't worn in years, a loose blue dress with a pert little collar and tiny red cherries appliquéd to the front. Cherries, I thought. Life is just a bowl full of cherries. No it isn't. It is pain and loss and grief and irresponsible, misplaced, confused and confusing anger. It is guilt and anxiety and betrayal and responsibilities violated. It is anything at all but a bowl full of cherries.

As I walked, ears ringing, hands and feet tingling, the one block to Malcolm's office, I remembered that seven years before I had worn this very dress when I was pregnant with Paul. I had worn it when I went into the hospital to have a stitch put in my cervix and when I returned to the hospital with an infection in the stitch. I had worn it when I was spotting and cramping and terrified and when I was drugged with alcohol and Valium to stop the cramping.

Walking that one block, I relived the whole course of the pregnancy, from the first slight bleeding at one month, followed by the hormone treatments, the surgery at three months, the infection of the stitch at seven months, and especially the cramping and contractions I had felt throughout the nine months.

But mostly I thought of the alcohol and the Valium I had been told to take to stop the contractions. "Don't be afraid of alcohol," my doctor had told me. "I have treated many women with threatened miscarriages this way. It does work, and it's perfectly safe for the baby. Intravenous alcohol drips are the treatment of choice for threatened miscarriages."

I had agreed to this treatment, remembering how he had tried to stop the premature birth with an alcohol drip. If I had just gotten to the hospital sooner, I thought, if I had just had a stiff Scotch at home before labor was firmly established, maybe I could have saved that child.

Dr. Berg also reassured me about Valium. "It's a muscle relaxant and it will stop the uterus from contracting. It's necessary for you to take it regularly. These are more than Braxton-Hicks contractions. They are not benign."

I remembered all this and how I had let myself be reassured. But I also remembered the sleeping pills I had been given at the very end of the pregnancy when I was so used to drugs and so dependent on them that I could no longer sleep for more than three or four hours at a stretch. I must have taken too much of everything. I must have damaged the baby.

Malcolm drove me the five blocks to the hospital and checked me in. Dimly I was aware of his great kindness, of the competent way he sped me through the process of hospital admissions, the quiet way he talked to the nurses and made sure I was safe at last in a private room behind closed curtains.

I was sick all during that night in the hospital. Every hour or two, I got up to be sick, then crawled back into bed. Occasionally nurses came in to check on me, and then left again quickly. I felt their disapproval when they came in to take my blood pressure, my temperature. I felt their fear, their embarrassment in the way they twitched the curtains open with a quick rasping sound, the way they looked away, staring out the window, after putting the thermometer in my mouth, as they stood there with two fingers on my pulse. They couldn't wait to get out of that room.

I felt very lonely there in the hospital room behind closed curtains, but the present moment was less real than that other time, one day in particular, a March day, when I was five months pregnant and we went to London for ten days. My doctor had said: "By all means, go to London. It will do you a world of good. Everything is going fine with you at the moment, and besides I don't believe in pregnancy invalidism."

Dr. Berg had also warned me about cigarette smoke. "Smoke is an irritant. It causes the uterus to contract. Stay out of cigarette smoke, any kind of smoke, as much as possible," he had told me. But on the long trip to London, there was no way to get away from cigarette smoke. After we took off from New York, the pilot turned off the NO SMOKING sign, and several people around us immediately lit up. This was before airlines offered no smoking sections, and I was surrounded by smokers, breathing the air that couldn't be cleaned and filtered fast enough.

I began to feel some cramping. I took a Valium, but the cramping got worse. I took another Valium. The cramping began to feel more rhythmical, coming in waves, like labor contractions. Flying over Newfoundland, far from safety and farther still from clean, pure air, I began to panic.

When the drinks trolley came around, I ordered a Scotch. Jim sat beside me, holding my hand. He knew I wasn't feeling well, but I didn't want to tell him how bad it was. I felt that his fear, if he knew the extent of my worries, would just increase my own fear. I had all I could do to stay calm and steady, to try to relax, not to panic.

One Scotch and two Valiums later, the contractions were still there. We were heading out over the long stretch of the Atlantic. It was eleven o'clock at night New York time, four o'clock in the morning London time. My uterus was now a tight, hard ball, clenched like a fist in my lower abdomen. I thought surely this is it, I am going to miscarry now, on this airplane, with a stitch that will cause terrible tears in the cervix. I might hemorrhage, bleed to death. I will certainly lose the baby. I will probably never have another child because the cervix will be too damaged from the ripped-out stitch.

And then I remembered that my doctor had given me yet another drug to use in an emergency. Quaaludes were newly on the market at this time, and Dr. Berg had given me a small packet of them, saying that they were perfectly safe for "pregnant moms and dads." I took one and eventually drifted off into a troubled sleep just as we were landing in London.

We went immediately to our hotel, had breakfast, and collapsed in bed. I slept the rest of that day and woke up the next morning feeling fully restored.

I felt fine, but I also felt that something was wrong. It was a few hours before I realized what it was. The baby hadn't moved, hadn't moved for a while. How long? A few hours? A day? A day and a half?

In a panic, I called a friend who was a mother of four children and who was living that year in London. Dagmar tried to reassure me.

"Don't worry," she said. "At five months, babies often don't move for several days. It's awfully early."

"But this one has been moving every day. I know." I put my hand protectively on my lower abdomen. I gave a little poke. Nothing happened. I gave another little poke. "This is different, Dagmar. I know it is." The lively, fluttery little butterfly movements were stilled, and I felt that a stone had been left behind, a dead weight without movement, without life.

"You're probably just tired. The baby is just tired. It's a long trip, a different time zone."

Letting myself be reassured, I laughed. "You mean the baby is still on Minnesota time?"

"Of course! The baby is still on Minnesota time. Aren't you?"

I hung up after that and pushed the worry to the back of my mind. And shortly afterward, the baby did start to move again, just as strong and lively as before.

But now, seven years later, the worry surfaced again. Was that the moment? The very moment when the damage was done? The moment when some hurt was done, some assault was made on developing brain cells?

Always, after that I thought: two Valiums, a stiff Scotch, and a Quaalude deprived a child of his very soul. It was then that I felt I understood the Faust myth. It is possible to sell a soul, not just one's own, but also someone else's. Someone, a new person, had been entrusted into my care, and I had violated that trust. I had deprived someone of his intellect. Why should I have the benefit of mine?

Finally, I fell asleep and slept through most of the next day in the hospital. Once I woke up to see a doctor we had known slightly for years standing at the foot of the bed. "Don't I know you?" he asked hesitantly. Puzzled, he stood there and stared at me with deep concern on his face. I had taken the children to him a few times when our own doctor had been unavailable. Dr. Smith looked again at my chart, at the admissions record made out the night before for an overdose case, a case of aspirin poisoning, self-inflicted.

"Yes," I mumbled, tears filling my eyes. I didn't want to admit that this disgraceful, rumpled person lying here in a wrinkled hospital gown, with a pale face and a lingering sour smell of vomit, was the same woman who had brought her children in for checkups, the same person as that competent, capable, cheerful young mother.

Dr. Smith stepped closer to the bed. "Are you getting help?"

"Yes." I mentioned Malcolm and how we had started going to him for counseling.

Dr. Smith nodded, and regarded me for a few moments longer. "Good." He seemed about to say something else. "Good. That's good," he repeated, and left the room.

The next day, a Sunday, when I got out of the hospital, I felt appalled at what I had done, and deeply ashamed. I was determined to forget my craziness and to get on with my life in a matter-of-fact, no-nonsense way. I wanted to run as far from the aspirin incident as I possibly could. Above all, I wanted to protect the children, to make a safe place around them, to restore something that had been threatened.

Jim told me he couldn't find a babysitter and that he needed to go to his office to grade some papers. I recognized the justice of this, although I didn't feel ready to be with the children and I wanted to protect them from my craziness. So I simply packed away my feelings, the terrible, shocking truth of what I had just done, or tried to do.

The real terror of that time, when I had stepped up to the razor's edge, when I had leaned over and flirted with the gods of destruction, didn't reach me until much later. At the time I was numb. My feelings were too scandalous, too shocking to admit even to myself, especially to myself. I felt my life depended on keeping them at a distance, and yet of course I was driven by what was denied.

I did everything I could to keep my guilt at bay, to tell myself I was stupid to believe I had damaged my son, stupid to believe that I had killed my mother by making her work so hard to send me to college. Those were the forbidden words, the forbidden feelings, and I could never allow myself to look at them directly. They were something from a soap opera, something that reasonable, educated people like me didn't feel. So why then did I feel that I had been brought up short, snagged on a rock in the stream of life? Why did I feel like a motherless daughter, a childless mother?

I knew why. I had been too privileged: too much had been given to me and too little to my mother. I also feared that too much had gone into the making of me and of Jim, and too little into Paul. Jim and I had had it all. Our parents, and now it seemed our children, had much less. I wondered if cosmic energies weren't after all limited, so that what is taken from one generation is given to the next, to be denied to the one after that.

*

"Want to go see Jesse," Paul said that morning, after breakfast. He was hanging on my arm. "See her silo."

Why not, I thought? I wanted the children to be safe and happy, and spending a day in the countryside at Jesse's farm was one of the safest things we could do. I didn't want to share with her the terrible thing I had done, and I thought I could get away with being silent. I also knew she would take the children off my hands for a little while.

And so we went to see Jesse and her silo. Paul and Kate looked inside the silo and shouted "Ooooo" over and over again into the fermented darkness, until they got tired and went into the orchard. Jesse helped them climb a ladder and pick apples. She helped them get one of each variety and taste each one, deciding which they liked the best. Then she took them into the kitchen for milk and apple pie.

Knowing the children were safe, I fell on the grass, face to the sun, too tired to lift an arm. The colors were too bright that day, the barn too red, the grass too green. And noises were too close, cicadas seemed to be in my ears, legs strumming, stripping my very nerves. Lying there, I knew I was two people. One was a competent and capable young mother and professional. She was matter-of-fact and in control of her life. The other was crazy, hysterical, out of control, and probably headed for destruction. The competent woman floated a few feet above the ground, looking down on the crazy woman lying in the grass. The crazy woman lay there raw and exposed, with stripped skin, damaged nerve endings, almost bleeding into the grass.

The competent young professional reminded the crazy woman that she had a busy week in front of her. "You can't just lie there in the sun all day. Remember, you have a women's studies conference next weekend. You've worked six months to set it up, remember that?"

The crazy woman grudgingly agreed.

"You lined up all the speakers and the panel discussions," the competent professional went on in a more insistent tone. "You arranged for accommodations and meals and transportation from the airport, for books to be ordered for a special book sale, for entertainment. Remember? You wrote all those letters. You filled out all those budget requests. You're not just going to throw all that away, now are you?"

"No. Of course not." The crazy woman lay there and tried not to bleed into the grass.

"Besides, your old friend from Bryn Mawr will give the keynote address at the conference. You want to be in good shape for her, don't you?"

"Of course I do."

"So what's your problem?"

"My problem? My problem is . . ." But the crazy woman couldn't quite say. She just lay there and remembered Bryn Mawr, remembered her mother.

One incident in particular the crazy woman remembered. I remembered. It was the summer after my junior year and I was living at home and working at the Folger Shakespeare Library. I had gone to see Mother's doctor with some minor ailment of my own. Dr. Owens called me into his office after he had examined my throat and written a prescription. He seemed nervous, or irritable, I couldn't quite tell which.

I sat down across from his desk, feeling nervous myself. I knew Dr. Owens reasonably well because he used to live in our neighborhood, and I had babysat for his three young children every summer when I was in high school. I felt close to those children because I had worked very hard for hours every hot summer day to amuse them. Later, after I left home to go to college, Mother started going to see Dr. Owens with her many illnesses — bursitis, nephritis, high blood pressure, allergies, bouts of flu.

Dr. Owens sat back in his leather chair and put his two hands together. He rested his fingers against his chin, almost as though he were about to pray. "I want to talk to you about your mother, not about you." Dr. Owens rocked forward in the chair and took his hands from his face. He stopped to stare at me for a moment. I felt more nervous.

"I'm very worried about her. She can't go on like this."

I started to say something, but he put up a hand to stop me.

"You're killing her."

That's what I thought I heard, but I couldn't believe my ears. And then he repeated it. "You're killing her. She can't go on working like this."

"I don't want her to . . ." I started, and faltered. "I don't want her to work so hard, but I am already on full scholarship aid, and it's still not enough." I stopped. Maybe he was right. Maybe I was killing my mother. Maybe she would die from the effort of sending me to college. So I believed; so the crazy woman in me believed. It never occurred to me that my mother could have asked for a letter from her doctor saying she was too ill to go on working. That letter could have been sent to Bryn Mawr with a request for more aid, and I would almost certainly have received it.

Later, years later, I wondered why my parents didn't think of this. They accepted it as a given that I must have this education, and that my mother must work to give it to me. Even more, I wondered why Dr. Owens didn't think of it.

But at the time, all I felt was guilt, and a rock-bottom determination to do well so I wouldn't jeopardize my scholarship. At Bryn Mawr I always worked late into the night. I worked all weekend in the library. To keep going, I looked for new places to study — the art print library under the eaves, where no one ever went, nooks in Goodhue Hall so I could listen to music practice as I studied. In good weather I climbed out onto the roof of Rockefeller Hall and sat up beside the chimney stacks or near the crenellated edges of the roof. An even better place was the top of Rockefeller Tower, four stories high, up among the wisteria vines. Studying all the time, I rarely let myself take a break, especially for the first two years. Work was everything. It was my only justification, it was my mother's due, my family's redemption, my hope, our survival.

Just once during term time was my mother able to visit me at Bryn Mawr, and that was for May Day and the awards convocation at the end of my senior year. Mother had read about the May Day celebrations for years and had always wanted to see one. She herself had dropped out of college as a sophomore to work and to help send her younger brothers to college. Now she wanted to enjoy the ceremonies of privileged collegiate life, at least as an observer.

May Day at Bryn Mawr was something special to her, and to me. I woke up at five to sing with my class the Magdalen College Latin hymn to the sun from Rockefeller Tower. Mother stood beneath the tower to hear the singing. And she was there at breakfast, when we ate fresh strawberries. She was there as we skipped in our silly white dresses with baskets of flowers and wove the ribbons together in our Maypole dance. She was there to laugh at the annual "immorality" play, written by a friend of mine and performed on the steps of the library.

This was a day to celebrate, to enjoy, to reap the rewards of four years of hard work. Later we met in the chapel for prizes and awards. I won the prize I most desired, the American College Poetry Award. I knew that my poems would later be published in a national magazine. My parents were there in the audience, sitting in the back, behind the senior class.

After the ceremony, I left the chapel and ran up the hill to catch up with my parents. But then I stopped. Ahead of me Mother struggled up the small hill, her black straw hat set at an angle on her head, her plastic purse knocking against her knees. She had recently had a strep throat, I knew. But I didn't know she was this slow, this tired. I didn't know she had become this old.

Holding the poetry prize in my hand, I stood there and stared. Mother seemed to be broken at her knees, broken in her shoulders. Through my sudden tears, the pink flowers on her dress seemed to spread like bloodstains across her back. Slowly, slowly, she walked up the hill. And I was seeing her for the first time. I knew then that she was dying, that it would not be long before she died.

I was graduating, and my mother was dying.

CHAPTER 19

Soft Sift in an Hourglass

I SAT at the kitchen table, a glass of sherry at my elbow. A copy of Edith Wharton's *The House of Mirth* lay open before me; I had one hundred pages left to reread before class the next day, but I didn't feel ready to face Lily Bart's agonizing death through an overdose of chloral. I was fed up with her this time around. Spread open on top of the book was a *Family Day* magazine that I had picked up earlier that afternoon at the grocery store checkout stand. A stew bubbled on the stove, Paul was playing with his pipes and the hose in the back yard, Kate was still next door at the day care center. I would have to pick her up in half an hour, but for now I was just sitting there, idly flipping through the magazine, sipping sherry.

I circled one page in the magazine, glancing at it, moving on, then flipping back: "Do You Have a Problem with Alcohol?" was printed in bold, blurry letters at the top of the page. Then underneath, the author suggested that I "take the easy ten-minute test."

Taking a large sip from the glass of sherry, I picked up a pencil and started marking the answers:

1. Have you ever felt guilty about your drinking? (Well, yes. Hasn't everyone?)
2. Do you drink to feel better about yourself? to handle stress? to feel normal? to reward yourself after a hard day's work? (Yes to all of these. What's a drink for, anyway?)
3. Have you ever had a blackout when you were drinking? (No, what *is* a blackout? Sounds awful.)
4. Has your family suffered financially because of your drinking? (No! Of course not.)
5. Have you ever been in trouble with the law because of your drinking? (Heavens, no.)

6. Have you ever missed work because of your drinking? (Of course not. But, I wondered, what about all those sore throats and cases of flu I am always getting?)

Well, what about them? I paused to look out the window. Paul was soaked, but I decided he was good for at least another ten minutes. He had built a dam on the sidewalk with rocks and sand, and he was absorbed with flooding it with the hose, trying to see how much pressure the dam would take before it gave. Sand and rocks were all over the edge of the lawn, as well as the sidewalk. I knew Jim would be furious when he came home, but what could I do, how could I take care of everything anyway? I poured myself another large glass of sherry and went back to the questionnaire.

7. Do you hide your drinking, or sneak drinks when other people aren't looking? (Yes.) I had another sip of sherry and thought about Jim coming in any moment now. I needed to finish this glass before he walked around the garage. (The answer was yes, I do. All the time.)
8. Have you developed an increased capacity for alcohol? (Sure have.)
9. Does your drinking cause trouble with your spouse? (I don't want to think about that one.)
10. Have you ever tried, and failed, to stop drinking? Do you attempt to control the amount or kind of drink you take? (The answer is yes, every single day of my life.)

Six yeses, three nos, one maybe. Or was that maybe really a yes? This was worse than I thought. The article said that three yeses qualified you as an alcoholic, and even two was cause for concern. I gulped down the rest of the sherry in the glass, then quickly hid the bottle in the cupboard behind the potatoes. Limp white sprouts were coming out of the potatoes, and they were starting to smell a rancid, rotten earth smell. Better get rid of them. I pulled the bag out of the cupboard and held it up: black fluid oozed out from the bottom of the sack. Yuk! I tossed the bag in the garbage. I looked at the clock. Five o'clock. Time to get Kate and clean up Paul.

This scene, or ones like it, happened not once but many times. I read articles about alcohol or drug dependency, I filled out questionnaires (while at the same time sipping sherry, or wine, or beer). After the episode in the hospital, I even talked to Malcolm about my worries. At his suggestion, Jim and I went to a series of lectures on alcohol abuse and kept diaries, daily accounts of our alcohol use. We did this for about three days, then stopped. I realized this was all a sham. I was dependent. Jim was not.

They say alcoholics don't realize that they are alcoholics. It is a disease of denial and, by definition, prevents self-knowledge. But I knew perfectly well, although of course I didn't *want* to know. Some mornings, after I had had too much to drink the night before, I sat in the bathtub, shaking, hung over, my bones aching, so fragile that it felt as if my skin would rub off under the washcloth. I knew. In fact, I felt *sinful,* then was immediately shocked that I could even think of such a word in the late twentieth century. But that was how I felt.

Years later, the children, particularly Paul, would ask me about my alcoholism, and I would try to explain to him what it was, what it had felt like. He would always say, "But you didn't hit us. Or fall asleep on the couch in the middle of the day. Or scream at us." And I would agree. Nevertheless, my feelings, the guilt, the shame, the sense that my life was out of control — all that was there. At the time, a poem by Gerard Manley Hopkins kept going through my head:

> *I am soft sift*
> *In an hourglass — at the wall.*
> *Fast, but mined with a motion, a drift,*
> *And it crowds and it combs to a fall.*

I felt that my very self was seeping away as if it were sand in an hourglass. Adrift. Undermined with emotion.

One night I woke up at three or four in the morning (as I often did, usually did). This time, Jim woke up, too, and I told him I wanted to go to treatment. There was no sudden flash of inner knowledge, only a slowly growing conviction that alcohol was no friend of mine. He told me he would stand by me and support me in any way he could. Then he rolled over and went back to sleep.

And that was that. I called Malcolm the next morning, and on the Monday following I drove up to the Twin Cities to the program that had agreed to take me. It wasn't easy; none of it was easy. I often thought during that time of the saying "The truth shall set you free — but first, it will make you bloody miserable."

For one thing, Jim seemed to think that the treatment program had given him permission to release a whiplash of anger at me, then at Paul. I felt crowded into a corner, as if it weren't my treatment program at all, and it took me many years of therapy on my own, and with Jim, to recognize and deal with my own feelings of anger and resentment which I had never been able to express in treatment. In treatment I was, of course, by definition the sick one and Jim was the victim; I was the wrongdoer and Jim was the sacrificed sufferer. And I found this very hard to take.

Recognizing and expressing anger had always been a problem of mine, and yet the rages that propelled Jim and me through sleepless nights were utterly destructive. There were times when I thought I would break down, and there was one time, weeks after the end of the program, when Jim did break and had to be hospitalized.

All that summer, Jim had been growing more and more rageful. Some of this was well-deserved anger aimed at me, and some was a compressed fury at Paul which had been there since Paul was three. But something else was going on as well. His eyes gleaming with a new and frightening energy, Jim began to say that alcohol may have been my substance of choice, but anger was his. Every day he got "higher and higher" on anger, until by the end of the summer he was hardly sleeping at all and was driven by some inner power that began to seem terrifying.

The woman who treated us in our couples' group said Jim reminded her of the poet John Berryman, who had been her patient several years before. Berryman had been an alcoholic, treated unsuccessfully at the same hospital, and eventually he had committed suicide one morning in Minneapolis, jumping off a bridge after waving good-bye to an unsuspecting pedestrian. I think this therapist, a kind, older woman, was haunted by the notion that she had failed Berryman. Something about Jim — his articulateness, the power and vividness of his personality — reminded her of the dead poet. Maybe she saw in him her own second chance as a therapist, a way of redeeming the past, even though Jim wasn't technically the patient. But I was scared by this new development. Jim had become too powerful. He threatened to overwhelm me by the sheer force of a personality heightened and transported by anger. I also felt that he had co-opted our therapist, taking her with him, careening down some new and dangerous pathway.

Our fights became more and more destructive. Several times that summer we were both awake all night fighting the most personally harmful battles of our lives. Jim began to tell me that I couldn't trust my instincts, that really I was very ill, even though I may have thought I had begun to put my life back together again. I felt that somehow he had managed to insinuate himself into my deepest self, my most private mind and soul. But then I realized that I was trying to do the same with him. We had both begun to say things we had always considered off-limits. We began to make insidious and unfair comparisons between our two families, a dirty way of fighting which would have horrified us earlier and has ever since.

Even worse, we began to threaten each other with seizing custody of the children. "Now that you have been identified as an alcoholic, I can take the children away from you," Jim shouted at me one night. Terrified, I flashed back with accusations about Jim's past which I thought would equally disqualify him in the eyes of a divorce court judge.

And then I think we both stood appalled at our own viciousness. So this is what it feels like to fight to the finish, I thought, to fight right up to that point and beyond, where divorce would be far saner, far kinder. How terrifying human relationships began to seem: to know so much about another person and to be so known by another person. This power was dangerous beyond any other.

Finally, at the end of the summer Jim virtually stopped sleeping for almost a week. He prowled the house at night, and during the day he began to seem more and more dissociated. He went out in the car one day to buy milk for the children and was gone a long, long time. An hour or so later, he came home and confessed that he had driven all over town, stopping in each parking lot, before he remembered what he had gone out for. "I just can't be by myself," he confessed, and he stayed beside me all the rest of that day.

The next morning he was up very early after sleeping only one or two hours, so he took the children for breakfast to a new McDonald's that had opened on the edge of town. In the restaurant, there was a grinning plastic anthropomorphic tree, as well as little mushroom seats around a table. Coming home later, Jim told me he was as fascinated by the tree as the children had been. He said he felt that he had just awakened in a new place and had seen it with a child's freshness of vision.

I found Jim sitting in a chair in Kate's room very early the next morning. She was in the middle of her bed, sobbing in a rasping, terrified, choked way. Jim was just sitting next to her, leaning his elbows on his knees, smiling in a knowing way at her tears. I realized then that something was terribly wrong. Jim would never, under any normal circumstances, have laughed or smiled at the pain of another person, let alone that of his own child. Clearly, something had to be done.

I called Malcolm, who agreed to see Jim that same day, but he thought there was nothing much the matter. Later a psychiatrist said

Jim had been "editing" at the time we saw Malcolm, presenting a more acceptable picture than the one he was really feeling. But by that time, I felt even more frightened.

The next night was even worse. Jim prowled the house all night looking for a gun, even though he knew of course that we never kept a gun. He woke me up several times, and when he spoke, I felt I was hearing his dreams spoken aloud.

I called good friends the next morning, as early as I dared. They both had degrees in counseling psychology; they said they would get in touch with a psychiatrist immediately and would try to find a hospital bed for Jim. As soon as I hung up I told Jim what I had done, and he agreed without protest to go to the hospital. His reason, he said, was to give me some rest, but by this time he was himself staggering from accumulated exhaustion, virtually a whole week without sleep.

Jim spent two weeks in the hospital, then he returned to teach his classes. But he continued taking an antipsychotic drug for several months, to allow memories and feelings to come to the surface, his doctor said. After a few months he went off Haldol, and then for months after that he was deeply depressed. I would often find him in the kitchen in the morning staring at the floor. He would go with me into bookstores and stare in disbelief at all those books, marveling that anyone could possibly find anything of interest there. "Nothing is interesting anymore," he would often say to me. "And nothing has any meaning whatsoever."

"I have lost my coiled spring," was an expression he often used at the time. I knew he meant he had lost everything that made him so energetic and forceful and vividly alive. It was many months before he felt he was even beginning to recover something of his old personality, and I ached for his sorrow, his loss of a whole year out of his life.

One day during this dark time, when Jim was still in the hospital and I was feeling more overwhelmed than ever, Kate, now three years old, came to me and took me by the hand. She led me to the bench by the kitchen table, patted the bench, and said, "Sit down. Have long talk."

I sat down beside her. Miraculously, I didn't burst into tears, even though I wanted to, badly, at that moment. Kate turned her small face toward me, her hazel-brown eyes wide open and full of questions, their thick lashes matted with tears. Quietly she repeated, "Have long talk." Staring into her sweet, concerned face, I started to try to explain to her what was happening, that Jim was sick, but that he would get well soon and would be coming back to us. She seemed satisfied, but I also realized how hard this was on her, how confused she must be, and how I was neglecting her as I dealt with more pressing crises.

That fall was also the time my tenure decision was to be made, and I had the pressure of constant class visits to cope with, as well as a seriously depressed husband and an autistic child who was becoming more and more uncontrollable. The tenure decision was negative. All that fall I could never relax, not for one moment. As soon as one crisis had been dealt with, another would spring up in its place. The day I learned I had been refused tenure, Kate found me in the kitchen in tears. I explained that I had lost my job and that this made me feel very sad. Full of sympathy and concern, she patted my arm, then gave me a hug. Then she went away, satisfied that I had been comforted. When she found me the next day, again in tears, she approached hesitantly. "Did you lose your job again?" she asked.

This was a terrible, terrible year, but by then I knew I could cope, now that I was no longer pouring sherry on my sorrows. I also began to think Jim and I would make it through together. When he came home from the hospital, we both felt chastened, frightened of our power to harm each other, willing to try again to resolve our differences, to try to pull together. I felt very protective of him, and I think he did of me.

I had a dream that my whole life was breaking up, like paving stones beneath me. First one layer of stone, then the next, then the one beneath that, crumbled and fell apart. I had an autistic son, a daughter with cerebral palsy, I was an alcoholic, and my husband had just had a manic breakdown. There was nothing now that could support me anymore; the very earth was crumbling beneath my feet. Finally, in my dream, all the paving stones cracked apart, and beneath me there was nothing but a great open space of air.

I was about to start a sickening free-fall through empty air, a little like Dante falling and falling through the Inferno, when suddenly large, strong, callused hands appeared beneath my fall. I was caught and held. And then again like Dante, I found myself coming out the other side. The bottom was now the top, and the open air was a place of safety, not of danger. I had taken the free-fall into sanity.

After that, I learned I could lean against the knife's edge during those necessary, unavoidable moments when pain is inevitable. And I knew that I could feel the pain without being destroyed.

*

One evening my father called to say a hurricane was headed for his home on one of the sea islands off the coast of South Carolina. He told me that he had decided to stay and ride it out. "They think it will veer north of here," he said over a crackling phone, a bad connection that made his voice fade and return, fade and return. "And anyway, I don't feel like getting in the car and driving inland to find a motel."

He paused. The phone crackled again, and when he started to speak, it seemed that his voice was swallowed up, lost in a great space very far from me. I wondered if his place would be flooded, if phone lines would soon be down. Daddy was seventy-nine and lived alone. But he was also quite capable of making a rational decision.

"The wind and the rain have started," he told me, a lilt of pleasure in his voice. "I think I should stay put. Just thought I'd let you know."

So he was going to settle in and enjoy the hurricane. I told him I wished I could join him, but then I wondered to myself: will I ever see him again? The phone line sounded as if it were already awash in wind and rain: crackling, snapping, ghostly voices sometimes crossing from another line onto ours.

"Daddy?" I began tentatively.

"Yes. I'm here."

"Daddy, there's something I'd like to tell you."

I paused, then took a deep breath. "There's something I'd like you to know. I just went through treatment for alcoholism. In a hospital. In the Twin Cities." I paused again, as the wind seemed to sweep across the lines. "And Daddy?"

"Yes? I'm here."

"I feel just fine. I'm glad I did it."

There was a pause, then slowly my father spoke. "I'm glad to hear it. You know, I've been worried about you. I think that's wonderful."

The phone crackled again, and I thought of the hurricane headed for the island, the outrider winds already sweeping across the beaches and the marshes, the palmetto trees and the forests of live oak. But now, somehow, I felt safer, almost thought my father was safer.

"Jane?"

"Yes. I'm still here."

"Bless you. You did just the right thing. And I'm glad you told me."

CHAPTER 20

Heights and Depths

I T WASN'T EASY. None of this was easy, but nothing was ever so desperate again. After this, Jim and I went to see Malcolm every week, and we started talking about what was bothering us. But even in therapy Jim and I were both out to win. Two first children still, we both had to be right, especially about what was truth and what was reality, and about who was coping best, who was acting most responsibly, and who was most put upon. Especially who was most put upon.

Jim started to talk about how they had changed the rules on him. When he was a child, he had to obey his elders. He had to be absolutely quiet whenever his grandfather, the old autocrat who ruled over the household in the west of Ireland, turned on the radio to listen to a scratchy BBC with news from the European front or the Asian theater. And the child Jim always *was* quiet and respectful during the years he lived with his grandfather and the later years at school with the priests. He didn't interrupt adult pursuits. But now that Jim was an adult, children had all the power, especially American children. "I thought it was going to be my turn," Jim said, "when I grew up. But it's not."

Jim knew he had no sympathy from me. I thought it was *my* life that was on hold. I was the one who mostly dealt with Paul's tantrums, who struggled to get time with Kate alone, who talked with Paul's teachers, and now Kate's nursery school teachers also. My old litany. My old song. I was the one who had been abandoned.

Paul started carrying a stepladder with him all over the house. He set it up, usually in the room where Jim was trying to work, climbed until he touched the ceiling, and asked, "Am I tall?" Over and over again, "Am I tall? Am I the tallest person in the world?"

"I am held hostage in my own house," Jim told Malcolm. "In my own house, I am under siege."

Off the ladder, Paul continued his obsession with heights, but he had more creative ways of expressing this interest. He spread scrap computer paper from the dining room floor into the living room. Then, at the bottom of the paper, he drew pictures of the world's tall buildings — the Empire State Building, the World Trade Center, the Sears Tower, the IDS building in Minneapolis — and labeled them all by height. Above the buildings, he drew Mount Everest, Annapurna, and other mountains, marking their heights. Then, above the mountains, he drew various clouds — cirrus, cumulus, cumulonimbus, stratocumulus — then the highest jet flights, the highest balloon flights, and above everything, the stratosphere, stratospause, troposphere, tropospause.

At other times, Paul simply threw tantrums, or engaged in private rituals. "One, one, one." He marched through the house, repeating this single word over and over to himself. Swinging through the kitchen one day, he grazed the doorjamb with his shoulder. Stopping dead in his tracks, he turned to hit the door with his fist, then to kick it with his foot. "That door is always hitting me." He glared at the door, ran into the living room, then back into the kitchen to kick the door again. A few paint chips fell to the floor. "Everything is always hitting me," he shouted.

"Stop it, Paul! Stop it!" Jim ran out of his study and grabbed Paul by the elbow. He pulled him into the study and slammed the door behind him.

Through the closed door of the study I could hear Paul starting to howl and Jim continuing to shout. I turned away and walked into the playroom and shut that door behind me. I wasn't going to watch this. Let them settle it between them.

And there was Kate in the playroom. "I'm going to run away," she told me. She was packing her little plastic doll's suitcase with her pink pig and her gray stegosaurus, with two cookies, a box of crayons, and a peach.

"Good idea," I said. "I wish I could join you."

Kate stared at me for a moment, looking uncertain. Then she grabbed her suitcase and marched to the back door. I followed at a discreet distance, watching out the window as she walked past the garage and the driveway, and out to the lawn next to the church. She sat down, then flopped onto her stomach, watching the house through the tall grass.

I left her alone for about ten minutes, then I went outside. Kate was feeding some cookie crumbs to Steggy. She had tears on her face.

"Sit down. Have long talk." Kate said, patting the ground next to her, just as she had done when Jim was in the hospital.

I sat down beside Kate and drew her to me. "Do you understand why Paul is so upset so often?" I began.

She shook her head, watching me with solemn eyes.

"Well," I drew a deep breath. "It's because he has so much trouble understanding feelings. You know, some children have trouble learning to read?"

She nodded. Maybe she didn't know this yet, but it seemed to make sense to her.

"And some children have trouble learning how to ride a bike, or a tricycle?"

She nodded again.

"Well, some children have trouble learning about feelings. And Paul is one of them."

Kate looked down at her stegosaurus. "Steggy doesn't have trouble learning about feelings." She smiled up at me. "I tell him about my feelings every day. And he always understands."

I smiled down at Kate. "I know he does. He's a wise one, is Steggy."

We saw a film about an autistic boy and his miraculous recovery. *Son Rise*, the filmed version of Barry Kaufman's book about his son, was shown on television one night. In the film, this family formed a plan for "recovering" their two-year-old lost child, for enticing him out of his totally self-enclosed and repetitive play with spinning plates. First they decided to join Raun in his obsessions with spinning objects, just to sit with him and rock with him, for hours if need be. They wanted to show him that they loved and accepted him, whoever he was, whatever he chose to do.

Then Raun's parents decided to strip down their bathroom. They wanted a small, enclosed room that offered few distractions so they could work with their child. The family developed a schedule in which they would sit with Raun in the bathroom for twelve hours of the day and teach him. Taking his work material and music to the bathroom each day, they set out to teach him to distinguish different sizes, shapes, and colors. They played with crayons, Play-Doh, chalk, and building blocks. Music exercises were used to identify body parts and to teach Raun to move his body to the tempo. Kaufman and his wife used books and pictures, everything you would find in a nursery school, or in a well-equipped, middle-class household. They did everything you do with children, but there was a difference.

This intensive, concentrated play went on all day. Locked in a bathroom together, mother and child worked and worked and worked together. I didn't see her answering the phone, or cooking, or talking to her older children. True, mother and child took short breaks to the park and for meals, but mostly they worked together day after day in the stripped-down bathroom on the cold tile floor.

Raun's mother had already given up her work as a sculptor, and then the father quit his own work to help. The two older sisters faded into the background. The family hired helpers, but everybody worked with that child for hours each day, intensively, with total concentration and dedication.

In the film, it seemed that nothing else existed in the lives of these parents — work, friends, vacations, their older children. Everything was focused on Raun and the massive intervention needed to bring him out of his autism. The movie argued that this ultimate sacrifice was necessary, that such children could not be saved except by total concentration on teaching. The end of the film showed a normal little boy of about nine. Raun had recovered completely, helped by parents who were willing to forsake the world at least for a time, by parents who cared enough to make every sacrifice for their child's health and well-being.

The next day, Jim and I had our regular appointment with Malcolm. He was concerned about us. He too had watched *Son Rise,* and as our therapist he was afraid that we would be vulnerable to the extremism of the message. He asked us, with real concern in his eyes, what we thought about the film. Jim dismissed it easily enough; it didn't seem real to him, was just a Hollywood fairy tale. I also told Malcolm that I thought it was excessive, yet privately, at the back of my mind, I worried just a little bit. Maybe I should have done more for Paul when he was little. I knew I was very vulnerable to feelings of guilt, but knowing that I was didn't always lessen the temptation to blame myself.

CHAPTER 21

One Friend

THE SUMMER when Paul was almost seven, the phone rang. "Is Paul there? This is Allen."

I pictured the little blond boy in Paul's class, with the engaging, shy smile. Allen said he was at home all alone. His dad was working and his sister was at a friend's house: could he come over and play with Paul?

I scribbled down his address, and Paul and I went to pick him up. Allen lived in a mobile home on the edge of town. He was waiting outside and ran to the car as soon as he saw Paul. Paul scooted over on the seat to let Allen in.

"You want to come to my house?" Paul asked him. He sounded disbelieving. "You want to play with the hose? You want to build a dam?"

Allen grinned and nodded.

The two of them dragged down Paul's plastic pipe collection from his room, and pulled out the old rusted pipes he and a babysitter had found at building sites and left littering our back yard. They started to set up an elaborate network of pipes, with junctions and shunts, spigots and fountains. Then they ran the hose into one end of the pipes and arranged a spigot so they could shunt the water in different directions, through different valves. They seemed so happy playing that I soon left them alone and went back into the house.

Later I went out the front door to check on them. There on the sloping sidewalk was a dam built of rocks and sand from the sandbox. Water from the hose had backed up behind it and was beginning to break through the dam, spilling sand into the lawn. The front steps down to the street were covered with rocks and mud.

Time to stop them. I got Paul to turn off the water, and we took

Allen home, promising to pick him up the next day. They had made an unbelievable mess, but at least Paul seemed to have found a friend.

During the next few months, Allen and Paul learned to go alone to junk yards and building sites to collect old pipes that had been taken out of buildings. They dragged them home and set them up in the back yard, along with the pipes Paul already had. They developed more and more complicated shunting systems with valves and spigots and fountains. Soon the whole back yard was covered with pipes. Jim grumbled, but paid the water bill.

The children at the day care center, Kate among them, often watched Paul and Allen through the gate in the hedge. They longed to come over and help with the waterworks. One day Paul was crying and hitting himself because he couldn't make something work. Kate was watching with two or three other children.

"What's the matter with your brother?" one asked.

"He's all right," Kate explained. "It's just that he has trouble understanding about feelings."

And then Kate came through the gate and hugged Paul. A teacher noticed she was gone and called to her: "Kate, are you at the day care center or at home?"

Kate stopped and looked guilty. "I'm at the day care center," she said, and returned through the gate.

When it was too cold to play with water, Allen and Paul looked for other things to do. I looked out the window one November day when the boys were in second or third grade and saw them riding their bikes up the driveway. They were carrying a long pole and something else that I couldn't quite make out. In a moment they came in the kitchen door and plunked an odd object down on the table. They stood there grinning at me.

"What? What in the world is that?" The object was round and gray-brown, with a woven texture and a few twigs sticking out from it. Suddenly I realized what it was. "A hornets' nest! That's a hornets' nest."

"Yup." They grinned proudly at me. "Don't worry, the hornets are dead."

They ran out of the kitchen, carrying the nest. "Now we have all of them, every single one," I heard them say as they ran up the stairs.

I followed them into Paul's room, and there, laid out across his bed were seven hornets' nests.

"Good grief! Where did you get all these?"

"Paul found them. He's been checking all over town, and he found them all."

"What are you going to do with them?"

"I'm collecting them."

Of course. What else. Paul, with his acute autistic's eye, had spotted every hornets' nest in town and had been just waiting until it got cold enough to collect them.

The two boys became like brothers, frequently fighting, but also inseparable. Allen, who was a year older than Paul, usually took the lead, with Paul two or three steps behind. He taught him how to go downtown without worrying about getting lost, how to talk to store clerks and use money. Paul, for his part, taught Allen all about maps, clocks, calendars, tape measures, scales, and speedometers. When the two boys worked together, this preoccupation with measurement became more than an autistic obsession. It became a way of exploring the world together, a way of interacting, taking turns, learning to respect the wishes of another person.

Paul clearly needed Allen, but Allen needed Paul just as much. Left alone much of the time because his father, his custodial parent after his parents' divorce, had to work long hours, Allen needed a home. For years I had tried to invite children over to play with Paul, or the two of us had gone together to playgrounds, where once or twice we found lonely children who were delighted to find an adult willing to play with them on the climbing equipment. But mostly these children drifted away, went home to their mothers, didn't want the kind of intense friendship Paul needed.

Allen was different. He began to stay for dinner most days. Then he began to spend the night at our house, then two or three nights at a time. Sometimes Paul stayed with him at his house, but more and more Allen lived with us. Sometimes friends brought over clothing their own children had grown out of for "our two boys." At times Allen forgot and called me Mom, and he often talked about "our house," "our garage." Once we took him on a family vacation back east. Everyone loved him, and we loved having him with us.

Even as a young child, Allen was a hard worker. He and his sister took care of their house almost exclusively, and when Allen was at our house he willingly took on jobs. I was delighted. Allen could concentrate in a way Paul could not, but when they were together, Paul learned to do some work for me — vacuuming, painting the fence, odd jobs that were always accumulating.

Allen needed to work for his self-respect. I think he was also trying to pay us back for our kindness. But also he had a number of ways in which he could demonstrate his superiority to Paul: he could work harder, he was more focused, he was more patient. He began to enjoy Paul's tantrums, even sometimes to tease Paul until he lost his temper. At such times, Allen was clearly "superior," clearly had the upper hand.

I would try to intervene, to treat them as equals and get them to work out their differences in a way that was fair to both. But Allen always knew, and felt keenly, that really when it came right down to it, I was Paul's mom, not his. There was a built-in imbalance here. Mostly when conflicts arose, Allen walked away from them, went home, wouldn't talk to Paul. Paul always wanted to resolve differences, hated being ignored, hated it even more when Allen was in control and he was not.

They had unhealthy ways of interacting, but I always knew that in this little boy we had found a gift of inestimable value. I could never have taught Paul as Allen did, nor could his teachers, or school psychologists, or therapists. Only a child can teach a child some things.

CHAPTER 22

Collecting

W ITH A FRIEND by his side, Paul's life started to improve; never-theless, he still had a long struggle ahead of him. His ways of playing remained different from that of other children, and sometimes this difference got him into big trouble. Like other autistic children, Paul was a collector. As he got older, his collections simply became more sophisticated. He discovered that *TV Guide* gave a complete record of what went on (on television at least) for twenty-four hours of the day. He started to collect the *TV Guides* I sometimes bought at the grocery store, then he asked us to take out a subscription. But there were still many gaps in his collection.

One day Allen and Paul came into the house dragging a large black plastic garbage bag.

"What have you got there?"

"*TV Guides*. Hundreds and hundreds of *TV Guides!*"

"Where did you find them?"

"Behind a dorm. We went through all the trash cans all over town."

"You did?"

"Yup." They looked very pleased with themselves. "We went to all the dorms and looked in all the dumpsters. But why would they want to throw out their *TV Guides?* They don't know how valuable they are!"

Paul and Allen bumped the bag up the steps to Paul's room.

Later that evening, I went up to check on them. They had stacks of *TV Guide* all over the room, and they were sorting them by month.

"There's a whole year here. Just think, a whole year!" Allen said.

"And now I can find out what was happening every moment, every single moment of last year!" Paul was so excited he could hardly hold still.

"And look," Allen said. "Now Paul can figure out the difference between crime drama, and mystery, and thriller."

"And there's comedy, and news, and game, and report, and documentary," Paul read out from one of the guides.

Paul and Allen started to collect pennies. When they had a few hundred, they went to the town library across the street to check out books on valuable coins. Sometimes I would find them poring over coins and books about coins on the floor of Paul's room. They never found any that looked valuable, so they decided to go downtown to the bank to exchange the pennies for nickels, then for dimes, then quarters, and fifty-cent pieces. Each time they returned from the bank they spread all the coins out on the floor and compared them with pictures in the valuable coin books. When they still failed to find anything of value, they traded the coins for bills.

Paul was getting an allowance by this time. He was supposed to use it to buy his own treats, but he never wanted to spend a penny. He saved everything and wanted us to spend our money on his treats. Understandably, the illogic of this infuriated Jim.

After a while, Paul reached one hundred dollars. He went to the bank to get a hundred-dollar bill. A few days after that I saw Paul and Allen trotting up the hill from the bank at Bridge Square, carrying a plastic bucket between them. They came into the house and set the bucket down. It was full of pennies. They had traded back to coins again.

I knew some kind woman was willing to honor their transactions. She did this for a long, long time. Often she would search for the shiniest pennies, the newest dollars.

Finally, one day when Paul staggered into the bank with two buckets containing one hundred fifty dollars in pennies and asked to change them into bills, she told him that the penny counter was broken down, and he wouldn't be able to trade his money anymore. And so Paul ended his banking transactions.

I never went down to the bank to talk to the sweet woman who was willing for so long to help Paul with his money. I simply felt grateful that it wasn't our bank and I didn't have to face anyone when I went in to cash a check. But years later I did want to thank her. I told a friend about this wonderful woman and she said, "Oh, I know who it must have been. That was Rebecca, a farmwoman who raised eight kids. It must have been Rebecca, it sounds just like her." My friend paused, then added, "She died three years ago."

Jim and I started to go to parents' group meetings at the Program for Autistic and Other Exceptional Children in the Twin Cities. We entered our first meeting nervously. Toys, slides, and climbing equipment had been pushed to the sides of the room, and small wooden chairs, supplemented with a few big ones, were drawn into a circle in the center. Jim and I didn't know what to expect, and we didn't know if we would be able to talk openly. We still had diametrically opposed instincts when it came to Paul, at least much of the time. Also, we didn't know anyone there; we knew only that they were the parents of children who were at different ages and stages of development and had different degrees of handicap.

We got coffee and found seats. Sheila Merzer explained that she and Lyle Chastain would try to arrange for parents' group meetings about once a month, depending on weather conditions, and that we could contribute any sum we felt we could afford to help to pay for renting the room. She said that the main purpose of these meetings was to help parents share the resources and expertise we had already developed (we were all surprised to hear she thought we had any expertise at all) and to support each other. Then introductions began with a small, pretty woman sitting next to Sheila.

"Hello, I'm Beryl and this is my husband, Tom. Our son is three and has just been diagnosed. Autism. And we don't know *what* to expect." Beryl's large gray eyes looked bewildered. Tom, a small man with a mustache, stared at the floor.

After a pause, the next man introduced himself. "I'm Larry. My son is fourteen, and he has just been placed in a group home. We couldn't cope anymore." Larry's voice caught on the last words. He pushed a small gum wrapper back and forth across the floor with the toe of his boot. Then, swallowing hard, he looked up resolutely. "Terry was banging his head against the wall until it was bloody. And he was hurting his little sister."

Larry was wearing a bright red polo sweater, a brave sweater, and big, lace-up boots. A tall man, folded awkwardly in his too small chair, he looked like a gentle giant, a Gulliver among the Lilliputians, snared in some net he couldn't begin to understand. He looked around at us. "We had to do it," he started to explain, but we all murmured our understanding. If anyone on earth could understand why Larry had to do it, we did.

After a pause, the next woman spoke. "I'm Kathianne. My daughter is three and she's . . ." Kathianne glanced at Larry. "She's self-abusive also. I think she'll have permanent scars on her lower arms. From biting."

We went around the room. "Hi, my name is Molly. I'm the grandmother of twin autistic boys." Molly sat up straight, her white hair a soft halo around her face. She was wearing a white cable-knit sweater embroidered with blue forget-me-nots on the front.

The woman next to her smiled. "I'm Annilee, and I'm the mother of the boys. They are seven years old and have just started in a special program at Pine Grove. At the moment I'm hopeful. And" — she looked at her mother and reached over to pat her knee — "I couldn't survive without *her*."

The woman next to her shifted uneasily in her chair. "I'm Susan, and my son Kevin is eight. And my mother is no help whatsoever. She thinks . . . she actually thinks we haven't prayed over Kevin enough. She thinks it's our sins and we are responsible . . ." Susan broke off and sucked the air in through her teeth. She glared around the room, at nobody in particular, at everybody, at everything. "*Now* she thinks we should have Kevin exorcised. To drive the devils out." She hunched her shoulders and opened her hands, palms out. "I guess. Who knows?"

Susan laughed a hard, brittle laugh, like glass breaking against stone. She looked around at us, almost challenging. She must have known she was taking a risk in telling us such a shocking story. We stared at her, and away from her. Then suddenly our shock turned into laughter. Susan relaxed and giggled, "Crazy, isn't it?"

The next woman was Jan, and her son, she told us, was five. "I can't cope," she said, twisting the rings around her fingers. She was wearing lots of rings, silver and turquoise, one on every finger of her left hand. "I have a six-year-old hyperactive boy, and Nathaniel, the autistic one, and now I have a new baby girl, three months old."

Jan paused, then gathered her strength to go on. "Jessica is all right. She's the only one in the whole damn family who *is* all right. My husband just left me," she finished in a monotone.

We waited, watching Jan, looking at the floor, not wanting to intrude on this sorrow. Jan went on, "Before I got married — hah! — I used to be a social worker. I used to *help* clients like me. Now I'm one of them. I'm one of the people I used to help."

Jim and I were next. We were quiet, not knowing what to say in the midst of all this grief. For a moment, I wondered why we were here. Our lives weren't nearly as hard as these. We hadn't split up, Paul wasn't self-abusive, he didn't bite his arms, he didn't hurt his little sister, Jim's mother was anything but a crazy religious fanatic.

I went first. "I'm Jane, and this is Jim. Our son, Paul, is eight and he has obsessions, many obsessions. He wants to know what *exact* temperature it is every fifteen minutes. He collects light bulbs, and *TV Guides,* and hornets' nests. Also pinecones and rocks."

"And maps, and clocks, and humidifiers, and coins, and power lines," Jim added and paused for breath. He looked at me. "Is there anything else?"

"He used to collect fire hydrants."

We both stopped and laughed. This wasn't so bad, when you considered head banging and arm biting, runaway husbands and exorcising grandmothers. The other parents started laughing, too, pressing us for details. Then others began sharing stories of their children's obsessions. Nathaniel collected fans, ceiling fans in particular. He would go into restaurants that had ceiling fans, but not ones that didn't. And Kevin collected vacuum cleaners.

"Vacuum cleaners?" Even Jim and I were stunned by this one. "He saves vacuum cleaners?"

Susan explained. "It all began two years ago when our old vacuum cleaner broke down and we had to get a new one. Naturally, this was not right. The new vacuum cleaner was all wrong. So Kevin saved the old one, and then he pestered us to get him a vacuum cleaner for his birthday."

We stared at Susan. "You got him a vacuum cleaner for his birthday?"

"Yup. A Hoover. He had an Electrolux already. And now he has two with a Sears brand name." Susan giggled. "Maybe that's why my mother-in-law wants him exorcised."

"It must cost a lot."

"Not really, I go to junk stores. I *haunt* junk stores."

"Maybe *you* ought to be exorcised!" I laughed. I felt so relieved to hear this story. "Actually, I used to haunt junk stores, too," I told her. "For telephones and answering machines. Then humidifiers."

I turned to Jim. "See, I wasn't crazy to go around to those stores, or to take Paul to see all those power lines. At least no crazier than Susan."

Everyone laughed again. Even Larry seemed more relaxed and happy, but I felt a pang of regret that we hadn't drawn him out more, or given him a chance to talk about his son.

Jim and I left the meeting that evening feeling better than we had felt for months.

By the following spring, Paul had collected 1,562 miles on the odometer of his bike. But he still hadn't reached the top speed shown on the speedometer. We told him not to try, explaining that the numbers, like the top numbers on a car speedometer, were never meant to be reached. They were just there as a possibility. We didn't drive the car at 120 miles per hour; he shouldn't try to ride his bike at 45 miles per hour. But this made no sense at all to Paul. If the numbers were there on the speedometer, that meant someone had one time gone that fast. And if someone else had once gone that fast, that meant he should be able to also.

I remember it was just after a rainstorm. We had returned home from a trip in the car, and I didn't realize Paul wasn't in the house with us. We had been home only a few minutes when the phone rang. I knew as I picked up the receiver that it was the call I had been expecting and dreading. A teenage boy was on the line. His voice was very shaky. Carefully he explained that I was not to worry, but that he was calling from the hospital emergency room where he had just taken Paul.

Jim and I rushed for the car, Kate running after us. In the hospital parking lot, as we got out of the car, we could already hear the crying coming through the double doors of the emergency room. Inside, we found Paul on an examining table, the whole right side of his face pulped and bloody. A doctor was feeling around in his mouth, searching in all that blood for missing teeth.

We turned to Kate before she walked into the room and told her to sit on a bench outside the room. We didn't want to frighten her.

The doctor looked up as we came in. "I think he's all right, but I want to find out how many teeth he lost. Three, I think."

I put my hand on Paul's arm. "We're here, lovey. It's all right now." I struggled to keep my voice strong, to smile down at Paul. But he looked terrible. The whole side of his face was smeared with blood. An open gash appeared just above his right eyebrow, and another one cut across his lip, and all the way down to his chin. His mouth was full of blood, and even the hair on the right side of his head was matted with drying blood.

The doctor pulled back Paul's upper lip. "See here? His front tooth is gone, and the lateral incisor, and one other. I think they are all gone."

The doctor turned to a nurse standing by the examining table.

"Would you get me some more gauze? And a butterfly bandage."

Then he turned back to Paul. "What did you say your address was, Paul?"

"I told you! It's 309 Washington Street."

"And what day is this?"

"I told you that too. It's Friday, April 22, 1980. Don't you know what day it is?"

The doctor turned to smile at us. "I keep asking him these questions because I want to make sure he doesn't have a serious head injury. I want you to check him every hour tonight. Shine a flashlight into his eyes to make sure his pupils aren't dilated."

I nodded.

"Why does he keep asking me these questions?" Paul was crying more quietly now. He tried to wipe the tears from his bloody cheek with the sleeve of his orange sweater. "Why do you keep asking me these questions?"

"Because we want to make sure you didn't hit your head too hard."

"I don't understand," Paul looked over at Jim. "Can I have a mirror? I can't see what they're doing to me."

The doctor shook his head slightly. "I don't think —"

But I already had my compact out of my purse and was opening it. "I think he'll do better if he can see what's going on." I handed the mirror to Paul.

He held it up and moved it from side to side. He stopped crying and stared, fascinated.

"See, it's not so bad," I said to him. My voice trembled. Paul's face looked terrible. Anybody could see it looked awful. He continued to stare into the mirror, turning his head from side to side. He opened his mouth wide.

"That's very interesting," he said suddenly.

We all burst out laughing. "*I* think it's awful. Bloody awful," said Jim, then he jumped up. "Kate. Poor little Kate has been sitting out there all by herself. Not knowing what's going on."

He opened the door, and there was Kate sitting in the middle of the bench, very small, very alone, her feet dangling above the floor, tears streaking her face, crying quietly to herself, so as not to make any noise.

Seeing her outside the door, Paul called, "Kate, come here, Kate. Look at this, Kate." The big brother, scaring the little sister.

"Look at this, Kate."

She approached slowly, then I picked her up in my arms.

"You see, sweetheart, he's going to be all right. The doctor is just going to put some bandages on his face to make it get better."

Paul stayed home from school for the next three days. His face puffed up so much he could only drink through a straw. I made him milk shakes of milk and ice cream, strawberries and Instant Breakfast. Paul was oddly calm that week, no longer pushing, battering at the world, asking questions insistently every moment. He was content to lie on the couch reading or listening to library tapes of *Curious George,* the little monkey who climbed too high, rode too fast, opened too many doors, explored too many new places, and got into so much trouble.

This episode did not bring an end to my magical thinking, however. I thought his guardian angel had been on duty but had let this accident happen for a reason. In one sense, his fall had simply been a reality check, a way of letting us know that bad could happen and we could still survive. But more importantly, it was the mishap that would prevent disaster. We had given up to the gods of destruction a little bit so that much more would not later be taken away. This was the sacrifice that would appease the gods, the broken teeth that would stave off broken bones, concussion, skull fracture, even death. In an odd way, it made me feel more confident, more secure.

But seeing the scars on his healing face, I wept for the end of his perfect looks, surprising even myself, who had so long before recognized that his mind, if not his body, was scathed, had always been scathed. In my injured mother's vanity, I had long been proud of his physical beauty, and now his one remaining perfection had been taken away.

CHAPTER 23

Nine Hundred Fifty-Six Feet above Sea Level

H OW HIGH am I above sea level?" Paul ran to meet me as I came home from my office. He had computer paper spread out from the kitchen to the living room. *The Penguin Book of the Natural World* was open on the floor, and Magic Markers were scattered all over. I could tell without looking at it that once again he had drawn all the highest buildings and mountains of the world.

"Oh, about eight or nine hundred feet, I would guess. Something like that."

"No, I mean, *exactly* how high above sea level. Right now!" Paul asked impatiently, jumping up and down. He was wearing the orange sweater he wore every single day and refused to exchange for any other. Blue ink marked his hands and was smeared across his left cheek.

"You mean right here?"

"Right here in the kitchen, in our house." Paul took me by the hand and led me to the bottom of the computer paper. "Right here. There's Paul and Kate."

At the bottom of the page there were two small figures, hands held up, outstretched toward the sky. They were standing beside a gray house with black shutters and a red brick chimney: our house.

Kate was drawing a row of flowers and a cat next to the house. "This is Vega," she said, pointing to a black cat among the flowers.

Jan came out of living room. "Paul has been pestering me all afternoon to tell him how high above sea level he is."

Suddenly I had an idea. "Let's go to City Hall and get copies of the maps for our area. We have an hour or so before they close." I paid Jan, and the children and I walked the two blocks to City Hall.

The clerk at City Hall wasn't happy to see us that day. She had a

bad cold, and we were obviously way up on her list of nuisance fac-
tors. She sat at her gray metal desk talking to a friend on the phone.
"Terrible," she was saying as she blew her nose. "The worst cold I've
had in years. Can't wait to get home and take a hot bath."

We stood at the front counter and waited for her to get off the
phone. Finally, she put her hand over the receiver and gestured toward
the clock on the wall. "We're just about to close," she said.

"This won't take long," I said.

The woman sneezed violently. "Let me call you back, Mavis. We
have to decide what to do about mother right away. I mean *right away*.
What's that? Oh, well . . . I think she'll just have to accept it."

Reluctantly, she hung up the phone and came over to the counter.
"What can I do for you?"

"We would like to get topographical maps for our area."

"You mean plat sheets?"

"I guess so. We need to find out how high above sea level we are."

"Sea level! You're a long way away from the sea."

"I know that. But we need to know how high we are. What the
height of Northfield is."

Paul pulled on my sleeve. "Our house," he said, "how high above
sea level our house is."

Kate repeated. "Yes. Our house."

The woman stared at us. "I'll have to Xerox them."

"That's fine. I'll be happy to pay."

"It'll take a few minutes."

"That's all right. We can wait."

"And we are almost closing."

"If you wouldn't mind?"

Finally, it was clear to the clerk that we weren't going away. She got
some rolled up sheets of paper and spread them out on the top of the
copier. She copied several, then brought them over to us. "Three-fifty.
That'll be three-fifty."

"Thanks so much! I really appreciate this."

We brought them all home, big maps with fine detail, and spread
them out on the living room floor. "The fire hydrants are the bench
marks, Paul. Do you know what that is?"

I didn't know too well myself, but between us, we figured out that
the hydrant closest to us was marked 923 feet above sea level. That
meant that the base of our house was just a little higher than that. How
much higher, Paul would have to calculate by measuring the retaining
wall in front of the lawn.

The next day when I came home, there was Paul on a ladder against the back of the house. The weather was starting to get cold, and a damp wind was blowing from the west. He was wearing his hat with the bobble at the back, and he had one end of a tape measure in his hand. Allen was standing at the bottom of the ladder, holding the other end of the tape, and shivering slightly. He was wearing a thin coat and his cheeks looked chapped with the cold. Kate was standing next to Allen, holding a basket full of plastic numbers. Marching up the side of the house at one-foot intervals were plastic numbers held up by sticking tape: 952, 953, 954.

I watched them for a while, then went in to cook dinner. Later as I was standing at the stove, they ran into the kitchen. Their cheeks were flushed with excitement.

"My bed is nine hundred fifty-six feet above sea level."

"Yeah, his bed is exactly nine hundred fifty-six feet above sea level."

"That's right. *Exactly* nine hundred fifty-six feet above sea level."

"But how high is mine?" Kate wanted to know.

"Yours is just the same."

"That's good." Kate sounded relieved. Paul didn't go to sleep at night at a higher altitude than she did.

Later that week, Paul took a ruler, a felt marker, and some masking tape with him to the college campus. He climbed the tallest evergreen trees there and marked their heights. I've often wondered if some of those marks are still there on the trunks of the trees, if they survived rainstorms and freezing winter winds, and if some future children at the top of the fir tree to the north of the music building might someday see exactly how high above sea level they are.

Mapmaking, we all know, was one of the earliest human endeavors. Maps bring order to the world; they help us to visualize a landscape and to locate ourselves, to place ourselves within the physical world in relation to other things. And for Paul, throughout his childhood, mapmaking was a primary means for comprehending the world. Often he simply obsessed over heights and depths, as he had done earlier over temperatures and weights, but this particular time, when he wanted to map the town in relation to his own room, I thought I could turn an autistic obsession into an opportunity for learning. And so I joined with him enthusiastically in going to City Hall for the maps.

By this time, I had learned to watch Paul for new interests and to catch him at those precious moments when the interest was still an opportunity for learning, before it had solidified into routine, into a repetitive ritual. I think I always sensed that the obsessions were where his energy was and where I would find his motivation for learning. And it always made more sense to me to try to use these special interests for expanding his world, for helping him to learn, than to oppose him and try to block his autistic fascinations.

Maps had a further significance for Paul's learning. They showed one thing in relation to another, not as separate, discrete, set apart. And this sense of relation, of relationship, was just what he needed most to learn. His troubles learning social relations, his difficulty in learning to generalize from one context to another, his trouble with sequential thinking, might all be addressed through his mapmaking — but I didn't quite know how to do this.

We went to Greenwich, near London, several times when Paul was growing up. We thought the Royal Observatory there would fascinate him, but really it interested Jim and me far more, in itself and also as a metaphor for some of Paul's activities. For there, on the top of that hill just outside London, is the designated center of the world, zero degree longitude, the prime meridian. It is the point from which the whole world was surveyed and laid out by nineteenth-century mapmakers, all in relation to London. It is also the place from which time is marked; Greenwich mean time is the reference point for standard time all over the world.

Visiting Greenwich one summer with the children, Jim and I talked about how Paul, mapping his world from the zero meridian of his bedroom, was no stranger than the nineteenth-century cartographers and the earlier navigators who went before them. And then that day I decided to take a picture of Paul and Kate and Jim on that one spot, that place on the path in front of the observatory where time and place "begin" for the whole world.

The picture shows a place of some significance, but also a lot of sadness, for Paul and Jim had been fighting all that day, every step of the way up the steep hill from the boat landing at the pier. I'm not sure now why they were fighting. I think Paul was very hungry and stressed, but then that was always my explanation for his bad behavior. Jim, I'm sure, would remember something else: Paul was obsessing over his watch, perhaps. Maybe it was fourteen seconds off compared to the time at Greenwich, and Jim, as usual, wanted to stop him from obsessing. Or maybe Paul was, for unknown reasons, simply out of control, miserably locked in conflict with Jim as he so often was. Anyway, it was one of those awful, awful days, like so many over the years when we traveled, dragging the children with us, determined to see the world in spite of the complications of an autistic child in tow.

When I took that picture of Jim and the children standing on the prime meridian of the world, Jim looked furious, and Paul had a twisted half smile on his face, an apologetic attempt at attention and cheerfulness. And Kate, in a little sundress, was standing just in front of Paul. She clutched her bear and gazed anxiously off into the distance, as if she were trying not to see what was just in front of her eyes.

Later, looking at that picture and noting the scowl on Jim's face, we tried to make a feeble joke out of it, to try to redeem a moment in time which might have been wonderful but wasn't: we called the picture "Greenwich Mean Time," but we meant it in another sense.

CHAPTER 24

"Why Do I Cry Every Single Day?"

PAUL RAN into the kitchen: "Why do I cry every single day? Why do I get so frustrated? Do other children cry as much as I do? Allen says other children don't cry as much as I do. I'll keep a record and see how long it is before I cry. I'll hit myself every time I cry."

Every day Paul came home from school talking about crying. Some days he came home and told us he wasn't crying. Then in ten or twenty minutes, stumbling against a chair or spilling some milk, he started to sob. And then he would hit the side of his head with the heel of his hand.

"Am I the only kid in Northfield who is clumsy? Who bumps into things? Does this happen to most children?"

Paul stopped and glared at us. "You mean you don't love me? Am I different from other children? I am so stupid, I can't believe it!"

Once, trying to eat his afternoon snack after school, Paul stopped: "My nose clicks! Listen, my arm is clicking. Does clicking happen to other children? I hate my nose. I want to cut off my arms."

"Do most children make seven mistakes in a row? Mama, I'm a mental retard. I'm stupid and clumsy and dumb. Mama, every single minute of the day I make mistakes."

He stopped to listen to the newscaster on TV. "See, she was perfect on the news. How does she do it? No clicking of noses. She must get into *The Guinness Book of Records*. I'm not normal, Mama. I'm clumsy and dumb."

Then, just before he collapsed altogether: "Mama, children make fun of me. They say *goll*." And Paul rolled his eyes to the ceiling, imitating the children at school.

I felt helpless, close to despair. How could I help this child? Over and over again, he came home from school and burst into tears. I talked to him, tried to comfort him, called the school to ask for yet another appointment.

Finally, one day I asked to see the principal of Paul's school. Paul had been crying now every day after school for several weeks. I had questioned his teacher and Paul himself, and still had no clues about why he was so upset after school. All I knew was that he was very ashamed of his behavior around the other children and that he was determined not to cry.

"I'm not crying," he would scream at us as the tears rolled down his cheeks. "I'm not crying. I haven't cried all week. See, I'm not crying," he repeated, as we stared at him in disbelief.

The principal, Mr. Breckenridge, was a large, confident man, who stood up to shake my hand when I came in his door, then leaned back in his desk chair and asked what he could do for me. He looked distracted as he handed some letters to his secretary to be mailed. He was clearly hoping this interview wouldn't last too long.

I started to tell him about my worries about Paul, that he was crying every day, that he was obsessed with not crying. Mr. Breckenridge rolled a pencil back and forth across his desktop. Then he looked up. "Crying? Did you say he was crying? Actually, I'm very proud of Paul at school. He has learned not to cry here. Just yesterday, I had to take him out of the classroom. This time, he held back his tears very well. Especially for an eight-year-old."

"He held back his tears? What do you mean? He held back his tears . . ." My voice trailed off. I hardly followed what I was hearing.

Mr. Breckenridge saw my face and faltered. He seemed to be genuinely surprised. "You know, don't you, that his teacher has to send him to my office at least once a week to be disciplined."

"No. I didn't know that." I was too choked to say more.

"He's just been out of control for the last few weeks."

"What's been the problem?"

"Well, one day he acted up when a substitute teacher was here. She put him out in the hall by the coats to stay for most of the morning."

"She did? He can't learn much that way."

"No, of course not. But he was keeping the other children from learning. And he wouldn't obey her and stay out in the hall. He started throwing a hat at the ceiling."

"What did you do then?"

"We made him sit in the supply closet all afternoon."

"You did what?" I could hardly believe my ears. I had an image of

Paul sitting all by himself in a closet with nothing to do except obsess over his watch. No wonder his watch was so precious and he was afraid to let it out of his sight.

"He left the closet. That's when I had to spank him."

"You spanked him?"

"Yes. And he's learning to take his punishment very well. He almost never cries when I spank him now. He's a real little man."

I stared at Mr. Breckenridge. This was appalling. I couldn't imagine shutting a child in a supply closet or spanking him at school. No wonder Paul cried every day and hit himself. And then shouted "I'm not crying."

Suddenly, I felt terribly guilty and almost overwhelmed with anger at the principal. I hadn't known about any of this. And Paul seemed not to be able to tell us, in words at least. His behavior, on the other hand, had been a clear signal, and I hadn't really looked for the underlying causes of his crying at home. He was trying to tell us something and I wasn't listening. "I want this stopped immediately," I said to the principal as soon as I could catch my breath. "Don't ever hit him again."

"But I thought this was what you and your husband wanted me to do," he sputtered, confused. "How are we supposed to discipline him?"

"Not this way. Maybe we can have another conference with you and his teacher soon. But I want the spanking to stop. Right now."

I was so angry, I didn't trust myself to say more at this point. I left soon after this, tears stinging my eyes, and hurried back through the corridors, through the smell of dirty socks and chalk dust. It seemed to me to be the smell of utter, abject, bewildered misery, the misery of a little boy who was made to sit in a closet and who was spanked, then praised for not crying.

As soon as Jim came home I told him about this conversation, and he was as appalled as I was. That evening he called the principal at home and repeated that we absolutely did not want Paul spanked again. "Never. Not ever," I could hear Jim repeating on the phone. Then he paused to listen to Mr. Breckenridge, who unbelievably still seemed surprised that we didn't want him to spank Paul.

When Jim hung up the phone, he called Paul to him.

"Paul, did Mr. Breckenridge spank you yesterday?"

"Yes." Paul stared miserably at the floor, then he hit the side of his head with the heel of his hand and turned away from Jim. "I'm not crying," he said in a high, thin voice.

"Paul. Look at me. I want you to know something important."

"Yes?" Paul glanced at him, then glanced away again, his eyes flat.

"We told him never, never to spank you again."

Paul turned to stare briefly at Jim, before his eyes skittered away again. "You mean you don't like that? You mean I'm not supposed to be spanked?"

Jim looked up at me. His eyes reddened, filling with tears. "Yes, I mean he isn't ever supposed to spank you again."

I knelt down on the floor next to Paul. I wiped the tears from my own cheeks. "And Paul, it doesn't matter, it doesn't matter *at all* if you cry. You can cry as much as you want to at home."

"I can?" Paul stared at me, then he turned away. "But I'm not crying. I won't cry for a whole month. I'll keep a record. You'll see, I won't cry. I won't cry ever again at school." And Paul ran out of the room.

I turned to Jim. "What do we do now?"

"I don't know. I don't know what else we can do."

Even though I knew Paul's problems at school were far from solved, that moment was a turning point for me. For one thing, I knew that I could count on Jim to act as an advocate for Paul, that I didn't have to do it all by myself. I also knew that we stood together on some important things.

We found out shortly after this that Paul's teacher was having a great deal of trouble controlling the whole class. The principal and others admitted this to us. We were also told that because the school year was about to end, it was too late to move Paul to another classroom.

Jim and I met with Paul's teacher. We came away from that conference feeling that he was basically a kind man, but he seemed to have lost his ability to control his class months before, and now he had a very real problem with discipline. But where the rest of the children were able to time their misbehaviors, to throw spitballs and paper airplanes when his back was turned, and to escape detection that way, Paul, who was always a step or two behind the others, repeatedly got caught. Then all the frustration the teacher was feeling at the behavior of the whole class boiled over, and Paul, most unfairly, was the one who received the full brunt of his anger.

The teacher next door to Mr. Curtis's classroom had been watching, it appeared, noticing Paul and his distress. One evening, he called and said he would like to give Paul some gerbils. He explained that Paul seemed to be fascinated with the ones they had in his classroom, and there were some new babies, just weaned, that he thought he might like to have.

I agreed happily. And Paul was overjoyed. He met this teacher at the door. "You mean I can have these gerbils? You mean they are for me? Just for me?"

"Just for you." He put the cage down on a table. And there in the cedar shavings were two little twitching noses poking out. One gerbil ran into the exercise wheel and started going round and round.

Paul was entranced. We thanked this teacher warmly. I hoped, however, that the gerbils weren't a gift sealing a bad bargain, that they were more than just a cover-up for a bad situation. The state had just passed a law forbidding corporal punishment in the schools, and a friend thought we should bring a suit against the principal and the school district. But Jim and I were too exhausted to think of a lawsuit. We also thought the problem of Paul's spankings had ended, and wanted now to rebuild trust in a small school district where he would have to remain for many more years.

Shortly after this episode, Paul started a summer school program in the Twin Cities for "autistic and other exceptional children," run by Sheila Merzer and Lyle Chastain. He went to this program for three years, through the summer he turned eleven. The school was a lifesaver for Paul and for the rest of us. He developed more during those summers than he ever had in regular school. In fact we began to look forward to the summer program as a time when Paul's psyche could be put back together again, when the wounding experiences of the regular school year could be healed.

In the summer school, each child had a teacher, a college student trained by Sheila and Lyle. This teacher worked individually with the child on many different kinds of activities, depending on his or her level of skill. For the high-functioning children like Paul, the day might include climbing ropes, board games, art projects, or trips to a nearby swimming pool or library.

At the end of each morning, just before the children left to go home, they all gathered for music therapy, musical games that taught them language, social interaction, and a sense of how their bodies moved through space. Often I joined the group at this time and sat in a big circle on the floor of the gym. Some of the children sat limply in the laps of their teachers; they couldn't really support their weight sitting or standing, let alone participate in clapping. But they too seemed to enjoy the music, to enjoy having their bodies moved for them rhythmically to the sound. They seemed to like it when their teachers would take their hands and clap for them. Others became confused and ran off. They had to be brought back, but they also seemed to enjoy the musical games.

Paul was usually rather passive during the circle games and music time. His early love for song, his perfect pitch, seemed to have disappeared, and I sometimes wondered if this was inevitable, a necessary shift of interest away from the early fluke of his musical talent. But I also knew that his music teacher in his regular grade school was very antagonistic toward him. Every time we had conferences this man expressed his annoyance: Paul would not sit still, he would not follow directions, he would not pay attention. Finally, at one of the conferences, the music teacher had said to me, sighing with relief: "I'm very proud of Paul. He stands still now during chorus."

"Does he sing?" I had asked.

"Sing?" The teacher looked at me as if I had lost my mind. "Of course he doesn't sing. But he keeps quiet now."

I wanted very much for Paul to learn to love music again, and to take the risk of trying to sing. I was delighted to see him one day move into the center of the circle with a little girl. Hesitantly, shyly, they both started to rock to the song "Rock to My Lou," then they ran back to their places in the circle, relieved to be out of the limelight. But later I noticed that Paul's lips were moving when they sang "Boris the Bear." Again, slowly, hesitantly, he started to participate.

There were other group activities, and these, as well as the music, Paul desperately needed. The children, together with their teachers, had treasure hunts, made popcorn, and traced the outlines of each other's bodies on large pieces of construction paper. They played games to learn how to share, how to lose, and how to accept failure or a lack of perfection.

This was one of the hardest lessons of all for Paul and the others. Because of their disability, or maybe because of their experience of repeated failure, these children were all perfectionists. They seemed to be fiercely determined not only to be right, but to be absolutely, one-hundred-percent perfect at all times. Paul, like the other children, had many rules for his behavior and for the behavior of other people. Things had to be done a certain way; no deviation was allowed. He constantly tried to control others, and this always brought him grief. His worst fights with Jim, or with anyone else for that matter, were always about control, about who was personally out of control, who was trying to control the other.

In the summer school program, the problems of each child were identified and some form of play was devised as an intervention. In this relaxed and very supportive atmosphere the children had many successes. Their strengths were singled out for praise; almost every time they did something right, they were commended for it. But they were also taught to accept occasional failures. Funny mistakes were built into play; silliness was used to help them accept their imperfections.

I watched one day as Paul made a mistake drawing his ears onto the big construction paper tracing of his body. The ears were too big and they were set too low. Paul looked over at the drawing of the child beside him, noticed his mistake, and started to hit the side of his head with the flat of his palm. "That's stupid," he said. "Dumb!" But instead of trying to correct Paul, one of the teachers turned the ears into a game. He drew big, floppy elephant ears on his paper. Paul laughed loudly, and he drew big glasses across the nose on his own piece of paper, then put a pipe in his mouth. Soon all the children were changing their pictures, drawing in mustaches, silly hats, crazy ears.

The atmosphere of the summer program was playful, nonthreatening. I realized that it was the opposite of so many other programs for autistic children, where they are taught by behavior modification techniques and by rote. Sheila had always said these children were exceptionally good rote learners, able to learn very readily in fixed patterns. Their problems came when they tried to generalize, to transfer knowledge acquired in one context to another context. For this reason, autistic children are often said to be rigid, rule-bound, and to lack humor, spontaneity, creativity, imagination.

But here, I could see children begin to behave with some spontaneity. In a few of the more high-functioning children, I saw a wonderful sense of humor emerge, an inherent playfulness. I saw the way Paul and some of the others loved to tease their teachers, although some of Paul's teasing was really a testing of limits. He sometimes threw a paper cup or plate out of a window into the playground and had to be taught to retrieve it and to learn to put it in the trash can. As soon as his teacher learned to be firm, without being threatening, Paul stopped throwing things out of the window. Watching him do this one day, I thought of how this behavior was so much like that of all other children. I also saw how he loved exaggeration, silliness, even some pretend play — all those things autistic children are supposed to be incapable of ever learning or acquiring.

*

Kate attended a sibling program during these summers. She went with Paul to the Twin Cities every day, and she joined with other sisters and brothers in field trips and in structured play activities, often built around their feelings. I was often worried about Kate during the children's grade school years. After her earliest years, when she once or twice allowed herself to get very angry at Paul, she became very protective of her brother. In fact, both children were protective of each other, or perhaps just very afraid of expressing anger.

"Are you mad at me?" Paul asked on every occasion, even when anger was the furthest thing from our minds. This was part habit, autistic learning in a pattern he could not get out of, and it was part anxiety. But none of us ever seemed to find a way out of this pattern of anxious questioning, followed by initial reassurance, then more anxious questioning. If it involved Jim, an explosion would result. If it was me, I usually tried changing the subject, or manipulating Paul into safer waters. But for Kate, retreat seemed safest. She just faded, dissolved into the background. She had learned early on to be very quiet and "very good," as she had told me that day Paul stole the light bulbs.

Kate was a caretaker. At her alternative progressive school, started by a coalition of parents in our community, she could always be relied on for her social conscience. When a child was rejected by the other children, Kate would stand up for that child and would refuse to join in the teasing. The teachers came to depend on her as someone who would be willing to sit next to Patrick, for example, who wouldn't be afraid of "catching Patrick germs." But then the other children would sometimes leave her out of their games. Apparently, she had picked up some contamination, after all, by refusing to go along with the crowd and by being friendly with the rejected child. So Kate sometimes ended up lonely, isolated, not a part of any group, and I almost wondered sometimes if her teachers weren't tempted to use her. Any teacher, or parent for that matter, would be grateful for Kate's maturity, would learn to rely on her to be always sensitive to others. We all appreciated her conscience, but I think it sometimes was a great burden to her.

Gradually, Kate learned to be more assertive, more "selfish," but she did it mostly with me, never with Paul. She sometimes took her frustrations out on me and blamed me for the unreliability of the world, the unfairness of having a brother who was often out of control. "The sun's in my eyes," she once snapped at me from the back seat of the car, "and it's all your fault." Another time it was, "My leg hurts. And it's all your fault!" After a while this became a family joke. Jim would sometimes wheel on me, saying, "It's snowing. And it's all your fault." Or "That letter hasn't come yet. And it's all your fault!"

Once I was driving home with the children at dusk, past a low-lying area near the river. A fog was gathering in the hollow, a fine mist rising up from the river bottom. I pulled over to the side of the road and stopped the car. The fog was so beautiful, with delicate bluish filaments gathering in whisps and in denser clumps, hovering about three feet over the surface of the field.

"Look," I said to Paul and Kate. "Look over there. See the cloud that has come down on the ground?"

They were both enthralled, and I told them they could get out of the car and run in the cloud. They were out in a flash, and then Kate hesitated. She came around to my window and stood there with her hands on her hips.

"You never took us to a cloud before!" She glared at me through the car window. "Not once. Not ever!" And then she turned and ran into the field after Paul.

Jim and I went to parents' group meetings as part of the summer school program. Some of the same parents we had met earlier had children in the program, and it was a pleasure to see them again. These meetings had become our lifeline at times when so many people seemed not to understand Paul or autism and seemed to blame us for his misbehaviors. The other parents always understood what we were saying; they never told us we were exaggerating or worrying unnecessarily about Paul, they never told us that we underestimated his abilities, or implied, on the other hand, that we had unrealistic expectations for him. They understood intuitively and accepted our accounts without asking for unnecessary explanations.

Even our closest friends, we sometimes felt, couldn't understand the way these other parents could, or the way Lyle and Sheila and the other consultants for the program understood. Not having had any experience with an autistic child, our friends tended, not surprisingly, to relate Paul to their own experiences as parents, to compare him with their learning disabled children, not understanding the vast differences between a learning disability and autism. Sometimes they offered us a sympathy that deeply offended me. "I don't know how you do it!" some people would exclaim, a comment that always annoyed me. I always replied, "You would do just the same! If you had to."

As we listened to the other parents in the group, Jim and I began to feel that we were lucky, very lucky. Measured against the broader population of autistic children, Paul was doing extremely well. In the summer programs he often stood out as one of the highest achievers. There he was a relaxed, bright, wonderfully inventive child, whereas in the regular school he attended during the rest of the year, he was a troublemaker, a disturbed child who was keeping up reasonably well academically, but only with the special help of the Resource Room teachers as backup.

In the parents' group, we heard mothers talk about how they couldn't leave their children unattended for even a minute. One child had fallen out of a window in the middle of the night. He had cracked several ribs but still managed to crawl to the front door and wait there until they got up in the morning and found him. Another had walked across the open flames of a gas stove. His pants leg, made of highly flammable material, had instantly melted in the heat and adhered to his leg, burning it horribly.

Other events weren't as terrifying, but they still caused stress. At one meeting, the group of parents started in on refrigerator stories.

"Jacob likes to get up in the middle of the night and take eggs out of the refrigerator. He drops them off our deck onto the deck of the apartment below. They make such a satisfying plop." Jacob, I knew, was ten.

"Annalee likes to pour maple syrup and catsup on the carpet in the living room. Then she turns on the vacuum cleaner to clean it up." Annalee was eight.

Some parents had ingenious solutions. "We've roped our refrigerator," one father confessed. "I never thought my Boy Scout knots would come in so handy."

Another remarked that ropes hadn't worked. "We have a chain and padlock. And not just on the refrigerator. The kitchen cupboards and the bathroom medicine chest are also padlocked."

"Sounds like a good idea," one exhausted mother commented. "Jeremy poured all our medicines down the drain last winter. That was when he and Lindy *both* had pneumonia at the same time."

At the end of one meeting, when Paul was about eleven, Jim quietly told the group that he thought he had sometimes overreacted to Paul, that he had trouble telling what was normal behavior and what was an alarming lack of moral understanding.

"I was afraid Paul would never learn the difference between right and wrong," Jim began quietly, "especially when he stole things or told a lie. I thought maybe he was a sociopath. And I was terrified."

Jim looked around the group and slowly continued. "He offended me. He violated my moral sense and my sense of reality. Above all he violated my paternity, the way I thought a son of mine should act."

He paused again, then after a moment went on. "I had to make everything a power struggle. I wanted to win and I wanted him to lose — because I was the father. I wanted him to change first. And he did. He did the changing."

The other parents were listening closely. No one attempted to say anything. Finally, in a low voice, Jim said, "And now, I think he is the most courageous person I have ever met."

One day, near the end of that same summer session, when I was dreading the end of this wonderful program but also looking forward to a trip to England, I sat on the steps with Sheila. She told me about a family she knew that had moved to California. These parents wanted to be close to the family featured in the film *Son Rise* so they could be trained by them to do the same intervention with their son. Sheila was telling me that this family had given up their jobs, sold their house, and moved their three kids to California to live in a motel — all of this so that their little boy could start training with Raun's father.

As Sheila talked, I remembered the film vividly. I could picture the stripped-down bathroom, and I remembered the intensive, highly programmed, very deliberate teaching that took place there. I felt exhausted just thinking about the effort required. Probably the film had exaggerated what really happened in the Kaufman family; nevertheless, Sheila and I agreed that the film sent a dangerous message to vulnerable parents looking for a cure. And I felt very sad about the family that had given up everything to go to California.

Then Sheila said something that surprised me. "Paul is doing just as well as the child in *Son Rise*," she told me. "And you didn't need to give up your lives for him. In fact, I think he is much better off because you didn't. I think he is better for the times you have spent abroad, for example."

The sun streamed in through the dirty, chicken-wire window set high up in the wall over the staircase. I watched as motes of dust floated up in a warm current of air through a sunbeam. Looked at in a certain way, the flecks seemed to be surrounded by tiny rainbows. Bright magenta, green, blue, sparked in the air, and I thought of a line from an Elizabethan poem I had read in graduate school: "Brightness falls from the air."

Sitting there watching the brightness in the air, I suddenly felt completely happy. I often had moments like this, but this time I was surprised by something else. I realized suddenly that there was nothing, nothing whatsoever, that I would change about my life.

I turned back to Sheila. She was asking me something about my alcoholism and chemical dependency, which I had long ago shared with her and with other people who knew me well.

"Have you ever thought of suing your doctor?" she was saying.

"Suing my doctor?" I was surprised and alarmed. "You mean for what happened to Paul?"

"No, I mean for what happened to you. What he put you through in treating your pregnancy with alcohol and Valium."

I paused. A cloud passed across the sky, and the sunlight was suddenly withdrawn, like a balloon deflating, collapsing, sunk down. Everything looked the same: the staircase, the green walls with their smudged finger prints, the poster about littering that hung near the door. But the life had gone out of it. And then the light went back up again, and it was as if the staircase, the whole scene, started to breathe again.

Sheila went on quietly, as she had so many times before. "It wasn't your drinking that caused Paul's problems, you know. The mothers of most of the children we treat had perfectly normal pregnancies, even where the children are seriously handicapped. I know lots of autistic children and none of them had alcoholic mothers. I also know a number of alcoholics and none of them have autistic children."

The bell rang. It was time to go and pick up Paul and Kate, to find Jim, who was still in the lounge talking to other parents. But when I left, I felt intensely grateful to Sheila for her wisdom and for her steadiness during all those years when we struggled with Paul and when I had struggled with my own guilt. Now I knew I was just about ready to give up that guilt, once and for all, and to move on with my life.

CHAPTER 25

Night Terrors

AT FIRST I didn't notice the old man leaning over the fence. It was a sunny fall day and I was cleaning the gerbil cages on the back porch. Usually this was a job I hated. Over the last few months, Paul and I had become more and more negligent. We waited longer and longer to clean out the cages, we waited in fact until they began to stink and we couldn't stand it anymore. The gerbils, once so friendly, now sometimes bit us, sinking their achingly sharp little teeth into our fingers right down to the bone. And now the mother had begun to neglect her new babies. She let the red skinned bodies lie helpless in the cedar shavings, as she ran over them, tumbling them over and over, as if they were nothing more than the cut-off ends of hot dogs. Then last week, Paul found her chewing through her latest baby.

The gerbils had become to me a symbol of overwork, disorganization, and my own inadequacy. Although I now felt far more in control of my life, I still sometimes felt overwhelmed. There were times when the dirty cages seemed to pile up with the unsorted laundry, the unwashed dishes, the unanswered letters. I could hardly bear to go into Paul's room. I knew Paul felt the same way about the gerbils, and I didn't want him to feel any more guilt or inadequacy. So I usually waited for him to help before I started on the cages.

But this day he was out on his bike, and I didn't mind the job. The sun was shining. It wasn't a day for guilt. In fact, I was feeling downright virtuous. The gerbils scuttled around in the unaccustomed and rather fearful freedom of a cardboard box. As I hosed off the last encrusted cedar shavings from the cage bottom, I looked up.

The old man was bent over the fence watching me. His face was deeply lined and stubbled with a day-old beard. His pants legs sagged over his shoes. He shuffled a little closer through the gate.

"Is this the parish house?" he asked, then seeing the confusion on my face, he gestured toward the church behind our house. "The parish house. For the Catholic church."

"Oh." I got up from the ground. "The Catholic church is across town." I waved my arm toward the front of our house. "Over there, in that direction, about half a mile."

But the old man wasn't satisfied. "I need to talk to the priests," he edged closer through the gate and down the walk.

And then he noticed the gerbils. A startled look of pure joy passed across his face. He bent to watch the gerbils and started to croon in a low voice.

"Baby rats." His voice was almost a whisper.

"Oh no, these are gerbils. My son's —"

"Baby rats," he repeated and glanced up at me. "I dreamed of baby rats. And a mother that took care of them."

"You did?" I was at a loss for words.

"Yes. Baby rats, and the mother took good care of them. She really loved them."

I watched quietly.

He went on. "I dreamed that dream last night."

I wanted to send him away as fast as possible, but I didn't. Something made me stop.

"Can I help you find the parish house?"

"Oh yes." His face lit up.

Then, in an expansive mood, surprising even myself, but knowing also that Jim was just inside in the kitchen, I said more generously. "Would you like a cup of coffee and a sandwich first? Then I'll drive you across town."

And so the old man came into our kitchen and talked to us as I made him a cheese sandwich and a cup of coffee.

"Nice setup you got here." He looked around appreciatively at our kitchen. I looked at it through his eyes: the Welsh dresser with the blue and white china, the polished copper pans over the stove, the children's bright artwork on the refrigerator door. The piles of books on the edge of the kitchen table.

"I been in prison," the old man offered. "When I start to drink, I always end up in the slammer."

Then he began to tell us of his many prison experiences, his longtime friendship with Dr. Sam Sheppard, the famous wife killer, his own attempts to live on the outside. We didn't ask what he'd done to "end up in the slammer," but he volunteered: "Oh, I just cash bad checks, bad checks and things like that. Then, slam bang, and back in I go."

He finished the last of his sandwich and leaned back. "I was afraid yesterday. I think it's starting to happen again."

His voice took on a musing quality. "But the baby rats . . . the baby rats. They was a sign. A message."

"So now" — he tipped forward, hands on knees — "now I go to see the good priests."

Jim and I drove him across town and dropped him off by the parish house next to the Catholic church. Then we drove slowly away, watching him shuffle to the door. His head was bent, and he looked unutterably sad.

For the rest of that day, I felt his sadness, his fear, his despair. I tried but couldn't shake off the sense of a life wasted, a life lived on the edge. Would Paul be like that in forty, fifty years time? Would he too be homeless, always on the move, driven from one community to the next, in and out of prison? If so, would he even have the skills this old man had: would he know to look for the "good priests" in every town he passed through, would he know what would keep him out of "the slammer"? The thought was too terrifying to confront directly.

That fall I thought a lot about Jim's two Uncle Jims, one on each side of his family. One Jim was a brother of his father, the other was a brother of his mother, and both had gone "bad." One ended up dead, according to the most reliable accounts. The other was a foulmouthed old man who lived in flophouses and carried his possessions around with him in a paper bag, occasionally showing up at Jim's mother's house.

Once, he inherited three thousand dollars from his brother, a retired meat packer in Florida. This Uncle Jim hadn't been seen in years, so the word was put out in the pubs around Ealing, Acton, North Acton, South Acton, Shepherd's Bush, and beyond. In two or three months, there he was, on Jim's mother's doorstep, come to claim his fortune. After this, he resurfaced once or twice a year. But of course his life never changed.

What had happened to this Uncle Jim to make him the way he was? And to the other Uncle Jim, whose life, according to family stories, was even worse? When I asked Jim's mother, I learned that her brother had been very like Paul when he was a young child — sweet, gentle, slow to talk, good with his hands. Later, he had been prone to outbursts, hard to control. He dropped out of school after five or six years. He became a skilled bricklayer. And then he wasn't heard from again, not for many years. This, of course, was just what I didn't want to hear. Especially the part about his childhood. It may have been comforting to think that autism was genetic or familial, and that I no longer needed to blame myself. But as a predictor of Paul's adult life, the example of his great-uncle was terrifying.

I wanted to think this couldn't happen to Paul. He was born in a more enlightened age, where children are appreciated and understood. He had the benefit of good schools, mostly, and good teachers. He didn't live in poverty in the west of Ireland. And surely, I thought, our good fortune, Jim's and mine, our own educations, our income, our skills in navigating the world, would help Paul.

But then I remembered a teenage girl I worked with when I was a graduate student in St. Louis. She was the youngest of four daughters, each of whom had had a breakdown the first year of college. Leslie had run true to family form, and when I met her she had just returned home from the psychiatric ward of Barnes Hospital. Before she was sent back to school, her mother wanted to hire a tutor-companion-good-influence for her. I was recommended. I set out hopefully to do the job. Leslie and I met once a week to read short stories and plays together, and to discuss them. And I, in my graduate school wisdom, chose unerringly wrongly.

This was the summer I was getting married, and I was making my wedding dress, adding bits of beautiful, expensive lace, whenever I could afford to go out and buy more. My cat had had kittens who were now big enough to wander all over my big, sunny apartment, sometimes tumbling in the snippets of fabric on the floor. I was teaching an upper-level class, my first, in American literature, and I was pleased that I was trusted with so much responsibility. Everything seemed to be going well in my life.

Gradually, in our sessions at my apartment, Leslie became more and more withdrawn. Her face, which had opened into a shy interest at first, closed down, became masklike. She began to skip our meetings and to forget to call. Sometimes she didn't wake up in time in the morning. I called her, then her mother, and eventually she just dropped out of sight.

The contrast between her life and mine had finally become too much to bear, and so she went away for good. But I continued to think of nineteen-year-old Leslie sitting motionless on my couch, watching with hardly a flicker of interest as the kittens tumbled in snippets of wedding dress on the floor.

Reluctantly, I gave up my dreams of helping her. I simply could not spend any of my good fortune on her. I had so much, my life was so full. I was surrounded by friends, by love, by hope. But I learned you simply cannot give your luck away; our luck is individual, highly selective, and very personal. And I learned another, harder lesson. You cannot heal another person through kindness, good cheer, or energy.

The visit from the old man happened at a particularly low time for Paul. He had outgrown the summer school program in the Twin Cities where he had done so well before, and he had entered sixth grade, his first year at the middle school. The new school and all the different classrooms and teachers were very stressful for him. Then, one day, Paul held a pencil over the side of his desk and sliced it suddenly with the side of his palm. It flipped high in the air and all the way out the classroom door. He got a roar of laughter from the class.

So, he learned, flipping pencils was clearly the thing to do in sixth grade. But after a few weeks, and then several months, this behavior had gotten him into a lot of trouble. The librarian had become so fed up with him that she decided to fight fire with fire. Only pencil flipping, intensive, continuous, unremitting pencil flipping, she decided, would cure him of pencil flipping. So she shut him up in a small supply closet with the instruction to flip pencils until she came to remove him.

But she knew nothing about autistic children. And of course this didn't work. Paul panicked when he realized he was late for his next class. He ran out of the closet and down the hall, where the librarian pursued him and pulled him out to return to the supply closet.

We didn't learn about this incident until much later, but in the meantime, Paul came home one day and announced: "They told me I can't handle the classroom situation. I'm going back to the Resource Room all day." He was clearly pleased and relieved to be pulled out of his classes and to spend the school day in the small, enclosed Resource Room with just a few students, some of them old friends.

If I had my private terrors during this time, Paul did also, although his were very different from mine. Ever since he was seven, he had sometimes awakened at night with nightmares. Or more usually, he cried out at night but did not awaken. These "night terrors," as eventually we learned to call them, were so extreme, so different from typical bad dreams, that we all began to dread them.

Some mornings after these events we noticed that Paul had no memory of the night before. Even if we mentioned it to him, he had no recollection of anything at all happening. At other times he did remember with acute pain and distress, and this of course made him more fearful of having another episode. We tried to treat the events casually, not to make too much of them, simply to reassure Paul that we would always be there when he woke in the night.

One night I remember Jim had heard the crying first, and when I reached Paul's room, he was already there sitting on the edge of the bed, one arm around his shoulder. Paul was up on his hands and knees, rocking back and forth. Sweat was pouring down his face. His eyes were wide open, staring straight ahead.

"What is it, lovey?" I dropped to my knees by the edge of the bed. "What is it? You can tell us."

"Nooooo," Paul moaned. "No!"

Jim put a finger across his lips. "Don't ask him. He's not awake. Remember, it will just frighten him if we ask."

I put my hand on Paul's back, as he rocked in a jerky, rapid movement. Sometimes he stopped and stared straight ahead at something that appeared to be just in front of him. "No! No, don't!" he said, then he resumed the frantic rocking.

"Turn off the light," Jim whispered to me.

I got up and flicked the light switch, then sat down again on the floor near Paul's bed.

Paul stopped rocking, brushed a hand across his face, then started again. Back and forth, back and forth. The muscles of his back and shoulders were tense, tight, beneath my hand. His pajamas were soaking. But we didn't dare bother him to change them.

"We're here, Paul. We're here." Jim spoke softly to him, monotonously. "We're here."

The rocking was less frantic now. Quietly, Jim went on talking to Paul. "It's all right. We're here, Paul. You can lie down and go to sleep."

Paul stopped and rested his head on the pillow, but I could still feel the muscles thrumming beneath the skin. I went on slowly massaging his shoulders. "It's all right, Paul. We're here, Paul."

Suddenly he let go, and without ever awakening from his terrifying dream, he lapsed back into a deep, quiet, soothing sleep. I could feel the tension leave his back. We stood up and pulled the covers around his shoulders. I bent to kiss the damp top of his head.

Jim and I went back into our own room and climbed into bed.

"I can't sleep."

"Neither can I."

"What is going on? What are these episodes?"

Once again Jim started to tell me about his own night terrors when he was a child. He told me that trying to wake up Paul was the worst thing we could do. Also asking him questions would just make it worse: the questions planted further doubts, gave him more material for elaborating his fears. But Jim also told me again about how frightening these experiences were: "With me, they were a terror so deep, it was unimaginable. Like being on the edge of the universe, like being lost forever."

I hated to think of Paul suffering that way. And I hated to think of Jim suffering so as a child, but I wanted to blame his Catholic education. Why then would Paul have such experiences also?

Then I realized that I did know something about these episodes. I had recently come across something that sounded very like Paul's experience in the *DSM, The Diagnostic and Statistical Manual,* the manual used by doctors to diagnose psychiatric disorders. It was called *pavor nocturnus,* popularly known as night terrors. It was a neurological condition, different from simple nightmares. After this, Jim and I discussed finding a neurologist and we drifted off finally, thinking we could deal with the problem medically, if not theologically.

Paul's class was scheduled to go to an Environmental Learning Center in northern Minnesota early that spring, in March before the warm weather arrived. Although the children would be gone only four days, Paul was very afraid of going. He had never been away from us before except to spend the night at Allen's house, but his teachers thought he was ready. We wanted to believe them. We knew how much he would learn and grow from such an experience. Paul had always loved the outdoors: taking walks in the woods, exploring trails, visiting all the state parks within a hundred miles of our house, these things had long been his favorite summer activities.

But we also knew he was full of anxiety, far beyond what most of the other children were feeling. He was tense, preoccupied, withdrawn, wary, even as we continued to argue the merits of camp. When Paul learned that Allen wouldn't be on the trip, he became even more resistant. What we didn't know, what he didn't share with us, was his fear that he would have one of his night episodes while he was at camp. He didn't know if he could handle it on his own, and he was terrified of the embarrassment of waking up everyone in his cabin. But he didn't tell us of this fear, and for some reason I didn't suspect it.

We continued to try to persuade him, finally giving him an offer he couldn't refuse. We told him we would give him an Atari game, the one he most longed for, if he would consent to go to camp.

"That's bribery," he said.

"I know," I replied.

Paul stared at me. He hadn't expected me to agree with him. "Well, I guess. Maybe. Maybe I will go. Space Invaders, did you say you would give me Space Invaders?"

"Yup. That's what I said."

Paul went to camp. We took him to school very early in the morning and watched as they loaded the luggage, then the children, onto three school buses. Paul sat at the window, his face pale and expressionless. He was holding on tight, determined to see camp through, but clearly not enjoying the prospect.

"Brains." I thought that was what the young doctor was saying. "What we need are brains." We were at an Autism Society meeting the second evening Paul was at camp. I was already feeling tense and worried about Paul, not quite in control, and this doctor looked ridiculous. What did he mean, he needed brains? We had come to this meeting because this doctor was going to talk about some new experimental drug therapies for autistic children. I glanced around the room at the other parents attending the meeting to see if I had heard correctly. They were shifting uneasily on their folding metal chairs. I saw them glance furtively at each other, then swiftly away again. I had heard right.

"Without brains," the doctor plunged ahead, "we'll never know what autism is. It may be a defect in the vermis, maybe the hippocampus, maybe the cerebral cortex, maybe the lateral ventricles."

I didn't dare look at Jim sitting next to me. His expressive face, which always showed everything that went through his mind, would set me off. Instead I concentrated on this doctor. He had very white, pasty skin. His plaid jacket was rumpled. He looked as if he had been in a lab for a very long time. Or under a log. His ears stuck out and glowed with a faint peachy sheen from the light behind him. They looked like apricots. I clamped down hard on that thought and struggled hard once again to concentrate.

"We used to think that autism resulted from a brain stem disorder. Bernard Rimland first theorized that autism was the result of some sort of malfunctioning of systems within the brain stem which regulate arousal, or attention.

"*But*" — and here he pressed his lips together, and his voice took on a smug quality, a just-between-you-and-me coziness — "the only brain stem abnormality ever reported was in just one single postmortem case where they found that the neurons of the inferior olive were reduced in size."

I strangled a giggle before it could escape my throat. I wanted to laugh or to cry, I hardly knew which. I thought of Paul's brain and of the neurologist I wanted to consult. I thought of the night terrors he was having, his unusual fear of camp, his suffering over little things that didn't seem to affect other children. Then I thought if I breathed deeply I wouldn't feel such an overwhelming urge to laugh hysterically, or to cry.

"So, you see, without brains, we'll never know."

By now my throat was aching with suppressed laughter. Maybe I shouldn't have come tonight, I thought. I've been on edge all week. I might have known this meeting would be too much.

"To conclude." He was winding down now. I looked up hopefully. "You parents need to know that postmortem neuropathology studies are desperately needed." The doctor took his heavy wire-rimmed glasses off, slowly unhooking them first from one apricot ear, then the other. He pulled his shirttail out of his trousers and slowly wiped his glasses, squinting at us nearsightedly down his nose. He wanted to make sure we parents got the point.

"So, if you know of any child or young autistic adult in a fatal accident . . ." He glanced away from us and stared at the light on the ceiling. Then, taking out his notes, he settled his glasses back on his nose. "Now I want to talk to you about Fenfluoramine."

Paul had to stay up all night, the receptionist told me a month later when she called from the Pediatric Neurology Department, where Paul was scheduled to have tests for his night terrors. A sleep deprived electroencephalogram was more accurate than the other kind. I was to bring him in at nine in the morning, after he had been up all night.

I hung up the phone and turned to Jim, frying bacon at the stove. "The EEG is scheduled for April twelfth" I told him. "And we have to keep Paul up all night before the test."

Jim didn't say anything. He flipped the bacon over with the spatula. I knew he wasn't as interested in this test as I was. He didn't expect to learn much from the results, but he was willing to go along with me, the detective mother who was always after answers.

At last he turned to me. "Well, he's been wanting to stay up all night. Now's his chance."

"Right, he can at last check out the *TV Guide*." I picked up the magazine from the kitchen table. " 'Tales from the Darkside': an atomic researcher in Utah traces radiation burns to throbbing mud from the center of the earth. Or how about this one? Retired Wall Street stockbroker decides to start a worm farm."

"Until the night crawlers." Jim scooped the bacon onto a plate just as Paul walked into the kitchen. "Until the night crawlers decide to craaawl in the night."

"What night crawlers? What are you guys talking about?" Paul asked, looking offended.

"What we're talking about is you, Paul Anthony McDonnell, staying up all night."

"All night? You mean *all* night? Why did you change your mind?"

"Well" — I sat down at the kitchen table — "you see, you are going to have a test at a hospital up in the Twin Cities. Not a test that will hurt at all. Just a test that will read your brain waves."

"Can I watch?"

"Sure. You'll be able to see the lines on the paper. First, they glue some wires on your head, then they turn on a machine and some needles, pens with ink, trace lines on a long piece of paper."

"That sounds interesting."

"It is interesting."

"But why do I have to stay up all night?"

"Because they get better test results that way. I don't know why, exactly, but you get to stay up all night and watch TV."

"Can I have a Coke?"

"Yup, you can have a Coke. It will help you to stay awake."

"Can I have some doughnuts?"

"Yep, you can have some doughnuts." I got up from the chair and gave him a quick hug. "But first you have to have a good dinner, a goooood dinner. Is that a deal?"

"It's a deal."

The morning of April twelfth, when Paul and I went to the hospital in Minneapolis, I felt bruised from lack of sleep. It had been a hard night, with Jim and me taking turns keeping Paul company, keeping him awake. Once, between our shifts, he had been left alone for a few minutes, and I knew he had dozed off.

As I sat on a stool beside Paul watching the technician glue the wires to his head, I remembered our earlier visit when he was two and was tested for a brain tumor. This time, there wasn't much to worry about. I just wanted to find out more about those night terrors. Maybe there was something we could do.

The technician finished with the wires. "We'll just wait now for him to fall asleep." She turned to me. "Let's leave the room and wait a few minutes."

I stroked Paul's forehead. "You go to sleep now, sweetheart. I'll be just outside the door."

We went into the hall. But Paul shifted restlessly on the plastic couch. I could tell he wasn't sleepy. We waited. And waited.

Finally, the technician gave up and went back into the room. She turned on the machine and flashed a strobe light across Paul's face. Click, click, click, the light flashed rhythmically across his face. On and off, on and off. I felt dizzy with tiredness. I wanted to lie down on the couch myself and go to sleep.

I picked up Paul's hand and stroked the back of his wrist lightly. "Maybe you'll get sleepy, lovey, if I do this."

"I'm not sleepy."

And he wasn't. The technician finished the test with Paul awake all the time.

An hour later I was called back to see Dr. Featherstone and get the test results. "You stay here, Paul. I'll be back soon." I hoped he would stay in the waiting room, reading a *National Geographic*.

"No, I want to go too. I want to see my brain waves."

"I'll tell you everything. I want you to stay here."

"No, I want to see my brain waves." I could hear the rising note of panic in his voice. "I have to see my brain waves."

"Well, okay then, but you need to be quiet and let the doctor talk."

So Paul came with me and stood close to my shoulder, as Dr. Featherstone went over the results of the test.

"It looks pretty good, no seizure pattern. And no, I don't think we will need to run another test anytime soon. It looks good to me."

So there was nothing there, I thought, as we left the hospital. Nothing of note, nothing to indicate any neurological problem that they could see. Could the problem be theological after all? I was so dead tired, I didn't know anymore.

We were crossing the street to the parking lot. I was dizzy, nauseated with tiredness. I couldn't wait to get home and take a nap. And then I saw a tiny child crossing the street in front of Children's Hospital. She looked about four years old. I couldn't believe that any parent could be so careless as to let a four-year-old cross the street by herself. I looked around for an adult. There was no one there, and a truck was turning the corner, bearing down on her. I knew what I had to do.

"Paul, you stay here."

I took off across the street. The light had changed now, and there was a stream of traffic. Dodging a station wagon, which swerved and braked suddenly, I came up to the child. She was about to step onto the grass of the median strip.

But something was wrong. The child had a large black plastic handbag hanging from her shoulder, bouncing on her hip. And she walked in a funny way. A rapid, lurching, hitched walk. Then I saw her face, turned angrily toward me. The four-year-old was a dwarf. I had been chasing after a grown woman to save her from the traffic. I turned on my heel and swept back through the cars. Paul was standing on the curb looking at me.

"Mama," he began, as I ran up to him. "Mama, that was a dwarf."

"I know."

"I think you need new glasses."

"I know."

We walked back to the car. I was deeply chagrined at causing the woman such pain. "What a stupid thing to do," I told myself. "You'd better stop rescuing the world and just let go of a few things."

We never did find out anything more about Paul's night terrors. And gradually they just went away. He says now that it was as if his brain were being scrambled, the wires crossed, like a computer malfunctioning. He said his mind raced, and his thoughts were uncontrollable. These are his words for an experience that was, and is, essentially indescribable.

The fear gradually lessened for Jim and for me also. After a while, we didn't have to watch Paul suffer, locked in a faraway place we couldn't enter, caught in the grip of a terror beyond comfort, beyond comprehension. Just as I had learned from Jim not to ask Paul questions because the questions themselves were agitating, so I learned to live with these night terrors, which seemed to come so thick and fast for a few years.

Paul stopped crying when he had the episodes. He learned to handle them himself. Much later, he told us that at camp he did wake up once in his bunk bed with that funny feeling in his head.

"Did you call the counselor in your cabin?" I asked.

"No."

"Why not?"

"Because I knew I could handle it. I woke up, and the feeling just went away after a few minutes."

*

Later that spring I decided to get rid of the gerbils. They still ate their babies even though we kept the cage clean now, and I had had enough. So one warm day, I called to Paul and Kate. "How about if we take the gerbils to the woods?'

"Why?"

Quickly, before they could ask too many questions, I started explaining. "Well, you know they really do come from the wild. The Russian tundra, I think. Their normal habitat is under the leaves. They really like to forage. I'll bet they can find all kinds of good things to eat in the arboretum. And they won't get cold. They can curl up at night under the leaves."

Stop it, I thought, you're overexplaining. Clearly Paul and Kate thought this was a good idea.

So we took the cage in the back of the car and drove to the edge of the arboretum. I drove down a dirt road and stopped just at the edge of a grove of pines and firs.

"This looks like a good place." I tried to sound cheerful. "A mousy place."

We put the cage on the forest floor and opened the door. But the gerbils, usually so eager to get out, were wary this time. They ran up to the open door, then back again, up to the door, then back again. Finally, one ventured out, whiskers working, then the other followed, sniffing the ground, sniffing the leaves, the pine needles.

Quickly, I picked up the cage and gave it to Kate to hold, before the gerbils could change their minds.

Paul dropped down to his knees. "Good-bye, Brownie. Good-bye, Puffy."

Brownie ran into Paul's outstretched hand, then away again. Then he ran over to my shoe and drew himself up into a tiny posture of inquiry. Standing on his hind legs, he seemed to look up at me, nose quivering, whiskers working, small hands held loosely in front.

"Can we come back and see them sometimes?" Kate asked.

"Sure. But they may not come when we call. They might like it here too much." Liar, you're a bloody liar, I thought to myself. "Let's leave now and give them a chance to get used to their new home."

I backed the car around, then headed for the main road. No more gerbil cages to clean out, I thought gleefully, disloyally. We pulled onto the highway, and I looked back once at the stand of pines. The wind was blowing gently through them, and high above, so high I couldn't be certain, I thought I saw a hawk circling.

CHAPTER 26

News from the Border

"THEY SAID I was daydreaming in social studies today."

"Were you?"

"No!" Paul was indignant. "I was wondering how long light would take to go from Longfellow School to Sibley School! Light travels at 186,000 miles per second, but I couldn't figure it out."

"Did you tell them that?"

"No. I couldn't. They put me in the hallway by the coats and said I had to stay there until I could concentrate."

Weighing, measuring, taking temperatures, recording dates, Paul tried to map a bewildering world, to chart its ambiguities and fluctuations, to give number values to its many varieties. And because he lived for so many years in a world that seemed unpredictable, chaotic, and uncontrollable, Paul sought out certainties with a vengeance.

Not at home in the world, not truly dwelling *in* it, Paul sought to dwell *on* it. Where he couldn't sense, he tried to know; where he couldn't intuit, he tried to gather information; and where he didn't feel comfortable, he fixated. Confused and frightened at school, and indeed all during his childhood, Paul found some consoling certainties in the natural world. He found out that every night when he went to bed, he was at 90 degrees longitude, 42.5 latitude, and exactly 956 feet above sea level. Every day he knew how many hours of sunlight we would have and whether the daylight was increasing or decreasing, and by how many minutes.

"What time is it there?" Paul asked me one day when he was six or seven. We were watching *Watership Down*, a very sad movie about some rabbits that were about to die in a huge conflagration. We watched as the fire licked first at the edges of the fields, then gathered in strength, and finally roared in a great snapping inferno through the woods and fields. The field animals, the rabbits, mice, ferrets, weasels, all fled for their lives, and Paul, turning to me, his face working with anxiety, asked with more urgency, "*What time is it there?*"

It wasn't that Paul couldn't feel the distress of the rabbits and the other animals. He felt it strongly enough. He just needed, once again, to locate himself in something tangible and known. Like time.

If I said, to any of his questions, "I don't know," Paul would demand, "Well, figure it out!"

"Why is the siren going off now?"

"I don't know, Paul."

"Well, figure it out!"

Perhaps, I thought, the autistic child has only knowledge, never imagination, hypothesis, intuition, belief, pretense. I couldn't say the siren might be blowing because a house was on fire, or a car had run off the road, or an old woman had collapsed with a heart attack, or any of a number of other possibilities. At such times, Paul would wait patiently while I explained, and then he would ask me which one it was. The house on fire, or the car off the road? I was supposed to know. If I told him I didn't know, he would demand, "Well, say it anyway!" All knowledge for him was a certain knowledge, never provisional knowledge, a knowledge of likelihood or probability. "Probably" was only "more yes than maybe," it wasn't a radically different kind of knowing from certainty.

The willingness to entertain possibility just for the pleasure of it, the "let's pretend" of his younger sister, were utterly foreign to Paul. One day he was standing with me in the kitchen, and we overheard Kate playing with two friends, just outside the back door.

"Let's play house."

"Let's. Let's pretend I'm the big sister." This was Kate.

"And let's pretend I'm the baby." This was Kris.

"And I'm the House Ghost!" This was from Amy.

"Yes. I'm the big sister and our parents died and I have to look after you. I have to look after my baby sister."

"But you don't look after me. I'm the House Ghost and I haunt the house. You can't look after me!"

"Why not?" Kate wanted to know.

"Because."

"Why does Kate always say 'Let's pretend?' " Paul's voice had a genuinely questioning tone. He was bewildered, as if at the sheer waste of energy on such useless activity. Kate could, after all, be measuring the height of a tree, or exploring the storm sewers. Instead, there she was *pretending*.

Play, in all its forms, whether it is acting out, imitation, or imagining, is the way children learn. We are told this over and over again by child psychologists, but any halfway observant person knows this to be true. Play is the way children test the world and bend the rigidity of its rules; it is the way they reassure themselves, gain competence in human interactions, assert their independence from adult control, make wishes, change "reality." It is the way they learn to be at home in the world.

I often watched Kate and one of her friends act out every family event, every human interaction, every crisis that they observed but could not understand. I also watched them invent traumas that they had never themselves suffered.

"This is an orphanage, and seventeen children live here." They used Legos to build elaborate buildings, with well-furnished rooms, with flowered and wooded grounds.

"This is where they sleep."

"And this is their swimming pool."

"And this is their merry-go-round."

"Sarah is the oldest. Her parents were killed in a car crash."

"And this is Beth. She has nightmares, *terrible* nightmares. And she also has pneumonia."

And on and on. These games lasted days, even weeks. The girls played with Legos or they pulled all the furniture out of the dollhouse and arranged it in separate houses on different shelves in my study. They made up characters and life situations, and they returned to their dolls over and over again, always picking up where they left off before. It was like a play, or a soap opera, with multiple characters and crises, whole lives that were carried on independently, parallel to the children's lives, and just as important.

When Paul was in first or second grade and had not yet learned how to "play," at least not in the accepted and approved ways, the school psychologist gave me a book to read: *How to Play with Your Child*. I felt insulted by the gift. *I* knew how to play. I had grown up playing elaborate games of fantasy: plays enacted on the back porch, treasures buried in the woods and treasure maps carefully drawn to show where they were. In a world of limited opportunities and before television, we spent our lives playing. When I was growing up, children were *supposed* to have imaginations. Our imaginations were our occupation, our refuge, our main attribute. And any child that couldn't amuse herself, who dared to come complaining of boredom, was quickly put to work.

"You're bored?" my incredulous mother would wheel on us, if we came trailing into the kitchen on a hot summer afternoon as she was boiling peaches for preserving. "You're *bored? I'll* find some work for you to do!"

I never even opened the book on how to play with your children.

Finally, one day when Paul was eleven or twelve or thirteen, I can't remember when, I overheard him say, "Hey, Kate. Let's pretend you're the mean teacher and I'm me." And the two of them disappeared into the TV room to act out a classroom drama. I felt this marked one of the most important moments in Paul's growth. But it was not something I taught him. He was simply ready for it.

Perhaps autistic children do not play in the usual sense of the word because the world is utterly confusing to them. The most fundamental distinctions that most children learn rapidly, and that are the basis for all play — the difference between objects and people, living things and inanimate things — are not readily apparent to them. The professional literature now puts it simply: "autistic children have unusual relationships with people and objects." When Paul was very little, he often seized someone by the arm and threw that arm and hand at something he wanted, a box of cookies, or a toy that was just out of his reach. Sometimes he would greet a new babysitter at the door in this way. Taking her arm, he drew her across the room and threw her arm toward the object he wanted.

You might say we were just useful tools to him and nothing more. But I always thought it was more complicated than that. People were never just tools to Paul. He always had very close relationships and unusually intense feelings for other people. In fact, the people he loved most dearly, especially if he rarely saw them, were simply too "esciting" to see. When his old friend and babysitter Jan returned to visit a year or more after he last saw her, Paul would hide in his room. The very sight of Jan would be too charged, too overwhelming; his nervous system simply couldn't sustain the excitement. None of my reassurances, none of my coaxing, would ever bring him downstairs. In the end, Jan would have to put him out of his misery. She would just walk in on him and give him a big hug, and then he could calm down.

But if people could cause intense, overwhelming, and sometimes insupportable feelings, so too could objects. "Baby Earth," as he called his globe, caused the same anxious tension as a beloved human object.

This globe had been given to him the Christmas he was six, because by that time he had developed his strong interest in geography. He studied it with rapt attention for several months, and then imperceptibly it slipped from educational object to sacred object, from something that could be studied and treated casually to something that must be set aside and approached with reverence. In a few months, it had acquired an aura, a power to compel attention, a power to express value, which we could only guess at. Paul had taken the globe off its stand, and the little hole that was left and which appeared just over the North Pole, was the part of the globe most sacred, most veiled from observation by the profane. He told us later it was like the eye of the earth.

The following Christmas Paul wanted to take Baby Earth with him when we visited his grandfather. I told him he couldn't, it was simply too big to carry on the plane and it wouldn't fit in any of our suitcases. Paul sadly bid good-bye to his globe as we left to catch the plane, but when we returned, instead of rushing into his room to see his precious Baby Earth, he hesitated and hung about anxiously outside the door. Finally, he confessed that it was just "too esciting" to see his globe, and he asked me to turn it so that at least the little hole would be invisible as he walked in the door.

Inanimate objects often were treated by Paul as if they were sentient beings. Perhaps this started when Paul was three and he approached the "sleeping" daffodils with such fearful attention. At that time there was also one special page in a book about a runaway train which could be looked at only when Paul knew he was safe in my lap, my arms around him. Something about that page and the picture of the little engine caught in the dark limbs of a tree at the end of the line was fearful beyond any meaning I could give to it.

I suspect all sensitive children do this; they ascribe special powers to inanimate objects. Kate woke up in the night crying about "wiggly things." She had a stick horse whose head was propped over the foot of her bedstead, and she said its nose wiggled at her in the night. Also her wallpaper was too wiggly, and for a long time she had to go to sleep facing away from that paper with its too complicated design. She also had a child's notion of value which guaranteed protection: "Am I too precious to get chicken pox?" she would ask. And I had to explain that, sadly, her dearness was no protection against illness, much as I or any parent would like it to be otherwise.

But the significance of the globe went beyond this. True, it was a "transitional object" like Paul's earlier stuffed animal, his panda bear, that somehow protected him from the world, or connected him with the world, or gave him magical powers. When he was two, Paul threw Baba, his panda bear, at a huge coon dog that barked at him, and then he felt safer. That seemed simple enough. But the significance of Baby Earth, hidden away in his room emanating untold powers, was beyond our ability to understand.

Perhaps it was simply the stability and dependability of objects in an otherwise confusing world which gave them such special powers for Paul. Maybe he needed to rely on them, as we did not. Many years later, when Paul was a teenager, the television broke. He helped me carry it into the repair shop. I knew he was unusually agitated, but it was only as we drove back up our driveway that I learned why. Paul suddenly exploded and started pounding the dashboard. I asked him why he was so upset. "Because" — he turned to explain to me as if I were a very slow child — "because I know people are unpredictable and they change. But not objects. TVs don't break down. They don't. That would be like the moon blowing up."

He finished and watched me to see if, even in my density, I had followed. And then I almost started to explain to him, once again. TVs do break down. You know they do. And refrigerators. We just bought a new one. And tape recorders. You get old ones at garage sales and you try to fix them. But this time, I didn't say any of this. Instead something clicked into place in my own head.

"So that's it," I said and stared at him. He stared back. "Of course."

Jim always said that what Paul lacked was a sense of the tacit, the intuitive, the taken-for-granted knowledge that the rest of us use every day to navigate the world. It was no surprise that Paul needed, desperately, to figure it out. That extra sense, that finely attuned echo-location by which we move and locate ourselves precisely in a world of human interactions, was lost to him. So Paul would ask over and over again, "How would you feel if . . . ?" How would you feel if you ran over that squirrel? How would you feel if lightning struck the house? How would you feel if Kate was lost? How would you feel if I died?

These are unanswerable questions, precisely because the answer is so patently there, so obviously obvious. But not for Paul. With him the questions had to be repeated and repeated, and then he would repeat and repeat my answers. "You would be just miserable, wouldn't you be just miserable?"

From his predictable crawling as a baby (up the stairs, pat the floor, turn left, crawl down the hall) to the more complex learning of human interactions, Paul, like other autistic children, learned in patterns. And anger was one of those configurations that he locked into early and immovably. Perhaps because he had attracted so much anger in his lifetime, he came to anticipate it always and everywhere. He even began to seek it out as a necessary part of every slight misunderstanding or disagreement, the only resolution that he seemed to understand. If the other person would cooperate, he almost always escalated every minor problem into an explosion. Only when he was exhausted would he stop.

Over the years, the patterns, the configurations of anger in our household, became so complex and bewildering, so impossible to unravel or even to understand, that we were all lost in confusion. Every day, it seemed, we entered a force field, a magnetic storm, where we were lifted off our feet and whirled around. The smallest things set us off, made us behave according to impulses we hardly owned, made us speak words we hardly recognized as coming from our own mouths.

For example: "Are you mad at me?" Paul followed close behind Kate as she walked into the kitchen.

"No, I'm not mad at you. I told you I wasn't."

"Are you sure you're not mad at me? You looked mad." Paul cracked his knuckles.

Jim, who had been watching, would probably intervene at this point. "She said she wasn't mad at you. Come and finish your dinner."

But Paul refused to sit down. "I don't like that food! I'm not hungry. Are you sure you're not mad at me."

"No! I told you." And Kate sat down to try to finish her dinner.

By this time, Jim was really annoyed. "Paul, that's enough! Stop it. You can't control other people's feelings."

"But she looked mad at me. Everybody's always mad at me."

"No they're not!"

"But you are. You're irritated with me now."

"Yes, I *am* irritated with you now."

"*See*. Everybody's mad at me. *All* the time!"

"Oh, poor little you," Jim would continue. "Trying to protect your precious little self. You don't have any right to care about other people's feelings. They are no business of yours."

"Other people's feelings are no concern of yours, except," and here I would glance pointedly at Jim, "*except* when they are directed at you." This was the point where I always intervened. Jim's sarcasm always infuriated me, and then I would step in to protect Paul.

But this was always too much for Jim: "*See*. There you go. You are always interfering."

And then I would suddenly lose control. "You just want to fight with me," I would yell at Jim. "You want to draw me into it. Go ahead. I'll fight! Pick on someone your own size."

But Jim saw it differently. "You're always interfering."

"I was with you all the way, until you became sarcastic."

By this time, Kate would have left the room again and Jim and I would be standing, facing each other over the table and over Paul, who of course had eaten none of his dinner, and would now not be eating any of it.

Paul would look up anxiously at both of us. "Now you are fighting about me." He would be rolling the carrots and peas across his plate, knocking some off the edge. Or he would be rocking back and forth in his chair.

"This is something between Daddy and me," I would say, which was by this time true, but Paul knew perfectly well that he was the occasion for the fight in the first place.

Maybe at this point, Kate would walk back into the room, carrying her swimsuit and towel.

And Paul would ask her anxiously again, "Were you angry with me, Kate?"

Then maybe I would say something like: "It's all right, Kate. You can tell him what you really felt."

Kate would say in a very small voice, so low that it was almost impossible to hear, "I *was* annoyed with you."

"*See*," Paul sounded tearful but also almost triumphant. "Everyone is angry with me. Allen. Ray. Mrs. Iverson."

Then perhaps I would add, making one last stab at working this thing out. "Maybe you are angry with them. If so, why don't you tell them."

"I'm angry with Daddy."

"Well, tell him."

"People don't have a right to be angry with me," Paul would say in a high-pitched, insistent voice.

"Yes they do!" This would be the final straw for Jim. He always saw this inevitable statement of Paul's as an attempt to control him, never, as I saw it, as an expression of Paul's anxiety.

But maybe at this point, Jim would be able to walk away from the situation. "I have to take Kate to the pool now." And the two of them would leave.

Some professionals have said that autistic children lack a "theory of mind," that it is hard for them to understand that other people have thoughts and feelings that are separate from their own, thoughts and feelings that nevertheless can be communicated and understood by other people. Young children, we know, see the world and others as an extension of the self. Only gradually do they come to see and recognize the sovereignty of each separate self, selves that indeed may be connected but are never truly merged.

Perhaps, I have sometimes thought, autistic children just get stuck seeing the world as an extension of self; they do this more persistently and for a longer period of time than other children. And if so, maybe there is some justice to the word *autism*. Maybe autistic children do experience a radical solipsism. The self is, terrifyingly, their only reality. If you are afraid that other people are mad at you, then they *are* mad at you, because that is the way you see it.

Eventually, Paul set out to rank the weight and seriousness of anger, to give the different gradations a number value that might somehow help him to understand what was for him a bewildering blizzard of emotions. And Jim helped him.

"Be critical," Paul began to say to Jim, at about the same time he asked Kate to be the "mean teacher." "Now be severe." And there would be a little anticipatory pause while Paul held his breath and Jim prepared to deepen the scowl on his face and lower his voice one notch down on the menace scale. Then, "Ooooooo," a little appreciative murmur from Paul, as he sidled backward from Jim. "You mean *business!*"

"Now be annoyed." At this point there would be a little catch in Paul's voice, a gulp. "Now, be *irritated!*" And he laughed nervously, jumping up and down in one spot.

And the final command, but only after Paul felt he was fully prepared, had gotten his nervous system well under control. "BE FURIOUS." Then Jim would growl and lurch at him across the kitchen floor, his voice now thundering an impressive bass-baritone roar.

Critical, severe, annoyed, irritated, furious. It would never have occurred to the rest of us that anger came in such minutely distinguished gradations. But this was one time when Jim's acting skills were put to good use at home. He drew himself up, seemed to puff out, as he stood on tiptoe and towered over Paul. Jim could modulate his voice, working from the peevishness of annoyance, to the rasp of irritation, to the white heat of fury. And Paul studied each minute discrimination with the pleasure of a confirmed theatergoer, but his pleasure was far keener because he knew he was playing with fire, flirting with the Real Thing.

And this was the beginning of play. It was of course a different kind of play, one that involved ranking and ordering, but it was play nevertheless. Only in play can you control other people's feelings. And for once in his life, Paul did have some control over other people, or at least of the situation itself.

The point for Paul, however, was that people were unpredictable. There was no way around this unpleasant fact. They got angry at the oddest things, at the most unexpected moments, and you could never be sure, at any given time, that you were entirely safe. As a child, before Paul learned to be very, very good and very, very quiet, anger was a familiar, although never understood, part of his daily world. Only in these moments with Jim was Paul able to play with his fears, and so learn some measure of control over them. In this way, he learned the value of play, of imitation, of imagination.

But Paul's control, once again, was a control gained through number, the ultimate language of order and degree. Sometimes he was explicit about this. Instead of "Be critical, severe, annoyed," and so forth, he would say, "Be angry at ten degrees. At twenty degrees," and so on up to one hundred. In a most obvious way here, he would quantify the gradations of mood.

Paul assigned arbitrary numbers to words and to abstract concepts, not just to events that can be understood according to statistical probability. He started to rank language and concepts according to numerical values when he was nine or ten, and some years later he even began to tell us his mood, ranking it on a scale from one to one hundred. Probability theory, which a math teacher had attempted to teach him when he was nine, gave Paul permission to do this. Soon he ranked not only anger, but all moods, his general emotional climate: "Kate, do you want to know what number I am today?"

"What number are you?"

"I'm only forty-two. Yesterday I was all the way to seventy-six."

"Why are you only forty-two?"

"Because we didn't have a storm. They said there was going to be a thunderstorm this afternoon. But there wasn't. So I'm only forty-two."

"Oh." Kate, as always, was sympathetic. "Maybe we will have a storm tomorrow," she added hopefully.

When he was twelve, Paul began to worry about whether the earth was in a cooling trend, moving toward a new ice age, or in a warming trend, heating up as part of the greenhouse effect. To find out, he decided he wanted to see all the temperatures that had been recorded for our area since the beginning of record keeping. So together we called the National Climatological Data Institute in North Carolina and asked them to send Paul a complete set of microfilm with all the temperatures by date, recorded since 1881.

After this, Paul set out for the college library and the microfilm room every day after school. I sometimes visited him there and found him bent over the machine, earnestly studying the numbers. Without a computer, without complex mathematical formulae, before Chaos theory, of course he could find no long-range pattern. But this was an interest worth pursuing, and once or twice I tried to find him a college student, a math or science major, who might work with him. But I never succeeded in finding anyone. So, for months, Paul simply read numbers.

The world is full of things that cannot be known in their particularity, but only in their generality. The thousands of leaves outside the window, winking in the sunlight, the dappled shadows, the millions of water droplets gathered into the filaments that we see as the clouds in the sky — all are a generality, seen massed together. Temperatures seen separately, one after another, are about as meaningful as water droplets. The "thisness" of things, their "Haecceitas," has its limits, in spite of what the poet Hopkins said when he praised the marvelous particularity of the world. You can have too much thisness and thatness, and when you do, you end up swamped. And that was what happened to Paul, at least at the time he was studying temperatures.

And yet Paul's memory, I discovered one day when he was in high school, was based on just this kind of particularity. One Saturday we were walking in the woods and we paused to sit for a while under a tree. It was one of those peaceful, quiet moments, which often happened in the woods when we were walking, when Paul seemed to reach some deeper part of himself. But on this day he came out with something that absolutely floored me. And then I could hardly believe I hadn't noticed it before. "I remember we were here once before, weren't we?" I asked Paul.

"It was Saturday afternoon, October thirty-first, 1987, and I was frustrated because there was no storm that day. Also I went trick-or-treating that night."

"Well, it was Halloween. But what else do you remember? How about the next day?"

"We went to Burnsville to shop. It was foggy. That was on Sunday. On Monday, November second, when I woke up, the temperature was warming up. I was getting interested in the weather. A friend of Kate's came over. They were playing the radio on the porch. I was watching *The Fly* one more time before I finally erased it. That night there was a big thunderstorm. On Tuesday, November third, I went for a walk in the Arb by the Cannon River. On Wednesday, November fourth, I went to a confirmation class, and they put white powder on my face and we had to go through an obstacle course. It was some stupid symbolic thing. I went to Allen's house later that night. And I can't remember anything on the fifth of November, but on Sunday, November eighth, I got into a fight with Daddy.

After this, we often asked Paul to tell us what happened to him on particular dates in the past. Frequently he could remember with an exactitude that astounded us. Sometimes we would check the accuracy of his memory by looking at a calendar or a datebook or diary, and always, unfailingly, he was right. Gradually we learned, as a family, to rely on his memory, to ask him when we had last traveled to a particular place in England, for example, and he always told us. He remembered all birthdays, including those of our cats. Usually, he could tell us what the weather was on almost any given date for several years running.

Paul couldn't, of course, explain why or how he remembered in this way. I asked him if he visualized a calendar, for example, and he was vague on the subject. All he would ever say was, "That was the only thing interesting to me — time going by."

Time was an absolute, and that meant it shouldn't speed up or slow down. Once Jim found an item in the newspaper about the "leap second" that astronomers were adding that year. "Look at this! Sunday will contain 86,401 seconds, rather than the normal 86,400."

He read out loud, " 'The extra second, known to astronomers and professional timekeepers as a "leap second," will be squeezed in just as the New Year begins in London. In other words, in Minnesota, sixty-one seconds will elapse between five fifty-nine and six P.M., making it the longest minute in the last two years.'

"We've outsmarted the sun once again," Jim chuckled, but then he paused. "Don't show this to Paul, will you?"

I agreed. How would we explain this one to him? A leap year and an extra day is hard enough, without having to cope with loose seconds.

Finally, Paul found a principle for the very unpredictability of the world, the inscrutability of fate, the perversity of human interactions: Murphy's Law. If anything can go wrong it will. If two things can go wrong, the worst will happen first. Two wrongs can never make a right, but two rights can and often will make a wrong. Murphy, that Irishman of obscure origins, came forward to supply the missing piece in Paul's world. And now Paul had found the very principle for unpredictability, the law for lawlessness itself.

Instead of disasters, we sometimes now had only Murphy. If it rained on a picnic, that was Murphy. Bread always falls butter side down. Cars never break down in the driveway. Just when you know all the answers, they change the questions. The day you are early, they have canceled the meeting. Murphy, always Murphy, that worker of insanity, that manipulator of events into the least reasonable possible, was satisfying to Paul and also very funny. But this was much later; Murphy appeared only when Paul was a teenager.

Eventually, Paul stopped mapping and measuring, at least in the simple way he had done as a child. He and Allen stopped exploring the sewers with flashlights and the countryside with their bikes and topographical maps. Paul stopped climbing the highest trees and testing swimming pools and lakes for the deepest depths. Scales, clocks, tape measures, speedometers, odometers, and thermometers were no longer his primary tools for comprehending the world.

Although I didn't realize it at the time, when Paul was near the end of middle school, he was not only ready to leave his childhood behind, but also he was making preparations to give up some of his autistic defenses. As he approached his fourteenth birthday, we planned a term away in Dublin. Unknown to us, Ireland was to be a turning point in Paul's life, a shifting, uncertain boundary between childhood and adulthood. When we were there he found the perfect metaphor for this transition in his life, the ideal spot on earth where he could examine and measure a shifting borderland before moving on: he discovered the tides and the tidal zones of the Irish Sea. But in other ways Paul was about to abandon the safety of numbers, the exactitude of measurement, and to enter, without guides this time, our confused and ambiguous and terrifying social world. I could never have anticipated how difficult and risky this journey would be, nor how much it would cost Paul, and indeed all the rest of us.

CHAPTER 27

The Hand of the Crusader

AUNT MAGGIE's stone cottage under the hill: we were there at last, on the west coast of Ireland, County Mayo, the last rocky outcropping of Europe, before the vast sweep of the Atlantic. I had heard about this place for years, the family home of Jim's father, and I knew it was as close to the old Ireland as I would ever come. When we crossed the threshold of this little cottage, and I saw the cross and cup for holy water standing just inside the door, I felt as if I had stumbled into a different world and had traveled back at least two hundred years.

So here we were, in a thatched stone cottage with a stone floor, a cottage with electricity but no plumbing, a turf fire at one end of the room, a television set at the other. The auld chat, a curtained-off bed for the old couple, was set into a nook of the wall near the large open fireplace. On the mantelpiece was a kind of household shrine: candles, mass cards, a picture of Pope John Paul and a picture of Aunt Maggie's eldest son who was a priest and lived in Meridian, Mississippi.

For almost twenty years I had heard stories of this house and these people from Jim. This was the house that was always full of music when Jim was a child: the melodeon, the tin whistle. Music and dance and never much food. Even Jim's mother's family, who lived twenty miles away on deeper soil, was more prosperous and had already left this way of life generations ago.

Now, walking through this door, I was struggling to realize that these gentle and warm but very different people were my people too. I lived in some vital connection with them. They were mine by marriage, mine now by that strangest of mysteries, the mystery of mingled genes. My children were their children also, their cousins.

Earlier that morning we had stopped with Paul and Kate at the old churchyard at Aghagower. This was the churchyard, beside the ruined church, where Jim's grandparents, his father's parents, had been buried. I say "had been buried," because in all probability they were no longer buried there. We had wandered around the graveyard and ruined church, picking our way through nettles, burdock, buttercups, and lady's smock, over the untended graves. Jim explained to me that in the west of Ireland, they sometimes dig up old unmarked graves in order to make a place for the newly dead. The bones from these graves, unmarked because the families were too poor to pay for a headstone, are then stashed somewhere in the churchyard or perhaps in the ruins of the church. Jim's own family had been unable to pay for a marker, and therefore a permanent resting place somewhere in this soil. But we knew his grandparents were still there somewhere.

We had stopped to examine the round tower, which was perhaps eight hundred years old. The entrance to the tower was set high above the ground so the monks could climb inside, then pull up the ladder to be safe from Viking invaders. But Jim also showed me the bottom of the tower where the invaders could simply remove a stone, then fire the tower, which became an inferno, trapping and killing every monk inside. Their safe hiding place was actually the most dangerous place they could have chosen.

Walking around the churchyard, we had missed the children sometime before. But now we heard stifled giggling from inside the ruined church. Going into the nave, where the walls but not the roof were still standing, we found them by a niche in the wall near what used to be the altar. Paul was batting at Kate with a bone, and Kate was fighting back with what looked like an arm bone. Approaching them, we found a cache of human remains — tibia, fibula, humerus, even a skull with teeth still intact. We instantly recognized that they may have been the bones of these children's great grandparents.

We made them put the bones carefully back where they found them. But driving away, I thought of the strangeness of this scene. And part of the strangeness was that we weren't shocked, Jim and I. This seemed like a natural occurrence: two children playing with the bones of their ancestors in a ruined church in the west of Ireland. Later, though, sitting down to tea in Aunt Maggie's cottage, I struggled to realize that these children were connected not just with me and with Jim, but also with some unknown, unfathomed past. Bone of my bone, they were also bone of a far different people, a people who had lived here on this land for millenia. And this feeling of strangeness, this odd feeling of connection with some unfathomable past, stayed with me all day.

*

We were in Ireland for our third sabbatical abroad because Jim wanted to develop a program for American students in Ireland. We would be renting a house during fall term in Dublin, and the children would be going to school there. But the return to Ireland was more than just an academic exercise for Jim: now, for the first time perhaps, the Cambridge-educated academic was meeting the country boy from the west of Ireland. These two sides of Jim were coming together in a new interest in the literature, history, and music of the country he had left so long before.

I had my own reasons for wanting to be in Dublin. I hoped that, by coming to Ireland for a term, we would also be traveling to a more accepting past. I hoped that Ireland would be a more tolerant place than America, more forgiving of difference in Paul, and indeed Jim's immediate family, with their steady warmth and acceptance of him, had long predisposed me to this belief. Jim thought I was being a romantic once again, but I hoped to get away from some of America's anxiety about success and getting ahead in the world.

We knew, however, that we had taken a big risk in coming to Ireland. We had spent a sabbatical semester in London when Paul was ten and Kate was six, and that had gone reasonably well, but this time Paul had made it abundantly clear to us that he was being dragged to Ireland very much against his will. He simply didn't want to go to a foreign land where he had no friends, where everything was new and strange and different. Now, at the age of fourteen, he was much more articulate about his wants.

During the whole previous year, Jim and I had agonized over this decision to transplant the family for five months. In the end, we decided to put the family first, before Paul, to consider the benefits for all the rest of us, above any distress the move might cause him. We had made decisions this way several times before, and thought that change, although difficult for him, had in the end made Paul more flexible.

Paul felt disoriented in Dublin, but he wasn't the only one who felt that way. I had expected to find the city a provincial London, full of cultural activities and street life, with a greengrocer and newsagent just around the corner. I had improbable dreams of a Georgian house, fanlit doorway, cavernous rooms, and a small but intensely blooming garden. Instead we found ourselves in a stuccoed suburb, part of a new development, houses built side to side, a thicket of cinder block walls out back. This was the new Industrial Revolution style, I thought,

Victorian artisan's cottages with plate glass front windows. Like thousands, millions, of others in Ireland and England, they were crowded together as if within sound of the factory whistle, close to the post office, the butcher. But here there was no reason for crowding, nothing was just around the corner. We had to get in the car and drive several miles to the nearest supermarket in an American-style mall. The mall, of course, was built to remind us of the cozy shops crowded together on the streets, which used to be just around the corner. But they had come back to Ireland by way of the United States.

School wouldn't begin for several weeks so, as always, we looked for tourist sites that would interest the children as well as us. We decided to take a day trip to the Boyne River Valley north of Dublin, to visit Newgrange, a Neolithic chambered tomb. Jim and I thought Paul especially would be fascinated with such a place.

When we arrived we discovered that the burial chamber itself is within a huge mound of earth, and can be reached only by walking down a long, claustrophobic passageway. We were warned by the guide that some people might find it hard to walk down the sixty-five-foot passage to the central chamber, and indeed one woman turned back after a few feet. The darkness as we walked along seemed almost total, literally the darkness of the grave, but we kept going, following the faint light of the guide's flashlight.

As we entered the chamber at the end of the passage, we were told that once a year on December 21, the winter solstice, light pierces the passageway all the way to the round barrow at the end. For twenty minutes, and only twenty minutes, at sunrise on the shortest day of the year, the light floods the chamber. We stood there, breathing the dank earth smell of a five-thousand-year-old burial chamber, trying to imagine ourselves into the heads of New Stone Age people. What fears, what hopes, were expressed in this huge mound of earth, this twenty-foot-high burial chamber that receives the sun's rays just once a year? Newgrange seemed to be a place that had something to say, if we could just listen and attend.

The guide told us that, like Stonehenge and Avebury, Newgrange might have been a calendar in stone. Certainly it was built with some knowledge of the sun's movements, but unlike Stonehenge, which was built with the summer solstice in mind, this court cairn was built to mark the swing of the sun at its lowest arc on the shortest day of the year. But we learned that Newgrange is older and even more baffling than Stonehenge. Emerging again into the broad daylight, we all took a deep breath and looked around at a series of stone circles outside the tomb. The guide explained: a much later people settling this same land, perhaps at the same time that Stonehenge was built, seemed to have been terrified of Newgrange. They built henges, stone circles in the fields outside, perhaps to contain whatever force or power was embodied in this mound of earth. At least, that's what scholars seemed to think.

Just before we left, the guide turned again to the spiral decorations on the kerbstones at the entrance to the tumulus. "These probably will never be read, never be understood," she told us. "All we know is that these early people liked spiral decorations, and such decoration remained a part of Irish art for the next four millenia."

And that was all. We left almost regretfully, knowing Newgrange had yet once again preserved its mysteries. More than anything else, this mound of earth, this heap of stones, had told us that the past is discontinuous and unreclaimable. And there are pasts behind the past, a bottomless time that can never be reached and understood.

We had thought Paul would be interested in all this. A five-thousand-year-old burial chamber, with human remains in niches in the walls, a long, narrow passageway that the sun reaches into just once a year, an astronomical calendar built of stone and earth, all this would have fascinated him years ago, as it did Kate right now. But there was a new passivity in Paul, a strange, new resignation. It seemed that the old gods of measurement no longer fascinated; the old dispensations were gone. He would go with us where we led, but he wouldn't necessarily enjoy it.

We had taken Paul from his home, his friends, his school, where he had at last settled in and started to do well. We wanted to find the right school for him in Dublin and were afraid as we set out to make our way through a new and utterly foreign school system with a special needs child. Would they understand auditory processing problems and social deficits? Would there be the equivalent of a resource room here? We were very aware of our American educational babble and wondered if we could begin to translate it across cultures. Letters we had sent in advance hadn't brought us much information.

We made an appointment with the headmaster of St. Kenneth's, a small Catholic secondary school we had heard good things about and had corresponded with. We all went to visit the school and were shown into the parlor of a large early Victorian house that served as private residence for the headmaster as well as administrative offices for the school. The parlor had two large Parian marble fireplaces, red Bohemian glass, pink Aubusson carpets, and paintings by Jack Yeats. We sat on the edge of our seats. Aubusson carpets and original Jack Yeats meant money to me, also intelligence, privilege, and high-achieving kids.

In our letter to the headmaster we had tried to give him a sense of Paul and what we thought he needed in a school. We had made an effort to be as honest as we could be, but we hadn't used the word *autism*, or even the terms *high-achieving autism* or *pervasive developmental disorder*. We had discovered in the past that these words frightened people and gave them the wrong impression. Paul never truly fit people's abstract notions of what autism was, and we had learned that if we called him autistic, no school would want him. Our compromise over the years was to try to give a careful description of the particulars of his learning style and personality. But now, sitting in the parlor on the edge of our seats, we wondered if we had made the right decision. Had we really lied in our letter, misrepresented Paul and his deficits and talents?

We need not have worried. The headmaster, Mr. McNamara, a cheerful, friendly man with an affectionate way of teasing the boys, immediately put us at ease. We talked a bit, then he took Paul out for a brief interview. He tested his reading, math, and science knowledge, then returned to tell us that he was mostly at grade level. After Paul was taken out to be shown around the school, Mr. McNamara turned to us. "Is he autistic?" he asked. Immediately, I began to think this man knew more than most school officials we had ever dealt with. It was reassuring now to hear the word in the context of acceptance and approval, not as grounds for excluding him.

We were, however, still worried that Paul wouldn't be able to keep up with this accelerated curriculum. These fourteen-year-old boys studied not only history and English and math, but also Latin, French, Spanish, and Irish. This would be way above Paul's head, so we agreed that he would do English, history, math, and try the Spanish class.

We had also written ahead of time to schools for Kate, who had just turned ten, but in a sense she took the initiative herself. The first Sunday we were in our new house, she joined some games, running competitions, in the little park nearby. She didn't know anyone there, but as usual she started to talk to some girls her age. Everyone told us about a wonderful Protestant girl's school within easy walking distance of our neighborhood.

The next morning Jim and I took Kate to visit the Claudia College for Girls. The school looked like a factory, but the headmistress's office was decorated with pictures of the Roman Forum and the Colosseum, the Borghese Gardens and the Capitoline Museum. We all sat down on the hard plastic chairs and accepted the cups of tea from her secretary. I looked around at the office. Dirty plate glass windows made up one wall; the desk was piled high with papers and half-filled mugs. Behind the desk was a sepia-tone map of the Roman Empire — Hispania, Gallia, Illyricum, and Britannia. Sipping my tea I studied it: interestingly enough, Hibernia, Ireland, that winter wasteland which the Romans never sought to conquer, was not mentioned on the map. Over the bookcase was a chart of the Roman emperors — Augustus, Tiberius, Caligula, Claudius, Nero — which I idly read as we waited for the headmistress to arrive.

Kate sipped her diluted tea and stared around the room also. Suddenly she seemed very small to me with her feet dangling just above the floor, and very American in her jeans and sweatshirt. I had strong doubts about this school. What was this culture we had stumbled into — intimidated Irish Protestant, postmodern classical? And what did this say about the headmistress and about the school as a whole? At that moment it all seemed very strange to me, almost unnerving, a little like the shopping center that reintroduced the old Irish shops by way of a new American mall.

Finally Miss Julian fluttered in, wearing a bat-sleeved academic gown over a pale and somewhat dirty lavender dress. Before we could open our mouths to ask a single question, she launched into a tirade about the school uniform. "Now you realize that even though you are American, your daughter has to wear the uniform? You realize that, don't you?" Kate was staring uncomfortably out the window. She seemed to be far away.

Not waiting for an answer, Miss Julian plunged on. "No child, no matter how temporary, should ever get away with not wearing the school uniform. Once, several years ago, a French girl didn't wear her uniform for almost a whole week because she had sent it to the dry cleaners. This must never, ever happen again." Miss Julian stopped at this point and glared at us from the other side of her desk.

We mumbled something, made our excuses, and fled. "Let's just go home," Jim said to me after we were out of earshot. "Remember that good Anglican girl's school we heard about? It's not so far away. Let's just go and call them for an appointment."

We stepped out of the administration building and headed down the sidewalk, past the classrooms for the lower form girls. On the pathway in front of us, two women stopped and smiled and introduced them-

Paul, a bright, alert baby,
at age ten months

Jane and Paul, age nineteen months

In Contignac, France, with his grandfather

It was at the Wolfson Centre
that Paul began to master language

This teapot provided
Paul with his first word

For years, Paul was fearful of flowers

Paul Hager

With baby Kate

Paul, always able to be affectionate, is
shown here with his beloved grandmother

Despite so many fears,
heights were never a problem

Even on the hottest days, Paul, sitting with
Kate and cousins Charlie and Graham,
insisted on long sleeves

Unable to understand the world,
Paul set out to measure it with numbers

At six, Paul used peripheral vision
to view the world

"How high am I above sea level?"

Kate with her Teddy,
Paul with his mileage meter

"Baby Earth"

With Allen and one of their many towers

Kate often comforted Paul

With Squeezy at Warwick Castle

"Greenwich Mean Time"

Jim and Paul — and his watch

Jane, Kate, and Paul on visiting day at camp

Paul's senior class photo

With Barry Morrow, who wrote
the screenplay for *Rain Man*

Having given up many of his autistic behaviors,
Paul began to clown and mimic, here with Kate

The family today

selves. "Can we help you?" one of them asked. "We are lower form teachers." As it turned out, these two charming, sensible, intelligent teachers were precisely the ones who would be teaching Kate if we decided to send her to the Claudia College. They showed us the classrooms they were preparing for the students' arrival next week. They explained the curriculum: history, English, math, Irish, and natural science. They told us Kate could learn Irish dancing and gymnastics. Then they dived into the lost and found, pulling out a jumper, a sweater, a scarf, just right for her. "You don't have to go out and buy a whole new uniform for her," they said. "That's a waste of money for someone who will just be here four months."

This decided the matter. We enrolled Kate in the Claudia College for Girls, and we never had reason to regret it.

And so we settled into Dublin, feeling we could relax a little now that the children were placed in good schools. We bought a modified uniform for Paul, gray slacks and white shirts, tie and sweater, as well as black shoes. We were afraid he would refuse to wear these clothes because they were so different from his usual blue jeans, but Paul accepted this change and a number of others with apparent ease. He now carried a book bag to school for the first time in his life, ate a hot lunch with the other boys, and sat quietly in the classrooms, even the ones, like Latin and Irish, which he wasn't officially taking. He was supposed to work on homework in those extra classes, but he started carrying books to read in the back of the room.

Later I realized that there was an important benefit for Paul in this school. Because he was with a new group of boys, people who didn't know him or his past, he felt almost for the first time in his life that he wasn't judged in advance. No one here called him "retard" or simply " 'tard," those terrible put-down words used both of children who are slow in their development and of anyone who is in any way different. No one sneered when he walked down the hall, or tried to work him into a frenzy, or laughed at the "weirdo" after they had made him angry.

I also learned sometime later that the headmaster had spoken to all the students in the school before Paul started about the fact that this new boy was an American, that he wouldn't know anyone and would appreciate some friendliness, and perhaps that he might be a little different, so they should be kind to him and not tease him. This kind of appeal to the better side of American teenagers would probably have backfired; they might have done exactly what they had been asked not to do, singling out a kid for special abusive treatment. But here it seemed to work, and Paul felt very comfortable among these boys.

Looking back on our time in Dublin, I realized that this comfort had given Paul the space he so desperately needed to calm down. Because he now felt accepted, he began to drop some of his odd behaviors, the pencil flipping and the loud yawns he had been known for in middle school. He started to melt right into the crowd, something most autistic people never are able to do. And gradually he became something he might not have been, had he stayed in his American school that term: he became a very well mannered, attractive boy, quietly interested in everything that went on around him, and totally unremarkable in his behavior.

This newfound calmness, however, did nothing to help Paul in his loneliness, a loneliness that in the end threatened to swamp him.

Jim was, by this time, attending a seminar at University College Dublin, where he was making a lot of friends, and he had also been asked to take over a class in contemporary literary theory at Trinity when the teacher became ill suddenly. It turned out that he was the only person in Dublin qualified to teach that particular class: his own syllabus, developed for our college in America, was very similar to that of the teacher at Trinity. So Jim was now very busy and very happy. He was learning a lot about Irish literature for his own teaching and he was making a lot of contacts, people who would later be able to help him when he developed his own Dublin program and brought American students over to Ireland.

Jim was very involved in the two colleges, but I had time on my hands. My book, which I had at last finished, had been chosen as one of the finalists for a prize and publication in a university press series in America. I was waiting anxiously to hear if they had accepted it, which meant I was really at loose ends. I was afraid the book would in the end be turned down (it was), and I didn't know if I should work on further revisions in the absence of the readers' reports or start on a new project.

Kate began to make friends, and we soon discovered our neighborhood was full of ten-year-old girls. She was invited to many birthday parties, and almost every day after school she went to a neighbor's house, or another girl came to our house to visit. She also loved her two teachers, who often combined the two classes of ten-year-old girls or traded with each other. She joined the gymnastic club and tried Irish dancing for a while. She began to do very well academically and enjoyed everything except the study of bogs. "I'm sick of raised bogs," she complained to us. "And the evolution of bogs! Who cares about bogs?"

Everything seemed to be going well for Kate. She had a circle of devoted friends, teachers who admired her and approved of her work, and she had started to become very interested in her own Irish background and heritage. The contrast between her life and Paul's began to seem more and more apparent to him. One afternoon one of Kate's friends stumbled on Paul alone in his room crying. After that he felt outraged, although it was no one's fault. He felt embarrassed, invaded in his only safe place.

We decided to buy secondhand bicycles for them both, even though the traffic conditions were terrible. Kate was young enough to be allowed to ride on the sidewalk, so she was safe, but Paul was supposed to ride in the street. I was terrified that something might happen to him in the heavy traffic, so I made him carry his name, address, and phone number in his pocket. We let him go, however, feeling that a bicycle would give him some freedom, some exercise in the fresh air and something to live for. We gave him a map of Dublin, a street atlas that he tucked into his sweater, and then he took off after school every day, bicycling all over south Dublin near us, then north Dublin as far as Phoenix Park. He told us he sometimes got lost, sometimes deliberately. "But then I just stop and look at the map, and I can always find out where I am," he told us proudly.

Jim drove Paul to school every morning. They were always stopped in heavy traffic, near a newsboy who worked the street up and down between the rows of cars, selling the morning paper. Jim made sure that Paul always had money ready to give the newsboy. And Paul began to check the paper for the time of the tides before he was dropped off at school. Then after school every day, Paul began to head for the Irish Sea on his bicycle. More and more, it was the sea that drew him, and finally it was the sea that helped him to survive Dublin and the loneliness and isolation of a foreign school, where he was kindly treated but where he had no real friends.

His favorite place was a small promontory, a sand spit near the main port of Dublin. This was an extension of land out into the Irish Sea, with nothing but a road, the electricity works, and a small encampment of traveling people, gypsies, who had drawn up near the walls of a gutted house. I sometimes worried that this wasn't a safe place, but I also knew that, except for the "troubles" in the north, Ireland is a very safe place. There is little personal violence of the sort we have come to expect in American cities. So I let Paul go to his favorite sandbank, the lonely spot out by the electricity works. Occasionally I went with him, but mostly he went by himself on his bicycle.

Wednesdays were half days at St. Kenneth's. The other boys did sports in the afternoon, but since Paul wasn't interested in any sports he came home. After lunch we would set out together to explore some part of the coast of the Irish Sea. Usually we didn't go to the electricity works but rather to some other part of the coast which I thought would be more beautiful, or which would offer us a tearoom later in the day. We sometimes went to Bray or to other resort towns to the south of Dublin, or to Malahide on the far north coast.

One of our favorite places was the coast at Howth Head, a beautiful rocky promontory, with a lighthouse and a cliff walk near the small village of Howth. W. B. Yeats, at Paul's age, had lived in a small, low house on the cliff. Sometimes we walked past it and stopped to read the poem on a plaque by the door: "I have spread my dreams under your feet / Tread softly, because you tread on my dreams." Once, looking in the front window, I noticed a sweater drying across a radiator and thought how strange it was that people still lived in that house.

I usually brought a book or some postcards to write and I sat on the rocks a little way out of the reach of the water, but Paul always went right to the edge of the shore. At Howth the tide came in over rocks, so there were always small pools of water left behind when the tide went out and each of these pools had myriad forms of sea life. Then the incoming tide would flood these pools and change their tiny perfect ecosystems once again. Paul was fascinated by this place, by the unstable, always changing intertidal zone. He wanted to mark the low tide and the high tide and to keep track of exactly where the water mark had been each week.

One Wednesday we went to Howth when a storm was threatening. We thought we could stand in a small lifeboat shelter on the pier and watch the approaching clouds as they swept over the landmass heading for the sea, and then still make it back to the village before the rain hit. But of course we were caught in the sudden squall and soaked through to the skin.

After the storm passed, we headed for the little tea shop where we often went after watching the tide. We sat there by a small electric heater, our clothes steaming as they slowly dried out. As we drank our tea, the woman who owned the shop started cooking a large vat of soup. She cut up carrots and turnips and dropped them in the pot and talked to her friends as they stopped by for a chat. The chicken soup filled the shop with a wonderful smell as it slowly simmered. Paul and I didn't want to leave. This place was safety, and neither of us wanted to head home to think of school and the responsibilities of the next day. We waited as long as we dared, then started our slow journey home, first traveling by train, then walking through north Dublin to the bus that would take us almost to our door.

I always found it hard to get used to the beggars in Dublin. It had been years since I had lived in a large American city, and the poverty I had seen over the past years in the small town where we lived in Minnesota was less obvious, less open. Poverty there was at least housed. But here in Dublin, we sometimes saw mothers and babies sitting in doorways, a shawl covering both their heads, looking for all the world just like the eighteenth-century poor that so concerned Swift and Handel. These mothers sometimes sent their older children after us to follow us down the street. And these children, their faces blotchy with rashes, would chase us, never leaving our side, until we gave them something. I often thought of the beggars for whose relief Handel dedicated the first performance of the *Messiah,* in the Council Chambers of Fishamble Hall, so close to where we now walked.

On this evening, as we walked to our bus in north Dublin, an old man came up to us to ask for some money. I gave it to him and then, in a very courtly way, he shook my hand, and Paul's hand, gave us his blessing and best wishes for all in our family, and shuffled away.

I thought no more of this old man, until later that week when I read Paul's English notebook from school. In it he had written a little story:

> I have been forced to leave my home and I have nowhere to go. I will cope with it by sleeping on park benches and try to find a job for some money to live on, hopefully to buy another home. Before I get that job, I will go and eat out of garbage cans. I don't think that is a very good way of living, but it is the only way of getting food and living. I tried to get a job as a newspaper printer, but they didn't want me for the job.
>
> I am wandering the streets feeling very angry, worried and depressed. I wish I could kill those people who said I couldn't stay in my house any more, because I did not have enough money to pay for it. I don't know what to do, it is very difficult to get a job if you're just a person who wanders the streets, eats out of garbage cans, sleeps on park benches with a newspaper or a very dirty old blanket

to cover yourself, and wears very filthy clothes that haven't been washed for weeks.

I haven't had a bath since I lost my house three weeks ago. I am very dirty and I am wondering if I should bathe in the river, even though it is full of raw sewage and chemicals. I decided not to bathe in the river. It is a real problem for me not to have a bath to wash in anywhere. I am thinking that a house that a stranger owns will have a bath that I could bathe in, but that person will almost certainly not allow me to use his bathtub.

I have no friends that would let me share their house with me. So I just wander around the city looking for a job and a home, feeling very sad and lonely. Maybe I could make a friend somewhere, but if so it could take a long time.

When I read this little story, I knew it wasn't just the old man in north Dublin that concerned Paul. He was beginning to be very preoccupied with his own future, to wonder if he would ever get through school or make it on his own, to wonder in fact if he might not end up like this old man. He didn't talk at this time of these fears, but later I wondered if they might have been part of his growing depression that fall.

Paul got a B on this piece of writing, but we knew he was having a hard time keeping up with the accelerated curriculum of a good Irish school. Even the average Irish students were at least two years ahead of their American counterparts, and this school took only the very brightest. They had no Resource Room, no tutoring or support program of any sort, and there were no parent-teacher conferences, no regular consultations over a child's progress. Nevertheless, at first we thought Paul was doing passably well. It wasn't until much later, the end of the term in fact, that we learned that his teachers had long since stopped asking anything of him.

As the days got shorter and he found he could no longer go to the beach after school, Paul began to get more and more depressed. Riding his bike, watching the tides, and reading Enid Blighton books had been his only pleasures. And now he discovered that he had only three Enid Blighton books left to go. We went to a secondhand bookstore and found the remaining three unread books, brought them home, and then Paul collapsed.

He cried for hours that evening, for hours and hours. Jim and I tried talking to him, but finally we were so frayed, we wondered if we could go on, if we shouldn't try to get in touch with a professional, someone who could help us with Paul, even though we were returning to

America in only three weeks. It didn't seem that he could last even for that long. But somehow he held on, and he continued to go to school, although one day they sent him home ill, pale and nauseated. I bought some jigsaw puzzles and together we worked on them after dinner. Paul was briefly interested, but I could feel him slipping away from us.

Earlier in October, Paul had asked us when our plane would leave for America. Then he took the calculator out of my purse and started counting days, hours, minutes, and seconds until the moment of our departure. Every few days he would recalculate his remaining moments in Dublin. Now each day when he came home from school, he recalculated the minutes until our plane was to take off. Sometimes he did this several times a day. He was fixated on simply getting back to America, counting minutes and seconds so that now of course the time was dragging more and more slowly.

Those last days in Dublin, I cast about desperately for interesting things to do with the kids, ways to occupy Paul in particular. One December day, we found ourselves walking in the rain on the north side of the Liffey. We had taken a smoky bus to north Dublin, then gotten off at O'Connell Bridge. Now we were walking along the river, past the warehouses, past Penny Farthing Bridge. The tourist season was over. The Americans had all gone home. So had the trinket sellers on the bridge, the transcendental meditators in their saffron robes, and the sidewalk artists chalking Rubens, Caravaggio, Titian, beside the gates of Trinity. The rain stung our faces. Gulls worked the sluices and sewers spilling into the brackish river. The Dark Pool: *dubh linn*.

We walked with our heads into the wind. We were going to St. Michan's Church, one of the oldest and most historic churches in Dublin. I had chosen this church for an outing because I thought it would offer something for everyone: some history and architecture for me, and for the kids there would be a dead Crusader, mummified and preserved in the crypt. We had read about this church and its mummy in our guidebook, *Exploring Dublin for Children*. The book told us that shaking the hand of the Crusader was the traditional way of acquiring good luck in Dublin, a little like kissing the Blarney Stone for the gift of gab. And I thought that acquiring a little luck at this time didn't seem like such a bad idea.

The rain let up a bit. Down a narrow street of dirty houses, we found the church. Corrugated metal was nailed into posts against the nave to shelter a garage next door. On the edge of the churchyard, several young men worked on a car engine. They turned the car on, and it ground and sputtered, choked and shut down again. St. Michan's, whose one-thousand-year-old tower was built before the Battle of Clontarf, was not a pretty sight.

We went inside. A sign just inside the church door said: TOURS OF THE VAULTS: DAILY, 2:00 TO 4:30 P.M. Another sign said: TOUR IN PROGRESS. WAIT HERE FOR NEXT TOUR. We settled down on the cold stone benches. There was a dank smell coming from inside the church.

We waited for a while, then decided to look inside. We dropped some money into the collection box to help, as the sign instructed us, to maintain the fabric of this ancient and historically valuable church. Looking around, we saw no evidence of a tour in progress, but there was one old man, the verger perhaps, polishing brass rails in a dark corner of the cold, dimly lit church. He looked over at us suspiciously. "Can I help you?" he asked, but every line of his body expressed resentment at our intrusion, a heavy reluctance to greet us. Clearly he didn't care for our being there.

I told him that we had come for a tour of the vaults. He told us there was no tour of the vaults. Or, if there was, it is only in the summer at the height of the tourist season and for busloads of visiting Americans who write well in advance. But we had come a long way, on a smoky double decker and through the rain, and I wasn't about to give up. I mentioned our guidebook, *Exploring Dublin for Children,* and his own signs just outside the door.

Defeated, he relented. Reluctantly setting down his Brasso and his rags, he offered to give us a tour of the church. He started in at the altar. "The church is Anglican," he said. "You know what that means? That's Episcopal in America." He peered into my face. I nodded.

On around the church. "You see that baptismal font? The Duke of Wellington was baptized there. You've heard of the Duke of Wellington?" He went on, "He defeated Napoleon at the Battle of Waterloo . . ."

Just as I was trying to understand this amazing record of English imperialism, which had somehow ended up here in this ancient church in the slums of north Dublin, Kate pulled on my sleeve. She had noticed a skull in the corner near the altar. Here was something interesting. "What's that doing there?" she asked me.

"That skull has been there since Cromwell's Rebellion." I noticed the verger said Cromwell's Rebellion, not the Irish rebellion that Cromwell put down. "You've heard of Cromwell?" He looked at me again suspiciously.

He didn't explain why the skull had been there since Cromwell. Was it a Protestant skull, one of Cromwell's soldiers? Or was it one of the killed Irish, a Catholic skull kept as a kind of trophy, a little like a headhunter's battle souvenir? He didn't say. And I didn't expect him to, but I was beginning to notice whose side he was on.

The verger went on, leading us over to the other side of the church. "This organ," he said, stopping beside a beautiful instrument in a dusty corner, "dates from 1722. In 1742, Handel gave the first performance of the *Messiah* on it."

I stopped and stared. I had thought the first performance of the *Messiah* was in the Council Chambers of Fishamble Hall, given for Irish poor relief. I happened to know this. Lots of people knew this, even some of the Americans the verger so despised. But then I thought he must mean Handel *rehearsed* the *Messiah*, probably composing large parts of it in those short twenty days, here on this organ.

Here. On this organ. In this dim and dirty church. Here Handel sat at the keyboard, working by candlelight, writing the score, playing the recitatives, directing the chorus. And right here the soloists gathered around him, the small chorus: "For behold, darkness shall cover the earth, and gross darkness the people."

The back of my neck began to prickle. "Yet once, a little while, and I will shake the heav'ns and the earth . . ." I imagined the music beginning to rise like pure air, like a clear exhalation to move through the moldy church. All around me, in this old air, crowded against these cold stones, that first audience would have listened to the same music I had later learned to love so much. This was the music that once, long ago, was played at the Foundling Hospital in London, that same hospital at Coram Fields which later became the site of the Wolfson Centre. This very music had raised money for the hospital and school that later benefited our child so much. And even before that this music had raised money for Irish poor relief, for those unknown ancestors of my own children.

But now the children were becoming restless. They had come to see the dead Crusader. We were led outside, where we briefly admired the one-thousand-year-old tower, the oldest part of the church, and the graveyard that, we were told, was "no longer in use." Then we followed the verger through a trapdoor and down the steps into the vault. We walked into a dense, earth smell. Stooping under several arches, we moved into a central vault. And there lay four bodies: the Crusader, one thousand years old; a nun, four hundred years old; a criminal, feet and right hand cut off, age unknown; and another body, age and identity unknown.

The children stood transfixed. Then the guide told us to shake the hand of the Crusader, but I noticed he didn't show us how. We stood there looking at the leathery flesh, the teeth grinning through the cheeks where they had fallen away, the flesh sunk and puckered on the bones of the hand. We looked at the thief, at the stumps of his legs, at the place where the right hand used to be. To reach the Crusader, one had to cross the nun. And the thief. I told Kate she didn't have to touch the hand of the Crusader. This was a silly superstition anyway. But then Paul was stepping over the stumps and reaching down to touch the rigid, curled, leathery fingers. Kate followed him and did the same.

Later that night, as I was tucking Kate into bed, she told me she had fears. Fears, as she explained, of her thoughts, fears that her thoughts would lead to a dream. She said that a man on television explained our fear of dead bodies by saying it was a fear of our own death. She told me that wasn't true. She didn't think of that at all. I asked her what she did think of. "What I do think of," she said "is that the Crusader was *very* unhandsome."

Thinking back to our time in Dublin, I am haunted by certain images. I see bones, the bones of my children's ancestors which they found and played with in that abandoned churchyard in the west of Ireland. And I see the gnarled finger bones of that dead Crusader in the crypt of St. Michan's Church, which we dared to touch in the hopes that we would get some kind of crazy Irish luck. Sometimes I see the bones in the burial chamber at Newgrange, touched only once a year by the sunbeams of the winter solstice; and then I think of the darkness of that tomb and of the even greater darkness of an unfathomable past, which will forever remain outside our knowledge.

But thinking of our time in Dublin, I also see Handel. There he is in the dusty corner of St. Michan's Church, his wig slipped to the side of his head, his face fevered with his last illness, but playing, perhaps even composing, those beautiful choruses of the *Messiah*. And when I think of Handel, I am flooded with images of his compassion for the poor and destitute of Dublin, for the sick and orphaned children of London.

But more than anything else, when I think of that term in Dublin, I see Paul on the edge of the sea. I see him at Howth Head on Wednesdays, studying with minute attention the intricacies of intertidal life, fascinated with the lives of creatures who are neither wholly of the sea nor wholly of the land, but rather are some borderland creatures who must adapt themselves to two elements at once.

I see him on the sand spit out by the electricity works beyond the gypsy encampment. And I remember how I would sit beside him on the bank as he dug in the sand. The sea was always aluminum gray, the electricity plant always a dull throbbing sound in the background. I knew that Russian submarines traveled in the deep channels of the Irish Sea just thirty miles off the coast, American Poseidons following in their wake. Worse still, the nuclear "reprocessing" plant at Sellafield on the north English coast was spilling cesium, plutonium, and enriched uranium into the Irish Sea. Clusters of leukemia among Irish children had been found up and down this coast.

I used to think of articles I read in the papers about Sellafield. The English had refused to allow on-site inspections of the plant, either from the Irish government or from an international nuclear regulatory board. And sitting there in the sand, just outside the slap of the waves, at the shifting margin of sea wrack, watching my son dig tunnels in the sand, I felt the same sense of frustration at the English which I read in the *Irish Times* every morning.

I wondered if I should keep Paul out of this sand, away from the slide of this corrupted sea. But I knew it was his favorite place. This margin, this always shifting edge of land and sea, was essential to his very sanity. Every afternoon here on this spit of land, he found a good observation point, a place to watch one of the most eternal, incorruptible events on earth: the changing of the tides. Still confused and bewildered by so much of what happened in his day at school, he needed to locate himself at some essential point on this ever-shifting earth of ours.

And so I sometimes sat there with him, staring out over this dull, misappropriated sea, thinking of the waves from Sellafield bearing their terrible burden, imagining the submarines trawling their death threats in the deep channels up and down the coast. But I also thought of how Paul had brought me in touch with the natural world, of how, without him, I was in danger always of not seeing. Over and over again, he brought me to a rim of the world, to one of those places for seeing and for knowing. And so I sat there with him and turned my mind from Sellafield and Poseidon, from the terrible poverty a quarter mile away at the gypsy camp, to watch with a lonely boy the elemental force of the tides.

CHAPTER 28

Below Zero

THE MIDDLE SCHOOL had promised to take Paul back into their Resource Room to finish out the semester and possibly the year, but after we returned home from Ireland, Paul felt very uncomfortable there. "I'm the tallest kid in the whole school," he told us after the first week in January. "And I really want to go to the high school with my class."

I knew quite well that Paul wasn't ready for high school, but we decided we would visit it anyway. I really liked the idea of his having an extra few months in the middle school where there were good support services and where he could have a class that focused on creative writing, public speaking, and art. This class, in the gentler environment of the middle school, was just what he needed, I thought, to gain confidence and more academic skills before he went on to the high school.

For years I had dreaded the time when Paul would be in the high school. I knew their Resource Room was excellent, but was worried that he would be utterly lost in the large, formal, regular classes, where he would need listening, note taking and writing skills that he simply did not have. The school was big and rather brutal: the kids, I knew, would be both competitive and highly conformist, insecure and impatient with difference.

Barbara Clark, the high school Resource Room teacher, was waiting for us in her room. Barbara was a warm, motherly woman who had raised four children before she started her career in special education. She had made a huge impact on a whole generation of learning disabled students, many of whom would not have graduated without her. Her students kept in touch with her for years; they returned regularly to see her, brought their wives and husbands to meet her, and even, so I had heard, named their children after her.

Barbara greeted Paul with genuine warmth, not with the slightly patronizing greeting I had seen so often from people in the past. She asked him what he wanted to do.

"Oh." Paul glanced at Jim and me and twisted his hands together. "Oh, I think, if you don't mind, I'd like to see around the school."

"Of course, Paul. Why don't we all go?" Barbara smiled at Jim and me.

We set off walking down the corridor, Jim and I trailing several feet behind Barbara and Paul.

"Is it very crowded between classes, the hall, I mean?" Paul asked hesitantly.

"It sure is, Paul. It's a madhouse."

"How many students go to this school?"

"About a thousand."

"Oh. That's a lot." Paul hesitated, then went on, sounding both frightened and determined. "I think I need to come to this school."

He moved fast down the corridor, hitching his right shoulder and his right foot forward slightly as he walked. I was so familiar with Paul's gait that I rarely saw it anymore. "The gimp," Jim called it with affection, using the Irish expression his father used for this gait. Sometimes Paul looked like an Irish "navvy," a construction worker like his grandfather.

Now suddenly I saw Paul as others would see him: a tall, very handsome boy, who was also a very vulnerable, very frightened fourteen-year-old who needed many more years to grow up. I saw the kid they would meet in the halls: a boy who swung through the corridors, flinching from contact with anyone, twisting his hands together nervously, asking in an anxious voice about the school.

Paul and Barbara paused before the door of the library, and Paul repeated, "I really think I need to come to this school." He glanced over at Jim and me, then back to Barbara Clark. "I have to face it sometime, and I might as well face it now," he finished earnestly.

"That's very courageous of you, Paul. I think you can start now, or rather on January twentieth, when the new semester starts. I think we can arrange that, if it's all right with your parents," Barbara said, turning to Jim and me. I didn't know what to say. Jim looked at me and said, "Well, it looks like it's settled, doesn't it?"

I wanted Paul to stay in the middle school, but he was so determined that I thought maybe we should let him go to the high school. He usually knew when he was ready for something. And I was so impressed by his pluckiness that I let it override my better judgment. "I guess so," I agreed. And so it was decided.

After our return from Ireland, Kate went back to her small alternative school in the country. But this school, which had been so good for her in the past, was now almost a disaster. Kate missed her Irish school, where she had had so many friends and where she had gotten along so well with her two teachers.

She came back to a combined classroom of third-, fourth-, and fifth-graders, under a teacher whose teaching style was totally different from Kate's learning style. Sharon, a very verbal, oral teacher, taught to the children's listening skills. Kate, who had trouble absorbing information verbally, needed written and visual materials. Sharon and I talked about all this, but not many changes were made.

In the meantime, Kate was becoming more and more anxious about math and she stopped writing altogether. The little books that she had enjoyed writing from the beginning of her time in this school were no longer a joy to her. Her last year's success with *The House of the Living Dead,* in which she had killed off her main character, Jessica, at the end, and which the other children had asked her to read aloud over and over, was too hard an act to follow.

I began to wonder if Kate's problems weren't related to her earlier developmental delays, her neurological problems when she was a baby. The principal of Prairie Creek also wanted to have her tested for a learning disability. We agreed that we would wait for the results, they would certainly provide some guidance about how to proceed.

Barbara called me a week after Paul started at the high school. "I wanted to tell you that I have given written information about Paul to all his teachers so they'll know what to expect. Also, he has permission to leave the classrooms at any time he feels overwhelmed. He can come back here to the Resource Room any time he thinks he needs to." She paused, then added with a laugh, "We tell all our Resource Room students that. It keeps them sane."

Barbara went on: "I also went back to the middle school and told them how well Paul is doing. He's nothing like the kid they described."

"Really?" I didn't know how they had described Paul, but I remembered how he used to flip pencils obsessively and yawn loudly so that his friend down the hall could hear him.

Barbara explained, "Here, of course, he doesn't have an aide in the classroom with him, and he doesn't need one. But he does need a lot of help getting around to his classes and following through on his assignments."

She paused again. There was something else on her mind. I wanted to know what the middle school teachers had said about Paul, but felt it might be unethical to ask.

Then in a rush, Barbara said, "Paul is so mannerly. He is so polite and sweet and so good-looking. He is nothing like what they said he would be!"

Ah, now I knew how the middle school had described Paul.

A few weeks later, when Paul walked in from school, he bent to unfasten the Velcro fasteners on his sneakers. I could tell from the impatient way he threw them down by the door that something was wrong.

"What's the matter, Paul?"

"Nothing! Nothing's the matter. Why do you ask me what's the matter?"

I decided to leave him alone, but a little later when I called Paul to dinner, I found him in the TV room, rocking back and forth rapidly, nervously.

"Come and eat, Paul."

"I don't want dinner. I'm not hungry."

I sat down next to him and tried to put my arm around his shoulders. He brushed me off impatiently and rocked more and more violently.

"Is it something about school?"

"I hate them! I hate the way they stare at me. The halls are too crowded, and they bump into me. Everybody is mad at me when they bump into me!"

That evening I talked to Barbara, and she confirmed that Paul was having a lot of trouble with the halls. He seemed to find the crowds very stressful. He also seemed to be very lonely, and she was trying to find someone who would eat lunch with him, one of the old pros from the Resource Room who might show him around a bit and introduce him to other students.

Every day after this, Paul went right to his room after school. He didn't seem to want to see Allen, who was also at the high school, or a new kid from the Resource Room who was very friendly with him. He didn't want to see anyone.

One day at the beginning of March, we took a long walk together in the woods, in a state wilderness area not far from home. The woods seemed very ugly that day. Some of the snow had melted and formed muddy rivulets or standing puddles. Ice still clung to the banks of the river, but in the center the water ran brown and dead-looking. All around us broken tree limbs, snapped off by storms or simply by the natural process of decay, looked like broken bones left exposed at odd, painful angles. As we picked our way through the mixed mud, snow, and ice, I wondered why we had come. This was one of our favorite places to walk during other seasons, when the forest floor was covered with May apples and cinquefoil, with Indian pipes and the last of the endangered trout lilies. But now the woods looked like a ruin, full of nothing but fallen trees and decaying stumps.

We walked silently, heads down, concentrating on our footing. Almost without noticing, we came upon a grove of evergreen trees, firs and long needle pines. A small wind sighed in the highest branches above our heads, but it was quiet and sheltered beneath the trees, with almost no snow on the ground. Our feet crunched the pine needles, releasing a lovely, spicy smell. Then suddenly the sun came out and shone in one long shaft of light through the trees.

"Let's sit down here," Paul said. "This looks like a safe place." He knelt under the trees and started raking the needles into a springy bed. "This would be a safe place to come and hide. Suppose there was a robber running away from the police; they would never find him here, would they?"

I sat down on a stump next to Paul and watched him rake the needles into a higher and higher pile.

"I would like to come here and hide and never come out again," he continued. "I'm such a terrible person. No one likes me, and I don't blame them."

I watched Paul, not trying at this moment to answer him, or contradict him, or reassure him.

"When did you decide you didn't like yourself?" I finally asked him.

"When I was four. That's when I found out I was a bad person."

Out of nowhere a memory came to me. It was about this time of year, February 18, 1943, and I was on our front porch steps in Richmond, Virginia. My fourth birthday and I was sitting alone. Slowly I kicked my heels back against the brick steps. I think I was wearing leggings, but even through the wool, I felt the solid, hard dependableness of the world, where it began just at the back of my legs.

The pale southern February sun warmed my hands. The trees were lacy against the sky, the city hummed in the distance, and my mother was just inside baking a cake for my birthday. Very early that morning, before I was supposed to be awake, I had hidden behind a curtain to watch her wheel a small black doll baby buggy, a secondhand carriage she had bought from a neighbor, up the walk and into the house. It was going to be my birthday present and I wasn't supposed to know it, but I was filled with joy, with the secret pleasure of a gift securely anticipated.

I was four years old and I felt an enormous satisfaction in that fact. My brother was just one, and I was pleased that he didn't even know it. And then, as if a kaleidoscope had shifted and a pattern suddenly came into view, I felt something I had never felt before. It seemed at that moment that I knew myself, knew who I was. I seemed to come into myself. I knew that I existed in the world. My heart was beating, the world glowed around me, and I was a part of it, a part of the living air, sitting there on the steps in the shimmering winter sunshine. And that knowledge alone was enough to fill me with an almost unbearable happiness. I stopped kicking my heels against the brick and held myself very still, held myself for a small moment at the heart of the living universe. And knew I had been blessed.

Now, sitting in the woods with Paul, on that cold March day, I wondered, What must it be like to know yourself for the first time, and to feel that you are bad, deeply flawed, wrong somehow? It seemed unimaginable; such a feeling would be too painful to sustain.

I thought of Paul when he was four — a sturdy, sweet, little boy with curly brown hair, but with too little language and driven by a frantic, too focused energy. But how did he learn such a low opinion of himself so early? And then I remembered how the other neighborhood nursery school children asked me questions when it was my turn to pick them up to drive them home from school. They were puzzled by Paul and would pull at my sleeve, or blurt out just as soon as we all got in the car: "What's the matter with Paul? Why does he talk so funny?"

The questions were genuine, spontaneous, innocent, uncensored. And they didn't happen just once or twice; they happened habitually, for years and years, all through Paul's childhood. As the children grew older, their questions only became more indirect, more encoded in complicated behaviors of rejection; they began to intend harm.

But when they were four, the children didn't mean to be hurtful, even though their simple innocence wounded me all the more deeply. As soon as the question was out, Paul would start kicking the seat. He would twist around in his seat belt; he would whine and hit the door. He knew perfectly well that he couldn't speak very clearly. He heard their questions, understood them, and learned that he was flawed.

I remembered Jan remarking to us once that Paul knew there was something the matter with him and that he blamed himself. He took it as a moral failing. Little children have no concept of developmental failures, they see their insufficiencies as personal shortcomings, as something they should change. Paul also thought he was disappointing us, and could, if he only worked hard enough, correct his failings.

And this had put us in a terrible bind, one that I think is classic for parents of disabled children. All through Paul's childhood, I had struggled with this dilemma: Should I work hard on "normalizing" him, and in so doing, risk teaching him that he was not normal when he failed or fell short of standard expectations? Or should I appreciate and value his differences and thus permit him to remain trapped in oddity, in loneliness? If I pushed him too hard to be like other children his age, wouldn't I simply be teaching him the deeper lesson that he was flawed?

Perhaps that is what happened. The standard for Paul was always created with other children in mind; there was never any way of determining in advance what he could do. We didn't know any other autistic children in our town; Paul met only one or two people vaguely like himself in his whole childhood, and he saw them only in the summers in the Twin Cities. And without a rough yardstick of what might be possible for him, we had to invent one, and reinvent it over and over again. I had to guess when I was pushing him too hard, when not hard enough.

I remembered the terrible naivete of a cousin's comment. To her, it seemed so simple: "Treat him like he's normal, and he will be normal." There was no point in trying to explain to her the destructive impossibility of this idea. And yet she merely said what dozens of other people thought but hadn't the courage to say.

Paradoxically, it was Paul's intelligence that allowed him to see that his mind was flawed. And by the time he was fourteen, he was a boy caught uneasily in a borderland between normalcy and difference, between autistic coping and typical teenage behavior. He had developed far beyond any other autistic child we knew, yet his very development had put him at risk for depression and self-hatred.

As we walked out of the woods that day in March, Paul seemed more cheerful. And then he turned to me suddenly, and exclaimed, "You could just walk into the woods at night in the winter when it is below zero and soon you would freeze to death. It wouldn't hurt at all." He stopped and looked all around him, at the broken trees, at the murky river, then added, "The earth is very generous in the ways we can die."

Hearing him say this, I felt cold to the bone, overwhelmed with such anguish for Paul that I was afraid I would myself be sucked into some dark place, into some dangerous helpless state where I could no longer help him. And I vowed at that moment that I would not let this happen. Whatever Paul was feeling must remain separate from me; I had to keep carefully to the surface, creeping around the rim of that dark, forbidden place of despair. Because it was only from some other place, outside whatever place Paul inhabited, that I would find a way of helping him to survive and move on.

CHAPTER 29

Camp

KNOWING how much Paul loved the woods, Jim, Barbara, and I discussed sending him to camp in northern Minnesota that summer, after his freshman year in high school. We had known of this camp for years; it was famous as a place for learning disabled children and teenagers. I had met some parents whose children went there year after year, and they praised it highly. The camp worked on outdoor skills, as well as crafts, and most importantly, on self-esteem. We read brochures and showed them to Paul. Then Eddie Brewer, the camp director, visited the high school to show a video and answer questions. The school system agreed to pay Paul's tuition and the tuition of one other boy who qualified.

But Paul was very nervous and resistant. That spring he and I went for many more long walks in the woods, and Paul asked me repeatedly about the camp. I tried to reassure him. Yet I worried that we were forcing him to do something against his will. Could we depend on his pluckiness, the courage he had shown recently in accepting a new school in Ireland, in starting high school a few months later? Or were we pushing him too hard, too fast, beyond his capacity? Camp would be the third new thing asked of him in one year. Everyone seemed so sure that he would love it there once he got used to it, but to me he seemed unusually frightened.

Finally, I wrung a promise from Paul that he would at least try camp. If he was truly miserable after a few days, he could come home. I called Eddie Brewer to tell him this. He complained that this was the wrong thing to do. "Paul needs to ride it out. If he thinks he can get out of camp after a few days, he won't even try to get used to it."

I saw his point but told him this was the best I could do. Otherwise, Paul would absolutely refuse to go at all. He had agreed to at least try it, so we got to work, buying the clothes he would need: walking boots, long jeans, shorts, swimsuit, pajamas. Paul had always refused to wear shorts and walking boots, and for the last several years, went to bed in his underwear. We simply accepted this as part of his autistic rigidity. We thought other battles were more important, such as getting him to eat or to go to school. But now he would be faced with a number of changes in his life, which other kids could take in stride and think nothing about but which Paul might find harrowing. His differences, even from the learning disabled population, were to us apparent, but we didn't know if the camp personnel would understand.

On June 15, we set out, all four of us, to drive Paul to camp. As we traveled north from the Twin Cities, past Duluth and up the north shore of Lake Superior, I began to wonder why we didn't come here every summer. I loved the cool, dry air, the crab apples and locusts blooming around Duluth, giving way to the mixed hardwoods of aspen, alder, and Russian olive trees, then the forests of pine and fir and balsam farther north. "It reminds me of Finland," I said to Jim.

"But you've never been to Finland." Jim looked at me, half surprised, half amused.

"I know, but it still reminds me of Finland."

Paul loved the landscape also. We stopped at Split Rock Lighthouse, spending the night in a motel in Two Harbors. The next day, a Sunday, we had half a day to do more exploring. We went to Temperance Bay on Lake Superior and spent some time on the rocky coast and following trails through the woods. Iron ore beneath the surface of the earth was leeched out by water running from springs and into the bay. We sat on the rocks in the warm sun for a while, beside the rust-colored water as it spilled down the rocks and into the blue of the lake.

There was a rib-rock strength to this cool northern landscape, I thought, sitting there in the sun. The veins of iron ore ran like hard bones under the earth, the land had been flattened by mile-high glaciers and scraped clean of anything extraneous, and the soil left behind now nourished a delicate, strong, persistent growth, a growth that came back year after year. I wanted to read the landscape as an outward sign of the strength that Paul would somehow find in himself.

Sitting there on the rocks, Paul seemed to relax just slightly, and I promised him, perhaps foolishly, that there would be beautiful places like this at his camp and that he could spend a lot of time outdoors exploring. But as we drove on, he became more and more nervous and frightened. I could tell he was trying hard to be brave, but he seemed bewildered. We parked the car and joined a line with the other kids and their parents waiting to register. Some children were running around with excitement, calling to old friends and waving and shouting. Paul became more and more quiet, wringing his hands, rocking back and forth slightly. His shoulders were slumped. He stared at the floor until it was our turn to fill out the registration forms.

"Hi, pal. Glad to see you." Eddie Brewer reached across the table to shake Paul's hand. "Want to know what cabin you're in?"

"Um." Paul turned from Eddie to look to us for guidance. Then he surreptitiously wiped at his eyes with the back of his hand and sniffed hard. "Yes, I guess so." His voice was so quiet, we could hardly hear him.

We were shown Paul's cabin and we helped him take in his bedroll and his bag. The cabin counselor, a college student with red hair and a friendly face, met us and showed Paul his bed at the bottom of a bunk by the window.

"Hi. I'm Sam. These are your shelves where you'll keep your stuff. And this is your locker. You can put the stuff away now, if you like."

I glanced at Paul. He had gone white and was swaying slightly. The rims of his eyes had reddened and filled with tears. He stared at me for a moment, an open, exposed look, before he sat down suddenly on the side of the bunk bed.

"I don't think I can take this."

"Paul, put your head down between your knees." I knelt beside him and pushed his shoulders gently forward. "Take a deep breath. You'll be all right." I struggled to keep my own voice from shaking.

Sam's face showed real concern. He waited a moment, then suggested we all go outside to talk, away from the crowd in the cabin. We moved outside to the back of the cabin, under some pine trees. Paul was still fighting back tears. He looked embarrassed, ashamed, frightened, and utterly vulnerable. I touched his arm lightly, but I longed to hug him, to protect him somehow from the terrible power of his own feelings. But I thought I might embarrass him in front of the other kids, so I just stood there, we all just stood there for a moment, not knowing what to say.

A cloud of mosquitoes swarmed around Paul's eyes, his face. He slapped at them and rubbed his neck, where big red welts were already forming. Mosquitoes lit on all of us, up and down our arms, across our foreheads, on our necks. A misery of mosquitoes.

"Let's go in the sun." Sam led us to the front of the cabin.

I wanted to cry, but I choked back my own feelings and tried to put on cheerfulness and determination. "You'll be fine, Paul. Once you get used to it," I said, but I thought my own voice sounded high and strained. "Everybody is scared at first. That's perfectly normal."

"That's right," Jim began in the same vein. "I felt this way too, when I went away to school."

"You did?" Paul glanced briefly at Jim, hardly believing him, but wanting to believe him. His eyes looked a little less dull.

"I did. And I did get used to it."

Sam turned to us. "Paul will be fine. I think you'd better leave now."

Jim and I each gave Paul a quick hug. He submitted limply, his arms at his sides. Then Kate, who had been watching all this while and saying nothing, came forward. Paul bent slightly to receive her hug, and she whispered earnestly in his ear, "Paul, you must face your fears." He pulled back and looked at her briefly, then his eyes skittered away again. But Kate hadn't finished. "Paul." She looked him in the eye. "You'll be just fine. I know you will."

Paul nodded slightly, then, without saying anything, he turned from us and walked into the cabin.

As we started to get in the car, we all turned to wave at Paul once again. I could just make him out, a very white face in the window, staring straight ahead, an arm raised to shoulder level, a limp wave. And as we drove away, it was the pale face I remembered, and thought I would never forget, the white, flat face of a drowning boy, going down.

We called the camp a few days later to see how Paul was. We had been told that he would be forbidden to call us, unless it was some emergency and he had their permission. So we called them, and a cheery secretary said Eddie Brewer was out, but she was sure Paul was fine. We knew she didn't know who he was, but "no news was good news," at least no child that she knew of had collapsed and been taken to the hospital, or had broken a leg, or had died of snakebite.

Paul had been asked to bring to camp ten stamped postcards addressed to home, and we knew he would be asked to write to us. I wrote him every day, little notes of encouragement. I wrote about what was going on at home, about the weather and the cats watching a wren nest. I sent him a few pictures, and we waited anxiously for his first postcard to us.

A heat wave moved into southern Minnesota, and temperatures climbed up to the lower nineties. I sat outdoors in the shade of our maple tree and tried to read, tried to work on an article I was writing, but the cicadas were everywhere, strumming loudly. Our next-door neighbors to the north decided to cut down a diseased elm, then they hired an artist with a buzz saw to strip the bark and shape the six-foot-high remaining trunk into a bear. For days we were assaulted by the high-pitched, maddening scream of the saw.

I thought obsessively about our decision to send Paul to camp when he was in such bad shape. Eddie Brewer had told us about a boy who was there the year before, who had been depressed and who had attempted suicide at camp. Eddie was angry with the parents for not informing him of this risk. I had listened to this story with a guilty nagging at the back of my mind: were we taking a similar risk in sending Paul to camp? How far could he be pushed before he too did something desperate? Were we being completely honest with Eddie Brewer?

Those first days were a nightmare of worry. Every day we rushed for the mail as soon as it came, hoping there would be a postcard from Paul, and hoping he would say he was beginning to enjoy camp. Finally, a card did come: "Dear Mama, Daddy, and Kate: So far I am feeling very miserable in camp. I am missing all of you, and I miss home a lot. I am writing this letter on the third day of camp, but I am only a very little bit happier. I had a talk with Eddie Brewer, and he said that if I try to like camp, I will like it. Even with him saying that, I am still counting the days until you pick me up." So he was still alive, not happy, but surviving. I relaxed a little and went over to my office and turned on the air conditioner to work.

Kate went to classes at a children's summer theater institute. She studied dance, scene painting, lighting, creative dramatics, and voice — all the subjects she loved and could excel in. She was given the part of the tortoise in *The Tortoise and the Hare*. Wearing a baseball cap turned backward and the painted cardboard carapace of a mud turtle, she bent down under the "weight" of her heavy shell and moved across the stage with a deliberation that caught everyone's attention. Every movement was in character, and I could see that she was recapturing her self-esteem after the last semester at Prairie Creek.

By this time, the results of Kate's testing for learning disabilities came through, showing that she had an auditory processing problem. In an end-of-the-year report, her teacher had written that Kate was no longer her usual cheerful, friendly self; she seemed anxious and withdrawn and claimed that she no longer had any friends. She had more and more trouble following oral instructions, and often had to go to her teacher to have the instructions repeated. The report, however, had noted that Kate's "creativity and dramatic expressiveness continue to be her greatest strength." She had invented the part of a punk weaver for a class production of *The Emperor's New Clothes*, and this had been a great success.

As soon as we got these reports, Jim and I began to talk of moving Kate to the public schools, where we hoped she would get some help with her auditory processing problems.

Paul wrote some more postcards: "I still want to go home and have everything back to normal, but with only 22 days to go, I think I will just try to enjoy them." Then, "I only sort of like this camp, but I am getting used to things." And then, gradually, the language changed, and he started to ask about us: "What is it like at home? Are there any storms there?"

We decided to visit Paul on July 4. He would have been at camp for almost three weeks by then and would be over the initial homesickness. The camp officials told parents that a visit on that day would be welcome. I wrote to tell him we would be there on the Fourth.

The next card said, "When you come on July 4, I will show you around the whole camp and we could also talk to Eddie Brewer about how I am doing." Then, "I am very proud of myself for going away from home!"

The day we arrived at camp, a tall, suntanned boy standing with a group of kids next to the crafts cabin looked up, waved, then turned back to the others to say something. Then, he started toward us, walking not too fast, that familiar, rather hitched walk we knew so well, swinging his right shoulder and arm. And there standing before us was Paul, grinning broadly. Except for the walk, we hardly knew him. Gone was the hand wringing, the hunched shoulders, the rocking back and forth on his heels. He was changed. And he was proud of himself.

Paul showed us all around the camp, even introducing us to some of the kids in his cabin. Then we sat on the steps of the cabin and talked. He told us that there were lots of fights in his cabin, and at first this had bothered him. But now he thought it was funny. He pointed to the mattress propped against the outer wall of the cabin to air out, and lowered his voice. "That belongs to my roommate. At first he slept on the top bunk and I slept on the bottom. Then we had to change places. You can guess why." He grinned at us.

CHAPTER 30

Depression

P AUL SURVIVED and, to a certain extent, he flourished at camp. Eddie Brewer told us at the end that Paul had eaten nothing at all for the first three days, and that he was very worried about him. But after Eddie had a long talk with him, he began to make a real effort to like camp. He had some trouble participating in some of the sports and activities, but he tolerated them and stopped complaining of boredom. And when they asked him to stop wandering off in the woods by himself, he did stop. After a while, he even seemed to enjoy being around the other kids.

Paul came home feeling a real but very fragile sense of achievement. And his success made him set some new, high standards for himself, not only for his behavior but also for his feelings. He got very upset with *himself* when he got upset about something else; he blamed himself when he felt unhappy; he seemed to think it was his fault somehow if he was sad or discouraged.

At the time I didn't relate this anxiety to his experience in camp, where he had been told that if he changed his attitude his life experiences would change. Only much later did I realize that he had learned an important partial truth: he did feel better when he tried to feel better. But now he didn't seem to realize that his feelings couldn't control his environment. And none of our reassurances that it was all right to feel bad sometimes seemed to work with him. Every little misfortune was yet a new opportunity for self-blame. The camp gave him an important first lesson in feeling good about himself, but I realized he would need many more such experiences before he began to feel more secure.

Paul and I took many walks in the woods in the late summer and early fall, and every time he said the same thing. "Don't send me back to that camp. Please don't send me back to camp next year. Promise me you won't send me back to camp."

There was such anguish in his voice, such earnestness, that I had to listen. But I was bewildered: we thought Paul would feel so much better about himself after his success at camp. It was clearly good for him to be with learning disabled kids and with boys who had more serious behavior problems than his own. That summer Paul had learned that he wasn't alone, that he wasn't the only person who had trouble with social interactions. He also saw that he had some skills that many of the other kids did not. And the structure and predictable routine at the camp was good for him; after the first few days he had a secure sense of what was expected of him at any given moment throughout the day.

How then could Paul be so negative about camp when he had done so well, when he had survived and learned to feel a lot of pride in his accomplishment? I was puzzled, but I began to wonder if Paul weren't more seriously depressed than we thought. Something was keeping him from benefiting from his success.

When school started, Paul was almost frantic. Barbara called one day after the first few weeks to say she would have to bring him home early. He was so miserable that he couldn't concentrate, and she was afraid he couldn't keep control for much longer. She didn't want him to have the experience of collapsing completely in school. If he did, he might really develop a school phobia. Paul came home early that day, but we made sure he returned to school the next day, and the day after, and the day after that. Some things just had to be done, and school was one of them.

That year Paul was in a school Work Adjustment Program, a class for learning disabled students who needed some supervised experience with the workplace. I was delighted that he had this class, but it seemed not to be helping him. At the beginning of the year, he was placed in the middle school snack bar to sell candy and pop after school. The job required him to make change rapidly, which was no problem for him, but he also had to attend to many different people and to rapid-fire demands.

Every day when he came home, Paul looked pale and drawn. He continued to complain about this job. "It makes my day too long. I have too much to think about." He began to worry that he would never be able to hold down a job as an adult. And he talked more and more about suicide as the only logical way out of the stress of his life. Although Jim and I thought that this talk was mostly an expression of his frustration and anxiety, not a real statement of intention, we were still deeply disturbed by it.

I spoke to the teacher who ran the program, who said she thought Paul should stay with this job. "He mustn't learn the lesson that he can get out of his commitments." Shelley seemed to feel so strongly about this that rather reluctantly I caved in. She was getting impatient with Paul, and I didn't want to come across as a meddlesome mother who overprotected her son and made excuses for him. Shelley was sure Paul "would settle down and get used to it." He had wanted a job in the middle school, she reminded me, because he liked to see the girls there.

But one day Kate came home from the middle school, where she was now a sixth-grade student, and said she had bought some candy from Paul after school. "He gave it to me," she said, "and he didn't even see me. He looked right through me, even though I stood right in front of him and tried to get his attention."

The next day after school I went to the hallway near the snack bar. Paul and one other boy were working there. Surrounding them were ten or twenty students, some in line, others pushing to get forward to buy a snack quickly before their buses came. Some were waving money, dollar bills, at Paul and calling out their orders. Many were impatient and showing it. Paul handed out candy, took money, made change, but all his motions were preoccupied and jerky, and at times he seemed to pause and stare off into space. He looked dazed, drawn, miserable.

I watched for a while, until the crowd thinned. When there were only two or three kids left in front of the stand, I approached Paul and stood in the middle of the hallway very close to him and within his line of sight. Paul continued to move like a puppet; he looked drawn, his movements were hitched, his eyes looked flat and blank. He never noticed me at all.

I turned on my heel and marched up the stairs and into the offices of the Work Adjustment Program. "I want to see Shelley," I demanded, and when she came out of her office, looking surprised to see me, I said, "I want Paul taken off that job today. It's not the right placement for him."

Shelley realized that I wasn't willing to discuss the issue any further. She agreed, and I turned and left the building.

Jim and I decided we should get in touch with a psychiatrist. Paul's depression and anxiety seemed to be getting worse, and we didn't know what more we could do to help him. We learned about a psychiatrist who was supposed to have some experience with high-functioning autistics, and I made an appointment.

Dr. Morley had a practice in the Twin Cities, and I took Paul there on a cold day in November. The doctor was a tall, very gentle man, with a kind, quiet way of speaking. I liked him immediately. He invited me in with Paul for the initial interview. The office had a soft beige carpet, and low, warm lights on the desk and beside the couch. Dr. Morley had already closed the shutters on his windows against the early darkness outside, but an azalea, which stood on the windowsill, seemed to glow, almost to give off its own light through the deep pink and magenta blossoms.

Paul and I sat down on the couch. Dr. Morley drew his desk chair closer to us. He held a clipboard on his knee and began to take a few notes from me about Paul's history and about any family history of depression or other affective disorders. Then he leaned forward and started to ask Paul some questions.

Paul answered Dr. Morley's questions with the slow, deliberate honesty I knew so well. "I don't feel like riding my bicycle anymore," he told him. "And I'm not really interested in anything else." He described how the kids at school got angry at him when he brushed against them in the hallway or when he spilled something at lunch. It was his impression that they were angry at him all the time.

"How does this make you feel, Paul?" Dr. Morley studied Paul's face with a searching kindness.

Paul twisted his hands together, then gestured suddenly, awkwardly, with his right hand. "I feel just terrible. I cry at school a lot, and the other kids tease me." He paused and stared at his hands in his lap. Then he looked up, his eyes reddening slightly. "I guess I'm just a terrible person. I mean, I know I'm a terrible person. I just want to grow up and get out of high school." He paused again, then said in a low voice, "Sometimes I think it would be better if I just committed suicide."

"Those must be very painful thoughts, Paul." Dr. Morley's voice was concerned and kind, but it was also even and level and calm. He paused before he went on. "Can you tell me more about what you are thinking? Do you have any plans?"

Paul looked up at him. "I think I am at the first stage," he began slowly, "but I am afraid that I will go on and find a way to do it. And then I will choose a date."

I felt chilled to the bone. Paul had never talked in such detail before.

And I knew that he wouldn't say what he didn't mean. He had always been honest as only an autistic person can be honest, utterly straight and "without side," as Jim's mother always said about him. With anyone else, any other unhappy, disturbed teenager, these words might be a threat, or an effort to manipulate, but with Paul at this time they could only be the truth, the terrible, unacceptable, terrifying truth.

After he finished questioning Paul, Dr. Morley turned to address me again. "I think, in view of Paul's thoughts of suicide and in view of the family history of depression, Paul would be a good candidate for medication. It's hard to tell in cases like this, but Paul's loss of pleasure in his usual activities, his exaggerated sense of guilt, and his fearfulness of his classmates . . ." Dr. Morley turned back to Paul, "And especially because of your suicidal thoughts, Paul, you might begin to feel a lot better with medication."

Paul nodded slowly, and Dr. Morley asked him, "How would you feel about taking an antidepressant?"

Paul turned to me, and I smiled at him. "I think, Paul, it is worth a try. It might just help."

Dr. Morley wrote a prescription for desipramine, fifty milligrams per day, to be increased to one hundred milligrams per day in one week's time.

We left the office and drove home. Paul seemed more cheerful for the rest of that day than I had seen him for months, for more than a year, except for that brief moment at camp.

Earlier that fall Jim had mentioned to one of his students that Kate was very interested in dance, and after that she was invited to join her Friday evening workouts. I usually went to pick her up in the car, and I often went early so I could watch. I was amazed to see that Kate could hold her own among these beautiful, lithe twenty-year-olds. She moved with a rhythmic grace that defied all the predictions of the neurologist who saw her at ten months, that exceeded all my hopes for her when I had done those many therapy exercises with her. She also had a confidence, a sense of self-possession that seemed ages beyond her years.

One day when I picked her up, Kate ran to tell me that she had been asked to do a solo in a dance performance in January. I was proud, thrilled, in fact, but as I thought about it, I began to be afraid this might put too much pressure on her. "Are you sure?" I asked Lisa, the student who was working with her.

"I won't let her try anything she isn't capable of doing," Lisa reassured me. She sounded completely convincing. Lisa was a petite young Japanese woman who had grown up in Hawaii and had danced from the age of five. She was enthusiastic, energetic, boundlessly happy, always in graceful motion, like a small butterfly.

Lisa turned and twinkled at Kate, who was almost as tall as she was. "Just keep a smile on your face and don't look at your feet. And the audience will never know if you make a mistake." Then she added, "Once I fell down during a performance. So I pretended I was picking flowers and that this had all been planned." She laughed. "The audience never knew the difference."

I could tell that Kate trusted Lisa and that she deserved to be trusted. Lisa would choreograph the piece and they would work on it on Sunday afternoons before Lisa left for Christmas break.

Paul started on desipramine, but he didn't get any better. We waited for one month, then two, and still no improvement. Now he was barely making it to school. Some days Barbara had to bring him home early. Once she couldn't reach either me or Jim, so she brought him over to my office, where my secretary watched him for an hour. We agreed Paul couldn't be left alone, shouldn't be left alone. He had begun to talk of wanting to walk in front of a truck.

Every month, I drove him to see Dr. Morley in the Twin Cities. But nothing seemed to help. A new friend of his, another boy in the Resource Room, had started coming home with Paul almost every day after school. Bill was concerned about Paul, and also clearly liked him a lot. But when they came in together, Paul usually went up to his room. "I don't want to hurt your feelings, Bill," he would say in a low voice, wringing his hands and cracking his knuckles. Then his eyes would fill with tears, and he would turn and run up the stairs.

But Bill knew that Paul needed to be alone, and he wasn't hurt. He would stay and talk to me until Paul felt able to come downstairs again, then he would leave to go out on his paper route. Bill and I tried to get Paul interested in taking over part of the paper route. I knew this would be much better for him than the snack bar at the middle school: he wouldn't have to meet the public and work under pressure in the same way. Also, his ability to work within patterns would make this a logical job for him.

Finally Paul agreed to go out with Bill one day. I drove him to the pickup points and waited in the car as he delivered the papers. But he got confused, couldn't read the map, couldn't remember which houses he had already done. This was unusual for him, very unusual. His map reading ability, his memory, had always been his most reliable talents. Now he seemed not even to have these skills anymore.

Paul was trying so hard to be just like the other kids, and he seemed to have made a conscious effort to discard many of his autistic habits and interests. No longer hyperactive, he now seemed to be hypoactive, too quiet, too polite, and much too sensitive to other people's feelings about him. At the same time, he had dropped most of his earlier interests — exploring, map reading, the weather, riding his bike, swimming. One day he said to me, "I seem to be between obsessions." I knew just what he meant. No longer did he have a single, all-consuming interest, as he had always had before in his life.

The desipramine made Paul's mouth very dry, and yet he was afraid of getting a drink of water at the water fountain at school. That meant braving the crowds of students in the hall, or possibly being late between classes. I took bottles of fruit juice to the Resource Room for Paul to drink during the day. Paul was incapable of bringing them there himself — that would be too different from what he was used to doing. Even taking a book bag or using a locker was too much.

Paul started making lists of his problems. One day I found one of these lists on the desk in my study:

1. I get frustrated over small things.
2. I ask too many questions.
3. I ask the dumbest questions.
4. I think people are being mean to me, when they are really not.
5. I think people are making fun of me, when they are really not.
6. When I accidentally hurt someone and they say "ouch," I get mad at them.
7. I expect everything to be perfect.
8. When I get into a fight, I can't stop. I continue the fight and make it bigger.

And so on, up to sixteen points. I was astounded by what I read. On the one hand, Paul showed enormous insight. No one could have done better. But on the other hand, he was so focused on the negative. I asked him to write a list of his good qualities, but he sat for half an hour before a blank sheet of paper. I told him what I thought were his good qualities — his sensitivity to other people's feelings, his lifelong courage and perseverance and willingness to try what was hard for him, his kindness, his remarkable memory — but he brushed me aside. "You're my mother. Of course, you think that!"

Kate's dance performances were in the middle of January. On the first night, we were all very nervous but trying not to show it. Jim, Paul, and I went early and sat in the front row of the theater. I was worried because I knew the performance was underrehearsed, especially for Kate, who was less experienced than the college students. I had left her backstage in her costume, trying to control her nerves, practicing her steps by herself. I decided not to stay with her but to let go. I thought a mother in these circumstances would just increase a child's anxiety, and I trusted Lisa, thought she would be better for Kate than I could be.

Kate's piece was the first after the intermission. Just as the lights went down, we all leaned forward to watch for her entrance. I glanced at Jim, his face just catching the lights of the stage in the center of the theater. He looked so stricken, so drawn, so terrified for her, that I whispered in his ear, "Lean back, Jim." I didn't want his face to be the first thing Kate saw as she danced onto the stage.

The music began, and Kate entered, in a blue satiny dress and white tights, her hair braided in ribbons and carrying blue ribbons in her hands. Oh, the grace of that small form! Kate smiled as she wove across the stage, dancing her beautiful child's dance, the ribbons floating behind her.

Here was the child with cerebral palsy, the child who was expected to walk with a limp, to drag her right foot. The child who would never dance. And Kate wove across the stage, through the ribbons, through the music, a floating image of delicacy and small perfection. I knew now she would be all right: I could almost relax and enjoy the performance.

In February, Paul had still not improved, and Dr. Morley put him on nortriptyline, another antidepressant. Paul continued to go to school, reluctantly but with a resigned determination. Barbara told me that during the times when he seemed most anxious and upset, she could usually calm him down by insisting that he do his algebra homework. He almost always lost himself, at least temporarily, in working through math problems. She also said he seemed a little less stressed around the other Resource Room kids than he had been earlier. He enjoyed listening to their jokes and their complaints about work, although he didn't ever join in.

Barbara wanted to give Paul a psychoeducational battery of tests. It had been several years since he had last been tested. On the basis of his earlier school record, Paul had started high school on a college preparatory course, a slightly adapted version of the program taken by the higher-achieving students. He had one or two special education classes, but mostly was in regular classrooms with backup tutoring help in the Resource Room. Now it was time to reassess whether this was the best placement for him.

Barbara gave him the Woodcock-Johnson test and shared the results with us. She told us that Paul had scored in the average to high average range for most of the tests of cognitive and verbal ability; only reasoning and visual-perceptual speed were low average. One score, for brief cognitive ability, was superior, and the score for memory was in the very superior range. The test results for academic performance were also encouraging: reading skills were average, mathematical skills were high average.

On the face of it, the tests showed that there was no reason for Paul not to do well with academic subjects at the high school level. Yet I knew the tests could not identify Paul's continuing neurological problems. They wouldn't show his auditory processing disability, his difficulties in listening and attending to lectures and verbal information, in processing information rapidly, in reading social situations, facial expressions, nuances of language use and gesture — all the many ways in which most of us pick up information.

The tests also wouldn't show the trouble Paul had in switching attention, or keeping in mind several things at once. He found it almost impossible to attend to several different tasks such as classes, a job, a friendship he was struggling with. And not surprisingly, girls were now becoming his single focus, his one all-consuming preoccupation. He noticed all the couples in the hallway between classes and said they made him feel terribly lonely.

New material was beginning to come out on autism, and I read it with some excitement, with a sense that at last professionals were beginning to offer a model for understanding this perplexing disorder. They were saying that autism was a problem of sensory integration, a disturbance in the reception, integration, or interpretation of sense impressions. Autistic children have abnormal responses to sensory stimuli, involving either hyper- or hyposensitivity to sensory stimuli.

Other professionals were pointing out that this sensory dysfunction was related to a problem with the regulatory system. These children felt too much of whatever it was they were experiencing at the moment — anger, sadness, excitement — and they were unable to modulate their feelings, but were simply overwhelmed by them. Then they shut down and withdrew from human contact, or they acted out their anxieties and frustrations.

Could it be that Paul's present problems with holding in mind so many different things — four or five academic subjects, a job, the wish to find a girlfriend — were just too much for him? Was he simply overloaded, the circuits about to overheat and short out?

One afternoon in mid-February, after having been away at a women's studies retreat the previous weekend, I came home early from my office to be there to see Paul when he came home from school. He walked through the door and brushed right past me, hardly acknowledging that I was there. He turned to give me a distracted greeting, then headed for the TV room, where he started to play a video game. I followed him and sat down on the floor beside him. He played for a few minutes, then began to get frustrated.

I watched, hating this game, hating all video games. The little man in armor was shooting at skeletons and monsters, was zapping huge spiders as they dangled from the ceiling of caves, was leaping over abysses, barely escaping huge boulders as they fell to the floor. Around every bend, up every staircase, there was always a new menace materializing out of nowhere. Paul was very good at these games, he learned patterns rapidly and retained the memory over long periods of time, but I thought the game was just making him more nervous and agitated.

I asked him to turn it off, and to my surprise he did. Even at fifteen Paul could rarely stop something he had started. He switched off the game and pulled out the cartridge, but he continued kneeling in front of the TV set, rocking back and forth, back and forth.

"What is it, Paul? Did you have a good weekend when I was away?"

He continued to rock back and forth, not looking at me. He was on his hands and knees now.

"Did you like seeing Mary?" asked about the visit from Jim's sister on her way back to London from Kansas City, where she had been training others in computerized booking for airlines.

Paul looked at me, and his eyes filled with tears. "I was very confused," he began hesitantly. "She gave me a present, a little digital clock, and I just looked at it. I didn't know what to say. I didn't even know where I was. I ran out of the room without even thanking her. Do you think she's mad at me?"

I stared at Paul. His face was pale, his eyes were red, he was rocking back and forth. His whole body seemed to vibrate with tension.

"You were confused, you say?"

He nodded but didn't stop rocking.

"How did you feel at school today?"

"My mind was racing. And I couldn't stop it!"

"Your mind was racing?" Slowly, something was beginning to dawn on me.

"My mind was racing and it was the most horrible feeling I have ever had in my life!"

Suddenly, I knew. "Paul, it's the drug. I think it's that drug that is making you feel that way. I want you to stop taking it now until I can talk to your doctor."

Paul stopped rocking and stared at me. "But that's what I've been trying to tell you!" His voice held real anguish and frustration, but surprisingly, no anger. "I know it's the drug. I hate that drug, and I've been trying to tell you!"

My own eyes filled with tears. I felt terrible, full of worry and guilt and self-blame. How could I have ignored the signals? How could I have ignored a kid in pain when he was trying to tell me something so important?

When I reached the doctor, I told him what had happened, and the decision I had made on my own to take Paul off the medication. Dr. Morley listened without saying anything. I could hear the sharp intake of his breath as I told him about Paul's confusion and agitation, about his description of his mind racing. "Thank God you made him stop taking the nortriptyline!" he said.

Then he went on to tell me that some depressions resolve themselves as manic episodes, especially those that are being treated with antidepressants. The agitation, the confusion, and above all the feeling that his mind was racing out of control, are the first signs of a manic episode. Paul had been on the edge of a psychotic breakdown, and by taking him off the drug I had pulled him back from the edge just in time.

"You were absolutely right to trust your instinct and you did exactly the right thing." Dr. Morley paused for a moment, then repeated, "Thank God for a mother's instinct!"

I too was grateful that I had noticed just in time. But I still wondered why Jim hadn't seen anything unusual in Paul's behavior that weekend, especially since he had twice been through the same experience himself. But then I realized that there was so much else in Paul's behavior, such a lifelong experience of agitation, that Jim understandably didn't think this last weekend was anything out of the ordinary. When I talked to him about all this, however, he felt terribly guilty. "I should have noticed," he said. "I guess I was just too busy with Mary's visit."

Dr. Morley wanted Paul to go back on nortriptyline, but only after starting on lithium first. I was very reluctant to start him back on the drug, but Dr. Morley explained that he thought it was necessary: "The suicidal ideation has been too strong to ignore." The lithium, he said, would stabilize Paul's moods, would keep him from developing that terrible agitation. At the same time, the nortriptyline, he thought, should lift the depression. The goal was for him to feel no depression, but also no agitation.

Increasingly, I distrusted these drugs. But the alternatives were even scarier. Jim and I talked and talked about what to do. We knew hospitalization was always a possibility, but it was a last step. We also felt that Paul would so hate being hospitalized that he would probably regress. And we knew that it would be difficult getting the insurance to pay. The shocking truth was that Paul might have to make a suicide attempt before they would pay for anything more than a three-day observation period.

I made phone call after phone call during this time, trying to gather all the information I possibly could about medical treatment and an alternative school placement for Paul. If school was the major stress in his life, as it seemed to be, perhaps we could find another, better, place for him.

Perhaps, I began to think, Paul needed a therapeutic setting. My sister-in-law, whose son had attended a school for emotionally disturbed children for five or six years, seemed to think so. I listened to her, but didn't know if her son's experience was really analogous with Paul's. Nevertheless, I called every school district in the Twin Cities, and every consultant, every advocacy group I could think of. There was no high school for emotionally disturbed teenagers, I learned, although later I did hear about one or two hospital-based school programs for such kids. There was, however, a very good school for learning disabled students. I called the director there and described Paul's difficulties, also his relatively high intellectual abilities. He told me point-blank, "I can't accept him. We don't accept autistic students. We had one once, and it just didn't work out."

I knew Paul was neither learning-disabled nor emotionally disturbed, at least not as these labels are usually applied. As a high-functioning autistic, he didn't seem to fit in anywhere, either in a regular high school, or with the truly learning-disabled. And he cer-tainly didn't fit in with the emotionally disturbed teenagers, who had tried drugs, alcohol, and early sex, who had been runaways, or who had been in trouble with the law. Once again, it seemed to me that he was on some border, some no-man's-land inhabited by no one but himself.

In the end, I called our old friend and consultant on autism, Sheila Merzer. She spent a day visiting the school and talking with Barbara Clark. Later she called me to say that she thought Paul already had a therapeutic setting.

"I can't imagine a better teacher than Barbara Clark," she said, "or a more appropriate setting than the Resource Room. Paul has all the advantages where he is now of a normal school placement, as well as all the backup services of a very skilled and sensitive teacher."

So Paul remained where he was. He continued on the drugs, he continued to see Dr. Morley, but I still worried. He was not getting better. For a year and a half now, he had seemed to be just hanging on by his fingernails. He was learning very little, developing very little. He was running, frantically, just to stay in place.

CHAPTER 31

Day Treatment Program

ONE DAY in early June, we took Paul to Riverview Hospital in the Twin Cities for an intake interview at their adolescent day treatment program. Paul was miserable but resigned. The month before, when we visited Dr. Morley I had asked him to take Paul off all the drugs. We had given them enough time, and they just hadn't worked. Dr. Morley had written our HMO to recommend that Paul get help at this day treatment program. This meant we would have to say good-bye to this kind, gentle doctor, since Paul would have to be put under the care of Riverview's own psychiatrist. He hated the idea of yet another change, and I worked hard at telling him that I thought the day treatment program would help. I stopped just short of saying he had to go there, or else. I was prepared to do an involuntary committal if it came to that, if in other words, his life were in danger. But it hadn't come to that, and I still wanted to work with him, not against his will.

We took the elevator up to the fifth floor of the hospital's west wing. The whole hospital had been taken over for adolescent treatment and included the chemical dependency program for both alcohol and drug abuse, the day treatment program that Paul would be attending, and the in-patient treatment program, which I assumed was for the more severe, perhaps psychotic, cases.

Paul's program, I knew, would be full of kids having trouble with their families, with their schools, with the law. Shoplifting, vandalism, running away from home, early sexual acting out, defiance of parents — I imagined these would be the behaviors of the other kids. I wondered if there would be any cases of depression besides Paul's. The hospital was on the edge of the slums and seemed to be a way station for all the destroyed young lives from this modern American city.

We were shown into a small lounge to wait. As we sat there, six or seven kids walked past with their counselor. The boys swaggered by on their thin, pipe-stem legs, glancing at us briefly. One of the girls, her hair in a high, teased beehive that I thought had gone out of style in the sixties, stopped and looked at Paul and punched her friend in the ribs. "Hey, Stacey, looks like we've got someone new." The two girls, both chewing gum, stopped in the doorway to consider Paul. Stacey slowly blew a big round pink bubble, then grinned when it popped. With her tongue, she slowly gathered the film of the gum off her cheek.

"Looks kind of cute." Stacey nudged the other girl, and when Paul looked up, they giggled and scuttled quickly down the hall, clattering on their impractical, their impossible, shoes. Paul went back to cracking his knuckles. He had barely noticed them.

Anne Hemingway, a short, pleasant, middle-aged woman, came into the room, shook our hands, and introduced herself as the director of the program. She led us to another room, where she began to ask us some questions.

Paul sat slumped over the table, every line of his body hunched. He answered Anne's questions in a very low, almost inaudible voice. "Yes. No. I don't know." Only rarely did he glance at her, his eyes looking flat, impenetrable. At one point, he explained simply, as if it were the most obvious thing in the world: "I'm not a very good person. That's the reason why I don't have any friends."

Listening to him, I wanted to cry. But I was determined to be hopeful, to support him in this chance to make a change in his life. I felt that I had to hope for him, if he wouldn't do it for himself. He must not see me cry or feel sorry for him or for myself.

Anne explained that the day treatment program would offer Paul occupational therapy, structured group recreational activities, group psychological therapy, exercise, and relaxational skills, in addition to some individual therapy. During the first week, he would have a medical evaluation and a complete psychological and neuropsychological evaluation.

Jim was teaching in a summer school program, so for the first two weeks I drove Paul early every morning to the Twin Cities. I enjoyed the ride with him through the early summer countryside, past fields of corn showing a foot or two above the soil, past fields of cows grazing, and the strawberry fields where the crop was beginning to come in. The mornings were cool and fresh, full of bird song and promise.

One morning, listening to the radio, we heard "Strawberry Fields

Forever" just as we were passing the strawberry fields outside of town. Several people were hunched over the low plants, carefully picking the delicate fruit and filling their pails. The sun, low still on the eastern horizon, seemed to string lines of golden light along grass blades, over spider webs. The light gleamed in thousands of places, along each blade, tracing the tracks of spiders and bugs and dew. It seemed a world of hope, newly created, one where Paul might also make a fresh start.

But each morning, as we neared the hospital, Paul became more agitated and nervous. Over and over, he asked me why I was taking him there. Again and again, I explained that they could help him feel better about himself and that he might learn how to make friends with the other kids. I walked him up to the fifth floor each morning and left him standing there, hunched, cracking his knuckles, staring at the floor.

One morning, as I was dropping Paul off, Marianne Flynn, Paul's therapist, asked to talk to me. Marianne was young, in her late twenties or early thirties. She had short blond curly hair and a sweet, open face. In her office, a tiny, windowless cubicle carved out of another room, we sat down next to her desk and started to talk.

"I really don't know anything about autism," Marianne began. I stared at her, feeling shocked, but also appreciating her openness. "But Dr. Nolan gave me a book to read over the weekend. He had marked lots of passages, and I did read them very carefully."

I waited. I didn't know where to begin. I had lived for so long with autism that it was hard for me to imagine anyone, let alone a professional psychologist, not knowing anything about it. And yet, in a way, I wasn't surprised. I knew, from my own experience and reading, that even when people did profess to understand autism, some of them didn't in fact understand it at all. And it was a relief to hear Marianne be so honest. As I sat there, trying to think of what to say, I felt grateful at least that she didn't have a Freudian model of autism: there was no danger that she was going to apply Bruno Bettelheim's theories. Ignorance, I thought, was better than false knowledge.

Marianne went on. "I have drawn up a program for Paul while he's here. I made up a list of ten behaviors for him to work on, and I wanted to share them with you first."

I nodded and she went on. "At the top of the list is eye contact. I want him to learn to look people in the eye. If he can look people in the eye ten times a day, he will earn one point for that day."

I was appalled. This was worse than anything I had imagined. How could I begin to explain what I knew about autism as a problem with sensory integration; how could I explain how the neurological problems of autism interfere with social knowledge, with learning to follow and understand social cues? How could I explain about Paul's anxiety and how he avoided eye contact the more anxious he became? Marianne did seem to be following the old model of autism as a psychological disorder, a deliberate withdrawal from social contact. I tried to explain some of what I knew, without sounding too opinionated and distrustful of her as a professional, but I gave up after a few moments. "I don't think focusing deliberately on Paul's eye contact will do much good," I told Marianne. "I really think he will have better eye contact when he begins to relax and trust the people here."

Marianne nodded. She looked puzzled, but she was listening closely, without any professional competitiveness. I went on. "It's my feeling that working on trust is really the best thing you can do, at least at first. Better eye contact will follow."

"But what behaviors do you think I should reward?"

"I don't know. But I do know that focusing on his eye contact will just have the effect of making him more and more self-conscious."

Marianne looked a little chagrined, but she accepted this. After all, she had asked. I went on to recommend that she call Sheila Merzer who ran the program that Paul had been helped by so often in the past. Sheila's office was just a few blocks away from Riverview Hospital. "I'm sure she'd be willing to talk with you on the phone. She might even be able to do an in-service training here, since no one here has much experience with kids like Paul."

We left it at this, but I went away not knowing if I could trust the day treatment program to give Paul the help he needed. Maybe this program had been a mistake, maybe I shouldn't have insisted so adamantly that he come here.

Shortly after this, Paul was given the psychological and neuropsychological evaluation. The staff was very open and they gave a copy of the results to Jim and me. The report explained that a doctor had administered a structured intellectual and cognitive battery of tests, along with personality and emotional functioning tests. Dr. Sheridan wrote that he had given Paul the Halstead-Reitan Neuropsychological Test Battery for Adults because of Paul's significant history of language and other developmental delays, and also because of what appeared to be his "current visual memory problems."

Paul's I.Q. test placed him in the fifty-fifth percentile and in the average range, but the Halstead-Reitan Test placed him in the "mildly impaired range." The overall test results, the doctor said, showed "higher order integration and visual motor matching difficulties." He also said he had found "quite clear information that there is an impaired organic substrate in cerebral hemispheres." The particular difficulties come in "higher order processes such as inductive and deductive reasoning, problem solving, concept formation and managing of problem tasks that require stepwise solutions."

The report also stated that Paul "simply did not have adequate social knowledge, social reasoning, practical knowledge or practical reasoning." His weakness in these areas, Dr. Sheridan pointed out, would naturally "lead to a sense of social ineptness on his part." Paul would be "expected to address the world in a fairly immature and perhaps even regressed manner on the basis of this organic-like involvement."

The doctor went on to urge the various therapists in the day treatment program to keep these test results in mind, and to be aware that they could explain Paul's discomfort in interpersonal relationships. The report concluded that Paul "feels very inferior and also demonstrates a lot of personal distress when he is in interaction with other people." In support of this statement, he quoted Paul: "I just act very stupid sometimes, I act shy and depressed and frustrated." Asked, on one of the tests, what he would change in his family, Paul had said, "I would change the way they force me into things I don't want to do." And when he was asked what he most desired, what his first and major wish would be, he had answered: "I would like to understand the world." And then he had added, "I would like to understand other people."

A few days later, the psychiatrist in charge of the program called to say he wanted to put Paul on Prozac, a new antidepressant that, he explained, was a serotonergic drug. Dr. Nolan told me that the drug blocks the re-uptake of the neurotransmitter serotonin, thereby leaving it in the synapses of the brain a little longer. This, they thought, was why it worked in cases of depression which were caused by a deficiency in serotonin levels.

Dr. Nolan went on to say the drug was also useful in relieving repetitive obsessive-compulsive behaviors, the kinds of behaviors that autistics typically show. He told me that he thought Paul would be a good candidate for Prozac in view of his dual problems, depression and autism. High-functioning autistics often have episodes of depression in their teenage years, he told me, and they frequently come from families with a medical history of affective disorders.

Ah, I thought, now we are getting somewhere. Even if the psychological part of this program won't help Paul, maybe the medical part will.

Jim and I had been fighting all summer. I had attacked him in our family therapy sessions, reminding him of those times when he had been so hard on Paul, when he had said things he really hadn't meant, such as threatening to leave Paul if he went on lying or stealing. I accused him of being too hard on Paul at times in the past, of sometimes being uncontrollably angry, of being cold and unforgiving at other times.

Beatrice, our family therapist, was genuinely puzzled. Jim's presence sitting across the table gave her a different story. His gentleness, his obvious concern for Paul, his willingness to come to therapy sessions and to try to help Paul: none of this added up to a man abusively angry or cold and withdrawn. She asked, "But is Jim doing that now?" And I had to admit that, no, he was not. He had stopped some years ago. He was now usually very tender with Paul, very patient.

Then Beatrice asked me, "So why are you still so upset about it?"

I told her I didn't know. But later that day, I realized I had my suspicions: I thought I was displacing my fears for Paul into anger at Jim. I was afraid for Paul, terrified that he really might try to kill himself, and I was afraid that Jim's harshness with Paul in the past had done some lasting harm. I was afraid that part of Paul's low self-esteem, part of his depression, came from Jim's earlier attacks.

I had a fantasy that if Jim apologized, Paul could begin to feel better about himself, could begin to understand that those things said in the past were the product of anger, and not a real and lasting judgment on Paul himself. They did not mean, had never meant, that Paul was a bad person. But the more I wished for this scene, the further it retreated from all of us. I was trying to force Jim into some Lear-like scene of apology and humbleness, and the more I tried to force it, the more resistant he became.

That summer a terrible thing had happened to a friend, and it cast a long, dark shadow over my own life. Lois, a doctor and a mother of six children, whom I had met several years before in a parents' group, lost a son, not her autistic child but an older son. One day, shortly after Paul started the day treatment program, I heard that Sam had been found dead of an overdose in a park near the river. He had taken a handful of antidepressant pills and crawled into a culvert, a cement drainage pipe that ran into the Mississippi. And there he had been found several days later.

Sam was twenty-two. He had been a model student through high school and had been accepted at Princeton. Then, midway through his first year, he had had a breakdown and had been hospitalized. Lois told us in our parents' group that many diagnoses had been given, ranging from depression or drug dependency all the way to paranoid schizophrenia. For four years professionals had tried to help Sam. He had been in and out of hospitals, day treatment centers, and halfway houses, and what had started as a depression and a simple breakdown began to seem more like a permanent condition.

We knew that, for years, Lois had tried to help him. Often in our group, Lois told us how Sam was trying to live on his own. "But his life is very lonely," she had said not so long before his death. "Really, it's marginal, he lives only on the edges of his old life."

Every week Lois called Sam and asked him over for dinner. Those evenings she tried to talk to him and help him fill out forms for public assistance, for job interviews, for rent. Often she did his laundry, or shopped for food, or picked up his prescriptions. A month before his death, however, Sam's therapist and caseworker had asked Lois to stop trying to help him. They had argued that he would never get better as long as she was looking after him. But privately, in our group, Lois shared her fears that Sam was incapable of surviving on his own.

"He's just too confused," she told us one day. "He can't seem to remember appointments. He writes phone numbers on scraps of paper, then loses them. I'm afraid he's going to be evicted from his apartment. I don't think he's paid his rent in three months."

That day in the parents' group meeting, Lois told us she would go along with the caseworker and the therapist, but she wasn't sure it was the right thing to do. Everyone, she told us, seemed so sure it was the right, the only, thing to do — her husband, her other sons and daughters, Sam's psychiatrists and the other professionals. Everyone else seemed so sure. Maybe they were right.

I went to Sam's wake. I had been to many visitations at funeral homes before this. I even knew three families that had lost children, and each of those funerals had been terrible. But this was worse. Even though I struggled to see all the differences between Sam and Paul, my mind kept returning to the similarities. Lois had told us that Sam was hyperaware of his new disabilities, his inability to concentrate or study as he used to do. He seemed to have lost his fine intelligence, the one that had gotten him to Princeton, and the contrast between what he was now and what he had once been had become insupportable. It was as if he were two people, Lois told us, the self that couldn't perform according to the world's expectations, and the self that knew it and felt it keenly. Lois also told us he had talked of suicide. "I know that for him it seems the logical way out," she had told us one day not too long before his death.

Inside the funeral home, I paused to sign my name in the guest book, then went into the main room, where guests were slowly walking down the line of family members, speaking to each in turn. Lois was standing slightly off to one side, her husband and five remaining children seeming to avoid her. She looked very much alone.

I headed straight for Lois and gave her a big hug. She held me for a long, wordless moment, her eyes brimming. Then she drew herself upright and wiped her tears. "Would you like to see him?" I nodded and walked with her to the far corner of the room to the open coffin, which stood behind the banks of stiff, awkward, too carefully arranged flowers.

Lois rested one hand on the edge of the casket and drew a deep breath. We both looked at Sam for a long time, then she turned to face me. "He looks very peaceful, doesn't he?"

"Yes. Yes, he does."

Even with his clayey, inert skin beneath the makeup, Sam was still a very handsome young man. He had thick light brown hair, a high forehead, neat ears tucked close against the side of his head. Something about those ears seemed so childlike, so exposed. He had been about six feet tall, with broad shoulders — Paul's build exactly.

Turning away from her son, Lois led me to some chairs in the corner of the room. "Part of me is happy," she said looking down at her hands in her lap. She glanced up at me. "Or relieved. I guess *relieved* is the word for it." She paused again, looking across the room at the open casket. "It's over now."

I nodded. This made perfect sense to me. Suddenly, I almost envied Lois. Yes, it's over now: all Sam's suffering, all his anxiety, his feelings of helplessness, his unending, unrelieved, hopeless struggle. "I know," I said, almost in a whisper.

And then I remembered the teenager I had tried to help when I was in graduate school in St. Louis. Leslie had also had a breakdown halfway through her first year at college, and she too had seemed beyond help. I remembered how her mother had agonized over Leslie's pain, over her loss of self-respect, her inability to concentrate. And I remembered all our sessions in my apartment, when Leslie and I read short stories and plays together. Nothing had ever made much sense to her, nothing that is, except one play.

I gave her Synge's *Riders to the Sea* to read, and then later we listened to the tape of a radio production. That day in my apartment, Leslie had listened quietly, and slowly her face had become less mask-like. She stopped picking at the sore beside her mouth. Her eyes opened wider, those lovely gray eyes that always before had seemed hooded, filmed over. A light pink color appeared on each cheek, and I began to see how beautiful she had been, might yet be with a return to health.

Leslie sat rapt, totally mesmerized. Only much later did I realize that Synge's message was the only comfort she could receive at that time in her life. When the old Irish mother says, after her husband and the last of her sons are carried away by the sea, "They are all gone now. There is nothing more the sea can do to me," Leslie listened with a light on her face. She seemed to understand that there was a point beyond fear, beyond desire, a point at which you stop grieving and simply exist. Thinking about it later, I wondered if maybe Leslie didn't envy the old Irish mother, didn't wish that she herself had entered that state of mind where there is nothing more to give up, nothing more the sea could take away from her. The safety of resignation, or perhaps the safety of despair: this is what had brought the pink to Leslie's cheeks, the unaccustomed light to her gray eyes.

I reached for Lois's hand. Maybe she had arrived at that place beyond fear, beyond desire, where she could simply exist, could accept the terrible fact of her son's death. Part of me longed to be there with her.

But then I drew back and sat very still, staring at my own hands. I was suddenly terrified and hoped that Lois hadn't noticed. I mustn't allow myself to be seduced by these thoughts. Unlike Sam, Paul was still alive. And I knew that with every cell of my body, every fiber of my being, I wanted him to stay alive. I knew I still feared. I still desired. There was still much more the sea could do to me.

In our family therapy sessions at the day treatment program, none of this got said. I never talked about Lois and her son, about Leslie and the old Irish mother who had finally reached that place beyond grief and pain, about my fear that Paul would be like Sam and my terror at being seduced for a moment by that vision of death as the welcome end to suffering.

Jim and I made no progress whatsoever that summer. All that ever happened was that I had attacked Jim day after day within our therapy sessions; and every day as soon as we left the hospital, Jim had turned on me with just as much ferocity, but also without witnesses. And so it had gone all summer: unclear, messy, unproductive fighting. Nothing had ever been clarified. The anger had seemed pointless, vengeful, hurtful. We never got to the point where we spoke our deepest feelings, our reasons for feeling so angry, so betrayed, each by the other.

All during that summer Kate was neglected. She kept telling us she wanted to go to the family sessions, and we kept asking Beatrice if she could come. But we were told that we weren't ready for that yet, that Jim and I had to work through some of our anger at each other before we would be ready to stand together and support Kate. Beatrice thought those sessions would be too destructive for Kate, too frightening.

I understood perfectly well what she was saying, but I also knew that Kate witnessed destructive anger at home also, that she wasn't protected from it. I also thought Jim and I might behave differently if she were at those therapy sessions. But because Jim and I never resolved our anger at each other, Kate was excluded all summer and it was a long time before she got a chance to voice her own confusion and terror and anger in a therapy session. We talked with her a lot ourselves, but it wasn't the same; she felt excluded and not valued as a part of the family because she wasn't allowed to be a part of Paul's therapy that summer.

Dr. Nolan called me one day to say he had some interesting information about Paul based on the results of an MRI, a magnetic resonance image taken of his head earlier in the summer. When I went to his office, he showed me the images made during the scan.

"See this?" he said, unrolling the paper and pinning the ends down with books on his desk so it would lie flat. "This, right here?"

I peered closely at the place near the back of the skull which Dr. Nolan was pointing to, but it meant nothing to me.

"This is the cerebellum," Dr. Nolan said, leaning forward, close to the paper. He paused, then added in a low voice, "And it's too small. You see this area behind it, this darker place?"

I nodded, studying the faint images on the paper.

"This is the cisterna magna."

"What's that?"

"That's just the empty space around the brain tissue. You see here

it's too large, there's too much empty space around the cerebellum."
Dr. Nolan stood upright again and started to roll up the paper.

"But what does this mean?"

"I don't know what it means. But I do know that we have found the same thing in every other autistic person who has ever had an MRI. They all seem to have cerebellar abnormalities."

"They have?" I was amazed. "You must be onto something now?"

Dr. Nolan nodded. "We think so. One hundred percent of all autistic people tested have had this same, or some similar anomaly, in the area of the cerebellum. One hundred percent. But we don't really know yet what this means."

Three years later, I heard a lecture given by Dr. Eric Courchesne at the National Autism Society's annual meeting. He pointed out that the cerebellum appears to be involved in the ability to coordinate voluntary shifts of attention and that defects in that part of the brain may explain the profound deficiency in social communication, including problems with joint social attention, which are a characteristic of autistic people. He suggested that researchers may go on to discover other systems of the brain which are involved in autism, but that at this point in time there was at least strong evidence of cerebellar dysfunction.

I had always known that Paul had trouble with social and behavioral cues, that when he was younger he found it very difficult to understand pointing, facial expressions, and other aspects of nonverbal language. When he was little, I had often noticed that he couldn't watch my face or look me in the eye at the same time that he attended to what I was saying. And even as he grew older, he couldn't easily be interrupted when he was telling me something. He had to finish whatever it was that he was saying before he could address my questions or comments. In other words, Paul had always had difficulty coordinating voluntary shifts of attention and he had some trouble integrating information received from several senses at once. Thus I heard Dr. Courchesne's lecture with a profound sense of excitement: at last professionals were beginning to understand the neurological basis for autism. But the summer of the day treatment program, Dr. Nolan apparently didn't understand the effect of the small cerebellum on Paul's behavior, nor could he interpret his findings to me when he showed me the results of the MRI.

Paul's depression did not lift. Weeks went by, and he continued to get up early, to put in time at the day treatment center, and to come home again. They complained that Paul was still behaving in a very "passive-resistant" way and that he was being manipulative and controlling. When I dropped him off or picked him up, Marianne would sometimes ask to talk to me.

Once, when I was sitting in the lounge waiting for Paul, Marianne joined me. It was a hot, humid day and the air-conditioned hospital seemed only slightly cooler than the outdoors. A pall of traffic fumes hung over the city that day, clamped down by a thermal inversion, a dome of hot air that wouldn't rise and move on.

That morning when I had dropped off Paul, he had seemed especially tired. It was the end of the week, and he had been getting up at five forty-five every morning, so we could have a decent breakfast, then drive the forty-five miles through heavy traffic to the hospital before the program began at eight. He had been almost swaying as he got out of the car that morning.

"How is Paul doing?" I asked Marianne. She seemed so earnest and so well intentioned, yet I didn't trust her. At the same time, I wanted desperately to trust her. I needed to believe that she would help Paul and not harm him.

Marianne slipped her sandals off, and pulled her feet up under her on the couch. She stared at her hands for a moment, then looked up at me. "Paul's still very passive. He just sits and waits until someone tells him what to do. He hasn't yet initiated any social interaction with anybody." She paused and looked down at her lap before going on. "I wanted to warn you that today he is likely to be pretty upset."

"Why?" My heart was thudding. I wanted to protect Paul from what I was beginning to think was an abuse of power, a distortion of therapy. At the same time, I knew that they thought I was an overprotective mother who was trying to shield Paul from anger and from the world. I wanted to preserve an image of myself as a "good mother": I didn't want to come across as meddlesome or as someone who made excuses for her son and held him back in his development.

Marianne went on. "Today in group therapy, we confronted Paul for being so passive-resistant. He fell asleep this afternoon after lunch, and we confronted him because he was being so disrespectful of the other kids. He wasn't paying attention to them when they were talking."

"But Paul was exhausted this morning," I interrupted. "He was really tired. I doubt if he meant to be disrespectful." I stopped for a moment, shocked by what I was hearing, yet hardly knowing what more to say. It seemed so obvious to me that Paul was tired. Why wasn't it obvious to Marianne?

She waved my objection aside. "That hardly matters. We were just using his falling asleep as an opportunity to confront him. He's been using the excuse 'I'm sad' or 'I'm depressed' to get out of group activities, and today we all got fed up with him. Some of the other kids told him he was tricking them into thinking he was 'dumb.' And they confronted him with specific behaviors."

"What were they?" My voice was very small. I knew what these behaviors were. I could picture Paul in the group.

"Minimal eye contact. One-word answers. Hanging his head. Playing with his hands. Staring off into space. You know the kind of thing." Marianne glanced at me, then away again.

"Yes, I know what you're talking about." My thoughts were spinning. I mustn't try to protect him, I kept saying to myself. Also I thought maybe Paul would respond to Stacey and the "Beehive." A couple of girls confronting him, who also thought he was "kind of cute," might be a way of reaching him.

Marianne went on. "We want him to get used to anger. We feel that this is his major problem." She paused to let this sink in, and then went on, picking her words carefully. "We feel it is very important that you follow through at home. When you are angry at him but denying it, he can still sense your anger and he becomes very confused. We feel that honesty and directness are by far the best way to proceed with him."

She paused again, and I nodded. She was right of course. I knew how dishonesty about feelings confused and upset Paul, as they would anyone. And he had always had a problem with anger. But was this the main problem? The one that was causing his withdrawal and anxiety, his depression and his low self-esteem? I didn't think so. At the same time, I didn't dare share my feelings with Marianne. I thought I would surely be discounted. And I wanted to come across as capable of the "tough love" that would hold Paul accountable, that would make no excuses for him, that would in the end cause him to recover and move on and accept responsibility for his life.

Marianne continued in a rush. She could sense my mixed feelings, even though I wasn't sharing them. "We feel that Paul will do significantly better when he is expected to act normally. We think he feels condescended to when he is treated as different, or as special — or as retarded."

"That's true . . ." I began. But I didn't know how to go on. I knew how terrible Paul felt when kids in school called him retarded. I also knew we shouldn't make excuses for him, that when we set higher expectations for him, he often did better. Of course. But the image of Paul struggling to conform to the world's expectations, struggling and always falling short, sometimes a little bit, sometimes a lot — this image kept rising up before me.

I recalled the test results, the findings that Paul had "an impaired organic substrate" that had caused his failures in "social knowledge, social reasoning." I remembered also that the report had said that he would naturally feel a "sense of social ineptness" because of this organic impairment. These words had been burnt into my brain, and now they seemed fundamentally, radically, at odds with what Marianne was telling me. What if Paul simply could not follow the complex social rules of the day treatment program? What if he were, in fact, trying very hard to understand, to figure out what they expected of him, but was continually falling short, not because he was being manipulative or passive-aggressive, but rather because he simply couldn't follow the rules of their social interactions?

I sat there staring at the floor and trying to focus on this new insight, then wondered why I hadn't thought of it before, and why I had exposed Paul to this frightening and disturbing experience. Wasn't Marianne blaming Paul for not doing things he simply could not do, at least not yet? Shouldn't she and the others be trying to teach him those very skills, the social knowledge and social reasoning that they were now blaming him for not having? Suddenly, and very clearly, I began to see that Paul's behavior, his anguished withdrawal in the day treatment program, was an aspect of his autism, the autistic's way of protecting himself from a confusing world, and was in no way a neurosis curable by these methods.

And then I was shocked and appalled as yet another new thought occurred to me. I stared at the linoleum-block floor, my eyes swimming, not wanting to look up at Marianne. The terrible truth was that they had made his autism worse. They had made him more fearful of other people, and they had impressed on him, even more deeply, a sense of his own inadequacy.

I thought of how Paul used to follow Allen all over town, watching him to see how he should behave, studying Allen as if he were his alter ego. That was how he had learned many of his social skills. This friendship, with its basis in trust, was the reason Paul had developed so far beyond other children like him. I also remembered how Paul and Allen used to fight. Paul was never quite quick enough. He was never able to fight back with the sophisticated skills of other children. He always ended up the loser, the victim, thinking there was something the matter with him. But he would always go back and try even harder to be like the other kids. He had never given up until recently.

I didn't share any of this with Marianne, and as soon as I left the hospital with Paul, I felt I had been co-opted. In the name of their view of honesty with Paul, I hadn't shared any of my own deepest feelings.

Paul was silent all the way to the parking lot. But when we got into the car, he exploded. "What did I do wrong?" He hit the side of his head with the heel of his hand, something he hadn't done for years. "What did I do wrong? I must just be a bad person. I don't do anything right." And he hit the side of his head again, hard. "I've been trying so hard," he went on. "I try to look at people and pay attention to them, but I just don't ever do anything right." Paul was rocking now, back and forth in the seat belt, as I started to pull out of the parking lot.

I kept silent as I took the entry ramp onto the freeway. I concentrated on moving into the fast traffic heading south. I knew I needed to make a decision, and I needed to make it quickly. Was I going to go along with the day treatment people and remain silent? Or was I going to say something to Paul? Listening to him go on and on about what a terrible person he was, I made my decision. Drawing a deep breath, I told Paul to stop for a minute and listen to me. He continued to stare straight ahead, cracking his knuckles and rocking slightly.

"Paul, listen to me. You need to know that you are not a bad person. Today they were just trying to get you used to anger. They needed to find an excuse to confront you. And when you fell asleep during group time, they decided to take that opportunity. They want you to cooperate more in the group. To talk more. To share more, and to listen to the other kids more. But mostly, they just wanted you to get used to anger."

He stopped hitting his head and looked at me. "So they were just looking for an excuse to get angry at me?"

"Yes. So that you would get used to it."

Paul stared at me for a moment, then said, "That's pretty stupid, isn't it? Don't you think that's pretty stupid?"

I couldn't help laughing. "Yes, I think it is."

CHAPTER 32

At a Crossroads

PAUL'S DEPRESSION did not get better that summer. We all attended the discharge interview, Jim, Paul, Kate, and I, as well as
Marianne, Dr. Nolan, and Paul's occupational therapist. Marianne
began the interview by confessing that Paul had met only one out of
the ten goals that had been set for him at the beginning of the program,
that of having a staff member check on his progress numerous times
each day. "And yet Dr. Nolan and I both think the program was a
success for him," she told us.

I stared at her. I didn't see how they could think this.

Paul sat hunched forward, gazing at the floor and cracking his
knuckles. She continued: "Paul was unwilling to initiate positive discussions with his peers. He appears to have some insight into more
appropriate interpersonal skills and insight into what he is feeling, but
mostly he continued his passive-aggressive and manipulative behaviors."

Paul glanced at her, then away again. He continued to rock and to
twist his hands together.

I had to speak: "Paul, you look upset. What's going on?"

"They got mad at me again today."

I glanced at Dr. Nolan and the others, then back at Paul. "What
were you doing?"

"They said I lied."

"About what?"

"I said I had played basketball with the other kids. They said I lied,
that I was just watching. I meant, what I meant was . . ." Paul looked
over at Dr. Nolan. "I thought when you asked, you meant was I out
there with the kids playing basketball . . ." He trailed off again.

In my mind's eye, I had a vivid sense of how this scene had gone. I pictured Paul on the playground watching the other kids play. To him, the question "Did you play basketball with the kids?" might well have meant "Were you out on the playground with them?" According to his lights, he might well have been answering truthfully. Even though I knew this wasn't the point they were making, I felt I had to say something. "I think he was trying to be truthful. Is that right, Paul?" I turned to him.

"Yes, what I was trying to say was I was outside with the others. I thought that was what Dr. Nolan meant."

I looked inquiringly at Dr. Nolan, who glanced over at me and gestured dismissively. He turned to address Paul directly. "Paul, you have been passive-aggressive all summer. You haven't really taken part in most of the activities. I needed to confront you about this."

Paul stared at the doctor as he was talking, then he looked down at his hands again and started cracking his knuckles.

"Stop that, Paul!" Dr. Nolan snapped.

"What? Oh." Paul looked down at his hands, then tucked them under his thighs, sitting on them, rocking forward slightly. He looked strained and miserable.

I felt rageful. And betrayed. I had worked so hard to get Paul into the day treatment program; I had made such an effort to support their plan even when I was doubtful of it. But now my anger was beginning to clarify all the complicated, confused feelings I had had all summer. The two voices in me — the compliant one and the rebellious one, the voice that spoke in support of the program and the one that told me it was all wrong — were no longer debating. They had become one voice, saying, Trust your instincts. You know this program has not been right for Paul. But he's leaving now, and you don't have to deal with these people anymore. I realized something in my own head had shifted. It felt like a pendulum weight had moved, a clock mechanism had settled into a new place, and now I could go on past this spot where I had felt stuck for so long. I knew I didn't have to explain to Dr. Nolan and to Marianne and the others what I was thinking. We could simply leave.

And that is what we did a few moments later. We left with a prescription for Prozac and a recommendation that Paul have weekly sessions with a therapist in our town. We had no trouble promising we would follow through on both the medication and the continuing therapy.

The next year was hard, but not as difficult as the one before. The only improvement we saw from the Prozac was that Paul immediately became less obsessive. He didn't "perseverate," persist in the same behavior or in asking the same questions over and over again, as he had done all through his life. He didn't get so upset over little things like spilling milk or unpredictable changes in the weather. He began to relax just slightly.

Paul's depression, however, didn't begin to lift for many months. Then in November, five months after he had started on the Prozac, I decided to add the amino acid L-tryptophan to his medication. I talked to professionals in the Twin Cities who had seen good, sometimes remarkable, results in autistic children taking this nutritional supplement. Also it was readily available without prescription in our local grocery store, and from all reports it seemed to be safe. L-tryptophan acted on the seretonergic system in the brain, increasing the availability of this neurotransmitter just as Prozac did. I had tried giving it to Paul off and on for several years, but had never given it to him consistently or at high enough dosages.

Within a very short time of adding the L-tryptophan to the Prozac, in fact within one or two weeks, Paul seemed very much better. He went to school more happily, he seemed to suffer less anxiety, he didn't dread the winter coming on. Barbara Clark, who hadn't known that we had started a new treatment for Paul, reported independently that Paul seemed better at school. He was beginning to talk a little bit to the other kids in the Resource Room. Slowly, slowly he was starting to improve.

Paul stayed on the L-tryptophan for a year, and then suddenly it was withdrawn from the market after reports that some people taking it had suffered a very rare disorder, Eosinophilia Myalgia. Later they traced this rare illness to contamination by some petrochemicals in some of the batches of pills coming out of Japan, but U.S. government officials claimed there was no way of guaranteeing that all future batches would be clean, uncontaminated. But by that time, the Prozac alone was enough to help Paul, and he continued year by year to improve.

Eventually we found a very good therapist in town for Paul. Usually he went alone, but sometimes Jim and I went to a session with him. From the beginning, I was impressed with Jerry: he had a straightness, a calm gentleness, a quiet respectfulness, that suited Paul very well and that was matched by Paul's own inherent decency. He seemed able to speak directly to Paul's better side, the side that wanted to stop being a victim of circumstance and to start to take some control over his life. I think

Paul sensed also that he was respected, even admired, for the efforts he had already made in his life.

The most impressive thing about Jerry was that he made no sudden moves, he never used irony or any kind of flippant, dismissive humor, and he never tricked Paul into anger or changed the social rules of the game on him. Even though he had no experience with autism, he seemed to understand intuitively the differences in Paul's thinking, and to respect them. He didn't try to cure the autism, as I think the day treatment people were trying to do when they interpreted it as neurosis. Instead Jerry made allowances for Paul's differences in thinking. He was willing to repeat his words over and over again; he never assumed that Paul should have heard him the first time or that he was being willfully obtuse, deceiving others by pretending to be stupid. Nor did he see Paul as manipulative, or passive-aggressive.

In other words, Jerry wasn't fooled by Paul's intelligence, fooled into thinking that he was being devious, pretending not to understand social expectations or the behavior of other people. He took his confusion at face value, saw it as one of the last symptoms of Paul's autism. Jerry seemed to think from the beginning that Paul didn't know, didn't understand, certain things about other people's behavior, but that he could learn.

When anger came up in these sessions, it came up naturally. With real admiration, I watched Jerry stand firm against Paul. I saw how he chose not to soothe him prematurely or to try to solve his problems for him, as I had sometimes made the mistake of doing. And he didn't try to stop him from expressing unreasonable anger as Jim had sometimes done. I saw how Jerry let Paul rage at the world, even when the targets of his rage seemed inappropriate. He even sometimes provoked the anger when he saw it was there just below the surface.

That year when Paul was sixteen, the film *Rain Man* was released. Jim and I decided not to preview it first but to go to see it as a family. We didn't know if the portrait of the autistic man would seem to Paul to be shameful or embarrassing, or if he would be frightened or confused, but we decided to risk it.

"I think I'm going to enjoy this movie," Paul mumbled between bites of Jujy fruits. Raymond Babbitt, the autistic character played by Dustin Hoffman, was becoming very upset, as Charlie, his brother, moved the books in his room. Raymond rocked back and forth from heel to toe, one foot slightly in front of the other. He answered his brother, whom he had never met before, in an agitated monotone. He clearly hated this interruption in the expected routine of his day, this messing with his possessions.

A little later during the movie Paul muttered to me, "I don't know how Charlie stands that brother. I wouldn't let him get away with that behavior." On the screen, Raymond was refusing to walk onto a plane, and Charlie was getting more and more frustrated at his odd and unpredictable behavior. But the more Raymond was forced, the more panicky he became. Finally, he started to hit his head and scream.

"I would just force him to get on that plane," said Paul, his voice rising slightly. "I would explain to the stewardess that I need to get to California, and I would *force* Raymond to get into his seat and shut up."

Hmmm, I thought, this is very interesting. All through the movie Paul strongly identified with the nonautistic brother. He shared Charlie's anger when Raymond refused to ride on the freeway, when he refused to go outdoors in the rain, when he insisted on eight fish sticks for dinner on Thursday because that was what he always had for dinner on Thursday. Paul laughed loudly when Charlie chopped the four fish sticks in half with a fork, creating eight sticks. "You want eight fish sticks? All right, here are *eight fish sticks.*"

A little later, as Raymond insisted that they drive back across the country one thousand miles because he needed some new boxer shorts "from K mart, 400 Oak Street, Cincinnati, Ohio," and as Charlie slammed on the brakes, jumped out of the car and marched down the country road shouting and swearing, Jim and I started laughing uncontrollably. All around us, people were turning in their seats, wondering at our insensitivity. What could we possibly see as so funny about this poor man's afflictions and his brother's crassness? But Jim and I were thinking of all those times we had traveled in England when Jim, distracted by Paul's questions or demands, had swung around the back seat and shaken his fist in Paul's face, when he shouted at him to keep quiet so he could concentrate on driving in very tricky traffic conditions.

For all of us, *Rain Man* was a healing experience. We didn't notice right away how it was helping. It had just been a pleasure to laugh affectionately at Raymond's autistic oddities and also to be moved by Raymond and Charlie Babbitt's experience together, the growing understanding and love between Charlie and his "main man," the older brother that as a little child he had named "Rain Man." A few weeks later Jim tried to get Paul to wear boots on a snowy day when he had to walk a mile to school. Paul wouldn't wear the boots because he had never worn boots; he had for years worn sneakers with Velcro fasteners and always would, as far as he was concerned, wear sneakers with Velcro fasteners. Finally Jim gave up trying to convince him, and said, "You know the reason you won't wear boots?"

"No. Why is it?" Paul had asked innocently, genuinely wanting to know.

"It's because you are autistic."

"Oh! Is that the reason?" Paul stopped to consider this interesting bit of information. And then he said to Jim, "Well, I think I'll wear those boots."

Hearing this story later, I marveled at it. Paul had just made what Alcoholics Anonymous calls a First Step. He had just accepted the fact of his autism and admitted that he was powerless over it. At the same moment, and in the same paradox recognized by AA, he had gained some power over his autism. By accepting that he was autistic, he was no longer quite so autistic.

Paul now had a name for what he was. The profound significance of this simple fact didn't immediately register with us. Years before we had been told not to call him autistic, mostly because the label didn't fit until it was expanded to include people like Paul. We simply called him learning-disabled when he asked us what he was, and that of course was how he was classified by the school system. But privately Paul had long since decided he was really retarded and that we were lying to him, had been lying to him all his life. Now at last he had a name for what he was, a name that for Paul neither evoked dreaded reminders of the swear word that other kids had used on him — *retard* or *'tard* — nor suggested that he was just like everyone else. He started to relax, and he began to accept himself the way he was.

I don't mean to claim that this was a sudden transformation. It was simply a tiny first step. Just as Prozac started a quiet revolution in Paul's life, so the term *autism* did. Slowly, bit by bit, he started to move forward again. When *Rain Man* appeared on television, Paul taped it and watched it over and over. He started to point out that he too rocked back and forth and got upset if things were moved in his room, that he also hated change and uncertainty. But at the same time, in that wonderful paradox once again, Paul was slowly getting used to change and to uncertainty, he was becoming more flexible, more willing to accept doubt and unpredictability.

Later still he began to do a perfect imitation of Dustin Hoffman as Raymond. "Time for Judge Wapner," he would say in that same stilted voice. "Five-thirty, gotta see 'People's Court.' " Or "Course that's not right. The syrup has gotta be on the table before the pancakes." These imitations amazed us. Autistic people aren't supposed to be able to act, to imitate others, and here was Paul doing an uncanny rendition of a screen character. He wasn't simply imitating his own former self because he never did sound like Raymond Babbitt; instead he had caught the exact inflections of a made-up character.

Sometime later, when the Irish movie about the young man with cerebral palsy, *My Left Foot,* was released, again we went as a family to see it. Unknown to me, Kate identified with the main character. I had long before stopped thinking of her as having cerebral palsy since none of the signs had been present for years. And later it never occurred to us to think of buying a tape of *My Left Foot.* One day Kate pointed this out to me. "You never think of me," she wailed. "We have a tape of *Rain Man,* Paul's movie, but we don't have a tape of *my* movie."

One day I overheard Kate talking to her brother. "Paul," she was saying, "you're autistic and I'm artistic." Listening from the room next door, I held my breath, waiting to hear what would follow. There was a sound of cereal shaken into a bowl, the refrigerator door opened and shut again. Then after a moment, Kate added thoughtfully, "And I think I would rather be artistic."

"Oh," Paul said, considering this. "Yeah, I think you're right. I'd rather be artistic myself."

I breathed again, then thought this was so typical of their exchanges. I need not have worried that either would misunderstand the other. I had never heard Kate criticize Paul or blame him for his differences; in fact she was usually too protective of him, too willing to put herself second and to consider his feelings first of all. Both children were usually very straight and direct with each other. There was no animus, no suggestion of gloating or hidden judgment in Kate's simple statement that she would rather be artistic; nor was there any anguish or envy in Paul's agreement. Kate's observation was simply the truth and nothing else.

Kate *was* artistic, there was no doubt about that. She had an interest and aptitude for almost all the arts: drama, singing, dance, writing, the visual arts. By this time she had acted in a number of Arts Guild productions and spent many summers in a children's theater institute. She sang the lead part of *The Little Drummer Boy* in a church Christmas performance, and she had danced her solo piece in the performance with college students. Once she and two of her friends had acted in a college improvisational performance. They were disappointed that they were given nothing more than the role of a wall; nevertheless, the three girls played a very animated and interesting wall, a wall worthy of the Rude Mechanicals in *A Midsummer Night's Dream.*

Now that Kate was a teenager, I began to understand that her talents were really the other side of her mild learning disability, perhaps an outcome even of her early cerebral palsy. Not only was she left-handed, but she was almost entirely a right brain person. She excelled in almost anything creative, and although she did well in school and loved learning, she showed an even more intense investment in all the arts. I also began to think that it was Kate's slight auditory processing problem that made her such a good actress. From the time she was little, she had been intently studying people's expressions and gestures as a clue to their meanings because she couldn't keep up with a conversation.

As soon as Paul started to recover from his depression, he told us he wanted to get his driver's license. "That's how you get a girlfriend," he told me. "It's really embarrassing if your parents have to drive you around on dates."

How right you are, I thought. The year before, when Paul had been so depressed, we had asked him if he wanted to take the driver's education class given at the high school. When he said he wasn't very interested, we dropped the idea. Privately, Jim and I also thought that putting a car into the hands of a suicidal teenager was the worst possible thing we could do. Furthermore, we were afraid Paul might have some perceptual difficulties, or a lag in reaction time, especially when he had to sort out a lot of information from different senses at once. We weren't at all sure he should be driving because we had never heard of any other autistic person, even high-functioning ones, who had their license.

Once again we had no models who went before Paul, no guides to help us make a judgment. So we let it rest until Paul himself brought up the subject again. Then we reasoned that because he had ridden a bike for years and especially because he was so very good at video games, which did require handling rapid-fire visual information and split-second decisions, he would also be good at driving.

Paul took the driver's education class the summer after his junior year, passed the written exam right after that, and got his learner's permit. We found out that he could take the behind-the-wheel test if he took lessons from a professional, so we signed him up with a driver's education company. When Paul finished the lessons, we made an appointment for the road test. We had been warned by the instructor not to try the office in our own county. "They don't pass many people there," she had said. "And the course is a difficult one." But this place offered the earliest appointment, and somewhat reluctantly I agreed to take him there. By now Paul wanted desperately to drive. He sensed, quite rightly, that a license was his only hope of independence *and* of getting a girlfriend.

We arrived early at the motor vehicle office, and Paul and I met the woman who would be testing his driving. She was heavy and was dressed in a tight military-style uniform. Her iron gray hair was pulled tightly back from her face, and she wore a slightly ironic smile, the corner of her mouth quirked up at one end. Heading for the parking lot, she asked Paul what color his car was. He stared at her for a moment, "Oh, umm, blue. I think it's blue." And he led her away to our car.

I knew perfectly well our car wasn't blue. It was gray, but I didn't want to say anything and embarrass Paul further. I realized, however, that if he thought our car was blue, he wasn't in very good shape, that he was very, very nervous and unfocused. I was suddenly afraid that he might have an accident or lose control in some other way, have one of his old autistic tantrums and start screaming and hitting the side of his head. I realized also that I too was very invested in Paul's getting his license. It would make all the difference to his future. Without a driver's license, he might not be able to work, and he would certainly be limited to only a few friendships with people who lived close by. Suddenly, all of this mattered very much to me.

Uneasily, I walked down the mall from the motor vehicle office and into a craft shop. Idly I picked up a few items that were for sale, hardly noticing what I saw: a birdhouse, potholders stamped with a bear design, an awkward clay soap dish, guest towels with more bears, wind chimes with loons cut out of the metal. There was a sad, impoverished look to this store, a brave attempt to please that fell far short of anything attractive or desirable. I drifted out of the store and noticed a small printed sign in the window: PRODUCTS OF THE WELCOME SHELTERED WORKSHOP. ALL ITEMS MADE BY HANDICAPPED WORKERS.

I sat down on one of the benches in the mall and stared at a potted palm. Which side would Paul fall on, I wondered: Would he be able to get a job and support himself or would he need sheltered living, sheltered work? Would he get his driver's license and develop all those other skills needed for independent living? Would he learn how to wash his clothes, cook his meals, and pay his bills? As always, there were no guides, no one who had gone before us who might point the way.

Paul returned with the examiner in a few moments. She walked briskly ahead of him, never glancing back. Paul followed a few steps behind, carrying a piece of paper in his hand. He looked very agitated.

"I failed," he announced flatly, his eyes avoiding mine. "She said I went too slow, twenty-five in a thirty-five zone." He paused and glared at the retreating back of the examiner. "I was just trying to be safe. There was so much traffic and so many things happening at once." He paused again and his eyes reddened. He angrily brushed the tears from his cheeks. I put my arm around his shoulder, and together we headed for the parking lot.

A few weeks after this, Paul did get his driver's license. I took him to the other motor vehicle office, the one that had been recommended to us by the driving instructor. He tried two more times, and on the third trial he passed.

And Paul was right: learning to drive did change his life. For one thing, his friends quickly started to ask him to drive them places. Sometimes it was to pick them up at school or the doctor's office, but at other times it was to take them to visit new people in other towns. Over the next year or two he gained a whole new circle of friends; he met new kids and their families within a far-flung radius, thirty-five or more miles from our home. Sometimes, picking up clothing at the dry cleaner or walking into some other store in town, I would be stopped by salespeople who wanted to know how Paul was. In this way, I found out that he had friends from all over, that he had visited their homes and met their parents. Paul had left our sphere of influence. We no longer knew all his friends and, from some of the things he said, we worried that some of them might not be trustworthy. But Jim and I decided to let him go, as earlier we had let him go on his bike with Allen.

As Paul's eighteenth birthday approached, several people urged us to take measures to protect his future. His Work Adjustment teacher at school told us one day that she thought it was imperative that we apply for conservatorship for Paul, to retain the right to make medical and financial and other decisions on his behalf. Otherwise, she said, he might fall prey to unscrupulous people and he might not qualify for some of the benefits and services he would need.

A few weeks later, we went to the Twin Cities to consult a lawyer who had a lot of experience in dealing with autistic and other handicapped people. It was a rainy day, dark, enclosed and shut down, the clouds so low they hung like a ceiling just over the street. As we walked into the office building, I noticed some homeless people huddled in a corner under an overhang of the building. They were sharing a Styrofoam cup of coffee, passing it between them as they tried to draw themselves in closer to the shelter of the building. But they couldn't quite pull themselves out of the driving rain.

The lawyer, in his beautiful glass office overlooking the street, began by asking us questions about Paul. We told him what Paul could and couldn't do: he could drive a car, he was working successfully at a library job, and he had almost finished high school, but there were many other ways in which he wasn't at all self-sufficient. He couldn't cook for himself or wash his clothes or go to a doctor on his own, and he sometimes tried to buy friendships by lending money to friends. He found it almost impossible to say no, and several people owed him quite a bit of money. Then we explained how he needed a very predictable, orderly environment, with clear instructions and expectations. Sometimes he was bewildered by too many instructions, too many things to do, too many places to go. We still did a lot for him.

The lawyer listened thoughtfully, taking a few notes as we spoke. Then he leaned forward across his desk and started to explain to us what a conservatorship was. "You need to know that it would probably be a lifetime legal condition." He paused to let this sink in. "The conservatorship would be a permanent and open part of Paul's record. Employers would have access to this information, and it does carry a stigma. You could apply to have it removed, but Paul would have to demonstrate to the court that he was no longer autistic in order to get back his civil rights."

He paused again, and Jim and I looked at each other. "But . . ." I began. "But that's an impossibility. Autism is a lifetime condition."

"I know that," the lawyer agreed. "Also, you need to know that under a conservatorship, there would be certain limitations placed on Paul. He couldn't buy car insurance, for example."

"But then he wouldn't be able to drive," Jim exclaimed. "And that itself would limit his job possibilities."

"True. True enough." The lawyer swiveled in his leather chair and stared out of the window into the pounding rain for a moment. Then he leaned forward again. "Also under a conservatorship, Paul couldn't marry without your permission. And he couldn't buy or hold property."

"But what are the advantages?" Jim asked.

"Well," the lawyer said, "without a conservatorship, you might have trouble getting public assistance for Paul — supported living if he needs it, or medical assistance. You can apply for it, but it might be harder to get."

Jim and I looked at each other. "That's a real catch-22," we both said, almost in the same breath.

"It is," the lawyer agreed. "On the one hand, a conservatorship is itself a limiting condition, and if it's added to Paul's autism (mild as that may be), he would then have to operate under two serious restrictions in his life. But on the other hand, a conservatorship would automatically entitle him to a number of crucial services, such as Social Security Supplemental Income and Medicaid."

He looked at us for a moment, then went on. "Paul sounds like one of those people who stands somewhere on a borderland, at a crossroads, neither completely handicapped nor truly self-sufficient, at the moment at least."

"But how will we get him the services he needs without the conservatorship?" I asked, trying not to think of the homeless people just outside the lawyer's office, huddled together on the edge of the rain.

"You'll just have to fight for them."

And that's what we decided to do. Jim and I left the lawyer's office that day without going forward with the conservatorship. On the other hand, we resolved to work hard on getting him those services like Social Security Supplemental Income which we knew Paul would need.

At the end of that summer, Barry Morrow, the screenwriter of *Rain Man*, came to town. He was scheduled to ride in a parade as grand marshal. My good friend Sandra, who had met Barry at a wedding in California, said she wanted to introduce Paul to him. I wasn't there to witness this meeting, but she told me about it later and also brought me a photograph.

In the picture, Paul and Barry Morrow are standing beside the brick wall of the bank, squinting into the bright sunlight. Barry had given Paul his parade top hat and Paul is wearing it, making him far taller than his usual six feet. Paul holds his head slightly forward with his chin thrust out. He is carefully balancing the shiny black hat, trying to keep it from falling off his head. But even without the hat, he would have towered over Barry.

There is nothing professional about this picture. It could be any-body's washed-out vacation snapshot, and that is what makes it so precious to me. The two of them have such a straight look as they stand together, eyes narrowed against the bright light. And it seems that both of them are smiling the same quirky smile, half innocence, half self-consciousness.

Paul brought an autograph home for me to see. "For Paul, my main man," it said. Signed, Barry Morrow.

CHAPTER 33

Mapping the Future

THE SUMMER of his nineteenth birthday, Paul went with some friends to the state fair. When he came home, he wanted to talk to me — not about the rides or the exhibits, certainly not about the animal barns or the craft shows — but about the freak show. And about one fat man, in particular. "I went in to see him," Paul told me. "And he looked so sad. His eyes followed me as I walked around him and out the other door."

Paul was very preoccupied with the fat man and he brought up the subject several times during the next few days. "He was so fat, he had to lie down in a bed. He was watching television. I felt so sorry for him. I wanted to talk to him, to ask him how he felt, but I was too shy." Then later Paul started to ask, "Will you come with me to the state fair. *You'll* know how to talk to him."

Paul seemed to be haunted by the man's sad eyes following him as he walked around the bed and out of the tent, and every day he begged me to go back with him to the fair. I didn't really want to go. It felt shameful, disrespectful to stare at a helpless person billed as a freak. I didn't want to encourage the economic exploitation of another human being or help to turn him into a curiosity or a monstrosity. And it seemed even worse to go in order to pity him or to feed off his misfortune.

Then I realized that Paul was on a different mission. He may first have gone to gape, to satisfy an illegitimate and intrusive curiosity, but now he wanted to return to reach across a boundary to another human being, someone in pain and distress, someone isolated by his very size. And he wanted me to go along with him. "Please come with me," he kept saying. "He looked so sad."

Reluctantly, I agreed to go with Paul one hot August Saturday a week later. We went to the freak show and found the tent with the huge pink picture of a man on a couch. I bought tickets from the hawker outside the door, and we walked up the metal steps into the stuffy caravan.

Immediately I noticed that there was no air conditioning, only a rotating fan blowing hot air across the narrow space of the tent. The air was close, barely stirred by the little fan. A hot floodlight hanging from the dark ceiling was fixed on a mound in the middle of the room. Dust motes and tiny bits of straw from the floor floated in the light. In a corner of the tent a color TV rumbled on, advertising Toyotas.

The mound shifted slightly, and then I saw the man's eyes. They were almost lost in folds and folds of loose flesh, flesh that spilled out over the edges of his cheeks, his chin, his neck. His flesh fell out of enormous clothes and flopped from his bones, entirely concealing the human form that lay somewhere in their midst. This man seemed lost inside himself, swallowed up. He had to lie half reclining on the bed because it seemed that his bones could no longer support his bulk. Looking at him, I had the sudden, bizarre thought that he could crush himself, that he might stop his own heart or his breathing from the sheer mass of flesh pressing down upon him.

Paul pointed to a collection box asking us to make a contribution toward thyroid surgery. This gave me an opening. As I slipped a bill into the box, I lifted my eyes again to those lost eyes in the sea of skin and fat. I started to ask him about the surgery he needed and about thyroid medication. I asked him if he were taking Synthroid and if it helped. I told him I was taking Synthroid, a very low dose for an underactive thyroid gland, and it had helped me. Paul's eyes were anxiously fixed on me, but as the man started to talk about the surgery he needed because the medication no longer worked, Paul looked back at him and visibly relaxed.

We talked for a little while longer. And then we left, walking out into the bright sunshine on our own solid bones.

Over and over again, Paul brought me in touch with human beings and with a side of our common humanity that I would not have known otherwise. I would never have gone to a freak show without him and I would never have made the effort to talk to this man who was so disabled by his very bulk. I would never have had the courage or the innocence to step across that line which my educated morality drew for me, telling me not to exploit people for their physical differences.

But Paul's innocence, his simple concern for another human being, had already led him across that line and he needed me to go back with him to talk to the man. And I went, as so often I went with him when he needed a translator.

Often Paul would ask me to talk to a friend of his, someone in trouble, someone who needed help. Sometimes I would and sometimes I refused because it seemed intrusive, but always Paul was concerned about these new friends of his and about the predicaments they so often found themselves in. And then, gradually, Paul stopped depending on me to speak for him, to express his concern for another human being. More and more he was learning how to do it himself.

For years Paul said he couldn't work on his homework. "I told you: I'm working on my social skills," he would explain. And so he was, deliberately setting out to make new friends, to learn how to talk to people, to get along with them. And then one day he appeared with a girlfriend. Meg, a little younger than Paul, had met him in the Resource Room. At first this relationship seemed blessed: two young people who had a history of learning disabilities and of loneliness and isolation had found each other. There was a gentleness, a tenderness, a quiet humor they showed each other which was lovely to see. Meg said she first became interested in Paul because he always teased Mrs. Clark, called her "Mrs. Run-My-Life" and pretended to refuse to do his homework. She admired his impudence, his gall.

But gradually the relationship became strained. Meg said she felt "crowded" and "needed more space." Paul couldn't understand why two people who cared so much for each other shouldn't spend as much time as possible together. He was always at Meg's house after school, often staying for dinner.

Finally, Meg tried to break up with Paul. He went wild, crazy with hurt and humiliation and anger. Over and over again, he tried to talk to her, to persuade her to come back to him. He sent her a big pile of family pictures and one of his most treasured possessions, a valuable coin his grandfather had given him years before. He wanted to empty out his bank account and give her every penny of his savings. Luckily the account required my signature, so he couldn't get at the money by himself.

This went on for several months. Finally, Paul learned to let go. Then a year or so later he met someone else, and once again the relationship seemed to blossom. Karen was another mildly handicapped person. She had been hit by a car ten years before and had been in a coma for months after the accident. Once again there was a real tenderness between the two, and very quickly Karen started talking about marriage. Then I learned something that Paul didn't know: Karen was a millionaire. She had won 1.6 million in damages after her accident. Understandably she didn't want Paul to know about her fortune yet because she had been pursued by unscrupulous men in the past.

Jim and I kept quiet, but I have to admit that I allowed myself about fifteen minutes of hope that this relationship might work out. If he married Karen, Paul could stay in school as long as he needed. He could afford to work part-time at a job he enjoyed. He wouldn't ever have to worry about medical expenses, or housing, or travel, or anything else that money can buy.

But once again, and to nobody's surprise except that of Paul and Karen, this relationship also started to deteriorate. Karen, we learned, had a far more complicated and traumatized history than we had known at the beginning, one that would pretty well guarantee that she would act irrationally, be abusively angry and hurtful. And so she was.

Paul, for his part, was again miserably confused, hurt, and angry. Driven to tears more than once, he just became more vulnerable to Karen's embittered, abusive, scornful anger. "Boys don't cry," she would sneer at him, keeping her own safe distance behind her contemptuous anger. But then after Paul finally summoned the courage to break up with Karen, she decided she wanted him back.

And so it went on for several weeks, maybe two months in all: messy, confusing, frightening anger and accusations from both sides. Neither yet had the ego strength to sustain a mature and self-respecting relationship. These were two young people who had been hurt badly by life, and they hadn't recovered enough, hadn't learned enough trust in themselves and in other people, to establish a workable relationship with each other.

With the breakup of both of these relationships, Paul again talked of suicide. Several times we took the car keys away from him, hid all the knives in the house, and put in emergency calls to Jerry. But each time he seemed to get over the trauma just a little bit faster, to come out of the crisis a little less devastated than the time before. Slowly, he seemed to be gaining some ego strength, some slight trust in himself. He was helped by the fact that his close friends, Bill and Allen and others, were always there. Every day they stopped by the house or called him. They gave him a little bit of perspective, let him know that breaking up with girlfriends wasn't the worst that could happen, was pretty normal in fact.

Friendships, girlfriends — these continue to be very important to Paul. But there is something else, another old interest, that has stayed with him. The weather still fascinates Paul, and he has always told us he wanted to be a meteorologist, preferably a "severe storm chaser." When he was younger, eleven or twelve, he taped weather forecasts and played them over and over, studying weather maps and the outlandish terms that meteorologists sometimes used. He told us when we were expecting a "cold core occluded front" or an "anticyclonic baroclinic vortex." For a while, he also collected high and low temperatures for a Twin Cities television network that needed some back yard meteorologists. And several times he visited Paul Douglas, the weather forecaster for that same station, Channel 11.

Today Paul still collects the weather pages from the newspaper, as he has done for the last six or seven years, and he reads the weather maps and information on these pages over and over again. He has kept his own personal calendar of the high and low temperatures for many years. He also has a large library of books on weather and climate, and he subscribes to *Weather Watch* magazine. Once I came upon him in my study carefully recording each storm from the prior year. He included the forecast and the actual storm, the time it hit, the amount of precipitation, the wind speeds, the duration of the storm, and any special qualities it had, such as large hail. This was all from memory.

For years, Paul has lived by this dream of becoming a meteorologist, or of working in the field in some capacity. This dream kept him going during the dark times of his depression and confusion in high school. At Barbara Clark's request, the associate principal of the high school gave him permission to leave classes to watch storms come up. This was a precious little opening during those bleak years, when he was shut up in a mostly windowless school, yet he was always too shy to take advantage of the permission. Barbara was also very cautious about encouraging Paul. "You'll need advanced algebra," she told him time and again. "And a college degree. Which means you'll have to work hard, to start to study and do homework. And right now you don't like studying."

Whenever she told him this, accurate as she may have been, Paul became more depressed and frustrated. I know he felt that he was blocked from fulfilling his one dream, and I wanted to keep the dream alive for him in some way that was also realistic. We hit on the idea of encouraging him to be trained in office or computer skills, so that maybe he could get a job in a meteorological center. For one year while he was still in high school, Paul took some classes in business technology at a nearby vocational technical college. But he was bored, didn't see how typing business letters would ever help him work in meteorology, and his teachers, I'm sure, saw him as lazy or stubborn. Another dead end.

We signed Paul up as a Post Secondary Options student under a new Minnesota law that allowed him to be educated at public expense, under the auspices of the high school, until he was twenty-one. The program calls for further education or vocational training, planning for independent living skills, and job supervision. We were delighted that Paul qualified for this service, as well as for services through the Department of Vocational Rehabilitation and Social Security supplemental benefits. But once again it was hard finding anything that matched his skills or interests. He didn't always have the capacities that the programs assumed he would, and he had some others that they didn't seem to value.

And then one day during a conference Barbara Clark decided to look at a community college catalogue on the off chance that there might be a course in meteorology. There was. And Paul could sign up as a Post Secondary Options student. Paul took the class, loved it, and got a B without even studying very much. This class was the start of a new beginning for Paul. His teacher told us that he thought there was real hope for Paul, there was "something there, a spark," he kept saying, something that would indicate that he might be able to get an associate of arts degree, possibly later a full college degree.

"Many students drop out of that class," he told me once. "It's not easy material to begin with, and I set very high standards. I rarely give A's or B's. Paul sometimes gets the highest grade in the class on the quizzes."

Then later he told us that Paul had the ability to glance at a weather map and interpret it. He knew instantly what the weather would be like across the U.S. for the next several days.

"Is that a useful skill?" I asked him, hoping it might help Paul get a job someday.

His teacher chuckled. "Well, no, by itself it won't help him get a job. But Paul seems to have a real intuition, an inner sense, an aptitude for meteorology. And more and more they are discovering that computers can't do all the work of forecasting. Weather stations always rely to a certain extent on the intuitions of people with long-term experience. There is no substitute for it."

Later this teacher told us about something new called the G.I.S., the Geographical Information System, which is a new computer-assisted mapmaking technique. Only one vocational college in the state taught this new skill, he said, but in a few years others would probably start a training program. Paul's teacher thought it would be ideal for him because he had shown such an aptitude for maps all his life and such an interest in meteorology. Possibly he could follow his associate of arts degree at the community college with training in G.I.S., which might put him in a good position to get a job working on weather maps in a meteorological center.

And this is where Paul is today: cautiously hopeful, allowing himself to dream once again, moving slowly, step by tiny step, but enjoying his classes at the community college and recognizing that he needs further education to get where he wants to go.

Paul has now traveled alone to South Carolina to visit his grandfather, and to Boston to stay with my brother's family. He has flown alone across the Atlantic to join Jim and me and Kate in Dublin, then by himself to Germany to stay with friends in the U.S. Army, then back to London to reconnect with us.

When he set off for Germany, I worried about whether his friends would miss him in the Frankfurt airport. I worried about Paul and a foreign language, a foreign currency, different phones and public transport systems. I wasn't even entirely sure he could ask for help. Years before I had had a nightmare, dreaming that we had just sent Paul abroad to Europe all by himself, and only then did we realize that of course he would not be able to buy food or to find a place to stay. He wouldn't even be able to call us or to ask for help. I woke up from the dream, shaking and soaked in a cold sweat, and the feeling of that dream, the sinking, stupefied awareness of Paul's helplessness and of my own utter powerlessness didn't leave me for a long, long time.

I remembered the dream as Paul got ready to fly from the Dublin airport to Birmingham, England, and there to change planes to fly to Frankfurt. Just before he left, as I was trying to explain who he should call, what he should do, if he was lost, and as Paul kept saying, "Why are you telling me all this?" and I knew he was shutting down, refusing to take in any more information because he was already swamped, overwhelmed with the things he needed to remember — at that moment I thought of writing a letter.

I wrote one of those "To whom it might concern" letters explaining that Paul was a high-functioning autistic, that he might find himself lost and confused, and asking the person who read the letter to please help him find his way to the address below. I gave the letter to Paul and told him it was his choice to use the letter or not and that if he did use it he should give it to someone behind a desk, someone in a uniform who looked official.

And then we sent him off into the blue yonder, the ether, the etheream, so to speak. The lap of the gods. He had nothing to protect him except a thin piece of paper in his pocket asking unknown persons to help in case of an emergency. Nothing else, that is — except (and this is a big except) — his own newfound confidence, his steadiness, his intelligent resourcefulness and competence in navigating the world. Paul, in fact, had a lot to fall back on besides that piece of paper.

Sometimes these days he says to me, "You just don't understand the real world." And I stare in disbelief at him. Perhaps I have just taught a women's studies class in which we discussed prostitution and pornography. Or I may have taken my students that week to visit shelters for the homeless or to eat in soup kitchens. Or I may have been working on a draft of a new sexual assault policy for the college, or talking to a friend about her son's breakdown. *I* don't understand the real world? What was he talking about? For after my negative tenure decision, I had been teaching women's studies and directing the program for many years.

But then I would realize that Paul lives in the thick of things in a way that I, protected by my middle-class academic life, do not. It is Paul who has been to many recent funerals and wakes, usually for the grandparents of his friends, and once for the younger brother of a close friend. It is Paul who took a friend who had been raped earlier that week to the police station to make a sworn statement, who had gone with another friend who drove his father to the hospital with a possible heart attack, who had stayed with them in the intensive care unit that night until five in the morning. This was Paul, the autistic kid who had had so much trouble figuring out the world of social interactions.

And where are the rest of us today? Kate has grown to be a beautiful young woman, too beautiful, Jim and I sometimes say, for her own good. "I don't want your face to be your *mis*fortune," Jim will sometimes warn her, half seriously, half in jest. And she will grin impishly back at him. "Oh, Dad. You don't have to worry about me."

These days Kate wears a long black cloak with a hood pulled low over her face. Around her neck are crystals, some on necklaces she has made herself. In her pocket are rune stones of smooth dark pebbles she picked up at the mouth of Merlin's Cave, at Tintagel on the north Cornish coast. She marked the stones herself with white paint after looking up the ancient symbols. She and her friends watch Mel Gibson in *Hamlet* over and over on our VCR. They love to write, and to act, and every few weeks they recreate themselves as characters in dramas that they spend all weekend acting out. Kate and her friends in high school are just as proud of their difference as Paul used to be terrified of his.

When Kate was fifteen, she and Jim played Cordelia and Lear in a reading production of Shakespeare's play. With each performance, I saw how Lear's mad scenes became more and more anguished, his assertion of his humanity more and more desperate. And watching from the audience on the last night, I witnessed once again that scene in the fourth act when Lear awakens in prison, and in that "other place," that place beyond madness, beyond patriarchal prerogatives. Lear looks down at his hands and wonders if they are his, and then slowly he awakens into sanity, into simple sense. And then there comes that moment when he knows, he realizes, everything — all the tragedy of rejection and betrayal and abandonment that has gone before.

Then kneeling before his daughter, he asks Cordelia's blessing, fearing that she can no longer love him, must now have cause to hate him. And Cordelia, played by Kate at only fifteen, speaks those wonderful simple words of forgiveness, of the love that survives and remains loyal: "No cause, no cause." A brief moment, before the tragedy sweeps to its bitter conclusion, but one that for me, as I watched from the darkened theater, seemed to be laden with an almost unbearable burden of feeling and of experience.

Watching the final act, however, I suddenly realized that Jim and I had long since moved outside of the range of this family's narrative, beyond the desperate, self-justifying anger and betrayal of the Lear story. For after the day treatment program ended, Jim and I no longer fought so ferociously. I don't quite know why. I only know that, at some point, we decided to pull together, decided that we had a common enemy in a world that doesn't understand autism, not an enemy in each other's possible misunderstandings of that condition. We had been saved, as Lear and his daughters, both good and bad, had not.

But the real surprise to me as I watched the final scenes of the play was that Kate, at so young an age, also seemed to understand the complexities of this family interaction. And she seemed to have moved to the other side of that grief, to a place where she could express the loyalty, love, and forgiveness that remains steady against all assaults.

I know now that I would not have known the world, or would not have known it in the same way, if I had not had children. I have discovered that to have children is to be open to the worst and the best that the world has to offer. I have felt a fear for my two children which goes far beyond any anxiety I have ever felt for my own life, my own well-being. To have children is to feel an ultimate vulnerability, but it is also to fall in love with the world all over again. And to have an autistic child is to learn to love difference, the humanity that runs far deeper than the success and achievement we are all taught to value.

This is a story of grief, yes, and of loss. But it is a different kind of grief from the one brought by the death of a child. For one thing the child isn't gone; he or she is *right there* flooding the back yard, screaming from the top of a tree, or pouring maple syrup all over the carpet and vacuuming it up. It is a complex and ambiguous grief parents must feel when they must mourn the loss of the child who might have been, while at the same time struggling to care for the child who is. And the terrible, extra burden that befalls parents of handicapped children is that they have no *time* to grieve. They are caught up from the beginning in a perpetual crisis that leaves them no time to reflect, no time even to feel their feelings for themselves. They must always be rushing to attend to a child in distress.

I was one of the lucky ones. Eventually I did have time to reflect, time even to grieve, and time to sort through the issues of guilt and overresponsibility. As I began to feel less guilt, gradually a new appreciation of my child as intact began to emerge. At first I thought of Paul as a changeling, a shadow of his real self, which had been taken away by genetic or environmental damage, which *I* had taken away by drinking during the pregnancy. Only later did I begin to see Paul as complete and whole, an entirely wonderful person in his own right, exactly and precisely the way he was.

Because I had a child like Paul, I was forced to confront my deepest prejudices. Beneath all the other differences which might define human beings, there was one which for me was unquestioned, and that was intellect. Living all my adult life in a academic environment, I had never been forced to consider that intellect is not the same as merit, it is not the same as virtue. It is a gift of nature as surely as any other. We don't ask for our intelligence and we certainly can never do anything to deserve it. It is simply given, a gift.

At first I almost wanted to divest myself of my own privileged mind because I felt so guilty about taking away my son's. I drank myself into oblivion every evening, blotting out both the consciousness of my pain and also my privileged mental capacity to feel that pain in all its complexity. But over time, I began slowly to redefine what I took to be our common humanity. I realized we are all only a car accident away from mental incapacity. People who are mentally handicapped are in no way essentially different from the rest of us. Our intelligence may seem to be an inherent part of our selves, but it simply resides in our bodies tentatively and always in grave danger.

To get to this place, I had to move away from self-sacrifice, and from guilt, overresponsibility and inner conflict. Eventually I developed a class called "The Politics of Motherhood," because I was so fascinated with the ways in which the idea and the institution of motherhood are imbedded in our cultural and political world. In preparing to teach the class I began to study the mythology of maternal neglect, to track down the prevalence of mother-blame in twentieth-century psychological literature. Not surprisingly, I found it especially in the accounts of autistic and schizophrenic children, whose mothers were almost always blamed for their children's handicaps in spite of a great deal of evidence to the contrary.

And so I began to reflect on why this mother-blame exists as a causal explanation for so many of the ills of society. What function did it play politically and socially? And why did so many "experts," mostly males who had never had the exclusive care or responsibility for young children, feel that mothers had done so much damage to individual children and by extension to all of society? Maybe, I began to reflect, such explanations came after the loss of earlier religious explanations, where madness and difference were understood as possession by devils or demons. In the absence of a notion of otherworldly influence, and left only with the psychological model of understanding human behavior, the twentieth century, it seemed, assigned all the extraordinary power to do good or harm which earlier had been seen as demonic — to mothers.

Recently I came across a reworking of the changeling story, a version of the myth in Swedish. In this retelling, the real child falls out of the arms of his mother on a woodland path and is snatched up by a crone, who leaves a troll child in his place. The mother, against the objections of her husband and all her neighbors and friends, takes this changeling home, where she nurtures him, cares for him to the point of exhaustion, all the time longing for her own child, who has been taken from her.

In the end, the child is returned to his parents. He tells them that he has been saved only because his mother had worked so hard to sustain the life of the changeling. Reading this little story, I realized that not only was this an account of the heroic struggle necessary to raise a handicapped child, but also that it was a story where the two children, the changeling and the real child, become one. The well-being of the one depended on the nurture of the other, and in the end the "real child" had survived only because the changeling had been loved and cared for. Perhaps, I thought, Paul too had been saved to "become" himself. The real child and the changeling had merged into one.

The house is full of Paul's friends these days. Two or three teenagers, boys and girls, troop in and out. Paul brings them by himself, or they stop here after work or school. And here they join the two or three come to see Kate.

Paul goes to movies with these friends, or to midnight bowling, or he spends time just cruising or hanging out with them. They all keep in constant touch with each other, and Paul, or our house, seems to be the humming center of all this activity.

He gets up early to go to classes at the community college forty miles away, and he works two or three nights a week. But between the two, he usually comes home to take a nap. His most faithful old friend, Allen, stops by several times a week between shifts at Hardee's, where he works long hours as a manager. Allen bangs the ship's bell on the porch as he marches in the back door. "Paul Dog," he shouts. And hearing no answer, he mutters, "Sleeping again," as he gallops up the stairs and into Paul's room.

During his depression, Paul learned that sleeping was a way of blotting out reality, but now that he is no longer depressed, it is just a way of waiting till his friends come over. And when Allen goes into Paul's room and pulls the blanket from his head, he groans good-naturedly. He isn't really unhappy to be awakened, and he grins, half in pleasure, half in protest, as Allen grabs his foot and pulls him back into the world.

Paul's Story

BY PAUL McDONNELL

I ALWAYS KNEW I was different from other kids, I just didn't know what that difference was. For years I guessed I was retarded, mildly retarded, and that my parents were lying to me when they said that I wasn't. That's what kids always called me: retarded. Finally when I heard the word *autism* and saw the film *Rain Man*, I felt that at last I had an explanation of my own life and experience. If you have seen *Rain Man*, starring Dustin Hoffman and Tom Cruise, you probably have an idea of what I am like. I am not as autistic as I was, but autism still shows in certain ways. For example, in the past I used to ask the same question over and over and I used to drive my parents crazy by doing that! I wanted to hear the same answer over and over because I was never sure of anything. I remember asking, "Is 'probably' more 'yes' than 'maybe'?" I wanted an exact answer to everything; uncertainty used to drive me crazy. My dad *especially* got angry at that behavior of mine, and we used to get into terrible fights. They were *very* painful for me at that time, and even now we fight occasionally. I may be autistic, but I am also a very gentle, kind person.

When I first saw the movie *Rain Man*, I thought, How could anyone live with that guy Raymond. Then when I watched the movie a second time, I saw he was doing some of the same things I did. Mainly rocking. Also at the beginning of the movie, when Charlie Babbitt pulled out the book from Raymond's shelf, Raymond got very anxious. I understood that feeling very well. When I was a child, I had a bunch of coins on a table by my bed. On top of the coins were a candle and a paper umbrella. Like Raymond, I also got very upset if people touched these objects and tried to change them in any way. I liked things to stay the same.

The movie taught me some things. I learned that my habit of asking questions over and over, my anxiety and uncertainty, were not just bad habits: they were aspects of autism. I also learned that my fear of change, my wish that everything stay the same always, even down to the objects in my room, was normal for an autistic person. After that, I didn't feel as lonely as I was, and I was a little less hard on myself.

These days I still rock back and forth as most autistic people do. I rock while I listen to music up in my room before I go to sleep. I also rock on the playroom bed in front of the TV. I find comfort in rocking. It helps me clear my head and think better. I realize that rocking would look very stupid to some people, and I sometimes feel self-conscious about it. Especially at twenty. But rocking helps me to relax, and I doubt that I will stop it any time in the near future. If other people think that it's weird, that's their own problem. I only want to be myself.

Because I am autistic, I have always had a very good memory for dates. I can remember what happened to me on almost any day in 1986 and 1987. I can also remember certain dates as far back as 1979. For example: On Monday, September 3, 1979, I remember climbing a ladder while a babysitter of mine was watching. Or on Friday, July 22, 1983, I got into a very big fight with my dad on the way back home from Valley Fair amusement park. I can also recite a couple of lists of one hundred song titles: for example, the "Top 100 Videos" of 1989 and 1990 on MTV. My memory isn't perfect. I sometimes find myself very forgetful. I used to forget to bring things to school a lot. I also have a lot of trouble remembering the names of people that I don't know well. I realize that I have some special talents, but I also feel very self-conscious about my weaknesses.

One of my main weaknesses is my social skills. They have never really been very good. I could NEVER just go up to someone at school and talk to him or her. I would always wait for them to come up and start talking to me. I started to work on my social skills in earnest when I was eighteen. I had some success, but not as much as I wanted to have.

Aside from having autism, I had to deal with a learning disability all my life. I found it extremely hard to listen to the teacher at school. I would sometimes get yelled at for daydreaming. I had to work twice as hard as everyone else in grade school and high school. I needed a lot more one-on-one teaching.

*

I want people to know about my life. I would like to tell them about autism: what it felt like from the inside and the difference it has made in my life. But I would also like to talk about the ways in which I am just like everyone else. Autism is often misunderstood, maybe because very few people have written about it from the experience itself. When I was a teenager, I began to think that even my parents didn't understand how autistic I had been as a child. It was a difficult and painful experience for me, but I know that I have survived it, and maybe my story might help others. I hope this story of mine will help teachers, school counselors, parents, psychiatrists, and everyone else understand autism better.

Early Childhood

My first memories are of being in London when I was three. I remember being left in a new place, it must have been the new school at the Wolfson Centre, and I was frightened. Of course it was a change and I hated change. I also remember at another time when I was three, my mom showing me a door to a closet and then a wall and rubbing my hand on them and saying "rough" and "smooth."

I was fascinated with certain things when I was three: flashlights and screwdrivers in particular. I have a memory of seeing the little screws in the chairs in my new nursery school (they were about the size of a dime) and wishing I had a screwdriver to take the chairs apart. I also remember taking an electrical plug apart, and my parents came in and stopped me.

I would only eat "ba ba boo" (chocolate milk) and "ma ma moo" (malted milk) when I was three. I liked to watch my mom beat up milk and eggs together with the hand mixer. Years later I put a gerbil in the bowl and spun it around in the mixer. The poor thing came out trembling all over.

When I was three, I had a babysitter named "E E." Her real name was Evelyn but I couldn't pronounce her name, so I called her E E. I took apart a flashlight and heard the bulb clatter around inside it. E E told me that I broke it.

Another memory of mine when I was three was the Christmas tree in the living room of our home in London. I remember taking the colored bulbs out and running downstairs to show my mother each color.

The outdoor toilet at my grandmother's house in London frightened me and I remember my uncle Tony telling me not to be afraid. Even when I was seven I was still afraid of the toilets flushing at Longfellow School. They used to flush automatically every five minutes or so and that really frightened me.

When I was little I noticed odors more than other people do. I used to be especially sensitive to the smell of food. That's probably why I was very fussy about the kinds of food I ate. On many occasions at home I used to just nibble at the food my parents cooked. My dad used to get very upset with me when I didn't eat the food he put out for me. He would sometimes tell me that he would force me to eat the food he cooked. I was always begging them to give me the dessert they bought at the grocery store earlier that day. I used to take very small bites and then say, "NOW can I have dessert" several times throughout the meal. I got very sick and tired of my parents' cooking after a while. One thing is certain about me when it comes to food, I get tired of the same kind of food year after year. Who wouldn't? These days I go grocery shopping with my mother and pick out different kinds of foods that I think that I would like.

When I was four, I was afraid of flowers, the insides of flowers, especially. Roses and tulips in particular frightened me. When I looked inside, it looked like I was seeing the guts of flowers, and so I was afraid to touch them. Carnations didn't bother me, however, or dandelions. Someone took a picture of me looking at flowers which shows me holding my hands away, afraid to touch them. I was maybe six at the time.

I loved hearing scary stories. After we returned to Minnesota from London I remember sitting with my favorite babysitter, Jan, as she told me scary stories. I loved the feeling that I got as she was telling them. On the other hand, I was too terrified to look at the picture of Princess Ruby in a big Sesame Street book when she had her face painted red. I never really knew why I was afraid of looking at that page of Princess Ruby. Maybe it was because I was afraid that my OWN face would turn red. Autistic people certainly have some unusual fears. Today I only fear what most people in this world would fear. For instance, Saddam Hussein dropping a bomb on the United States.

When I was four, I developed a big interest in pipes. I collected all sorts of pipes. I would connect them all through the back yard and run water through them with the garden hose. I would go to the hardware store with my parents and beg them to buy me a set of pipes that I didn't have. I also loved to collect spigots. I would love to open and close the valve on each spigot. It made me feel very happy to collect and to play with these "toys" of mine.

Every time the plumber came to fix a sink in the house, I would watch him with fascination. After the plumber left, I would want to take the pipes off myself. "Paul, the plumber already fixed it," Jan would say to me as I grabbed a wrench and started working on the plumbing myself. I refused to let anyone stop me from what I most liked doing.

I had chicken pox when I was four, and we were visiting relatives in Greenville, South Carolina. I remember seeing red spots on my chest and my face. That was one of the very few times in my life that I ever really got sick. I was one of those lucky people who didn't get sick very often.

When I was five I went to kindergarten. Each morning I was supposed to catch the bus. Daddy used to get very frustrated with me when I was slow. He said, as he was trying to put a mitten on me, "Get that bloody thumb in there." Before I went on the bus, I used to have chocolate granola bars. Once, when I was late, Daddy ran up to the bus with me, and the bus driver closed the door and was about to drive away. Daddy gestured very angrily and shouted, "Open that door!" I was very embarrassed. I remember being terrified if I had to go on a different bus, with a different driver. The numbers on the buses helped me remember which one was mine. If we changed buses for any reason, I panicked.

Grade School Years

When I was six, I went to first grade. There I met Ray and Allen, my two best friends. Allen and I spent a lot of time together when I was in first grade. In the spring of 1979, we would fill the sandbox in my back yard with water from the garden hose and make dams. We would love to see how big we could get the pool of water before the dam burst. When the dam finally broke and the pool of water drained, it would flood the neighbor's back yard. We spent many warm sunny afternoons making dams. Another time when I was standing up in the big room (the Transition Room), Allen had pulled out the chair from behind me. I didn't know it and I fell down and hit my head and started crying. And then Mrs. Austin gave me a little sticker in the shape of a star to make me feel better. That incident was quickly over with.

I wanted to collect all the Tiger, Lion, and Dinosaur work sheets for different reading levels. I brought them all home and worked on them. I wanted to collect them, the way I like to collect Garfield cartoons now. I've collected Garfield cartoons for over eight years now. I couldn't STAND to have even just one missing. When I miss one, I search the old newspapers at people's houses all over town until I find it. I also search the newspaper recycling areas behind buildings. If that doesn't work, I have the public library save their old copies of newspapers for me.

I made two friends who were girls in the same first grade class as me. Tianne and Abby. I don't remember them very well. I DO remember, however, visiting Tianne's house one day and being very frightened of getting into her mother's car. I was scared probably because her mother was a complete stranger to me. The car seemed strange to me because it was very different from our own car.

Another memory of mine when I was in first grade was when other kids used to hit me. I would get very frustrated and start hitting MYSELF! I know this was wierd behavior on my part. The other kids thought that this was very funny. I didn't think that it was very funny at the time. Today, as I look back on it, I laugh at it.

When I was six, I wanted to find out where all the power lines went. I wanted to follow them to the end. I used to have my mother drive on a dirt road alongside a set of power lines that ran north out of Northfield. We went for about fifteen miles, then we lost sight of them. I remember being very fascinated at the different shapes and structures each section had as we drove out of Northfield. In Cambridge, when I turned six, I started to run past picket fences. I looked at them sideways because I wanted to see how fast they would go by. It was like looking at spinning things. I felt I was in control. I also enjoyed playing records on the record player. I played them at different speeds — 16, 33, 45, and 78 rpms. I loved to hear the sounds at the different speeds.

Once when I was six, I was trying to count with a calculator as high as I could. I counted all day, then I left it on all night. The equals button, which I kept pushing, finally broke. I think I reached somewhere close to one hundred thousand when it finally quit. I remember Allen was over at my house at the time and was trying to make me lose count!

I used to love to climb trees, beginning when I was seven until I was thirteen. I wanted to see how high I could get. I marked off the maple tree in the back yard with stickers, measuring each foot up to around thirty feet with a ruler. I used to be able to climb almost half the trees on Carleton College campus. Once I got upset when I hit my head on a branch above me, and some students heard me yell. They stood at the bottom of the tree and thought that I was stuck in the tree. I tried telling them that I could climb very well and that I wasn't stuck at all, but I don't think that they heard me. I was too far up. I wished that they would've just quit staring up at me and left when I was just fine. That really aggravated me. Then I climbed down the tree and just walked away without saying anything to them. I was really embarrassed and angry. I felt like yelling at them to mind their own business, but I didn't.

The first day in second grade, I remember crying and my tears falling on the paper on my desk. It was the newness of it that overwhelmed me. I almost couldn't handle it, but I got through. I was changing schools, which I don't think should have happened. It frightened me and made me feel very overloaded.

During second grade I had very silly fears. One very frightening incident that I had in school was because of the toilets in the boys' room which flushed by themselves. I refused to use those bathrooms. I would always wait until the afternoon until it was time to go to the Resource Room, where there was a teachers' toilet that I was allowed to use. My classmates always said to me, "Paul, you've got to go to the bathroom." One day I needed to go to the bathroom, but I decided to hold it in until I got to the teachers' toilet. But as I was standing in the lunch line, my urge to go to the bathroom increased dramatically. When I had just started to go through the line with my tray, I couldn't hold it any longer. I felt myself peeing in my pants and I started crying. The cook said, "What's wrong, Paul? What's wrong?" I didn't tell her, nor did I tell anyone for the rest of the day. Later, that afternoon, Mrs. Carlson told me that one of the cooks reported that I was very upset about something. But even then I didn't tell her what was the matter. That was one of the most frightening moments of my life. I didn't know what to do. I was frightened, confused, and embarrassed.

Another fear of mine was the phys ed teacher when I was in second grade. I don't think that I really had anything to be afraid of, but I felt afraid anyhow. I seemed to picture him as a brute, or a monster. Once he came up to me and said I wasn't holding the basketball right and he was frustrated with me. He never hit me or hurt me in any way, though. He just looked really big and tough to me.

One of the biggest fears of all was on the school bus in the morning. When I was in first grade, someone I knew at school wouldn't let me get off at my stop. He held his arms out to stop me and I panicked. I finally yelled at the bus driver and she stopped and let me off. After that day I was afraid of the bus and of that kid. In second grade this kid rode the bus with me in the morning, but I got on before him. Every day I was hoping someone else would sit next to me, not him. I was afraid that he would keep me from getting off at my stop again. I remembered where his house was and I MADE SURE that somebody would sit next to me before the bus came to his house. I was rigid with fear almost every morning of that year when I was on that bus.

One day class was late getting out, so I ran as fast as I could to the bus stop. When I got there, I saw the bus pulling out onto the road. I knew that I couldn't catch the bus and cried out in panic. I went back to the office of the school crying. The teachers there helped me by calling my parents to come and pick me up at the school.

Another time when I was in the second grade, my Resource Room teacher, Mrs. Carlson, yelled at me and I was really scared. Tuesday, December 11, 1979, was the date when she got mad at me. I don't remember what it was about, but the date really stands out in my memory.

I never really liked Mrs. Carlson. She seemed to "follow" me from Greenvale School when I was in first grade, to Longfellow the next year. To me, Mrs. Carlson was a very hot-tempered lady. If I misbehaved just the tiniest bit, she would let me have it! She didn't hit me or anything like that, but she spoke to me very harshly a lot. She probably thought that it is good to discipline little kids, but I never agreed with her method of discipline. She used to frighten me a lot when I was in grade school.

In third grade, I remember the school principal spanking me and threatening me with a wooden paddle. He would say, "Go ahead, cry!" He said it in a "you deserve it" kind of voice. I was spanked because I hit a girl in my class. I was afraid of crying in school. I felt like I was a baby. I could tell that other kids thought that I was a crybaby. I tried to see how many days I could go without crying, but I never could go more than two days at a time. Allen hardly cried at all. I wished that I could be like him. I felt very different from everyone else my age. I felt ashamed of myself.

For four years I attended a summer school up in Minneapolis, from the time I was eight to eleven. There were autistic children like me who were at the summer school also. At that time, I wasn't told that they were autistic. I was just told that they had learning disabilities. I never even heard of the word *autism* back then.

I really liked this summer school. For one thing, there was a teacher for each student. Another was, I never got teased while I was up there. The whole atmosphere there was relaxed, not tense like regular school. I enjoyed many of the activities that I did while I was up there. I also went on field trips. I misbehaved for a while the first summer that I was up there, but after a couple weeks or so, I started participating in group activities. I also had the chance to do things with my teacher. I had the same teacher all summer long. I loved the individual attention that I got. I think that having a summer program where there is one-on-one teaching for each child is the best way to learn. Especially for autistic children.

The first girl in my whole life that I really noticed was Tammy Albers. She was more than just a friend. She was a special friend, someone I got along with almost perfectly. I remember her coming over to my house and me going over to her farm. She always used to say I was "super cute" and gave me a kiss on the cheek. However, by the time I was in fourth grade, Tammy and I had drifted apart.

In second grade, I remember being fascinated with the clock on the wall. I watched each tick. It jumped at every minute. Whenever there was a change in seating arrangements in the room, I was afraid that I would be seated away from the clock where I could not see it. Once I was moved away from the clock and I had to lean over my friend Unity, who was sitting next to me, to see the clock. I heard whispering behind me that said, "Look, Paul's in love with Unity!" But I was only trying to keep the clock within my sight.

Another person I spent a lot of time with, when I was seven, was Ray. We used to always go to Carleton College. We explored every building on the campus. We had this favorite tree that we used to climb. One afternoon we were there for five hours and my parents didn't know where I was and called the police. Ray used to bring this puppy that he had over to my house. My dad got very sick and tired of it because it wasn't toilet-trained and peed all over everything. One day, however, when we were at a park, Ray lost his temper with me and beat me up. I will always remember how frightened I was that day. I was scared of him for a few weeks after that incident. He has always had a bad temper. I suspect the reason he beat me up that one day was because for the past few days I was teasing him mostly by saying "Ha-ha, Ray!" whenever he got upset about something. I never teased him again after that incident. In the next couple of years he moved to Cannon Falls, a town east of Northfield, and we didn't see each other very much. Eventually, he moved to Wisconsin to live with his dad and I didn't see him at all for several years. These days he is living up in the Twin Cities and I visit him every two weeks or so. To him, I'm his best friend and that makes me feel very, very good.

I used to tease my cousin Charlie unmercifully when I was eight and nine. At that time he and his family lived just outside of Chicago. My family would visit them for Thanksgiving. They would also come up to Northfield to visit us.

Whenever I was around Charlie, I would tease him about the "Bogey Man." I would shut him up in a dark closet or the basement and tell him that the Bogey Man was waiting for him. He would scream and start crying and bang on the door. "The Bogey Man looks just horrible, Charlie," I would say to him. "His intestines are hanging out of his stomach, one of his eyeballs is hanging out, and his brain is oozing from his open skull."

Charlie believed every word I said. It was so much fun for me to tease him. He was SO vulnerable! This weakness of his encouraged me to go on teasing him. Charlie took every little thing seriously. I also did some really nasty things to him that I won't even mention.

As I look back on this, I feel sorry for what I did to Charlie. I realize that he used to be like me in a way. Maybe I teased him because I was teased myself in school. Children who are teased often tease other children.

These days Charlie and I are very good friends. We get along quite well. He now goes to a college in Maine. I sometimes write to him or talk to him over the phone. I never tease him anymore whenever I see him. I don't think that I will ever tease Charlie again. I really respect him now.

Allen and I remained best friends, even though he was in a different school for second, third, and fourth grades. I don't think I would have been able to cope with life without him. He was the main reason I kept going. It was like we were brothers. For a few years when I was a teenager, he was the ONLY friend I had aside from Phil Gordon, who I saw only at school. Even now we are best friends. We will always be best friends.

During the time we were in third grade, Allen and I used to throw a pitchfork at the sidewalk to watch it make sparks. That's when my fascination with fire began. We used matches at first, and when my parents took them away from us, we got lighters down at the grocery store. When Mama and Daddy took the lighters away, we started using the magnifying glass. We loved to set dry leaves on fire with it. I used to call it a "sun ray." The week of February 16, 1981, we set lots of fires out in the back yard. We wrote pictures by burning holes in the wood of the house. Fortunately, we never burned down my house or had our clothes catch on fire.

On Monday, September 22, 1980, I pretended there was a fire at home. I called the operator and said, "Help, help, fire! My little sister is burning up." A policeman came to the door. I remember him telling me not to do it again. I was told by my mother that almost every kid tries that at some point in his life. I didn't feel so guilty after I was told that.

Allen and I also used to explore the storm sewers under Northfield. We sometimes went as far as half a mile into them. Once we sat under the manhole of our favorite sewer, which drained into the Cannon River, which runs through Northfield, and looked at *Playboy* magazines. Another time I got terrified when we heard some water draining farther up the tunnel and I panicked and ran up to the top of the manhole. Allen stayed at the bottom and waited for the water to come. He was a lot less scared than I was. We found out where the water was coming from when we headed out the tunnel. It was spilling out of a very small tunnel only about a foot in diameter a couple of hundred yards from the entrance where we came in. Someone was obviously washing their car or something and the water was just draining into the storm sewer like it always does. I was afraid that the whole tunnel that we were walking in would fill up with water and drown us both. The loud echo of the water scared me greatly.

I also started a light bulb collection when I was eight. I would buy all different types of light bulbs with my allowance money. I have to admit now that I also stole some money out of my mother's purse once when I saw a light bulb at the hardware store that I really wanted but didn't have enough money to buy. I was always afraid that my mother would see the light bulb in my collection which I bought with the money I stole from her. I would always try to keep it hidden from her view. My collection grew fairly big over the months during the time that I was eight.

One night in December of 1980, Allen and I saw a house across the street all lit up with Christmas lights. I wanted very badly to have those colored bulbs, so we went over to the front yard of that house and started taking the bulbs out of their sockets. We were always watching for someone to run out the front door of that house, but no one did. We were taking bulbs for almost an hour and we had quite a collection in my room. We would take about twenty or so colored bulbs, stuff them into our coat pockets, and run back to my house and add them to my already big collection of light bulbs in my room. Then we would run back to the house and fill our pockets again. I said to Allen, after our third time of filling our pockets with bulbs, "Should we steal some more light bulbs?" Allen had an evil-looking grin on his face, and said, "Sure." We were just starting to unscrew the first couple bulbs from their sockets, which were hanging on a bush in front of the house, when someone came bursting out the front door. Allen took off like a rocket, but I delayed a couple of minutes getting a blue bulb out of the socket. I then ran across the street and saw the man running close behind me. I remember thinking to myself, He's got me, I can't outrun him. He came up to me and said in a rough voice, "Your butt's gonna warm up!" I started crying then, and he told me to hand over what I got. I drew out the blue bulb I had out of my coat pocket. He then asked me if I had any more and I said that I did. I couldn't lie. He followed me to my house and entered the kitchen, where my parents were eating dinner. I remember the man was so tall that he had to duck under the back doorway into our kitchen. He informed my parents what I did. I stood at one corner of the kitchen while my dad shouted at me: "You thief! You will never do something like that again! Do you understand?!" He also pointed a finger at Allen and told him the same. I'll always remember the scared look on Allen's face when my dad was shouting. My dad has always had a very bad temper, and he looked and sounded very scary to both me and Allen. We gave all the light bulbs we stole back to the man. My mother was very calm the whole time. She was handling it a lot better than my dad. However, I continued stealing light bulbs from various places, such as the funeral home parking lot two houses down from mine. I loved light bulbs and HAD to get as many as I possibly could.

During the summer of 1980, my parents got me an odometer for my bike so that I could keep track of the miles. Instead of putting it on my bike, I started turning it manually. I noticed that it started counting and I was delighted! I decided to just keep it as a kind of "toy" to play with. I called it a "mileage meter." The numbers on it grew from 500 to 1000 to 2000, and eventually, at the end of the summer, over 10,000. That summer, the "mileage meter" was by far my favorite toy.

One day, however, the "mileage meter" started screwing up. One set of numbers started going backward while another started going forward very rapidly. Unity was over at the time, and she noticed that I was in tears. She asked my mother, "What's wrong with Paul?" My mother explained to her that my mileage meter was goofing up. I doubt that Unity understood just how frantic I felt. I cherished this toy with all my life, and now it was breaking. I don't think that anyone else in the entire town of Northfield felt so dependent on a silly little odometer.

Probably one of the most traumatic experiences I had was the time I wiped out on Allen's sister's bike. His sister's name was Jeannie, and her bike had a speedometer on it. I just LOVED going fast on her bike. I wanted to see how fast I could go. On the evening of Sunday, March 29, 1981, I was racing down a hill toward Main Street, when I lost control of the bike and fell off of it. The next thing I remember was riding in the back seat of a car. I thought to myself, I just KNEW that this would happen to me sooner or later! Then, the next thing I knew, I was lying on a hospital bed in the emergency room. I cried out to the nurse who was bending over me and tending to my wounds, "Where am I?! What happened to me?!" The nurse said in a kind voice, "You are in the Northfield Hospital. You've had a little accident." I remember seeing my reflection on the glass on a light that was hanging over me. Half of my face was covered in blood. A few minutes later, my mother came in, and I felt a little less scared.

The day after my accident, President Reagan was wounded by an assassin. I tried over and over to ask what would happen if there was no president. My mother didn't understand what I was trying to say because my mouth was completely numb and swollen, and I got very frustrated with her for not answering my question. I eventually had to write the question down on paper. I went back to school that Thursday, and everyone gasped when they saw me. They kept asking, "What happened to you?" and I replied by simply saying, "I fell off my bike." I had big scabs all over the right side of my face. I was the focus of attention for one day at school.

Later, when I was twelve, Allen and I rode our bikes around Northfield a lot. I had a speedometer on my bike and I kept track of my speed at all times. I couldn't understand how Allen never seemed to get tired as much as I did from biking all over town. When we would arrive at my house, Allen would be way ahead of me and would be sitting quietly watching TV, seeming not in the least bit tired. I would run in two or three minutes later almost completely out of breath and covered with sweat. Allen would say, "What took you so long, Paul?"

I would look at Allen and be furious with him for not waiting for me. I would say, "Why aren't YOU tired?! You're supposed to be tired!" He would look at me with amusement on his face and just laugh. I would explode in fury and he would seem to enjoy my anger very much. He would say, "Paul, you're just weak." Sometimes this would lead to a fight between us.

In fourth grade, I remember acting out in class, saying funny but mostly rude things. I repeated rude comments that the other boys in my class asked me to say, without knowing what they even meant. Then all the boys laughed. I thought that they were laughing at what I said. Now that I look back on it, they were probably just laughing at ME instead. The girls in my class, on the other hand, were disgusted at the things I said.

I also had a great number of habits that were annoying to other people when I was younger. I've cracked my knuckles from the time that I was ten up to the present day. I find it VERY hard to stop cracking my knuckles. This is another thing that helps me to relax. Allen tells me that I will get arthritis by the time I am thirty. I try not to listen to him when he says that. I hope he is wrong because I doubt that I will stop cracking my knuckles any time in the near future.

In sixth grade I flicked my pencil over and over again, but it was only funny to the other kids for a couple of days. They got very tired of my constant flicking of pencils and started getting very upset and angry with me. Even the teachers got very tired of it and sent me out in the hall a lot. By the time school was about to get out for Christmas of that year, everyone, including the teachers, was sick and tired of me and looked down on me. One teacher, Mr. Curtis, said, "You're a pain in the butt." This really hurt me. I was never trying to be a "pain in the butt" to anyone that year. I was just very, very bored.

In the spring of 1982, I got my first wristwatch. It was digital and played music, "Hey Jude" and "Yesterday." It was extremely precious to me. Once when it got lost, I panicked and felt like my world was coming to an end. It was almost as if my watch was human and was my best friend. I even gave it a name. "Spongy" is what I called it a few weeks after I got it. I used to always say, "Good night, Spongy," and then pretend that Spongy would say good night to me as well. I performed this little ritual for several months. Not very long after I got my watch, it started losing its parts. First I tore the wristband off and used it as a pocket watch instead. Then, one of the buttons fell off, which was a great shock to me at the time. Eventually, I got another watch that Christmas, and I named this watch "Squeezy."

Later, when I was almost thirteen, Squeezy needed a new battery. So I took it to the hardware store downtown to have the battery replaced. The person at the counter tried to replace the battery by himself and screwed up the whole inside of my watch. To me, it was like watching my mother have open-heart surgery right in front of my eyes. I felt panic slowly entering my throat when I saw it being put together wrong. I then took my watch to the jeweler a few stores down the road to see if he could correct the problem. Unfortunately he could not fix it properly, so it had to be sent back to the manufacturer. For five months it was gone. During that time, it got lost twice in the mail. I was very upset and preoccupied with the watch, and I stopped by the jeweler every week to see if it was in. The jeweler was very kind. He kept calling the manufacturer in New Jersey. Finally, after five months, I got it back.

In the fall of 1982, my family went to London for a term's sabbatical. First we traveled to Ireland for a short vacation. The first night in Ireland, I woke up in the middle of the night with a horrible nightmare. I can't quite remember what it was, but I felt really dizzy. I panicked and I didn't know what was happening to me. Nothing my parents said helped it to go away. I felt a rocking sensation. I could have sworn the bed was going back and forth, swaying violently. I was soaked with sweat. Later, next spring, I had an EEG to try to find out what these nighttime spells of panic were. They went on for several years and always frightened me, but no one could ever find out what they were. They were at their peak during the spring of 1983, when I was ten. I felt a horrible feeling like a whole bunch of thoughts were crowding my mind at once and nothing I could do would stop it. I sometimes felt the strange feeling come on when I was lying in my bed awake. Then I would usually get up and turn on my bedroom light in an attempt to get rid of it. I don't think I could ever explain in detail what these strange sensations were. I will never know what caused them or what the hell they really were. My theory is that they are somehow linked to my autism. All I know for sure is that I don't ever want to have horrible experiences like that at night again.

That fall, in London, was a very hard time for me. The first day in the new school, I had my hands in my pockets and the teacher yelled at me, "Get your hands out of your pockets; I can't bear boys who do that!" I remember being really scared. I didn't like the newness and the difference of that school.

Every Wednesday was "Games Day." Our teacher made us run a mile and a half to the playing field, where we had to play soccer, which they called football. As usual, I wasn't interested in team sports, so I tried to stay out of it as much as possible. I didn't know the rules of the game, and the other kids got very angry at me. Every Wednesday when my parents picked me up at the field after the games, I would run to them in tears.

I made one friend during the time I was there, whose name was Mike. But mostly I was very lonely. I used to take a book with me to the playground and read while the other children were playing. I read *The Lion, the Witch and the Wardrobe* during that time. That was the year my mother read me and Kate a lot of Nina Bawden books, including *The Secret Passage* and *On the Run*. I loved those books.

I used to play with Legos in London. They kept me going. Every day after school, Kate and I built things together. I loved to build towers with the Legos. I also wanted to have ALL the Lego spaceships that were out in the toy stores. I also got interested in rock music that year. A song that I loved and listened to over and over was "Abracadabra," by the Steve Miller Band. That was my favorite song back then. I recorded songs off the radio for over a year. I felt very excited when one of my favorite songs came on the radio. I would immediately tape the song and listen to it over and over again on my tape recorder. I watched "Top of the Pops" every Thursday evening. I would love it when a song I knew was played on the show. My teacher at school taught me to do needlepoint, and I made something for my parents for Christmas. She and I got along better after the first day. That made things a little easier.

I started being very mean to my sister, Kate, when we got back from London just before Christmas of 1982. In the fall of 1983, when I was watching TV before school, she would try to come into the playroom. I would yell at her, "Get out of here, Kate! You are such a little baby!" One morning, she was standing right outside the door for at least twenty minutes, afraid to come in for fear that I would yell at her again. My dad got very angry with me when he found out that Kate was standing outside the door. I was worried that Kate was retarded because she was still sucking her thumb when she was seven. I was afraid that I would have a retarded sister, when I was already feeling really bad about myself. I wanted Kate to act more grown up. After Christmas of 1983, I started being nicer to Kate.

Throughout my teenage years, Kate and I got along fine. Kate would be very sympathetic to me during the times that I was depressed. Every day she would ask how I felt. It helped me through those hard years in my life to have a little sister who genuinely cared about me and showed it. I am very glad that Kate didn't have to suffer through the hard times that I've been through, both at school and at home. I'm very happy that she wasn't born autistic like me.

In the spring of 1983, Allen and a new friend of his, Bill Frykman, used to tease me with a game called "Same Same Different." They sat on one side of the table with everything the same for the two of them: plate, food, what they were drinking, and so on. I sat on the other side of the table with a different plate, and a glass of water instead of milk. This game used to make me furious. They kept saying, "Look, Paul, you're different." I would get more and more upset and when I started crying I would always ask, "Do most people cry as much as I do?" They would reply, "No, Paul, I've never seen anyone cry as much as you do. You are just different." I would then have a tantrum, and they would fall out of their chairs laughing.

I first met Bill in February of 1983. I was very jealous when he started coming over to Allen's house, and I wanted him to leave. I felt that he was trying to take Allen's friendship away from me. He wouldn't leave, instead he stayed and teased me unmercifully. Once he tried to make me drink goldfish water. Another time he let the air out of my bike tire and I had to walk my bike all the way home from Allen's house carrying my heavy tape recorder in my hand. He also threatened me with a "Wet Knot," which was a towel tied up into a big knot and soaked with water. Fortunately he never used it on me.

Bill and I became good friends later that same year, but he still liked to tease me. I remember once, a few years later, he would not let me go to see Ray, who then lived in Wisconsin but was visiting his mother in Northfield. He said that I could only go if I solved an Atari video game called "Raiders of the Lost Ark." Allen and I had worked on that game for over a year and could not solve it, so I knew that there would be no way to solve the game by myself. Bill then locked me in a room at Allen's house and tied the door shut with ropes. He also took the handles off all the windows so I could not climb out a window. In a very mean-sounding voice, Bill said, "You will NOT go to Ray's house!" I screamed back at him in tears, "Yes I WILL!!" I eventually managed to get the door open and slipped out when Bill was not looking and walked downtown to Ray's mother's place. On another occasion, both Bill and I were spending the night at Allen's house. I needed a fan to help me sleep more easily and more comfortably, but Bill would only let me have the fan on low. I complained that I could hardly hear the fan at all and it also gave out barely any wind for me to feel. He said, "The fan will be on low, if the fan is turned on high, the cord will be cut and the fan will be DEAD." So it had to be his way, and I just cried myself to sleep that night.

Once when I was in the fifth grade, Allen and I got into a fight in front of the whole class. I said, "Oh, Allen!" loudly, in an exasperated tone of voice. I was upset because he put a sad face on the work sheet of mine he was correcting. I had worked very hard on that work sheet. He knew I didn't like negative criticism, and he put the sad face on in a kind of taunting way. I was very upset that day. Now, when I think back to that day, I see that I shouldn't have embarrassed Allen in front of everyone like that. I had it coming.

Allen used to love to tease me and watch me get angry. Once he put one of my temper tantrums on tape without me even knowing it. This particular tantrum was about an Atari game cartridge that was missing from Allen's collection. I was furious because the only game that I really wanted to play was the ONLY game that was missing. I just couldn't believe how anyone could have such bad luck. I remember screaming, "Why do I always have bad luck!!" Allen was enjoying every minute of this tantrum of mine mainly because he was putting it on tape.

I will always remember the time Allen told me that he would be moving to a different town. His dad got married to someone from Farmington, which is thirteen miles away from Northfield. The summer of 1983 was coming to an end when Allen broke the news to me. I started crying. I thought that I would never see him again. My mother reassured me that I could still see him. She said that she would drive me up to Farmington to visit him in his new home, or pick him up and bring him back to Northfield. It turned out that I still could see Allen every weekend, and sometimes during the week. He would spend every single weekend with me for the next few months. Later, in the spring of 1984, Allen's dad got a divorce, and they moved back to Northfield. I was delighted to hear this. Allen has lived in Northfield ever since.

*

Sixth grade was one of the hardest years of school for me. It was the first year of middle school, and I also had to change my clothes and take a shower in gym class. This was a nerve-racking experience for me. I was embarrassed to be seen naked in front of thirty other boys. And when I was playing volleyball with the others, I was daydreaming during the middle of the game and I was yelled at by everyone on my team for missing the ball. I felt furious inside at the other kids for getting mad at me when I wasn't trying to let them down. I then thought to myself, if this is the way you want to treat me, then I'll just quit trying altogether. So then I got my own revenge by missing the ball on purpose and being as uncooperative as possible. They were fuming mad at me then and said things like, "PAUL!! You FAGGOT!! You LOSER!! Get off our team!" I was never good at team sports and probably never will be.

As my sixth-grade year was under way, I kept thinking about the line from John Cougar Mellencamp's song that went: "Oh yeah, life goes on." These words were going through my head as I walked down the halls of this new school. I thought of my life as just going through the years of elementary, middle, and high school. To me, each school year so far had taken forever. There were so many bad, scary, and interesting things that happened to me throughout each year, and it seemed that my entire life was just based on going to school. It seemed to me to just go on and on and on. I felt that I would NEVER grow up and get a full-time job that I would enjoy.

The middle school also had a Resource Room. It was there that I met Mrs. Gellie. I thought that she was extremely nice and very patient. She made it easier for me to adjust to the newness of the middle school. With her help, I found it easy to get my homework done. She would sometimes bake me a cake at her house and take it to school if I got a big assignment done, or if I just behaved myself for a couple weeks. Her cakes tasted delicious! The other kids who were in the Resource Room seemed jealous of me. I wasn't trying to be a "teacher's pet" or anything like that. It was just that Mrs. Gellie was trying to get me motivated in school by giving me rewards.

When I entered seventh grade, I became very good friends with Phil Gordon. We ate lunch together every day that year. We would make yawning noises in the Resource Room and then go on to a whole bunch of other different noises. It wasn't very long before I got carried away! I would be making all sorts of funny noises all day at school. It seemed that I could barely control myself. It was like I was stuck in a "rut." I wasn't trying to make myself look stupid at school by making noises.

It was just a way of "letting off some steam." I was also just trying to be funny, in order to pass the long hours at school.

During the spring of 1984, I started becoming fascinated with elevators. I used to ride them up and down with Allen in a twelve-storey building at St. Olaf College campus, which was on the west side of Northfield. I was thrilled when my mother took me up to downtown Minneapolis so I could ride the elevators in the forty- and fifty-storey buildings. Unfortunately, there was tight security and I couldn't ride the elevators on a lot of the tall office buildings. The security guards would question me and Allen whenever we were walking alone in some building and stop us from going any farther. Or they would stop us from riding the elevator after they saw that we'd been up and down it twice already.

Once, however, Allen and I got stuck in an elevator at the Twin Cities airport. We called on the elevator phone for help. We had to wait at least thirty minutes while a mechanic fixed the motor that ran the elevator car. I was very shaken up by this experience. Thank God I didn't have to use the bathroom during those thirty minutes. My interest in elevators continued for several months and then died out.

My parents got a couple of cats when I was twelve. One of them, named "Tiger Eyes," ran away and never came back. The other, named "Cushion," had three sets of kittens. I absolutely LOVED playing with the kittens. I would also love to tease them. I used to turn on the vacuum cleaner and point the suction nozzle at them and scare them. Kate and I would give them all names. We couldn't find a home for two of the kittens and had to keep them. One of them died from swallowing a chicken bone. The other, named "Stripes," I still have today. Ever since Stripes was a kitten, I would hold him like you would hold a baby. He has grown used to my special way of holding him and would just lie in my arms and purr. We also have Cushion and I just LOVE to tease her, even though my mother hates it when I do.

When I was eight I began to rate people by numbers, from one through one hundred. I rated myself 66, Allen 70, I rated my dad somewhere down in the forties, and my mother around 68. Tammy Albers was at 80 (I liked her a lot). I would rank every person that I met. These days, I would rate myself as 50, my mom as 70, my dad as 60. I used to rank myself higher when I was a child, but during my teenage years, my self-image dropped greatly. Even today, I look down on myself. It just seems that whenever I think to myself, Hey, maybe I'm a pretty decent guy after all, someone comes along and puts me down again. It just isn't fair at all. I have tried to get respect by making jokes, driving people around, listening to them when they were upset about something, or just being with them, and I always get looked down on or just ignored. This has happened several times in my life. I wish I could find a way to make people see the good side of me.

I had lots of rules when I was a child. One of my rules was that people weren't allowed to get angry at me, or even irritated at me. However, I didn't have any silly rules like Raymond's in *Rain Man,* where the maple syrup had to be on the table before the pancakes. Most of my rules had to do with controlling people's feelings. I've tried to control everyone's feelings for years. I still try to do that, but I am realizing now that I am always going to lose if I keep trying. I think this is because, all my life, people have seemed to try to put a big guilt trip on me, to make me feel bad about my behavior and what I did wrong. I didn't want to feel guilty about anything. I was always trying to please people, and to do everything right. I tried so hard that it had the opposite effect on everyone, including my parents. When people got upset with me, I felt like a failure. Even today I feel the same way. I feel it isn't fair that people get angry with me when I never TRY to do anything bad. I just CAN'T understand human emotions, no matter how hard I try.

For many years I would ask people, "Are you mad at me?" Usually I asked my parents that question several times a day. My dad would occasionally get upset with me for asking that question over and over. I would feel very anxious about certain tones of voice. I would think that a surprised tone, or an emphatic tone, would mean anger. Sometimes, I would get very upset and angry and blow things way out of proportion. This would usually lead to a fight between me and my dad or my mother. Even today, I still ask that question a lot. I always feel uncertain about peoples' emotions.

This is how I would get into big fights with Allen. I would carry on and on about Allen being a little irritated with me about something. Eventually he would get very angry with me and tell me to shut up. Then I would start crying and he would call me a big baby. Every time Allen and I fought, it would be very hard on me. We have fought less and less during the past couple of years. Today we hardly fight at all.

When I was a kid I had many rules about how things should be done. One rule had to do with walking through a doorway and not bumping my elbow. My rule was that I would be put in jail if I bumped the doorway more than two times a week. I used to scream, "I'll be put in jail if I bump my elbow again." If I accidentally bumped my elbow when I walked through a door, I would have to go back and repeat it; I would have to walk through the door again and get it right that time. I used to be in tears sometimes just because I hit my foot on something or knocked over a glass of milk. I would try to pretend to turn back time and pretend it never happened. I would get upset when my mom walked around the side of the dining room table closest to the wall. I was upset because this was different and I didn't like anything that was different. When my mom moved the furniture in the house I got very, very upset. I hated the change. I felt like I was not at home anymore. These days I still get upset sometimes over small accidents and behave in the same childish way. I realize that I should be less hard on myself about small things, but I still find myself getting upset very easily.

My dad and I used to get into terrible fights all during my childhood years, especially when I was eleven. We used to get into a "naming game." I didn't want to face the fact that we had a fight, and I would say, "You weren't really mad at me, were you?" and, "We weren't in a fight, were we?" I would want to call the fight just a little argument. I wanted to see how long I could go without getting into a fight. One incident back in the summer of 1983 was especially bad. We were in England and I was fighting with Kate in the car while we were on our way to Devon. My dad completely lost his temper with me and screamed, "Shut up! Shut up! Shut up!" over and over again for almost five minutes. I was crying and I was very frightened at his outburst. I was also very angry at the way he lost his temper. I wanted to swear at him and call him every name in the book.

Whenever my dad and I fought, he would make me feel very small and powerless. I would be filled with rage at him during a fight. He would be trying to put a guilt trip on me a lot. He never hit me, although he threatened to sometimes. He spanked me sometimes when I was a child. I thought that was wrong. One time I said to him, "I don't think that you are a very good father." He got very angry at me for saying that, but I felt at that time that it was true.

My sister, Kate, rarely fought with my dad at all. It would seem that he would concentrate most of his anger onto me. He would say things that he later said he didn't mean, such as "If you go on about this any longer, I'll beat you!" or "Yes, I'm going to force you to eat that food!" Sometimes, after a really bad fight between us, we would resolve things with a long talk and my dad would tell me how much he loved me with tears in his eyes.

Sometimes, when my dad and I fought, my mother would jump into the whole thing to defend me. I would like the fact that she defended me, but then my dad would get furious with my mother for interfering and then they would get into an argument just as bad, sometimes even worse! I didn't like it at all when my parents started fighting about me, especially in front of me. It made me feel very confused. I wanted to scream at them to shut up!

I used to have violent thoughts about my dad, usually after we had a fight. I would feel so much anger at him for the way he sometimes treated me. That anger inside me slowly built up over my childhood and teenage years. It was painful for me whenever I had those thoughts.

It was just last May that I got into a terrible fight with my dad. All the anger that was built up inside me suddenly came out. One night I came home late and walked into my parents' bedroom to discuss a problem with my car. My dad and I disagreed on something. He was annoyed with me and told me to leave the room. I didn't want to leave the room. I couldn't! Leaving on a bad note, I felt that I would never get to sleep. I wanted to stay there and resolve things. I NEVER like to leave an argument unresolved.

My dad started getting very angry with me for refusing to leave the room. I tried to tell him that I wanted to resolve the argument, but he was getting so angry that he wouldn't listen. I asked him if he still loved me and he said that he didn't right then. Things started turning ugly then. He leaped out of the bed and slammed me up against the door. He then opened the door and tried to shove me out of the room. He had a very rough hold on me.

That's when I completely lost my temper too. I didn't fight back, but I started swearing at him and saying very nasty things to him. My dad then threatened to kick me out of the house. "Jim, I'm going to call the police if you do anything to Paul," my mother said in a frightened voice. She watched the whole thing happen.

My dad then got dressed and left the house to "walk off some of the anger." I tried to stop him from leaving the house. I had a sudden fear that he would never return. I told him that I would kill myself if he left, but he got past me and left the house. My mother reassured me that he would return. He did return after only about twenty minutes.

"You have really disgraced me," he said to me when he returned. "I feel very little now. You should honor me because I'm your father. You should've left the room, Paul." "I wish you would understand that I couldn't leave the room. I NEEDED to work things out," I said then. "When I tell you to leave, please just leave," my dad said through tears.

We finally resolved things that night. I then went to bed trying (without much success) to forget about the whole thing. I hope that my dad and I don't ever get into another fight that bad. I love him, but I can't seem to tell him that. I find it very hard to look him in the eye whenever I talk to him. I know that he loves me, he tells me that almost every day. I really want to tell him that I love him too. I don't ever want any more hard feelings between us. I want to be able to trust him more.

Teenage Years

Let me talk more about my teenage years. Shortly after I went to Dublin, Ireland, in the fall of 1986, I went through a period of depression. I thought that it would get better when I came back home from Ireland, but it just got worse. I was feeling very down for over two years before I finally felt better about life around the end of 1988.

When I was in Dublin I never stopped wishing I was back in Northfield. I kept track of how many days were left until we were due to go back home on the plane. I tried to pass time by reading books a lot. I even got a calculator from my mother's purse and started figuring how many hours, minutes, and even seconds there were until the plane was scheduled to leave Gatwick Airport in London.

The plane was scheduled to leave at one-twenty P.M. on Monday, December 15, 1986. From early October I focused my attention on that day and that time. I don't exactly know why I hated staying in Dublin so much. Maybe I was just afraid of being overwhelmed by boredom. Extreme boredom is like a hellish nightmare to me, although my fear of it is a lot less now than it was at that time.

When I was fourteen and fifteen, at school and at home, I always kept looking at my watch. I wanted my day to be uneventful. I felt any incident that happened, whether good or bad, would make my day too long. I wanted the days to pass by quickly. Any change at all made me feel overloaded. I felt this way mostly during 1987 and 1988 when I was going to the high school. I got overloaded very easily during that time.

I used to rate my feelings, my mood, on a scale from one to one hundred. This started on Tuesday, October 6, 1987. I began doing this when I was depressed and I was helping my friend Bill Steele with his paper route. Usually I rated myself around 52; it went below 50 often during this time. I wanted to "measure" my feelings in hopes that it would keep my mind off of things such as the time and maybe in the long run help me to overcome my depression. It still took awhile to feel better, though. Today I feel better about things, and I would now rate my moods at around 60.

For a few years I got emotionally involved with the weather. I know it sounds silly, but this was one of my obsessions during that time. I used to scream and cry whenever a thunderstorm missed Northfield. Even when the forecast said just a thirty percent chance of a thunderstorm, I always got my hopes up very high. I would be in a very good mood whenever the weatherman said that thunderstorms were likely. My depression would be temporarily lifted. I wanted every storm to hit Northfield. So I would be ESPECIALLY angry when the forecast said a seventy or an eighty percent chance of thunderstorms and they would ALL miss Northfield. Also I would get very upset if the temperature didn't reach what the forecasted high was. I used to think that the weatherman was lying when he was really just giving an estimate. As I look back on my behavior, I see that I must have been trying to control the weather, which is obviously impossible. My dad would always tell me that I couldn't control the weather, but I didn't believe him at the time and I kept screaming and crying whenever the weather didn't do something that I wanted it to do.

I've wanted to be a meteorologist since I was twelve. These days I collect the weather section in the newspaper every day and record the high and low temperatures on a calendar on my wall. I also used to tape the weather broadcasts each night on Channel 4. My favorite weather occurrence is when a thunderstorm comes! I just *love* to wake up in the morning to a thunderstorm. Thunderstorms fascinate me greatly, especially the ones that spawn tornadoes, even though I have never seen a real tornado yet. My favorite type of storm is a hailstorm. It fascinates me to hear stories from other people that are weather-related.

We had a big storm on July 27, 1987. I was very annoyed when my mother kept me in the basement during the height of the storm. She thought that I was going to be killed! Isn't that a big laugh! Many trees in Northfield were knocked down by the storm, including a tree across our driveway. I sometimes wear a tee shirt saying I SURVIVED THE

STORM. That was a *very* memorable storm for residents of Northfield, and definitely for ME also.

After I got back from living in Ireland for four months, I was told that I was going to the middle school right after Christmas. I didn't like this idea at all. I argued that I was the tallest person in the whole school and that I wanted to keep up with my own grade. Fortunately I won the argument after a week and started attending the Northfield High School.

It was there that I met Mrs. Clark for the first time. She taught in the Resource Room and she seemed very nice to me. She and a friend that I made in seventh grade, Phil Gordon, helped me get used to the high school. For the first couple of weeks of the new semester I followed Phil around to his classes. Then in the third week I started classes of my own. I started feeling very overloaded that week.

That same week I started talking to therapists. I remember one particular day, Thursday, January 29, 1987. It snowed about three inches, and my parents and I went up to the Twin Cities to have me see a therapist. I answered all his questions and we talked for a while, but I felt that no professional would help me overcome my depression. I didn't quite know WHAT would help me feel better about life in general during that time.

Two days later, on Saturday, we went to a movie in Burnsville. On the way back home Daddy and I started bickering about my obsession with the weather. He started to get very angry with me after I started yelling about the weather and about him being irritated with me, and he shook his fists at me from the front seat while he was driving. He was so angry he had to pull over to the side and let Mama drive the rest of the way home. Later Mama told me that it was the movie that we just got done watching which caused him to get so upset. The movie was *Crimes of the Heart,* and it showed an attempted suicide. I had talked about suicide that week and he was obviously frightened.

During the time I was feeling most depressed, Bill Steele started to hang out with me. I was so unhappy about things that I hardly noticed him. He seemed to be very sympathetic toward me. He used to ask, "Paul, are you depressed?" whenever I was walking ahead of him toward my house. I am surprised that he continued to hang around me and stay my friend after all those months of my being a "bum." Most people would think that I would be "no fun" to be with, but Bill stayed with me until I finally got better. We will always be good friends.

I continued to feel overloaded in the high school during the rest of that winter and into that spring. It didn't help at all when Phil started getting angry with me and saying mean things like: "Why do I even hang around you?" and "You're a little wimp, Paul." He also hit me over and over and told me to fight back. I didn't want to because I was not at all used to being a "tough guy." I never was and I probably never will be. Phil and I stopped our fights, but only after I ran to Mrs. Clark and told her to set up a meeting with her, me, and Phil. We had a few more bad arguments, but today we get along just fine.

My obsession with the weather stayed the same during this time. I hated being cooped up indoors at school all day during the spring, and I wanted to be outside to watch the sky for storms. I used to stare at the clock on the wall all day and didn't hear a single word my teacher said. I felt boredom overcome me a lot. Each day seemed to last forever. Having to go to school and sit through boring classes where no one talks to you or is friendly to you certainly doesn't help a depressed person feel any better. Also, no one at all in the entire school seemed to share my interest in the weather.

I want to say more about just how bad high school was for me. Despite Mrs. Clark, who was always very kind and would listen to what was bothering me, I found the Northfield High School to be a confusing and very unfriendly place. I only had two real close friends there, Phil Gordon and Bill Steele (Allen and I hardly talked at school, we had a completely different schedule). Almost everyone there would act like they were such "superstuds." They acted like they were better than everyone else. There would be certain groups of people: Dirtballs, Jocks, Preps, Nerds, and Outcasts. I fit into the group of Outcasts. It was like I was the "invisible boy" in the school. I was almost completely ignored for a while. No girl seemed to notice me at all until my senior year. They all seemed very stuck-up to me. They wouldn't smile at me or anything. I would always worry about how I looked when I walked into the school every morning. I was told by a number of kids in the Resource Room that I was the "teacher's pet." They told me that I was a little baby and that I should "learn to fight my own battles" instead of running to Mrs. Clark whenever they picked on me. They looked down on me and made me feel absolutely terrible about myself.

In June of 1987, I went off to camp for a month. When my parents told me about Camp Buckskin I didn't like the idea at all. I tried to tell them I didn't want to go, but they insisted strongly that I give it a try. So that's just what I did. It was a warm sunny Monday afternoon up in northern Minnesota when we arrived at the camp. It wasn't until I stepped out of the car that I began to feel the first knot form in my stomach. Nothing at all for the next month looked good for me right then. That evening after my parents and sister left and the next day was one of the worst times of my life. I constantly felt homesick, and I was terrified. It felt like a bad dream had come true. Everything had changed so suddenly. Everyone around me was a stranger. I could hardly eat anything in the cafeteria for the first three days. I cried many times during the first week. I thought about running away from the camp during the night and hitchhiking my way home.

After the first two days, I started to feel less homesick and I began to get used to my new surroundings. I talked a lot with my two counselors, who slept in the same cabin as me. "Morris" and "Radar," as my counselors were nicknamed, kept telling me to "think positive." I tried to, but there were so many activities I had to do during the day that I didn't like, that I continued to think negative about everything at camp.

There were eight of us in our cabin, including me and Morris and Radar. I made friends with Ryan, who was in my cabin, and a younger boy named Zachary, who stayed in another cabin. One day Zachary said to me, "You're my best friend, Paul." I liked hearing that from someone. I guess he saw how gentle I was.

On July 4, my parents came up to camp to visit me. When I saw them I was very excited and happy. I told them everything about camp. I was only happy because my parents were with me. But I WAS proud of myself for surviving the first two weeks of camp. I could see that my parents noticed that when they were with me that day. After they left, I started feeling very excited about going home. The whole time I was up at camp, I was counting the days until I left.

When the day finally came when I could go home, I was very happy and very relieved. The kids from my cabin were crying because they hated to have to say good-bye to everyone from camp. Ryan gave me a hug and said that he would write to me (although he never did) and got on a bus. Before I left to go home, one of the head counselors, Muffy, came up to me and my parents and said that I had come a long way since the first day. I realized that he was right, even though I can never say I "enjoyed myself" while I was up there.

A couple weeks later, my parents told me that it would be a good idea to go to Camp Buckskin the following year. I felt scared when they told me this. Why the hell should I go through it all again next summer?! It will not be any different from this year for me. I will most likely feel the same way next year about Camp Buckskin that I felt this year, I thought to myself. Luckily, I was able to dissuade them from sending me again.

I started taking medication for my depression in December of 1987. The only change that I noticed was I didn't keep track of dates as well as I had before. I first started on desipramine, then a year or so later, I switched to nortriptyline. The nortriptyline had some very bad side effects for me. First I noticed that my mouth was extremely dry, which I found very uncomfortable. Then I started feeling very agitated. My mind was racing a lot during school, and I was shaking a lot also.

I first felt these side effects when my aunt Mary from London was visiting for a weekend. She gave me a present, and I said "Thank you." I didn't know what more I could say to her. At that moment I felt EXTREMELY awkward. I didn't know whether to walk out of the room or say something more to her, so I just stood there repeating "thank you" over and over again. "Are you all right?" my dad asked me. I wasn't all right, I was feeling confused and very agitated. I left the room then. "Is it something I did?" I overheard Mary ask my dad. It wasn't anything she did, it was the drug, although at the time, I didn't know it.

The next day, I went to school. My mind was racing all day. I couldn't seem to sit still in any of my classes. I was very relieved when the bell rang in the afternoon. I ran home on the edge of tears and started playing "The Legend of Zelda" on my Nintendo. My mother came in and sat down beside me and watched me play for a few minutes. She then told me to shut off the Nintendo. I shut it off and turned to her with tears in my eyes. "Paul, what is it? What's wrong?" she asked. "I feel my mind racing out of control!" I said to her in a desperate voice. "It must be the drug, Paul. That's got to be what it is," she said. I realized that she was right. It WAS the drug that I was taking. Relief flooded over me then. I had no idea that it was the drug I was on. I thought that I was starting to go crazy.

Later, I was told that lithium would help ease the side effects of nortriptyline. So I started taking a couple of lithium tablets with the antidepressant. It helped a lot. After that day, I felt no more side effects from the drug. Unfortunately, neither desipramine or nortriptyline helped me feel any better. I was still feeling very depressed the rest of that winter and all through that spring.

When my sophomore year at high school ended and the summer of 1988 rolled around, I was sent to an adolescent day treatment program in Minneapolis. I was there because of my continuing depression.

While I was up there I started the medication Prozac. I strongly objected to the idea of having to spend my summer days there. My mother told me to give it a week. After the first week was over, I told her that I still didn't like it, but she didn't seem to hear me. "Just give it a little more time, Paul," she kept saying to me over and over.

Dr. Nolan, who was my psychiatrist there, talked with me every day for a few minutes. I didn't like his attitude at all. He kept noticing EVERY little mannerism I had, such as cracking my knuckles or rubbing my face, while I was talking to him. He kept asking about them, and it REALLY made me feel embarrassed about myself. I wanted to scream at him, "Mind your own fucking business!"

I met a lot of kids my age up there and I got along with them fine. I hardly talked to anyone up there, except for one day when I was playing cards with this girl who was also in day treatment with me. I kept beating her at a game called "War," and I couldn't stop smiling. I thought that it was very funny how I kept beating her on every hand.

A couple of days later, while we were in group therapy, she told me that I had really opened up that day. Right then, I saw that she was right. Almost all the time, however, I kept to myself while I was there. I hardly enjoyed any of the activities that I had to do during the day. I felt I was doing time for just being depressed. It was like I was being punished for being unhappy at home and at school. At the end of July I finally got out of day treatment.

That same summer, my interest in girls began with a vengeance. Ray was visiting me for a week toward the end of June. One evening we were at Sayles-Hill, on the campus of Carleton College, when a girl I had seen flirting with Ray earlier started flirting with me. She came up to me and asked if she could borrow fifty cents from me. I gave her the money and she came back with a can of Coke for me. As I was drinking my Coke she asked me what my name was. Then she asked me if she could try something. I said okay, and she started tickling my neck. "Are you ticklish?" she asked me. "No," I replied, feeling extremely shy. Ray came along then and said that we had to go. As I was walking out the front door of Sayles-Hill, the girl said "Bye, Paul" in a friendly voice.

Ray left the next day, but I hardly took any notice. I was preoccupied with the girl from last night. I found myself thinking about her all that next week. Why didn't I talk more to her?! Why was I so damn shy?! I should've asked her name and asked for her phone number! I thought to myself over and over that week. Even though I would probably never see her again in my life, I suddenly felt that I HAD to see her again. I thought about her every single day for the rest of that summer and into that fall. "Mama, I keep thinking about that one girl," I would tell her. "This is your first experience, Paul, it will happen again," she would say to me. She didn't quite seem to understand. No other girl was interested in me. I wanted to see this particular girl because she was the only one in the whole wide world who seemed to have an interest in me. Why else would she have flirted with me?

In early September, Ray came to visit me again, and I found out that he had gotten the phone number of one of the girls, Tasha, who was there at Carleton that day in June. He called up Tasha and asked her for the girl's phone number, but to my great dismay, she didn't have it. But at least she had the girl's address. I learned that her name was Wendy, and that she lived in Ham Lake, just north of the Twin Cities. If I was to ever see Wendy again, I would have to write her a letter.

I wrote Wendy a letter, telling her how nice she seemed to me. I wrote down my phone number in the letter and was hoping with all my heart that she would remember me and write me back or call me. All through the month of September, I was waiting impatiently for Wendy's response. In the middle of the month, I decided to have a party at my house. I thought, maybe that would be something of interest to her. She would then be more likely to come down to Northfield. I sent a party invitation to her immediately. I also looked through the yearbook of the Northfield High School and sent invitations to some people that I hadn't talked to since grade school. I planned the party for October 1. Finally, on the twenty-eighth, Wendy called me. I was absolutely overjoyed when she told me that she wanted to come to the party.

I only felt overjoyed for a while, however. When the day of the party came I started feeling very nervous and overexcited. My mother and I went to pick Wendy up at her house. When the door opened I saw a total stranger, a girl I didn't recognize at all. This was obviously Wendy, but she wasn't how I remembered her. I developed an image of her in my head over those long weeks during the summer. On the way back to Northfield, I barely said a word to her. My mind was racing at one hundred miles per hour.

When we got to my house, Ray made things worse by saying, "Brought your bitch, Paul?" I didn't find that the least bit funny! I was about to take a walk with Wendy when Ray asked if I would like him to come along. I felt that if he came along, he would help break the silence between us. I was very wrong. Ray started blurting out obscenities when we were walking downtown. I felt very embarrassed.

Halfway through the walk, Ray left us to be alone together. Wendy and I walked toward the park together in utter silence. I could never remember a time in my whole life when I felt more awkward. We circled back to my house, and I sat down at the kitchen table and felt my eyes filling with tears. My mother was in the kitchen and told Wendy to go to the TV room for a few minutes while she talked to me. I told her that I felt so shy and confused around Wendy that I didn't know what to do. Then I ran up to my parents' room and sat there crying. Ray came up a few minutes later, and I told him to send Wendy up to talk to me. When she came into the room, my back was turned to her. "I just feel so shy, and I find it so hard to talk to girls," I said to her through tears. "At least you can talk about what's bothering you," she replied.

That night, as the party began to get under way, Wendy hardly talked to me at all. Instead of showing any interest in me, she started showing interest in Shawn, a kid from school that I had invited to my party. That night I was almost overwhelmed with jealousy. Everyone else, including Wendy, had a lot of fun at my party, except me. It was a tragic night for me.

I met Wendy twice more in the next few months, but she hardly talked to me at all. My mother called her the "Lump" and advised me to forget about her. Finally, in the summer of 1989, I wrote her a letter and told her that I really liked her. She wrote back saying that she only liked me as a friend. I have never seen or spoken to her since.

In November of 1988, after my obsession with Wendy died out, I tried DESPERATELY to find a girlfriend. Mrs. Clark set me up on a date with Peggy. She thought that I would like her. Peggy went to school with me. I didn't think that she was very pretty. I went through with the date with her, however. We went to a movie and had pizza together. When Allen picked us up from Godfather's Pizza and gave Peggy a ride home, she said to me, "Thanks for everything, Paul." I was glad that she enjoyed herself, but I was not attracted to her in any way.

It never worked out either with Bonnie, who was the next girl I went on a date with. The first date was during the middle of November; it went pretty well for both of us. I, as usual, felt very shy and didn't know what to talk about. A week before Christmas, we were eating at Pizza Hut, when Bonnie figured out what I wanted. She told me that she was my friend and no more. Another turndown!

I didn't completely give up, though. New Year's Eve, Ray and I went to a dance at Sayles-Hill. He was flirting, as usual, with a bunch of girls. He introduced me to them and two of them sat on my lap. I loved it when they did that. It felt good! I also danced with a girl that night. I enjoyed those few minutes dancing with her a lot. It was a fun night for me.

That January, I started receiving phone calls from a couple of girls that I didn't know. One afternoon, a girl named Amy called me up and asked me out. She told me that she was looking through the yearbook of the Northfield High School, saw my picture in it, and thought that I was cute. At first I felt excited and happy, but a couple minutes into the phone call, she told me that it was probably a bad idea. She said that she heard some bad things about me. My mother came on the phone then and told her not to tease me. She then said to me that my mother was an asshole and hung up.

This wasn't the end of it, however. Another girl, who called herself "Cindy Dawanta" asked me if I would like to meet her at Buck Hill ski area at Burnsville. I told her that I didn't know how to ski, and she said that she would help me learn. I again felt excited by this invitation. I told my mother about the invitation, and she told me that it was probably a prank. I felt angry with her for saying that, but later I found out that she was right. I went to the Northfield Public Library and copied out the phone numbers for all the Dawantas in our area. I called them all until I found a Cindy, and she told me that she didn't know what I was talking about. Later, in the high school counselor's office, I confronted the girl who had teased me. She didn't really apologize, and I could tell that she looked down on me for telling on her and getting her into trouble. I quickly forgot about the whole thing, but I still felt very hurt deep down inside.

After that incident, during the spring of 1989, I tried to ask several other girls out. I almost always wrote notes to them because I still didn't have the courage to go up to them in school. I was always turned down! They were just NOT interested in me. They either wanted to just be friends or weren't interested in having anything to do with me at all. I started to feel very bad about myself. It seemed that no one AT ALL was interested in me. Not even the tiniest bit! I began to wonder if I would ever find a girlfriend!

There was a girl that I really noticed and fell in love with in the spring of 1989, during my junior year at school. Her name was Olivia and to me she looked like my dream girl. I always saw her at lunch in the school cafeteria. She sat and ate with her friends one table over from me. I just didn't have enough courage to talk to her, so I started writing her letters. First I wrote one short letter, then the letters got longer and longer and more frequent. I told her everything about myself and hoped with all the energy I had that she would either write me back or come up to me at lunch and start talking to me. I started writing Olivia in January. By the time the middle of March came around, I was thinking or dreaming about her nearly twenty-four hours a day. Olivia finally wrote me in late March and basically told me that she was not interested in me. I was absolutely crushed! I felt that the only thing I was living for is gone. I was too upset to go to school the next day. After a week of being upset, I began to feel better.

That next fall, another friend of mine, Becky, told me that Olivia liked me. I excitedly wrote to Olivia to ask if this were really true, but when she wrote back to me, I found out that it was a big lie. She was NOT interested in me. I was very angry with Becky for a couple of weeks for lying to me about Olivia. I felt that Becky was lying to me on purpose just to get me excited. A couple of weeks later Becky told me that someone else told her this. I quickly got over my anger with Becky and went on with my life.

Aside from being very preoccupied with trying to get a girlfriend during the fall of 1988, I also had a lot of stress to deal with at school. I would say that the main source of my stress that fall was my Work Adjustment class. It wasn't the actual class that was stressful, but more the class requirements, which included having to go out and find a job. The job would then count as school credit.

My teacher for that class, Mrs. Gilbert, thought that working for an hour after school at the snack bar at the middle school would be a good job for me to try out. I wasn't very thrilled with the idea of sitting at school for seven hours and then going to a job right after that. The first day of my job, just before I started, I told Mrs. Gilbert that I would like to just try it for a couple of days. "I think you should try this job for a month," Mrs. Gilbert told me then. I dreaded what the next four weeks would be like for me.

After the first week of working at the middle school for an hour after a long day at high school, I told my mother that it made my day seem very, very long and complicated. I just could NOT handle the stress of a job and going to school the same day. It was too much for me. After a month, I quit the job at the middle school, much to my relief!

Mrs. Gilbert didn't seem to understand that having a job and going to school at the same time was ten times more stressful for me than for anyone else in her class. Because of my autism, I got overloaded much more easily than most people.

In January, I tried out a job at the Northfield Historical Society; a couple of weeks later I helped out at Radio Shack. I had both these jobs during the middle of the day. I found this a little easier than after school. I told Mrs. Gilbert that I didn't find either of those jobs very interesting. In March, Mrs. Gilbert told me that I should try a job at the Northfield Hospital. Phil Gordon worked there after school, and she said that I would have a friend there to work with.

I found out that I would have to work after school again. This time for two hours! That would mean that I would not get home until after five! Mrs. Gilbert told me that I should try this job for a month. I immediately told her that I thought that that was a very bad idea, but she insisted. After the first couple of days of working after school at the hospital, I felt overwhelmed. I then started to feel VERY angry at Mrs. Gilbert for forcing me to work at the hospital after school. To me, it seemed that she didn't at all care about how I felt.

After the second day of working at the hospital, I told my parents about all of it, and to my relief, they came to an agreement with Mrs. Gilbert, and I didn't have to work at the hospital anymore after that. This was the same time that I was obsessed with Olivia. With someone always on my mind, I felt that going to school and then going to a job for two hours after that would make my head split wide open.

It felt like I was being controlled and told where to work and how many hours a week I should work. I began to wish that I had never agreed to be in the Work Adjustment Program. Even Mrs. Clark was trying to force me to work at the hospital. "No pain, no gain," she told me. I don't think that even Mrs. Clark understood how stress affects me MUCH more than everyone else in school. I felt angry with Mrs. Clark for not understanding. It seemed to me that she thought that I was just being lazy. I was NEVER trying to be lazy.

Finally, a week later, I settled down with a job that I could at least stand. During the middle of the day, I went to work for an hour at the Northfield Public Library. The people who worked there made me feel at ease, but the job coach, Amy, that was with me did NOT! She constantly criticized any comments I made while I was working. She also treated me like I was four years old.

When the second semester of my senior year at high school began, I went up to the Dakota County Vo-Tech in Rosemount. I would ride up there with five others in a van, which would pick me up at my house every morning. I would then ride back to school with the same people in the late morning and go to a couple classes at the high school. I would be in a career exploration class up at the Vo-Tech and would try a different class every week until I found a class that I liked.

Phil Gordon was one of the people who went up to Vo-Tech with me. We would try out classes together each week. After several weeks of exploring different kinds of careers, I chose business technology. All the other classes seemed very demanding to me, but business technology was quiet and easy. I took that class for the rest of the year and all of next year.

The ride to and from Vo-Tech was very stressful for me. I rode up with a guy named Dan. He would always pick on me and call me a "fucking retard." But whenever I EVEN STARTED to say something back to him, he would hit me really hard and get very angry with me. One day, I threw a whole bunch of insults at Dan on the way back from Vo-Tech. When we got back to the high school, he was furious and chased me right into the school building. I felt a little scared at Dan's temper, but I felt very satisfied for getting back at him. Another day he gave me a bloody nose in the van. That day, Dan and I were called in to talk with the assistant principal, Mrs. Brock. She told me that I was in trouble as well as Dan. After what Dan did to me and I'M in trouble?! I thought angrily. I wanted to say something, but I knew that I could just get into even more trouble, so I didn't say anything to Mrs. Brock after that.

In 1990, after I got my driver's license, I began to make a lot of new friends, although I was never sure that some of them weren't just using me as a chauffeur. That summer Chrissy started hanging around me; we never dated, we just stayed friends. She obviously felt that being friends was better. We used to go out to Lake Byllesby in Cannon Falls together, usually with a small child that she was babysitting. Chrissy's mother didn't have a lot of money. I would witness the lives of people who lived in lower-income housing every time I went to visit Chrissy.

I was shocked at the ways some of the little kids were treated by their mothers. Chrissy used to babysit Todd and Stacey often, and every time their mother was with them, she would scream at them and slap them very hard. Stacey at the time was barely two, and Todd was at the tender age of three. I will tell you one thing, I will NEVER treat my kids like that if I ever have any. Mothers or fathers who would hit their children were probably abused by their own parents, but I think that even that is hardly a good excuse for hitting or slapping a small child. I was shocked and disgusted when I watched Todd or Stacey being slapped. I also felt some anger at their mother.

One warm, sunny day in June, Chrissy and I were at Lake Byllesby with her neighbor and her two small children. Chrissy started talking to a couple of guys who looked like they were in their middle twenties. I saw that she liked one of them. She got into their white van and went with them to their place. I rode home with Chrissy's neighbor.

Later that week, Chrissy called me up and told me that she had been raped. I asked by whom, and she told me it was those two guys she met at the lake. Somehow, I wasn't surprised to hear it. I felt very sorry for her when I heard this news. She went to the police the day after the two men assaulted her and filed a report. I couldn't imagine that such a terrible thing could happen to one of my friends. I felt a little guilty for not warning Chrissy about those guys. They DID look a little creepy to me.

Chrissy never had an easy life. She was looked down on all through school. Almost everyone around me in Northfield who was my age said that Chrissy was a lowlife. They were just looking down on her because she and her family were poor. They tried to get ME to hate Chrissy as well! I wasn't going to let them change my mind about her. I think that deep down inside she is a wonderful person. I hope Chrissy realizes that I will ALWAYS be a good friend to her.

Some people have said that autistic people don't care about friendships. That wasn't true at all for me. I tried to make as many friends as possible, especially after I turned eighteen. I just want to say that people mean more than anything to me. I always try to be as friendly as I can to people I meet. However, I still need to work more on my social skills. They are not as good as a lot of people's.

When I was seventeen I had my first relationship with a girl. Her name was Meg. I dated her for four months. Things were going fine between us until I started being obsessed with seeing her very often. I felt an urge to be with her every day. One weekend she didn't want to see me, and I argued with her until she gave in and let me spend that Saturday evening with her. She told me that she needed space and time to relax, but I refused to accept her wishes. I just couldn't understand why she didn't want to see me when we were boyfriend and girlfriend. That's when things started going bad between us.

One weekend in the middle of April, we were taking a walk around her neighborhood when she gave me the "let's just be friends" lecture. It took me a few minutes to realize what she was getting at. When I finally realized what she was saying to me, I felt the biggest pain in my heart that I ever felt in my life. I loved her. My stomach hurt and I couldn't stop crying that evening. I tried to make her change her mind, but I realized that she wasn't going to change it any time soon. For the next week we were bitter toward each other. That very next weekend we seemed to be getting back to the way things used to be. We went to a movie together in town and during the movie we started holding hands. I continued to push her into spending time with me every weekend again by writing her a note at school telling her that I was coming over. That note was a bad mistake on my part. She was furious with me and we got into a terrible fight when I came over later that afternoon after school. She said to me, "I don't know if I even like you as a friend anymore." I realized then that it was over between us. I cried for hours and hours that weekend.

For the rest of that school year and almost that entire summer I tried to get her back. I wrote her many nice letters, I sent her hundreds of pictures of myself and my family, I tried to sound friendly to her over the phone. I talked with her mother about what was going on. I even had my friend Bill Steele talk her into going back out with me, but nothing worked.

Later that summer, Meg and I ran into each other at McDonald's in Northfield. At first I tried to be friendly with her. But when she told me to leave, I got extremely angry. She and her friend left the restaurant, half their food uneaten. I chased her to the Super America right next door and then back to McDonald's, where she and her friend ran inside the ladies' room. One of my friends who was with me at the time went into the bathroom and told her to come out and at LEAST talk to me. I got to talk to her, but I was so angry with her that I could barely control myself.

Two days later I tried calling her, but her mother found out what happened at McDonald's and wouldn't let me talk to her. It was then that I realized that I had to quit this endless fight with Meg. She wasn't going to change her mind. I pushed her too far. I WAS NOT going to get her back. I was just going around in crazy circles.

When I was eighteen my friend Bill Steele found a girlfriend. I would go to Hastings with Bill to visit Jenny and her family. For a while I enjoyed this, but I started getting extremely jealous of them. They got along together perfectly while I used to have so many problems with Meg a year before. I felt it wasn't fair. While I was up there, I kept bugging them about finding someone for me.

Then in April of 1991, I met Mary at a dance at Hastings High School that I went to with Bill and Jenny. Not long after that, Mary and I started going out. She was the first girl in my life that I kissed. It felt great. Unfortunately, it only lasted a month between us. When we broke up, I again felt my heart breaking. She told me that she wanted to go back out with her ex-boyfriend Tom, who she had been going out with for a year and a half. I understood and accepted it. Thankfully, it took me only a few days to get over her. This relationship wasn't as serious as the one with Meg. Ironically, the most I did with Meg was hold hands. My mother told me later that breaking up with your first girlfriend is the hardest. That certainly is true.

After Mary and I broke up, I continued to go up to Hastings with Bill to see his girlfriend. I continued to feel very jealous of Bill and Jenny, however. In September of that year, Bill and Jenny told me that they wanted to be alone with each other. I felt that I was being pushed out and that it was something against me. Bill kept telling me that it was nothing against me, but I didn't think he was telling the truth. A few months later, I found out from Bill that Jenny was most likely using me just because I had my driver's license and Bill didn't. It really hurt to hear this. I had to agree with Bill, however. There just didn't seem to be any other explanation. Once Bill got his driver's license that October, I never went up to Jenny's house with him again. I felt worthless. I had thought I was a friend of Jenny.

In July of 1991, I went with my parents to the National Autism Society conference in Indianapolis. While I was there, I was hoping to meet a nice girl. My wish came true. We were having a fancy dinner when I was introduced to Barbara. I immediately felt comfortable around her. I had no trouble at all talking to her. We talked and talked that evening. I told her a lot about my life. She told me that her dad is autistic like me, and he gave a talk in front of a big group of people at the conference. I listened to him talk earlier that day; I thought that his speech was very moving and I told Barbara that.

The next evening, Barbara and I had ice cream together. We seemed to get along almost perfectly. Later that evening, she had to leave. Just before we said good-bye, I gave her a big hug. I then promised that I would write to her. I could easily tell that she liked me.

Barbara lived in Indiana, a long way from Minnesota. She was also going to a college in the same state. I realized that I might never see her again. As I went back up to my hotel room, I felt my eyes brimming with tears. Barbara was by far the sweetest girl that I had ever met. I felt very disappointed that she lived so far away. In that short time that I was with her, I developed real feelings for her.

I immediately wrote Barbara a long letter when we got back to Northfield. I told her exactly how I felt. I might have even come on a little too strong in the letter. I felt that my heart would break if I didn't get to see her again! I talked with her over the phone a couple of times in the next few weeks, and I found out that she already had a boyfriend. It bothered me to hear that, but she lived so far away that probably nothing more than friendship would ever develop between us. I haven't talked to Barbara in over a year, but I will always remember her.

Some other friends that I made when I was eighteen were Roxanne, Sarah, and Mindy. "Paul, you're the sweetest!" Roxanne would tell me. This made me feel absolutely wonderful. It meant so much to me to have these new friends of mine who wanted to spend lots of time with me. The downside to all this is that they already had boyfriends at that time (whom I met and got along with just fine) and only wanted to stay friends with me. I was always hoping that one of them would break up with her boyfriend and go out with me.

They DID break up with their boyfriends, but they either found someone else to go out with or wanted to stay single. After a while, I could see that they only wanted to stay friends with me. Sarah told me that she wanted a close friend to talk to and that if we went out, we might break up and therefore ruin the friendship on top of that. I understood that after going through the painful breakup with Meg. Sarah also told me to "cool my hormones" and be patient. "You'll meet someone soon enough!"

Roxanne, on the other hand, didn't want to go out with me because, she said, "You are more like a brother to me, Paul." I felt hurt by this. How am I more like a brother to her? I thought to myself. I wanted to be more like a lover to her instead. I eventually accepted this over time, and me and Roxanne stayed very good friends.

One night, just after Christmas of that year, Mindy, Roxanne, Sarah, and Mindy's brother, Jeff, were cruising around town with me when we came across Sarah's ex-boyfriend, Patrick. Ironically, this was also at McDonald's. Patrick was extremely angry. He just stood by the building smoking a cigarette, looking furious. What happened was that Sarah had dumped Patrick for Mindy's brother, Jeff, earlier that day.

Right then, I suddenly understood just how Patrick felt. He must have felt as angry and as heartbroken as I felt when Meg dumped me.

For a while, I thought that I was the ONLY person in Northfield who got dumped by his girlfriend. I was glad to see that I was not alone. I also felt very sorry for him. Roxanne stepped out of the car and tried to talk to Patrick, but he didn't seem to have much to say. I hope people realize that even though relationships rarely last long at this age, it can still hurt like hell when they end. Love can be just as strong during adolescence as any other time in a person's life.

That spring, very early on Easter Sunday, a tragedy occurred to Roxanne. Her house caught fire and burnt to the ground. She and her youngest brother, Scott, woke up to flames all around them. Scott ran outside while Roxanne ran upstairs to wake up her other brother, Brian. The smoke was so thick that she could not see anything and called Brian's name, but he didn't wake up and Roxanne had to run out of the house if she was to get out alive.

Brian died in the blaze. Roxanne told me the news Easter morning. "My brother is dead! I just couldn't save him!" Roxanne exclaimed while tears were running down her cheek. I was so stunned that I felt sick. I couldn't believe that something that bad would happen to any one of my friends. I felt so bad for Roxanne. I cried for the next couple of days. A house fire has always been my very worst nightmare.

I went to Brian's funeral three days later. When I saw Roxanne, I gave her a big hug. I wrote both her and her mother a letter telling them just how sorry I was and that I would always be there for them if they needed someone to talk to. I think Roxanne is the bravest person I have ever met. She handled the tragedy extremely well. She did NOT deserve what happened to her that Easter.

Finally a very good thing happened to Roxanne later that year. She met someone named Kelly and fell in love with him. Just after Christmas of 1991, they got married, and on Easter of 1992, she and Kelly had a baby daughter named Rachael. Not long after Rachael was born, Roxanne and Kelly moved to Germany, where Kelly was stationed in the army. I felt jealousy tugging at me, but I also felt very happy for both of them and ESPECIALLY Roxanne. Roxanne and I are still good friends. I stayed in Germany with her and Kelly and Rachael during August of 1992. I'm very glad that things turned out well for Roxanne. I wished I could've found a real love that she found.

I thought that I found what I was looking for when I met Karen in October of 1991. Chrissy went to class with Karen at the Rosemount Vo-Tech. Karen was looking for a boyfriend and was VERY eager to meet me. When I met her, I saw that she had a very bad limp and couldn't use her left arm properly. Her voice also sounded strange to me. I wasn't sure if I wanted to go out with someone with a handicap, but Karen seemed very sweet to me and in no time at all I fell in love with her.

Karen told me about why she had this handicap. When she was nine, she and a friend were hit by a car. Her friend died, but Karen survived, although she was in a coma for three months. She had to relearn to do everything. I was stunned after I heard this story from her.

She and I would often go up to the Camel Club, which was just north of St. Paul. It was a nonalcoholic bar, where you could dance to music. I enjoyed going to the Camel Club. Karen loved to dance with me to slow songs. We met some friendly people there, who go up there every Saturday night.

Karen was living at a foster home when I met her. Her foster mother, Donna, seemed strict and got upset easily, but I liked her tremendously. She was firm with Karen, but she was also very loving. She was very hopeful about me and Karen. "You two make a BEAUTIFUL couple," she said. I thought to myself, This could be it, this could very well be the girl I'm looking for. This may be the girl I marry!

I couldn't have been more wrong. Karen was not at all what she seemed to me to be like. We were getting along just fine until she moved to her aunt's house in Eagan, just south of Minneapolis. Three days after she moved in, we got into a big fight. Karen told me that it really bothered her when I tried to get her to quit smoking. She said, "I feel like you're trying to control me." It was only because I cared a lot about her. She seemed to find that hard to understand. We were downstairs at her aunt's house when she whispered something to her aunt. I KNEW it was something bad about me. At that moment, I felt just horrible! Her aunt told me I had better leave. Just before I left, I asked Karen if she wanted to break up with me. She just stood there and cried. I then left in tears myself.

We didn't break up immediately. Things went back to "normal" between us and she spent Christmas with me at my house. I was feeling very happy and I had almost completely forgotten about our fight two weeks before. But on New Year's Eve, Karen and I got into another big fight. This time it was partly my fault. We were visiting Donna when Karen called her aunt and told her where she was. Her aunt was furious with her for visiting with Donna and told Karen to come home immediately.

That's when some difficulties arose. I just HAD to get back to my house to change a tape in the VCR. I was recording the "Top 100 Videos" of 1991; it lasted for a total of eleven hours. I thought about calling my parents, but I was afraid that they wouldn't know exactly what to do. Instead of going back to Karen's aunt's house, I drove to my house so I could change the tape myself. Karen was very angry with me about this and told me that I was trying to get her in trouble with her aunt. The last thing I wanted to do was to hurt Karen. I was just obsessed with that video countdown! I changed the tape and then drove Karen up to her aunt's house. When we came in, her aunt started screaming at her about going to visit Donna. I just stood in the doorway watching it happen. Soon after that, Karen started telling me how I got her into trouble. I told her I was sorry about what I did, but she didn't forgive me. "This is strike two for you. Three strikes and you're out!" she told me.

I knew what she was talking about. I started feeling very guilty about what I did. Maybe I should've just driven Karen straight to her aunt's house from Donna's place, but I didn't know that it would affect our relationship. We had a long talk with her aunt after she cooled down about everything. After that talk, I felt better. Karen didn't seem angry anymore. We rang in the new year together. We kissed each other good-bye and I went home.

The very next day, we started fighting again. I was so upset by it that I told Karen that I would kill myself after I dropped her off. I didn't intend to do anything stupid like that, I was just threatening it. Karen called me as soon as I got home and she said that she was very worried about me. I was on the phone with her the next day and she started saying something about us breaking up. I again threatened suicide over the phone. She told me not to talk stupid. That's one big mistake I made. I was told later that you should NEVER threaten suicide to anyone, ESPECIALLY your girlfriend. It's not fair to do that. It makes them feel trapped.

During the month of January, I started going to therapy sessions with Karen. We wanted to get help from someone. Karen had been seeing this therapist for several months. We told her therapist about our fights and she gave good advice. She helped us, but only up to a point. Karen and I started fighting more and more that month.

When we finally broke up, Karen was the one who ended it all. The first weekend in February, we got into a terrible fight. I told her a few nasty things that I won't repeat and gathered enough strength to tell her that I wanted to break up with her. "Good-bye forever, Karen," I told her. My parents took her home that evening while I was at home throwing anything away that reminded me of her. I was just starting to listen to some music when the phone rang. I answered it, and it was Karen. She asked me if I meant what I had said, and I said that I wasn't sure. "Let's just get back to the way things used to be between us," she said. She wanted to see me that night and talk things out. I just couldn't resist, her voice sounded so sad. I drove up there and we went to a Perkins family restaurant to talk. She told me that she would try and stop the things she said that would get us into bad fights. I realized then that I still loved her and that I would do anything to help her feel better. We went to my house and she spent the night there. My mother called her aunt and told her that I was way too tired to drive Karen back up to Eagan. Karen had to promise that she was not to sleep with me because that was her aunt's rule. The next morning, Karen came up to my bedroom and slept with me for a couple of hours. Later that morning, my mother told Karen that she had broken her promise and that she would call her aunt and tell her what she did. Karen was angry about this while I drove her home that morning. I dropped her off without saying much. What could I tell her?

It wasn't until I called her up ten days later that I found out that Karen had decided that our relationship was over. "What are you calling me for? We broke up. I've got another boyfriend who's a lot better than you." When she told me this, I told her that I've been thinking about her a lot during the week. "But Karen, I love you," I said. "Good for you!" was her answer. Then she hung up on me. "Wait, wait, Karen, please!" I pleaded. I was crying then. I was so hurt by this. It wasn't fair. I COULDN'T let her go. I immediately called her back. She then told me it was what my mother said that ended it all between us; she said good-bye and told me never to call her again. Karen is gone forever and there is nothing I can do to get her back, I thought to myself that night. Talking to my friends or with ANYONE would not help the pain go away. I've lost everything! I NEED her. Then I did something very stupid. I started thinking about suicide. I wanted to at least hurt myself so I got a bottle of Wite-Out and started inhaling its fumes. I read on the bottle that inhaling the fumes can be harmful or fatal, so I just lay there on the playroom bed with the small bottle up to my nose. I really wanted to die that night. I felt as if no relationship with a girl would ever work out for me. I felt like giving up. The bottle of Wite-Out didn't hurt me at all. It didn't even give me a headache. Fortunately, I didn't try anything else, though I thought of swerving my car in front of a truck, but I realized that I shouldn't let one girl ruin my whole life.

The relationship I had with Karen lasted a little over three months. I had a lot of anger toward her for the next couple months. As I compare this relationship to the relationship with Meg, I would still say that breaking up with Meg was more painful. I look back on it now and see that Karen had a lot of problems of her own and that staying with her, I would just be miserable. We would be fighting all the time. However, it still hurts a lot to lose someone you love.

Present Day

Today, things are much easier for me. I go to Inver Hills Community College, where I'm working for my associate of arts degree. I am very hopeful about my future. I've taken some very difficult classes in geography, but I have passed all of them with a fairly decent grade. Mr. Brothen, a teacher that I had for two of my classes, seems very fond of me. My mother and I had breakfast with him one day, and he told me that my future looks very good. I felt very hopeful when he said this. I've always been afraid that I would be stuck with a job that I hate. Mr. Brothen has always been a positive influence for me. I visit him at his office these days, just to talk to him.

In September of 1991, I started working at Hardee's fast food restaurant. For the first few months, I didn't mind the work I had to do. I met a lot of new people, which was one of the main reasons I started to work there. Allen worked there also, and I usually worked with him. I liked working with my best friend a lot. It made it more fun.

I found washing dishes the easiest. I didn't like it when I had to close down the backline, which had the grill and the food station. Backline seemed extremely complicated to me. I found it very hard to remember how to clean some backline areas, especially the grill. Allen had to show me over and over how to clean it, and I felt stupid when I had to be shown how to do something more than once.

When the spring of 1992 came, I started feeling the stress of working at Hardee's get to me. I would get upset very easily over small mishaps. I would hate it when I had to be on backline alone. A small rush of people would come in to Hardee's and order lots of different sandwiches. The "frontliners" would be calling back three or four different sandwiches at once. Even if I rushed as fast as I could to make all the sandwiches, they would still be getting impatient with me. It seemed that I had to do everything at once. I would get overwhelmed and yell for help. Allen would then come back and shake his head and say, "Paul, Paul, Paul. What's wrong? Can't handle this by yourself? We're hardly even busy!" I knew that he was giving me a hard time, as usual.

Jason, the assistant manager, always liked to tease me. To him, my name was "Pauly." He was extremely good at magic tricks, and he drove me out of my mind with them! I just couldn't figure them out. Jason would make things literally disappear in front of my eyes! He would never tell me his secret to his magic tricks.

I quit for a while last summer because I wanted to relax more and concentrate more on my education up at Inver Hills. Lots of good things came from working at Hardee's: I learned to handle a very stressful job. I also made good friends with a few people I worked with. Joe and Rick in particular.

This last spring, I often went to a casino called Treasure Island, mainly with Allen. I used to spend twenty dollars up there every time I went. Just about every time I lost that twenty dollars, either on the slot machines or on blackjack. During the summer, I dropped my spending down to five or ten dollars. I felt extremely frustrated that I couldn't win any money, especially after Allen won a thousand dollars on one of the draw poker machines there one day in February, when he went alone.

Draw poker was my favorite game at Treasure Island. I could put from one to five quarters in the machine at a time. You also had the option to double your money every time you got a pair of jacks or better. I tried to double my money more than once, but the dealer's card just kept beating me. Blackjack was not much different from draw poker. My luck was no better. The dealer would always get twenty-one, or I would go bust. A couple of times I got angry and started being compulsive. I would spend an extra ten or twenty dollars on top of the twenty dollars I already lost.

Today, I hardly go to Treasure Island or any other gambling casino. As I look back on all the times I went, I figure that I lost somewhere around four hundred dollars or so. I would like to say that gambling can be extremely dangerous for high-functioning autistic people. They can easily get angry at losing and get very compulsive, or just have the mistaken notion that they can start making a slot machine pay out a lot of money by putting lots of money into it. I consider myself lucky that I did not lose all the money I have in the bank to gambling.

*

A very terrible thing happened to me at the end of spring 1992. Sarah wanted me to meet a new guy from Cannon Falls that she was dating. His name was Nick, and I thought that he was very friendly and courteous. When he and Sarah came over to my house, I showed him my room, where he noticed all the change that I had in one of the drawers. "Hey, Paul, you don't suppose I can borrow that money? I've got a speeding ticket that's overdue and there will be a warrant out for my arrest if I don't get it paid," he said. I told him that it would be a hassle to cash in all that change and that I wanted to fill up the whole drawer.

He then had a very disappointed look on his face. I felt that if I was going to make another real friend, I should help Nick out on that speeding ticket. "I've got a paycheck for four hundred fifty two dollars in the mail, and I'll give you fifty dollars extra if you lend me three hundred dollars," Nick said in a confident voice. I took out three hundred dollars from my safe, which was hidden in my parents' room. I hesitated giving Nick so much money, but he reassured me that his paycheck would be at his house the next day. I couldn't resist the deal he made with me. Fifty extra dollars for me sounded nice. When I handed him three one-hundred-dollar bills, he took them with a smile.

Just a couple of hours later, I started feeling that I had made a terrible mistake giving him that money. I had an appointment with my psychologist that day, and I told him how worried I was. He told me that I might not get any of the money back from Nick. He explained to me that there are people out in the world who just love to rip other people off. I could hardly sleep that night.

The next night I spent at Nick's house. When I went back to my house with him in the afternoon, I went to get something from my room and noticed that my change drawer was slightly ajar. To my horror, I saw that most of the change that I had collected for months was gone. I counted what was left and found out that two hundred twenty-five dollars of it had disappeared. I asked Nick if he took the change and he told me that he didn't have anything to do with it. I immediately told my parents about it, and they called the police. A police officer came to my house a few minutes later and my mother and I gave the name of the suspect, which was Sarah.

Nick had a party at his house that night. He told me that a girl, Dorothy, liked me and wanted me to spend the night at his house. She was supposed to be staying the night as well. Nick told me that Dorothy wanted me to get drunk. Then, after that, she would sleep with me. I felt excited about this and wondered how much Dorothy really liked me.

I started playing a drinking game with Dorothy and two other girls in the kitchen. I finished a whole bottle of Strawberry Hill liquor, and I started on a second bottle, but then everyone was getting pretty drunk, so we quit the game. I felt myself getting very dizzy. The room was spinning. I don't remember what exactly happened to me then, I must have passed out. When I came to, I was vomiting.

"You guys are nothing but trouble," I said. "We're trouble, huh?! Then get the hell out of here!" This angry response came from Nick, and I felt myself being lifted out of my chair very roughly and thrown outside onto the grass. He then carried me to my car and threw me in the back seat. "You can sober up in your car," Nick said. So there I lay in my car, half conscious. Suddenly, I felt glass crumble and fall onto the seat next to me. Someone had smashed my car window. Dorothy then got in the back seat next to me and started yelling about the bad things that were happening to her that night as well. Dorothy was obviously the one who broke the window. As she was yelling, I noticed that my car stereo was gone. What more is going to happen to me?! Is my life going to go next?! I thought.

I felt very frightened all of a sudden. It was like I was being stripped of all my money and all my belongings. I didn't know who took my car stereo. Sarah came to my car and helped me stagger back into the house. I then crawled on my hands and knees upstairs and reached for a phone in a room which was at the far end of the hallway. I was still so drunk that I could barely see the numbers on the phone, but with some effort, I dialed my phone number. My mother answered, and I suddenly felt some comfort. "Mama, I'm in real trouble here!! Please come and get me!!" She told me that she would call the police. She asked me if I knew the address of Nick's house. I told her that I didn't know. In fact I discovered later that the police were on their way to the house. Some people from the party earlier that night had been followed to Nick's house by a cop car. The cops suspected drunk driving.

Sarah and her brother came up to the room I had phoned my parents from and helped me back downstairs. I remember starting to vomit again on the floor downstairs. One of the cops was in the house then and saw me. He obviously decided that I needed an ambulance. I was still very drunk and was on the verge of passing out. The next thing I remember was looking up at the faces of a doctor and a nurse while I was riding in the ambulance to the Cannon Falls hospital.

Not long after I arrived at the hospital, my parents walked in. I reached for my father's hand and held it tight. I was overcome with relief to see the kind and familiar faces of my mom and dad. I was starting to sober up then and I could walk on my own out of the hospital. We went to the police station, and an officer named Rich got a taped statement from me. I told him everything I remembered that happened to me that night. Finally, my mother drove me home after we stopped by Nick's house to pick up my partially vandalized car. My dad drove it back to Northfield.

As Mama and I were driving home, I saw that the eastern sky was growing light. What a horrible night for me! I thought then. When I got home, I went right to sleep. Later that week, I found out from Rich that Nick confessed to him about stealing the money from my drawer. He and Sarah had both gone up to my room while I was taking a nap and had taken the money. Nick was also the one who ripped the stereo out of my car that night.

Nick told me a bunch of filthy lies that weekend. He betrayed my trust in people. I can NEVER trust new people I meet the way I did before. Nick humiliated me and made me feel very small and stupid. I realized painfully that I would probably never see that five hundred twenty-five dollars again. It was nearly two months of hard work at Hardee's, all lost to Nick. I NEVER should have lent him that three hundred dollars! I have to admit that he was good at conning me. He certainly had me fooled. Later that week, I also found that my radar detector, which was under my car seat, was gone too. At least the police got my car stereo back that night. This will always be a very painful memory for me for the rest of my life. I will never EVER forgive Nick for what he did to me!

This past October, I gave a talk in front of nearly three hundred people up in the Twin Cities about my autism. I was very pleased to have the opportunity to tell everyone about myself. For the first time in my life, I felt good about myself. I talked about what autism felt like for me, and I told some funny stories. My talk was about ten minutes long. After I talked, I answered questions. I found it a little hard to answer some questions, but I did so in the best way that I could. On the whole, this talk was a very big success for me. My talk brought tears to the eyes of many. It was a big step forward for me.

As I look back on my life so far, I see that I have been very brave. There were many obstacles for me to cross. Sometimes I felt like giving up. At times there seemed to be no hope for me at all. Now I see that there is a lot of hope for me. I've made it this far, and I'm NOT going to give up. I've got a lot to live for. I'm very proud of what I have accomplished so far.

I want to help other people who have autism. I know how they must feel sometimes, and I want to help guide them in the right direction. Autism is a disorder which can affect your whole perception of the world. For some people, it can be a crippling disability. For others, it is a disorder which interferes with their whole life. It limits their social abilities. It can also limit their progress in learning. I know that a lot of people out there who have autism feel like giving up. DON'T give up hope. Keep trying, because someday things might very well get better for you. Just take one day at a time and believe in yourself.